RESEARCH SERIES, NO. 43

The Apartheid Regime

POLITICAL POWER AND RACIAL DOMINATION

Edited by
ROBERT M. PRICE
& CARL G. ROSBERG

INSTITUTE OF INTERNATIONAL STUDIES
University of California
Berkeley

Library of Congress Cataloging in Publication Data

Main entry under title:

The Apartheid regime.

(Research series—Institute of International Studies, University of California ; no. 43)

Bibliography: p.

Includes index.

1. South Africa—Race relations—Addresses, essays, lectures. 2. South Africa—Politics and government—1961-1978—Addresses, essays, lectures. 3. South Africa—Politics and government—1978- —Addresses, essays, lectures. 4. Blacks—South Africa—Politics and government—Addresses, essays, lectures. I. Price, Robert M. II. Rosberg, Carl Gustav. III. Series: California. University. Institute of International Studies. Research series ; no. 43.

DT763.A725 320.968 79-27269

ISBN 0-87725-143-6

CONTENTS

Foreword vii

Notes on Contributors xi

EMERGING STRATEGIES FOR POLITICAL CONTROL: NATIONALIST AFRIKANERDOM
André du Toit 1

THE NATIONAL PARTY AND THE AFRIKANER BROEDERBOND
Hermann Giliomee 14

THE FAILURE OF POLITICAL LIBERALISM IN SOUTH AFRICA
Heribert Adam 45

CONTEMPORARY AFRICAN POLITICAL ORGANIZATIONS AND MOVEMENTS
Roland Stanbridge 66

THE STIRRING GIANT: OBSERVATIONS ON THE INKATHA AND OTHER BLACK POLITICAL MOVEMENTS IN SOUTH AFRICA
Lawrence Schlemmer 99

THE "APEX OF SUBORDINATION": THE URBAN AFRICAN POPULATION OF SOUTH AFRICA
Martin E. West 127

CURRENT LABOR ISSUES IN SOUTH AFRICA
Francis Wilson 152

BLACK TRADE UNIONS IN SOUTH AFRICA SINCE WORLD WAR II
Philip Bonner 174

CONTENTS

SOME IMPLICATIONS OF AFRICAN "HOMELANDS" IN SOUTH AFRICA

Newell M. Stultz 194

STRUCTURAL INEQUALITY AND MINORITY ANXIETY: RESPONSES OF MIDDLE GROUPS IN SOUTH AFRICA

Kogila A. Moodley 217

CHANGE IN SOUTH AFRICA: OPPORTUNITIES AND CONSTRAINTS

Lawrence Schlemmer 236

SOUTH AFRICA IN THE CONTEMPORARY WORLD

Colin Legum 281

APARTHEID AND WHITE SUPREMACY: THE MEANING OF GOVERNMENT-LED REFORM IN THE SOUTH AFRICAN CONTEXT

Robert M. Price 297

NOTES 333

SELECTED BIBLIOGRAPHY 360

INDEX 370

FOREWORD

The Republic of South Africa presents the analyst with what is the world's most fully developed racially dominated state. The state is controlled by and exists primarily to uphold the privileges of a White minority of somewhat more than four million people in a society of about twenty-eight million. Whites thus make up less than a fifth of the country's population. The politically, economically, and socially subordinated majority is comprised of approximately three-quarters of a million Indians, two-and-a-half million Coloreds, and twenty million Africans. About 60 percent of the ruling Whites are Afrikaners and 40 percent are English-speaking. The subjugated African majority is composed of numerous ethnic groups, of which the largest are the Zulu, Xhosa, Tswana, and Sotho, who together comprise about 60 percent of the African population.

The establishment of a modern, organizationally efficient state to maintain the exclusive interests and values of the White minority has defined the character and dynamics of political life in South Africa. White domination has historical roots reaching back three hundred years to the earliest settlements in the Western Cape, but only since 1948 has an ideology been pursued through which successive regimes have built up an oppressive legal order to sanction and define a system of racial domination and separation. Law upon law has been enacted by the South African Parliament to build the legal framework of apartheid. To implement and enforce such a complex system of statutes and regulations, the government has had to develop a substantial bureaucracy. In the West administrative states have been built up to provide for the national welfare; in South Africa such a state has been developed primarily to secure and uphold the dominance and privileges of a racial minority. The Whites enjoy a liberal-democratic substate, while the subordinated majority is ruled by a modern authoritarian state.

The ethnic group that controls the government of South Africa is the Afrikaner—a people of Dutch, French Huguenot, and German descent who settled the region beginning in the seventeenth century and who today constitute a genuine "nationalist" force. Unlike other settlers of South Africa, the Afrikaners have a distinctive history as a people, speak a distinctive language, share a common religion (Dutch Reformed Church), have their own literature—in sum, possess all the attributes of a *people*. Moreover, their collective consciousness has been forged in the crucible of historical conflict—both with the British who established their presence in the region at the end of the eighteenth century and with the African peoples whose territories they conquered. The political party that rules the South African state today and is the organizational expression of Afrikaner nationalism is appropriately called the National party. What has evolved in South Africa over a period of three centuries, but at an accelerating pace in the twentieth century—especially since the 1948 electoral victory of the National party—is a framework of growing confrontation between two racial estates and the nationalisms they have given rise to: a confrontation between Afrikaner nationalism, pursuing strategies to retain control of the state it captured just a little over three decades ago, and African nationalism, determined to bring about an end to the apartheid regime and institute in its place a political order based on majority rule, one man-one vote. It is this confrontation that animates political and social conflict in South Africa today and is the dominating theme addressed by the contributors to this volume.

This book is the end product of a colloquium on contemporary South Africa held at the University of California, Berkeley, during the Winter and Spring of 1978. Sponsored by the University's Institute of International Studies and organized by the editors, the colloquium met once a month, bringing faculty and graduate students from the San Francisco Bay Area together with leading scholars on South African affairs. This volume consists of revised versions of papers originally presented for discussion at this colloquium. Since the final intellectual product represented by this book benefitted substantially from the colloquium discussions, the editors wish to acknowledge the participation of the regular colloquium members: from the Berkeley campus of the University of California, Professors Kenneth Jowitt, David Leonard, William Shack, Elizabeth Colson, Andrew Jameson, Raymond Kent, Thomas Metcalf, and Michael Burawoy, and graduate students Pearl Marsh, Jean Freedberg, Michael Clough, Ruth Milkman, Karen Johnson, John Ravenhill, Owen Kahn, Ann Lawrence, Michael Halderman, Tom Callaghy, and Ardath Grant; from the University of California at Santa Cruz, Professors John Marcum and Isebill Gruhn and student Richard Sergay; from the University of California at Davis,

Professor Donald Rothchild; and from the greater Bay Area community, Barbara Pelosi, Jean Bachrach, William McClung, Suzanne and Allan Hershfield, Elaine Windrich, and Peter Dreyer.

The skillful editorial assistance of Paul Gilchrist, as always, has proved indispensable in the preparation of the manuscript. Ardath Grant contributed to the volume in a number of ways, particularly in putting together the bibliography and a preliminary index. Bojana Ristich prepared the final index and expertly typed the text on the Composer for publication.

The Editors

NOTES ON CONTRIBUTORS

ROBERT M. PRICE is Associate Professor of Political Science and Associate Director, Institute of International Studies, University of California, Berkeley.

CARL G. ROSBERG is Professor of Political Science and Director, Institute of International Studies, University of California, Berkeley.

HERIBERT ADAM is Professor of Sociology and Political Science, Simon Fraser University.

PHILIP BONNER is Senior Lecturer in History, University of the Witwatersrand.

ANDRÉ DU TOIT is Senior Lecturer in Political Philosophy, University of Stellenbosch.

HERMANN GILIOMEE is Senior Lecturer in History, University of Stellenbosch.

COLIN LEGUM is Editor of *Africa Contemporary Record* and Associate Editor of *The Observer.*

KOGILA A. MOODLEY is a member of the Faculty of Education, University of British Columbia.

LAWRENCE SCHLEMMER is Director, Centre for Applied Social Sciences, University of Natal.

ROLAND STANBRIDGE is a Researcher at the Scandinavian Institute of African Studies, Uppsala, Sweden.

NOTES ON CONTRIBUTORS

NEWELL M. STULTZ is Professor of Political Science, Brown University.

MARTIN E. WEST is Professor and Head, Department of Anthropology, University of Cape Town.

FRANCIS WILSON is Senior Lecturer and Head of the Research Division, School of Economics, University of Cape Town.

THE APARTHEID REGIME

EMERGING STRATEGIES FOR POLITICAL CONTROL: NATIONALIST AFRIKANERDOM

André du Toit

Thirty years after it came into power the political hegemony of the National party and government in South Africa is increasingly challenged—both internally and internationally. Facing up to the steadily deepening crisis—from Mozambique and Angola in 1974, to Soweto in 1976, to Rhodesia and perhaps South West Africa in 1979—Nationalist Afrikanerdom has not (yet) lost the will to rule. While internal opposition groups have been spawning models for "political alternatives," and external movements have been planning strategies for liberation, the ruling oligarchy has been evolving and adapting its own strategy for maintaining political control. The nature of this strategy and its relation to earlier phases of National party ideology and policy is not yet generally well understood, though the groundwork for the new strategy has been prepared for some time now. The purpose of this article is to analyze the Nationalist government's emerging strategy for maintaining political control, and to comment briefly on the implications for alternative strategies. The discussion will of necessity be summary, impressionistic, and somewhat speculative.

Undoubtedly a major reason for the general failure to perceive or understand the Nationalist government's evolving strategy has been the marked prominence of a rigid racial ideology at earlier stages of Afrikaner Nationalist politics. In the 1950s the ideological doctrine of *apartheid* provided a guiding principle for government action and legislation. From this ideology followed the systematic barrage of laws which imposed requirements for separate facilities, separate group areas, and racial classifications, which prohibited sexual relations and various other forms of formal and informal contact be-

Earlier versions of this paper were presented in Cape Town in November 1977, Berkeley in May 1978, and Grahamstown in August 1978.

tween different racial groups, and which provided for separate cultural organizations, separate academic societies, separate education, etc. In the 1960s the ideology of *separate development* provided both long-term policy goals and the ideological justification for the continuation of current policies. On the basis of this ideology, it was possible to claim that denying Blacks the franchise in Parliament was not a clear case of racial domination and discrimination because—in terms of the ideology—they would one day become fully self-governing in their own independent states. The migrant labor system and the pass laws could similarly be viewed as temporary transitional measures; it was claimed that through homeland development the Black influx to the cities could be reversed by 1978. Thus the ideology of separate development required that urban Blacks could not have property rights or political rights in their areas of residence because this would preclude their separate freedoms in the future.

The historic prominence of the racial ideologies of apartheid and separate development in government policy has misled many observers into regarding them as the main dynamic force in Afrikaner Nationalist politics. Accordingly, great significance is attached to indications of more "enlightened" or "liberal" views on racial issues by government spokesmen and supporters. It is assumed that a weakening of the traditional racial ideologies must lead to a general liberalization of government policy and/or a substantial erosion of the base of its political strength. Both of these assumptions are mistaken. In a variety of ways traditional ideological notions have declined in importance in the policy and practice of the Nationalist government. On a number of fronts the *official* policy and ideology no longer corresponds with the convictions of an increasing number of National party supporters, and in more and more cases, it no longer serves as a guiding principle for generating political action or determining the conduct of government. But this does not mean that Afrikaner Nationalism is now a spent force, or that the National party is becoming weak and impotent—as would have been the case had it been primarily an ideological movement.

While questions of ideology have become much less important than in the past to the National party and the government, there has not been any general liberalization of policy and practice—any easing of coercive measures or breaking down of authoritarian structures. As a political organization the National party has never been stronger. It will be argued here that its weaker ideological line may well allow it to become even stronger still. Conversely, a resurgence of ideological issues may prove a major threat to party unity and hence immobilize the new strategy for political control. As long as separate development remains the official policy, and to the extent that important sections of the government bureaucracy and its supporters retain a vested interest in upholding it as such, a renewed salience of ideological issues remains a real possibility. In any new strategy it may evolve, the party may thus still prove to be a captive of Nationalist Afrikanerdom's own past. No predictions will be offered here, but simply an attempt made to outline the main features of the new strategy for political control.

THE ORGANIZATIONAL BASE

It is a very interesting exercise to look at the South African political scene solely in organizational and institutional terms, forgetting for the moment about policy and ideological differences. This may seem wrongheaded, since substantive issues are traditionally so central to everyone's perception of South African politics. Still, it is quite instructive to consider the current situation purely in terms of the existing political organizations, their quality of leadership, total membership, nationwide distribution, available resources, etc. A senior Afrikaans newspaper editor recently claimed that there is only one political organization in South Africa that is effectively organized on a nationwide basis, that has local branches throughout the country in the rural areas as well as in all the major cities, and that has a large active membership and a unified leadership—i.e., the National party. All other political organizations have only local and sectional bases, are not effectively organized, and have weak and divided leaderships with little control over their followers. There is undoubtedly a large measure of truth in this, though one must hasten to add two very important qualifications.

First, the National party, though organized on a countrywide scale, has a decidedly sectional base. It is primarily the political organization of the Afrikaners as an ethnic minority group, and though it has somewhat broadened its base in White politics, no Africans or other Blacks can vote for it or become party members even if they wanted to. Second, the disruption and weakness of internal political organizations outside of White politics are largely the result of deliberate government policy and actions. The major African organizations like the African National Congress and the Pan Africanist Congress were banned, others were systematically infiltrated, and the leadership was constantly eroded through bannings, detentions, and other means of political intimidation. There is little freedom of political association. Through the homelands policy a traditional and conservative leadership has been encouraged on a decentralized basis. It seemed for a short time in the early 1970s as if a common front of homeland leaders could develop, and there was a striking proliferation of cultural, educational, and parapolitical organizations associated with "Black Consciousness" in the urban areas. But since the Transkei chose independence the fractionalizing of homeland leaders has proceeded apace, and with the bannings and detentions of October 1977 the government struck hard at the organizational core and the key leadership of the Black Consciousness movement.

Whatever the causes may be, the present internal political situation in South Africa is clearly dominated by a strong and unified National party. This party has a well-disciplined ethnic power base through its close alliance with the Afrikaans churches, the Afrikaans press, and a wide range of Afrikaans cultural, academic, student, professional, and business organizations and societies (the Broederbond, etc.); it has at its disposal a huge government bureaucracy; it is backed up by a loyal military, police, and security force; and it is in league with organized commerce and the White trade unions. What is there to counter this imposing organizational strength with its considerable resources?

The White opposition has not yet recovered from the total disarray caused by the prolonged demise of the United party. Though the Progressive Federal party (PFP) has, with the hesitant help of sections of the English press, made considerable gains in recent years, its base is both sectional and fragile, and its organizational resources are weak. The major urban Black organizations have been removed at one stroke, and the splintering process of the homeland leadership continues. In "Colored politics" only the Labour Party has the beginnings of a viable political organization, and it is severely handicapped by having to work within the framework of government policy.

Organizationally the only potential counterforce in sight at this moment is Chief Gatsha Buthelezi's Inkatha movement, which claims a registered membership of more than 150,000. And looking further afield, perhaps the churches. Otherwise South Africa seems to be moving toward something like a one-party-dominant state, with a strong basis of popular support within the White group and various captive clienteles from outside the White section.

But what are the possibilities of further spontaneous mass uprisings of the majority Black groups on the pattern of Soweto, bringing about a revolutionary situation? Whatever one's hopes or sympathies may be, it is necessary to face the hard questions of how this could come about without any effective organizational framework, without a unified national leadership (or even an effective local leadership), without any common ideology or clear policy objectives, and without the necessary military and economic resources. There may indeed be many more sporadic uprisings on the pattern of Soweto, probably in large measure triggered by external developments, but the organizational preconditions for an effective internal resistance movement seem to be quite lacking. Accordingly, if an effective underground organization or urban guerilla warfare is to take shape in the next few years, it can hardly be organized or controlled by any *internal* leadership. Training, resources, and strategy will have to be supplied by external organizations. The support or cover provided by the local Black population will of course be vital, but that would seem to be the total internal contribution possible at this stage.

STRATEGICAL OPTIONS FOR THE PRESENT REGIME

For the present regime, as for White politics generally, there seem to be three main strategies available at present to respond to Black pressures, expectations, and challenges:

1. Maintenance of direct Afrikaner supremacy;
2. (National) Party hegemony with indirect rule;
3. Negotiated power-sharing.

Corresponding to these are a variety of strategical options for Black politics, including self-interested collaboration, collaborative opposition, separatist opposition, unified alliance in opposition, etc. (As indicated, the organizational base for more radical forms of internal resistance or revolutionary challenge seem to be lacking at this stage.) Let us deal briefly with each of these strategies and touch on possible Black responses as they bear on each.

The strategy of maintaining direct Afrikaner supremacy is the one most closely linked with the ideologies and policies of apartheid and separate development. Consistent with this ideological heritage, it can be expounded as an insistence on full White supremacy over the South African heartland as a quid pro quo for relinquishing control over the peripheral "homelands": an exercise in internal decolonization. Shorn of its ideological trappings, it amounts simply to the quest by Nationalist Afrikanerdom for exclusive control of the South African state, which excludes any need either to broaden the political base of Afrikanerdom within White politics or to seek political alliances with any groups outside White politics. The coercive machinery of the state, including the civil service bureaucracy, the police and judicial system, the security forces, and ultimately the military forces, can be depended upon to impose the political order of Afrikanerdom on the entire South African society, and to defend it against internal and external challenge. This strategy can be seen as a remnant of an earlier stage of the history of the National party and Afrikaner Nationalism, when ideological concerns were much more central to it and when it did not have to recognize such serious challenges as now exist in the current political situation. Or it can be seen as a possible *last resort* in some future extremity: the "Masada complex" or "garrison state" model. In either case, substantial political *change* is ruled out: it is either not necessary or no longer possible.

An alternative to this is the strategy of National party hegemony with indirect rule, in which the National party is viewed as the vehicle for political change and accommodation. Given the need for political change in the current crisis, and given the organizational realities of the present, only the National party can initiate and control the transitional process. It is recognized that such a transition cannot be achieved by coercive measures only—that it must be a political process involving some kind of participation or collaboration by key figures from other sectors of South African society. Therefore it is necessary to broaden the base of the National party in White politics, and to form alliances with appropriate leaderships outside the White group as well. Such incorporation or alliances, however, must be clearly based on the recognition of the hegemony of the National party. Within the framework laid down by the Nationalist government—a framework which is ultimately supported by its monopoly of coercive force—there is scope for alliances with leaderships from outside the White group. Black leaders need not be only the *objects* of government policy: they can be given access to the highest level of executive decision-making—though only on a consultative basis, not of power-sharing. In addition they can be granted considerable delegated authority and powers, particularly on the local government level within their own communities.

Optimally this would relieve the central government from maintaining order by direct administration and coercive rule, and in the case of opposition and resistance the local Black leadership could be interposed between such action and the government. Appropriate elites can be recruited with the help of the considerable resources of patronage at the disposal of the government, and once installed they can be backed up and protected by coercive force, if necessary. In terms of this strategy, the "homelands" policy need not be aimed at complete decolonization and transfer of control; rather it can be a form of indirect rule which can be extended to Soweto and other urban complexes as well. There are two complements to this strategy from the point of view of the Black leaderships. On the one hand, there is the option of *self-interested collaboration* open to individuals who are prepared to function within the limits allowed by the government's framework, which offers both the limited powers inherent in these leadership positions and additional status, wealth, and privileges for themselves and their immediate followers. On the other hand, there is the option of *collaborative opposition*, whereby the opportunities for legitimate political action created within the framework are used as a means to build political organizations and mobilize popular support which can then be turned against the framework and the government itself. The latter alternative has been most consistently and imaginatively exploited by Chief Buthelezi, and might be termed the "Buthelezi strategy."

Theoretically, the strategy of "negotiated power-sharing" might also be an option for the present regime. At this stage, however, it is a strategy proposed only by the opposition PFP. For this reason discussion of it here is confined to a brief comment at the conclusion.

THE *NEW* STRATEGY OF PARTY HEGEMONY AND INDIRECT RULE

At present the National party and the government is still unresolved between the two strategies of maintaining direct Afrikaner supremacy or of working toward party hegemony within a collaborative alliance of other elite groups, though the trend is perhaps more and more to the latter alternative. What would follow if the latter alternative were adopted? What are the prospects for the party as a vehicle for change and accommodation? How much and what kind of change could be expected? Leaving aside the social and economic reforms that could be forced on the government from other quarters, internal or external, it is clear that the adoption of this strategy would require certain kinds of change if it is to work at all. But the kinds of change for which the party would be the vehicle can be very limited. The strategy need not be very ambitious. The aim is not to win support for government policies among the majority of the Black groups, but only to gain the cooperation of certain elites in running the institutional machinery. Moreover, even these collaborative leaderships need not be personally committed to government policy or ideology; as long as they are prepared to function within the imposed framework, they can be allowed considerable scope in voicing their opposition to the government and its policies. In fact, given the political climate of the communities within which they will have to function, such a public stance will be necessary if they are to establish any credibility.

The strategy is, after all, based on the need for at least minimal legitimacy and credibility of the collaborating elites within their own communities. If they were appointed and nominated by the government, there would be no political gain over a system of direct rule and administration; the only difference would be in the personnel. The local leadership must be produced by some kind of representative machinery. It is not necessary to gain wide popular participation in such representative institutions; that might even be dangerous in mobilizing popular support and providing an independent power base for the elected leaders. A total boycott of elections would turn them into a farce; what is required is the minimum turnout sufficient to provide them with some credibility—say 20 to 30 percent.

The basic requirements for the success of this strategy are that the political institutions created in terms of the government's framework—whether this be the homeland governments, the Colored Persons Representative Council, or Urban Councils in the African townships—do not break down completely, and that some public order be maintained in the Black communities. These two requirements are obviously closely connected. Prolonged riots and public disorder on the pattern of Soweto 1976 would tend to cause at least a temporary breakdown of these institutions. Conversely, though the coercive order remains basic, the function of these institutions is to constitute a safety-valve to prevent the recurrence of such prolonged and widespread civil disorders.

The coercive machinery of the state can also ensure that no serious rivals emerge for these collaborating leaderships. Obviously they would soon lose all credibility if an effectively organized political movement with a unified leadership and wide popular support emerged outside the framework of separate development. In this perspective the connection between the government's plans to allow some form of self-government in Soweto and other urban African communities, on the one hand, and the security measures of October 1977, on the other hand, becomes intelligible. The failures prior to October 1977 to restore civil order by coercive means only must have brought it home to the government that some political accommodation was necessary. However, the strategy of hegemony required that it could not negotiate with leaders produced outside its own framework who would be drawing support from the forces of resistance. Before an alliance with a collaborative elite could be formed, it was therefore necessary first of all to take decisive coercive steps to restore civil order, and to remove rival leaderships within the Black community. This was not necessarily thought out as a conscious and deliberate plan at the time. The crucial point is that it would have been one thing for the government to enter into open-ended negotiations with the Soweto Committee of 10 in the early part of 1977 *before* the security clampdown terminated the overt challenge to the established order, and a very different thing for the government subsequently to request the Committee members to collaborate in the introduction of the government's plan for representative institutions in Soweto.

The political accommodation sought through this strategy thus may be very limited indeed. At the same time it entails certain adaptations in the structure of the apartheid state. Any alliance with collaborating Black elites, however much under the hegemonic control of the party, is incompatible with strict maintenance of exclusive White privilege and social segregation. Moreover, given that full social incorporation or direct political or ideological mobilization of these Black elites is ruled out, the major resource available to the government to win their cooperation consists in the range of patronage it is able to dispense, of which granting access to privileged facilities can be one of the most effective means. Certainly at an elite level the system of racial discrimination cannot be retained. It seems paradoxical that the National party, as the party of apartheid, can be required to move away from racial discrimination, but to the extent that questions of racial ideology have become less important within the party, the obstacles to such adaptations and reversals are not insuperable. On the other hand, the strategy of hegemonic alliance does not require that these movements away from racial discrimination proceed any further than is necessary to gain the cooperation of the Black elite groups. It certainly does not require the systematic dismantling of the apartheid state; on the contrary, there are very real limits to the extent to which the National party can be the vehicle for change away from racial discrimination.

The major consideration that recommends the party as an instrument for change—i.e., its organizational strength, resources, and above all its unified leadership and disciplined membership—also serves to limit its contribution to possible change. Party unity is the key to power, and therefore any change that would threaten party unity will not be undertaken. Due to ideological slack there is currently a certain amount of room for piecemeal and ad hoc political accommodations, but any moves toward radical reform of the apartheid structure will repoliticize the ideological issues and intensify the conflicts of interest and orientation now contained within the party. Thus, *the need for (National) party unity is the most serious obstacle to any radical change coming about through this strategy.*

Of course, the National party itself is only one part of this picture. The "collaborative alliance" strategy may well prove to have unintended consequences; in particular, the scope it allows for "collaborative opposition" on the part of the Black leaderships drawn in as part of a larger alliance may produce unforeseen outcomes. It is not possible to provide a full discussion of this response (or counter-strategy) here. In any case, its effectiveness would seem to be largely a matter of creative improvisation by key individuals—a kind of political jiujitsu. In general it can be said that for a prospective Black leadership it combines the advantage of a legitimate public platform and institutional protection for political action and mobilization with the major disadvantage of alienating potential support from the Black community by working within the government's framework. The collaborating Black leadership seeking to get leverage from its position within the framework in order to oppose the government and perhaps force some more radical changes on it is caught in a classic double bind. If it could succeed in mobilizing substantial support within the Black community, then it would achieve a more independent power base and its dealings with the government could take the form of negotiation rather than mere consultation, but because of its participation in the government's framework, such a collaborating Black leadership is unlikely to gain substantial support in the Black community. The alternative strategy of non-collaboration is, in fact, more effective against these collaborating elites than as direct opposition to the government itself. Theoretically, perhaps the most effective strategy from the Black perspective would be a unified front of Black solidarity cutting across all ethnic, political, and ideological divisions—thus an alliance including the homeland leaders, the urban Black leaders prepared to work within the framework, the Black Consciousness groups, the ANC, the PAC, etc. *The lack of such a unified front of Black solidarity is the other major obstacle* to any radical change coming about through internal political accommodation.

A NOTE ON THE GOVERNMENT'S CONSTITUTIONAL PLAN

The government's new constitutional plan can be cited as both an instance of the shift from ideological politics for party hegemony and an illustration of the nature of this strategy. Since the 1950s the established pattern had been for the Nationalist government to follow a strong ideological policy line while carefully refraining from specific constitutional blueprints. The final goals of the policy of separate development were deliberately kept quite vague and ambivalent insofar as any constitutional specifics were concerned. At most there were some suggestions of a possible "commonwealth of separate states," a "confederacy," etc. There was a similar vagueness concerning the policy of parallel development for the Colored and Indian groups: much was made of metaphorical references to parallel lines that would never meet, or that might move closer or further apart, etc. In this way, while the meaning of separate development or parallel development could be made clear in ideological terms, the practical details of implementation could be left open.

Recently the Nationalist government somewhat surprisingly turned the tables by producing a constitutional plan, at the same time that many of the main tenets of its ideology became much less significant. This constitutional plan is an exercise in institutional piecemeal engineering, not a declaration of faith; at the same time it indicates the trend and thrust of the new strategy.

This is not the place for a detailed discussion and critique of the new constitutional plan. Only a few general comments are possible. The government's constitutional plan is a rather remarkable piece of work of its kind—both in what it says and in what it does *not* say. It provides, for example, precise details about the exact number of the elected and nominated members in each of the new constitutional institutions, including the income and age qualifications for members of the politically quite unimportant President's Advisory Council. On the other hand, it provides no information whatsoever on such crucial constitutional questions as the functions, powers, and competences of the new executive president and his "Council of Cabinets" in relation to the existing White Parliament and its executive cabinet (e.g., which of these institutions is to be in control of the administration and civil service). The practical significance of the new constitutional plan hinges on the answers to these questions; on them depends the determination whether the plan proposes a radical break with the present parliamentary system or whether it is nothing more than a slight consultative variation on the present system. But on these crucial issues, the plan gives no information whatsoever. In short, whereas one would have expected that constitutional proposals coming from a government rather than a perennial opposition party would give higher priority to practical than to symbolic issues, the practical import of the plan remains totally undetermined—at least at this stage. The symbolic meaning, on the other hand, is fairly clear, though not without some ambiguities. What the plan signals about the Nationalist government's strategy is the following:

1. It indicates an attempt at *inclusion* of the Colored and Indian groups in a quasi-federal structure while *excluding* the urban Africans, and thus a move toward some form of alliance with these minority groups against the African majority;
2. It indicates a willingness to allow limited access to the Colored and Indian political leadership to *executive* decisionmaking, at least on a consultative basis (and perhaps even more than that), but not to any shared *legislative* institutions;
3. It indicates a resolve to guarantee some form of built-in White majority by the prominence given to the 4:2:1 numerical ratio of White, Colored, and Indian membership of all the shared institutions;
4. It indicates a resolve to prevent any possible alliances between the White opposition and the other ethnic groups against the Nationalist party by the exclusion of minority parties from such shared institutions as the presidential electoral college and the Council of Cabinets.

In all of these instances one can begin to discern the outline of a specific strategy—that which I have termed party hegemony and indirect rule.

CONCLUSION: NEGOTIATED POWER-SHARING

It remains to say something about the third alternative strategy—that of "negotiated power-sharing." This strategy has been proposed primarily by the White opposition party—the PFP. In general moral terms such a proposal of "negotiation, not confrontation" is, of course, very attractive. Coming from a minor political organization without any major power base or realistic hope of becoming an alternative government in the near future, it is, however, a somewhat paradoxical political strategy. The PFP is not in any position to be a major participant in any negotiated power-sharing. In fact, this strategy would make political sense only if adopted by the ruling National party or a major Black protagonist. This is not to say that the PFP is not fulfilling a vital function as an opposition party by keeping this option alive and spelling it out for the benefit of those to whom it would be more relevant. In the meantime, the White opposition's main objective might be, like that of the various Black leaderships functioning within the system, to build as effective a political organization with as wide and cohesive a membership as possible in the circumstances, with a view to playing a more vital role in a future alliance when (and if) National party hegemony breaks down and negotiated power-sharing becomes a realistic strategy. Such a breakdown of National party hegemony is unlikely to be forced by internal political pressures alone. More probably it will come about through a combination of external developments and structural changes in the wider South African society and economy. But at this stage the internal actors have a responsibility to prepare for their vital roles at that critical juncture.

THE NATIONAL PARTY AND THE AFRIKANER BROEDERBOND

Hermann Giliomee

In 1971 René de Villiers, a liberal Afrikaner, commented on the expanding support the National party had attained since it was founded in 1934:

> [It] must be ascribed to its skill in persuading Afrikaners and particularly non-Nationalist Afrikaners, that *die party is die volk en die volk is die party* (the party is the nation and the nation is the party), or as Dr. Verwoerd was to assert almost without challenge during his premiership, "The National Party was never and is not an ordinary party. It is a nation on the move!" This identification was perhaps the chief magnet which finally drew and kept the overwhelming majority of Afrikaners together after generations of schism and squabble.[1]

It is one of the ironies of the South African political scene that the strongest supporters and the fiercest opponents of Afrikaner nationalism both regard it as a monolithic movement which mysteriously produces an unchallengeable *volkswil*, an ethnic consensus. This essay will attempt to analyze how the National party and Afrikaner Broederbond captured the Afrikaner nationalist movement for themselves and the role they play in the political structure of South Africa. After winning power in the 1948 general election, the National party had to operate in a much larger context than before, but it has succeeded in keeping its ethnic base intact and overcoming cleavages within Afrikanerdom.[2]

HISTORICAL SURVEY

In the 1930s the Afrikaners' political struggle entered a new stage when the United party was established, fusing J.B.M. Hertzog's National party with the pro-Empire South African party of J.C. Smuts. At this time there was a vast influx of Afrikaners into industry in semiskilled operative positions. For the followers of D.F. Malan's "Purified" National party, Fusion constituted a material threat. They anticipated that big capital, especially mining capital, would become predominant in the United party. This would split the Whites into a capitalist and a working class, and would enable the capitalists to replace unskilled or semiskilled Afrikaner workers with cheaper Black labor. Moreover, South Africa's almost neocolonial economic dependence on the British Empire would make a mockery of formal political independence. The attack on the joint enemies of imperialism and capitalism was led by a group of men usually labelled in a class analysis as "petty bourgeois": Afrikaans lawyers, teachers, professors, and lower level civil servants, whose career opportunities were limited by the increasing influence of English cultural and imperialist values under United party rule. Especially in the Transvaal this group was politically isolated because farming capital in the north supported the capitalist United party. This left the White workers as the only potential political allies. For the petty bourgeoisie, Fusion posed the threat of Afrikaner workers becoming denationalized in the process of mobilizing themselves on a class basis. Should this happen, there would be no hope of an Afrikaner party winning power and using the state to promote the interests of the Afrikaners at large and those of the petty bourgeoisie in particular.[3]

An orthodox class analysis, however, does not provide an adequate answer to the question of why the "purified" version of Afrikaner nationalism became a driving force in such a comparatively short time. As important as material interests were cultural and psychosocial fears and needs to which a strategy of ethnic mobilization could address itself. Fusion presupposed competition on an equal footing between the young and fragile Afrikaans culture and the rich British world culture. The purified nationalists claimed that this would result in the Afrikaans culture being swamped. Fusion also embodied reconciliation with English-speaking South Africa. The nationalists argued that this was a chimera before the Afrikaners had asserted themselves economically and culturally against the richer and more worldwise English-speaking section of the White population. Finally, Fusion represented the strengthening of the political ties with Britain and an entrenchment of imperial symbols such as the Union Jack and British national anthem. For the nationalists the imperial symbols did not evoke a sense of pride in membership of the British empire, but on the contrary reminded them that their nation had not yet taken its place among the independent nations of the world.

For the Afrikaner goals and sentiments to be understood, they should be viewed in the context of the deep psychosocial fears and resentments which many Afrikaners experienced in the 1930s and 1940s. The dislocation of rapid urbanization at a comparatively late stage in their historical development instilled in them a deep sense of insecurity. In a society in which urban and capitalist values predominated, the Afrikaners were not only of rural origin and the poorest of the White groups, but also were perceived as culturally backward and lacking in sophistication. Middle-class Afrikaners, particularly educators and clergy, were strongly attracted to a strategy of ethnic mobilization to overcome their feelings of insecurity and social inferiority, and they disseminated the ethnic gospel that self-realization and self-esteem could only come through group identification and assertion. It was because the 1930s was such a traumatic period for them that the Afrikaners were attracted to the "radical solution" of apartheid.

Both Hertzog and Malan tried to mobilize the electorate by exploiting the concept of Afrikanerdom, each defining it in a way that suited his political strategy. Hertzog, in attempting to build a cross-ethnic middle-class base, tried to make it an inclusive political concept. He proclaimed the rise of a "new Afrikanerdom" consisting of Afrikaans and English-speaking Whites—"equal Afrikaners"[4]—who subscribed to the principles of South Africa First and of full equality between the two White groups. In contrast, Malan's political strategy was to unify the Afrikaners, who constituted more than 50 percent of the electorate.

Malan's Purified National party hoped to mobilize the Afrikaners by staking group claims based on the notion that Afrikaners occupied a special place in the South African society. Politically it rejected the compromise of Fusion and called for republican independence. It argued that justice would not be done to the Afrikaners until a republic was established. National unity was possible only if the English-speaking section became part of a new South African nation of which the indigenous Afrikaner people were the core. In the economic realm the Afrikaners were urged to unite to close the gap between Afrikaner and English wealth and to protect the poor Whites from competition with Blacks, which could lead to the disintegration of the White race and "semi-barbarism." In the cultural sphere, the party demanded a two-stream approach involving mother-tongue education and separate educational, cultural, and religious societies in order to restore the Afrikaners' self-confidence and liberate them from their sense of inferiority.[5]

The most significant achievement of the National party in the

1930s was to rally most of the intellectual elite of the Afrikaners behind its cause. Its leaders were "cultural entrepreneurs"[6] who made extensive use of the Afrikaner Broederbond, a northern-controlled secret organization with extensive influence in Afrikaner educational institutions, to ideologize Afrikaner identity and history. The Broederbond view was that only by imbuing the Afrikaners with the sense that they were members of an exclusive *volk* could they be mobilized to pursue the National party goals aimed at safeguarding the future of Afrikanerdom. According to the Broederbond doctrine of Christian-Nationalism, nations were products of a Divine Will, each with a diversity of allotted tasks and distinguished from each other by their separate cultures. From this it followed that certain political, cultural, and spiritual values were a prerequisite for membership in the Afrikaner ethnic group; however, these were predominantly petty bourgeois values, with little appeal for workers. Concerned with winning the workers' support, Broederbond thinkers such as Nico Diederichs and Piet Meyer defined the volk in almost preindustrial terms: the Afrikaners were an organic unity in which workers and capitalists had assigned places and functions with corresponding rights and duties, and true Afrikaners would never exploit a fellow Afrikaner, but would protect and support him.[7]

The cultural entrepreneurs also ideologized Afrikaner history. In a recent study, Dunbar Moodie points out how central events in the Afrikaners' history, such as the battle of Blood River during the Great Trek, the wars of independence against England, and the concentration camps in which more than twenty thousand Afrikaner women and children died, were woven together in a "sacred history" in which God repeatedly revealed Himself to the Afrikaners as a chosen people. Moodie argues that the sacred history constituted a civil religion, and that after the emotion-charged commemoration of the Great Trek in 1938, the ordinary Afrikaner had made the main themes of the civil religion part of his own identity; indeed by 1938 "most Afrikaners believed that they belonged to an elect People."[8] Moodie's work is the most scholarly study of Afrikaner ideology to date, but it is difficult to believe that by 1938 the majority of Afrikaners conceived of themselves as an elect people with a sacred history. What happened in the 1930s was that growing numbers of Afrikaners began to believe that they were a separate people with particular interests that could best be promoted through ethnic mobilization. This feeling of belonging to a distinct political entity was greatly intensified after 1939, when Hertzog's concept of an Afrikaans- and English-speaking volk united in a new Afrikanerdom was shattered by the decision of the Smuts faction of the United party to take South Africa into World War II on the side of Britain. This rekindled all the old anti-British and anti-imperialist sentiments, and was ultimately decisive in persuading the majority of the Afrikaners to go it alone politically.[9] Afrikaners now more readily accepted civil religion as part of their identity, but even the leaders did not subscribe as faithfully to its tenets as historians imagine. By 1946 Malan, leader and prophet of the Purified Nationalists, observed that the Afrikaners did not, as outsiders alleged, consider themselves a uniquely chosen people:

> The truth is that the Afrikaner . . . generally speaking retained his sense of religion. As a natural consequence his nationhood is rooted in religious grounds: in his personal fate, as in that of his people, he sees the hand of God . . . . But that he claims this as his exclusive right and thus raises his people above others as God's special favourite is a false and slanderous allegation.[10]

In 1948 the National party won control of Parliament. The common assumption is that they achieved this by exploiting the Afrikaners' racist sentiments. From this perspective the election of 1948 was clinched by the ideology of apartheid, but there are serious difficulties with this interpretation. In the political campaign preceding the election, the Nationalists often urged that racial policies not be allowed to become a political issue between the two White parties, arguing that the only hope South Africa had of solving its racial problem lay in taking the issue out of politics.[11] The electoral victory was indeed ensured by Afrikaner unity. The appeal of the apartheid platform to the workers and the farmers was no doubt an important factor in attracting support for the National party, but equally important were the party's demands for South African national independence, its promotion of Afrikaner business interests, and its championing of the Afrikaans culture. Or, to put it in different terms, apart from "putting the Kaffir in his place," 1948 meant to the Afrikaners—particularly the professionals, educators, and civil servants—"getting our country back" or "feeling at home once again in our country."

After 1948 Afrikaner political power and ethnic unity gradually reinforced and consolidated each other.[12] It has often been assumed that the cohesiveness of the National party was due to a rigid adherence to the ideology of apartheid. However, central to the party's concerns was not so much the apartheid ideology but the need to maintain Afrikaner unity for the promotion of Afrikaner interests. If there was a dominant ideology it was one which stressed the values of *volkseenheid* (folk unity), which transcended class and regional (the North-South antagonism) differences, and *volksverbondheid*—the notion that the realization of the full human potential comes not from individual self-assertion but through identification with and service of the volk.[13] The indispensable support English-speaking Whites provided in maintaining the racial order worked against advocating Afrikaner hegemony too openly, but Afrikaner power was ensured by simply espousing Afrikaner unity. The policy of apartheid should be seen as an instrument which structures the South African polity in such a way that it fosters yet conceals Afrikaner hegemony.[14] However, the apartheid policy is not considered untouchable, and it is unity that is of decisive importance.

ORGANIZATIONAL FRAMEWORK OF THE NATIONAL PARTY

In some respects the National party has changed remarkably little since the 1930s, when it was a small opposition party and merely one of the constituent parts of the Afrikaner ethnic movement (*volksbeweging*), to the present, when it rules South Africa and stands as the guarantor of ethnic interests. It has always been a well-disciplined party, in which the decisions are made by a small elite while allowing members the freedom to express dissenting opinions within the party structure. The organizational framework has remained basically the same. It is a decentralized party in which each provincial party is almost completely autonomous, having its own constitution, party organization, and annual congress which chooses its leader. On the constituency level the party is organized in several branches which compete with each other in the raising of funds and the enrollment of new members. In the continual demands it makes on its members, the National party is a "standing" political party rather than one which is resurrected for each election. A large proportion of Nationalist supporters are card-carrying members of the party. In 1966, for instance, while the party's estimated total strength in the Cape Province was 274,678, it had 166,390 enrolled members. In the Transvaal the corresponding figures were approximately 516,000 and 300,000.[15]

Candidates for Parliament and the provincial councils are nominated by the branch committees of the constituencies and approved by the provincial leadership. In general, branches favor as candidates staunch party supporters known for their orthodox views rather than independent minds from the business and professional world, who usually stand aloof from the party organization.

In policymaking the party has remained elitist. The highest authority on party policy in a province is the provincial congress, which must ratify all policy changes of the party made in Parliament before they become the official policy of that province. However, provincial congresses do not have the power to make final decisions on the National party's program of principles. They can discuss proposals and submit them to the Federal Council, the supreme body of the party, in which the various provinces enjoy equal representation. Since the leaders of the party in Parliament are strongly represented in the Federal Council, they are able to block resolutions approved by a congress or submit proposals to the various congresses. During the past forty years all the proposals by the Federal Council have been accepted by the congresses without much opposition. The party leaders have sometimes bypassed the congresses in major policy changes. Without consulting the congresses, Prime Minister Verwoerd in 1959 committed the party to self-government for the various homelands and the abolition of African parliamentary representation. In 1967 Prime Minister Vorster decided to establish diplomatic relations with Black states without consulting the congresses. In practice, the annual party congresses of the four provinces are forums where policy and party matters are discussed and where cabinet ministers can explain and justify decisions made in the preceding year. Even in ideologically sensitive matters such as the "multinational" sport policy introduced in the early 1970s, congresses (after expressing some reservations) almost unanimously gave their approval to new policies initiated by the cabinet.[16]

The caucus, comprising National party representatives in the House of Assembly and the Senate, chooses the party leader. In its functioning, the caucus reflects the party's character of an elitist body which at the same time maintains a democratic forum. The caucus is not a policymaking body, but one which determines the strategy of the party during a parliamentary session. Ministers can be asked to explain decisions or statements, but the cabinet is not obliged to lay everything before the caucus. Verwoerd, for instance, in 1959 announced the government's decision to abolish African representation in Parliament before consulting the caucus. Challenged in the caucus, he conceded that bills ordinarily should be presented to the caucus at an early stage since it is a "combat unit which must know beforehand what is going on and then have to decide about the manner in which the struggle will have to be conducted in Parliament."

If members of the caucus express objections, the cabinet ought to discuss them because "it would be foolish for the cabinet to insist on things knowing that it cannot take its own people along on an issue";[17] however, Verwoerd added, the caucus did not have the competence to reject measures which the cabinet had decided on.

This touches on an important feature of the decision-making process during the past two decades. Decisions are taken in neither an authoritarian nor a democratic way. The first step in the process is the establishment of a consensus on important matters in the cabinet before they are taken to the caucus. The caucus is not the place for cabinet ministers to express their differences about ideology or strategy with their colleagues. About this, several cabinet ministers were adamant in personal interviews: "The Prime Minister will never take a divided cabinet to the caucus, and ministers will never attack each other in caucus."[18] Once a cabinet decision has been taken, all ministers are bound by it. Their task is then to win the support of the caucus for the cabinet decision. The caucus generally ratifies cabinet decisions without serious objections. The system works smoothly except in the case of crucial policy shifts.* To resolve differences Prime Ministers have used the device of appointing a cabinet committee to produce a general agreement, which is then submitted to a full cabinet.[19] In the cabinet's deliberations, the caucus is important in an indirect way: its members embody *die volk daarbuite* ("the people outside"). Ultimately a cabinet decision rests on an evaluation of whether it will "play" in the caucus and by extension in the provincial congresses. However, once the cabinet has reached a measure of consensus, neither the caucus nor the congresses can deflect it from its course. The system has been described by a cabinet minister as follows:

> Both cabinet and caucus operate within the confines of trust and obligation. The caucus has faith that the cabinet with its access to superior information will act in the general interests of the Afri-

*B.M. Schoeman (*Van Malan tot Verwoerd*, pp. 62-75) records an instance when a minority faction in Malan's cabinet took a matter directly to the caucus: it tried to get a decision in the caucus to remove the Coloreds from the common roll which would be binding on the cabinet. Motions that the caucus immediately discuss the matter and that it not be bound by the cabinet's decision were carried with large majorities. However, eventually it was decided to defer the discussion in caucus until the cabinet had the opportunity to consider the matter.

kaner people; the cabinet trusts the caucus members to fulfil their obligation to defend unpopular decisions to the people at large.

If this system breaks down, there is still very rigid caucus discipline; those who flout it are sure to be expelled from the caucus and the party. Only very rarely are members allowed to speak or vote in Parliament in a way which deviates from the party line. For any member hoping to gain promotion, the pressures to conform are enormous.

Thus virtually the sole impetus in the decision-making process comes from the cabinet—either guided by its own assessment of the situation or prevailed upon by the top bureaucrats. In such a context the composition of the cabinet is of crucial importance. The Prime Minister does not have a free hand in forming a cabinet. With the party becoming increasingly bureaucratized, it has in recent years come to resent the practice of bringing in technocrats or business leaders from the outside and quickly promoting them to the cabinet. For the sake of party unity, the Prime Minister is obliged to appoint to the cabinet the provincial leaders of the party who are chosen by their respective congresses. To make the call for White unity credible, he has to appoint an English-speaking minister or two. He is also under pressure to balance his cabinet in such a way that it reflects the different intra-ethnic divisions. Verwoerd is reported to have said that he sometimes found it difficult to reconcile the divergent interests and views of the various members of his cabinet. For him the task of the Prime Minister was "to keep your team together and unite the *volk* behind you."[20] Vorster also subscribed to this strategy, but his cabinets have reflected the shifting class and ideological base of Afrikanerdom. With the sacking of Albert Hertzog in the late 1960s, the representation of the Afrikaner working class was distinctly weakened in the cabinet, which became more middle-class oriented and ideologically less exclusive with respect to the Whites.

Verwoerd and Vorster differed in terms of their personal involvement in the process of decision-making. After he had established his undisputed authority in the party, Verwoerd became an authoritarian leader who forced through major changes. A towering personality, he overruled ministers on departmental matters and in general created the impression that he alone was making all the decisions—an impression which was not far from wrong. When Vorster became Prime Minister he is reported to have stated at his first cabinet meeting: "Verwoerd was an intellectual giant. He thought for every one of us. I am not capable of being a second Verwoerd. From now on each of us will have to know his own field, immerse himself in it and control it."[21] In departmental matters Vorster allowed a large measure of autonomy to ministers. Insiders in the party considered Vorster a man who in general policy matters was like a chairman of the board whose government did not run unless there was a large measure of consensus. It was a process of accumulating accord through patient listening, persuasion, and building of support. Unlike the years of Verwoerd, when decisions were made in accordance with an all-embracing master plan, Vorster's deliberations were pragmatic, experimental, and tentative. If serious divisions arose, an issue was shelved or delaying tactics were employed as far as possible. The overriding concern in the decision-making process was always the maintenance of unity.

The rise to power of P.W. Botha as Prime Minister in 1978 illustrates some significant trends in the party. First, it reflects the rise of the professional politician and the increasing bureaucratization of the party. To take the party in the Cape Province as an example: In the 1930s and 1940s the party organization on the local level was largely in the hands of volunteers. In 1936 the party appointed three full-time divisional organizers, one of whom was P.W. Botha, to assist the chief secretary in promoting the interests of the party and the Nasionale Pers (the nationalist publishing house in Cape Town). These organizers struggled to win respect for their office, often being referred to contemptuously as "paid agents"—people who worked for the cause only because they were paid a salary. When Botha resigned as assistant-secretary in 1946 to become propaganda officer of the Federal Council, he felt it necessary to express his gratitude to the Cape head-committee for the fact that "every member always has made me feel like a comrade—which I want to be—and not a paid agent who only seeks to make a living."[22]

During the 1950s party organizers were often under fire for interfering too much in the nomination of party candidates or using their office to promote their own political careers. Only after Botha became Cape leader in 1966 were these difficulties resolved. Under him the Cape party ran as a smooth and efficient machine. By 1978 there were sixteen full-time organizers under the chief secretary, who in a very professional way orchestrated activities throughout the province. Opposition to the nomination of party organizers for political offices had all but disappeared. The number of Cape parliamentarians who had started their career as full-time party organizers rose from three (one of whom was Botha) in 1948 to eleven in 1978 (out of a total of fifty-five). More important is the fact that Botha through the party machine has been able to influence the general pattern of the nomination process in the province. Unlike the former Transvaal leader C.P. Mulder, who had encouraged the recruitment of capable professional men as candidates, Botha favored party stalwarts tied to him through bonds of personal obligation and loyalty. In the election of the National party leader to succeed Vorster in 1978, this played a major role. While some of Mulder's "professional men" defected to R.F. (Pik) Botha and ultimately to P.W. Botha, Botha's "party men" backed him to the hilt. (It is estimated that at the most three or four Cape members did not vote for him.)

Botha's accession to national leadership indicates the weakening of ideological divisions within the National party. Power has come to rest increasingly on a provincial rather than an ideological base. The provincial parties have become the personal fiefdoms of their respective leaders, with enormous patronage at their disposal and the power to protect their followers. The situation was different in 1958, the most recent previous occasion on which an election was held in caucus to determine a national leader. (Vorster was appointed unanimously by the caucus in 1966.) Then a decisive number of Cape parliamentarians supported Verwoerd, an ideological hardliner, over T.E. Donges, a moderate Cape leader. In the 1978 election, Piet Koornhof—the most *verligte* (reformist) cabinet minister—proposed Mulder, who was probably the *least* verligte candidate but Koornhof's provincial leader, as national leader. (Mulder had protected Koornhof in the past when he was under fire in the cabinet for his deviant views.)

Transvaal is so strongly represented in the caucus (eighty votes against fifty-five for the Cape, twenty-four for the Orange Free State, and thirteen for Natal) that Mulder could have won despite the loss of those who defected to R.F. Botha. However, on the eve of the election, Alwyn Schlebush, the Free State leader, stated that "twenty and possibly twenty-one Free State members of the caucus would support P.W. Botha and tip the scale in his favour." With the votes Pik Botha and Schlebush delivered, P.W. Botha was able to clinch the election with ninety-eight votes against seventy-four.

In terms of ideology and resistance to reform the Free State has traditionally been much closer to the Transvaal than to the Cape. Both in 1954 and 1958 it supported the Transvaal candidate in the election of a national leader. In 1978, however, the Transvaal candidate (Mulder) was vulnerable because of the scandal surrounding the Department of Information, of which he was the head. Another factor in the election was a cleavage formed by competition between the two large Afrikaans pressgroups—the southern Nasionale Pers (with P.W. Botha as director) and the northern Perskor (with Mulder as director). Nasionale Pers publishes dailies in the Cape, Free State, and Transvaal, while the Perskor dailies are confined to the Transvaal. Explicit provincialism is taboo in Afrikaner politics, but the Nasionale Pers papers may have contributed materially to Botha's victory by subtly disseminating the message that the Cape represented more "civilized" values and a greater sense of responsibility than the "brash and volatile" Transvaal.

As Prime Minister, Botha can be expected to build his national power base on the model of his rise in the Cape party. People will be bound to him through personal loyalty rather than ideological affinity. Whereas Verwoerd bound Afrikaners through ideological mastery and Vorster through the image of a protective strong man, Botha will tie people to him through commitment to the party organization and ultimately to him as its personification. He has much of the dynamism of Verwoerd, and like him appears to be moving toward an ideal, which in his case may be to bind the Coloreds more closely to the Whites. (He has not expressed himself clearly on the position of the urban Blacks.) However, like Vorster, he is a pragmatist who believes in making adjustments to the exigencies of the times. Whereas Vorster sought to achieve the greatest measure possible of consensus before making a decision (in his last major speech in Parliament he stated that the primary task of the Prime Minister in the cabinet was "to achieve the maximum consensus"),[23] Botha's record indicates a tendency to get his way by overpowering his opponents or eliminating them politically. In some ways he resembles Lyndon Johnson in the early years of his presidency—someone who can control the party organization, who realizes the need for rapid change, and who seems destined to grow as a leader, provided he is not tempted (like Johnson) into a disastrous war beyond his borders or some other serious mistake.

THE RISE OF ONE-PARTY RULE

Since winning power the National party has steadily increased its representation in Parliament. After the 1948 election its majority —in alliance with the Afrikaner party—was only eight. (It had received only 37.2 percent of the votes cast compared with 47.9 percent for the United party.) In the 1966 election it won 126 of the 166 seats in Parliament, attracting 57.8 percent of the votes compared to 36.3 percent for the United party, and in the 1977 election it captured 134 of the 164 seats, drawing 64.5 percent of the votes.[24]

Against this background two constitutional trends have become manifest in recent years. First, the party has increasingly usurped the functions of Parliament as the link between the electorate and the executive. During the urban upheavals of 1976—perhaps the greatest crisis the South African state has yet faced—Vorster did not recall Parliament but summoned a special meeting of the caucus to discuss the situation and sample the mood of the Nationalist constituency. Parliament still functions according to established procedures, but its debates have little influence on the course of legislation.

Second, there has been a decline in legislative control over the executive. Effective judicial control is also lacking. South Africa has inherited the British system of the sovereignty of Parliament, and the courts at present have the right of review respecting only one clause of the constitution—namely, that referring to the equal status of the two official languages—and subordinate legislation (e.g., municipal ordinances). During the past two decades the executive has accumulated increasing powers to bring about fundamental social, economic, political, and legal changes by administrative action, and no attempt has been made to provide for the supervision of the way these powers are exercised. According to a leading constitutional expert (W.H.B. Dean), South Africa has already moved so far in the direction of the centralization of power that a constitution providing for a presidential-style chief executive will make little difference in practice.[25] With the party having largely supplanted Parliament and the executive overriding the legislature, the executive can crush extra-parliamentary political opposition to the system without being challenged in the courts or in Parliament. Parliament retains importance as an arena in the Nationalist succession fight: it remains essential for a Prime Minister or potential Prime Minister to demonstrate his ascendancy in debate, confounding the opposition and successfully defending his policies. Parliament also enables the government to publicize and legitimize its decisions.

"MOVING AWAY FROM APARTHEID"

Cabinet ministers have used the vast powers at their disposal to remove some of the crudest forms of discrimination and segregation (so-called "petty apartheid"). Ministers committed to such reforms have evolved a political style which differs distinctly from that of the 1960s, when apartheid legislation was boldly proclaimed and enacted. The assumptions and actions included in this new approach can be summarized as follows: First, it is accepted by the leadership that for the sake of party unity these reforms should not be presented as breaks with the past. Second, it is believed that any declaration of an intention to institute far-reaching reforms will only harm the cause of reform; thus to have publicly announced five years ago that the government was committed to mixed sport on club level, the abolition of job reservation, or the desegregation of theaters countrywide would have raised such an outcry in the party that any reforms would have been killed. Third, the leaders in the particular fields to be affected by the reforms (for instance, the sports administrators and trade union leaders) are called in by the ministers to have the case for reform presented to them; after consensus has been established, everyone is bound by the decisions. Fourth, the press is persuaded not to publicize the gradual implementation of reforms. This entails the incorporation of new influence elites within the party's decision-making process. (A minister who had spelled out the secret agenda of his plan for a reform in his field to the Afrikaans and English press remarked afterwards: "I talked to them more confidentially than with members of the Broederbond"—*Personal communication.*) Fifth, the caucus is confronted with a *fait accompli* of the reforms but assured that control will continue to be exercised by way of permits. Existing legislation has rarely been repealed: it is the administration not the law that has been changed.

While these strategies could be employed for pragmatic adapatations to the separate development blueprint, a proposed new constitution for South Africa is too much of a break with the past to be introduced in this way. This constitution provides for (1) three separate parliaments for Whites, Coloreds, and Indians, which will have control over their own respective affairs and will make laws on matters of common concern; (2) a State President appointed by an electoral college consisting of fifty members of the White parliament, twenty-five of the Colored parliament, and fourteen of the Asian/Indian parliament (the ratio of representation is fixed according to the present population figures), and (3) a cabinet council consisting of the State President, seven Whites, four Coloreds, and three Indians. Some of the more verligte spokesmen in the party argue that the plan provides for discussion by representatives of the three racial groups about common affairs. On matters of national concern a measure would become law only if passed by all three parliaments: each of the three parliaments would then have a blocking or veto right in respect of every piece of legislation touching on national issues. These spokesmen have publicized this as "consensus politics" and the "sharing of responsibility"; at the same time Vorster publicly stated that control would remain in the hands of the President. He explained that the proposed cabinet council, where consensus will have to be reached before draft legislation is laid before the various parliaments, will function in the same way the South African cabinet does now:

> Even if the majority of the cabinet feels that legislation should be introduced, the Prime Minister can still say in practice that it shall not be introduced. That is how cabinet government operates. If one were to count votes in a cabinet, or if one were to argue in a cabinet until one has reached consensus on every detail, there will be no governing.[26]

The President could thus veto draft legislation the National party opposes. However, he does not have the power to legislate by decree. Should the party wish to pass new legislation, it may have to secure the consent of the governing parties in the other parliaments. The basic difficulty for the party is that the veto right is split among three separate bodies which are rigidly stratified along racial lines.*

In putting forward their constitutional plan in 1977, the National party leadership adopted the following procedure: (1) a cabinet committee was charged with the task of drawing up a draft constitution; (2) the committee operated in isolation without engaging any sector of public opinion except perhaps the Executive Council of the Broederbond and a few academics; (3) the cabinet's deliberations remained private until it made public its completed recommendations. The editors and senior political correspondents of the

*The Progressive Federal Party has tried to resolve this problem by declaring in favor of the principle that groups should be able to form under conditions of free association: all laws enforcing ethnicity would be repealed. The PFP proposals provide for a federal government responsible for national matters, such as defense and finance, and several self-governing states which would be autonomous in matters such as health and education. The federal assembly would comprise political party representatives elected on a proportional basis within each self-governing state. The cabinet, or federal executive council, would include representatives of all significant parties in the assembly chosen proportionally, in contrast to the "winner takes all" system in which the majority has a monopoly of power. While budgets and money bills would be decided on a majority vote, most other decisions would be by consensus. A minority of 10 to 15 percent would be able to veto a measure in parliament and the cabinet. The hope is that cross-cutting affiliations would develop in such a political dispensation which would remove to a considerable extent the need or inclination to organize groups or parties on an ethnic basis. However, if the Whites chose to form a racial front they could still protect their interests, but a purely Afrikaner party would be too weak.

Afrikaans newspapers were called in to attend the meeting where the plan was presented to the caucus, and were thus put in a position of trust and corresponding restriction of freedom to report and express opinions on the plan. Commenting on the process whereby the constitutional plans were conceived, Marinus Wiechers aptly observes that it illustrates their nature:

> They are basically guidelines for future party political action aimed at constitutional reform, and do not, in themselves, constitute broad proposals which have to be considered by all interested groups and parties concerned . . . . Instead of being directives for a future development which will affect all the people in the Republic, they represent the outcome of rather parochial party political policies.[27]

The proposed constitution, based as it is on the cornerstones of the apartheid system (population registration, group areas, etc.), makes it unlikely that authentic Colored and Indian leaders, who reject these cornerstones, could be successfully incorporated in the scheme. Moreover, the plan is being introduced in a political climate in which goodwill and the unity of common purpose are conspicuously absent. Consensus government is being introduced without securing the consent of the participants in the first place, and there is no sign of a political unity emerging among the three groups upon which consensus politics can be based. Third, the plan runs counter to what the West would consider a prerequisite for easing outside pressures on South Africa. William Foltz has pointed out that the most important single consideration for Western policymakers in this matter is that of procedure:

> How a new constitutional order is drafted and implemented is at least as important to outside—and particularly American—opinion as the content of the final package . . . . Discussion and drafting of constitutional proposals ought to involve open and highly visible participation by domestic black leaders. . . . The leaders participating in the process must be able to speak for substantial constituencies and to demonstrate convincingly that they have mass support.

Above all any new order "must be presented clearly as a major break with the past."[28] The fact that Blacks are excluded from the plan greatly undermines its credibility.

However, despite all the flaws, the new constitutional plan has the potential to break the impasse in the South African political system, provided that a President emerges who is determined to make the system work, exploiting the considerable scope he has within the party and utilizing the party's strict discipline. G.E. Devenish has remarked that the status of the State President will be directly related to the extent to which he can make the constitution work: one deadlock after another will destroy the legitimacy and credibility of the constitution, and he cannot resolve all deadlocks in favor of Whites. "What the constitution sets up is a State President whose ability to effect essential and radical political reforms through compromise and simultaneously retain the confidence of the white electorate is a prerequisite for success."[29]

At the beginning of its administration, the Botha government promised to take a more conciliatory stance on the proposed new constitution. In distinct contrast to the Vorster strategy, which allowed discussion only after basic principles had been accepted, the verligte elements in the Botha cabinet referred the proposals to a parliamentary commission of enquiry. It is assigned the task of also considering alternative proposals submitted by representatives of all interested parties. Compared with the unilateral decision-making of the past, this procedure indicated a greater desire to seek common ground. However, the question remains whether a Prime Minister, or State President, heading the National party as presently constituted is structurally capable of embarking on fundamental reforms.

CLEAVAGES WITHIN THE PARTY

There is a complex of reasons for the failure of major reforms to emerge from a party commanding an overwhelming majority of White votes and finding itself under strong pressure both internally and externally to produce fundamental change. In the case of ethnic parties, it is particularly important to focus on the hidden cleavages and interests among their supporters because such parties often do not have ideological coherence. From recent opinion surveys a picture emerges of a whole array of political attitudes existing among Afrikaners, of whom more than 80 percent support a single party (the Nationalist) which claims to be ideologically consistent. On the basis of these studies, a number of generalizations can be made. In the political field the Afrikaners in the late 1970s are divided equally between those who favor consolidation of the homelands or radical partition and those who wish to retain the status quo; some 40 percent support a form of qualified franchise within a common political system; less than a tenth support power-sharing in a federal state with no group predominant. In the economic field two-thirds favor the abolition of the traditional racial privileges, while a third wish to retain them. In the social field a fifth favor the lifting of racial barriers in state schools, marriages, and residential areas, but nearly four-fifths oppose such measures.[30] This is hardly a clamor for fundamental reform. In a Market and Opinion survey conducted in December 1976 and January 1977 in the wake of the Soweto upheaval, National party supporters responded as follows to the question of whether drastic changes were needed in the party's policies to solve the problems of the country: 23.7 percent said yes, 53.5 percent said no, and 22.4 percent were uncertain.[31] Thus there is obviously no clear consensus for change in the party.

However, a distinct characteristic of an ethnic party is the large degree of loyalty and trust leaders command. A recent survey found that 60 percent of a sample of Afrikaners interviewed would support their leaders even if they acted in ways their followers did not understand or approve.[32] This indicates that if the leadership could agree on the nature and direction of change, they would be able to take their following with them. However, any significant split at the leadership level would be duplicated at lower levels. Assuming for a moment that the leadership is much better informed than the public of the need for change and of escalating pressure, why has it failed to introduce far-reaching reforms? The answer is that the party leadership does not have the necessary consensus to embark on such a course. In fact, since the early 1970s it has been characterized by what may be called a permanent succession crisis, in which most of the internal debate and politicking has been concerned with the prospects of rival claimants to be the successor of Vorster.

This raises questions about whether this kind of infighting is merely a matter of political ambition and rivalry, or is indicative of the party's structural condition. In the National party there exists no mechanism through which ideological and other conflicts can be resolved except by the leader. Through his disposal of patronage, his power to choose the cabinet, his responsibility to decide whether or not legislation should be introduced, and his brief to formulate the party consensus, he is in a position to determine the pace and direction of change and resolve conflicts in favor of one side against its ideological rivals. Through all these means Verwoerd propelled the party into acceptance of the "homelands" policy. Under him there was ideological coherence, unity of purpose, and little talk about who his successor would be. However, if a leader assumes the chairman of the board approach, as

Vorster did, the ideological differences in the party will surface at all levels, with each ideological faction seeking to prevail over the others by blocking their initiatives and ultimately by winning the struggle to elect the next Prime Minister. The position of the Prime Minister remains unchallenged, but within the party's structure several rivals for the succession emerge. Rivalries also exist in Western parties, of course, but are usually significant only when a leader falters or when a new one has to be chosen. In the National party of the late 1970s, however, there has been a continuous rivalry and jockeying for position in which the issue is not so much a conflict of different ideological approaches as an attempt to outbid rivals in assuring the Afrikaners that their interests are safest in a certain pair of hands. In such circumstances, there has been little possibility of firm political action in the direction of set political goals.

The National party also differs from traditional Western political parties in the narrowness of its political base and its limited responsiveness to the larger electorate. In recent decades most large Western parties have spread their bases to incorporate interests and views across a wide political spectrum. Despite substantial English-speaking support in the 1977 election—some 30 percent of the English-speaking voters who voted supported the Nationalists—the National party is still fundamentally ethnically based and is primarily responsive to ethnic pressures. English-speaking big business, to cite but one important interest group within the White section, is not represented in the party. Neither are Afrikaner-based groups which have recently risen to prominence, like the military and the state corporations. With rare exceptions the Afrikaner business, educational, and professional elite do not go to Parliament, and their thinking is only indirectly brought to bear on the caucus or cabinet. And of course the Black voice is not heard. Very few caucus members know middle-class Blacks intimately; fewer still are confronted with Black anger and frustration. The Minister for Plural Relations does not represent Blacks: he simply "administers" them. Conceivably his dealings with the Black population may convince him of the need for reform, and he may persuade the cabinet or caucus to accept policies which might stabilize the political situation, but within his structural context he is hardly in a position to get something accepted which will damage his own constituency's interests, and those remain firmly within the ambit of White politics. Members of the caucus are predominantly concerned with policies which will further the interests of the people they represent and who can return them to Parliament. Above all the National party represents an ethnic group which is determined to protect the political power which safeguards its material interests, and that depends largely on control of the state.

Because of the cleavages within the party, its narrow base, and its primary concern with protecting Afrikaner interests, it is clear that the party under its present leadership would not be able to introduce reforms which go beyond the limits of party consensus even if the leaders themselves were persuaded of the need for them. It is clear, however, that the leadership is not convinced of the pressing need for major changes. Though a sense of urgency has crept into some ministerial pronouncements in the late 1970s, probably the majority of the cabinet is of the opinion that there is still plenty of time to deal with the issues of statutory racial separation. Certainly the political accommodation of Blacks has a lower priority than the need to maintain party unity. The dominant feeling is that the prevailing consensus would almost certainly be threatened by ideological conflicts if any serious attempts at reform were initiated.

What are the main ideological tendencies within the party at present? It has been standard practice to discuss ideological cleavages within the party in terms of a *verlig-verkramp* dichotomy, but these concepts have become somewhat meaningless since verlig is used to refer to any relatively enlightened view in White politics. Historically the term *verlig* is related to those Nationalists who during the late 1960s and early 1970s advocated greater White unity and "harmonious" race relations through mixed sport and the abolition of petty apartheid measures. *Verkramptes* during this period championed undiluted Afrikaner domination and racial exclusiveness, but the verkrampte leadership was purged from the party in 1969. While they were still members of the party they formed the internal opposition within the whole range of Afrikaner institutions against the more "open" policy of the verligte leadership.

While the terms *verlig* and *verkramp* still have currency, they have become obsolete as indicators of present cleavages within the party. After the verkrampte leadership had been purged, the verkramptes were considered by the Nationalists to be excised from the party. In fact, at grassroots level many remained or subsequently returned. Members of the party who still favor undiluted White supremacy and social discrimination consider themselves the *behoudende* (conservative) faction—i.e., people who wish to retain the status quo. In the period 1967 to 1974, verligtes claimed to work and think within the framework of separate development, but during the watershed period of 1974 to 1977 they began to see separate development as an instrument rather than a goal. In the words of Gerrit Viljoen, reputed head of the Broederbond, there was a realization that "apartheid's original formula cannot cope with [the present] situation."[33] Verligtes still insist on the party as the only vehicle for change. Whereas verligtes in the late 1960s emphasized the positive and dynamic aspects of the ideology of separate development, they are now proposing some changes in the social and economic foundations of apartheid—e.g., the repeal of the Immorality Act, the Mixed Marriages Act, and statutory job reservation. While they favor some social and economic liberalization, they still reject all forms of power-sharing. What further distinguishes them from Progressives in their approach toward constitutional change is their insistence on (a) using ethnic groups (rather than regions) as the basis of any new political arrangements and (b) initiating change through the program of the National party rather than calling a national convention to work out a new constitution.

With one or two exceptions, cabinet ministers and members of Parliament have spurned a verligte or verkrampte tag. While the present impasse exists in the party, ministers have tried to build up a centrist image—speaking verlig on some issues and verkramp on others. The leadership is not much guided by an enlightened vision or moral concerns, but reacts mainly to political and economic imperatives. At the moment the main imperatives confronting the leadership are (a) the need to strengthen South Africa against any assault from the outside, (b) the need to prevent Black unrest (above all another Soweto), which could lead to escalating international demands for sanctions, (c) the need to promote economic growth to accommodate the growing numbers of Black unemployed and prevent further instability, and (d) the need to reach an accommodation with the Coloreds and Indians as possible allies.

Within the party at large two general approaches to meet these imperatives can be discerned:

1. *The ideologues*: Separate development should be implemented as an end in itself. The various non-White groups should exercise authority only through their separate homeland structures, and all Blacks who are not essential for the "White" economy should be settled in the homelands. Racial equality in the job market and further sharing of public facilities should be opposed.
2. *The pragmatists*: Separate development should be considered only a means to achieve the end of political stability. In order to create a stable Black middle class with common capitalist in-

terests and a stake in containing Black unrest, job reservation should be rapidly abolished and economic growth promoted. In the social field, separate state schools and residential areas should be maintained, but public facilities, living conditions, and business opportunities should be improved in the Black group areas.

In the political field there is serious disagreement within the party about the strategies which should be adopted to accommodate the various non-White groups and achieve a greater measure of stability. The main problem is that the government still considers the various homelands structure as the basis of decision-making, which leaves the situation of the urban Blacks an unresolved problem. Three basic positions can be discerned:

1. *Paternalistic consultation*: Whites should consult with Black leaders, but Black political rights should be restricted to responsibility for their own communal affairs in the homelands and Black townships.
2. *Indirect rule*: The various non-White groups (first the Coloreds and Indians and then the urban Blacks) should have a voice in their own communal and certain common affairs, but White sovereignty should remain intact in White affairs and almost all common affairs.
3. *Medeseggenskap*:* There should be a gradual evolution toward power-sharing—most likely in a consociational system in which various ethnic groups will participate and make decisions on the basis of consensus.

The new constitutional plan has been represented by the right wing of the party as indirect rule and by the left wing as an approach which implicitly entails common decision-making. To win acceptance for this plan, the party finds itself in a double bind. Only if a new dispensation provides for real power-sharing will Colored and Indian leaders be persuaded to participate in attempts to negotiate for change; however, if a new dispensation does involve power-sharing, the right wing of the party will threaten to break away, raising the specter of a divided Afrikaner group.

It is possible that chronic instability may prompt a faction to explore strategies for genuine power-sharing or even a form of supra-

*The Afrikaans word is ambiguous: it could mean only a "voice" or it could refer to common decision-making.

ethnic class rule, which is the antithesis of what the Afrikaner ethnic movement embarked upon. For the present, however, the primary significance of the proposed new constitutional dispensation is that the government has accepted the fact that the status quo is unacceptable, at least insofar as the Coloreds and Indians are concerned. As for the Blacks, who are still excluded from any proposals for constitutional reform, it is difficult to predict how the party will respond to pressures to accommodate them in a common political system. As pointed out earlier, the elitist nature of the party and its loyal following make it possible for the leadership to introduce major changes provided they are willing to accept party disunity. But it is impossible to anticipate under what circumstances a leader would emerge who would be willing to embark on fundamental reforms of the apartheid structure as it relates to Blacks.

The government's initial reaction to two new important commission reports in 1979 seemed to indicate that it was about to embark on reforms which went beyond mere adaptations to the apartheid policy. The Wiehahn Commission recommended that Black workers be allowed to unionize freely, while the Riekert Commission proposed greater freedom of movement to Blacks permanently resident and permanently employed in the so-called White areas. Broadly speaking, both reports aimed at creating and stabilizing a privileged group of Black insiders of some one million men and half a million women out of a total Black population of eighteen million. Implicit in the reports is the assumption that this "labor aristocracy" could be won as allies of the Whites by phasing out the reservation of certain jobs for Whites, accepting the principle of equal pay for equal work, and ending legal requirements for separate facilities for Black and White workers in factories and offices.

The Botha cabinet, which is much more verlig in composition than any of the Vorster cabinets, immediately announced that it accepted both reports in principle. However, because they "undermined" the position of the White man, the reports met with stiff resistance from both the White trade unions and the party's caucus, where Botha has not yet consolidated his position. As a result the bill introduced in Parliament embodied only those recommendations of the reports on which consensus had been reached. Several key recommendations were modified or rejected. Instead of the proposed freedom of association for all workers in a unified system of collective bargaining, the bill maintained the policy of segregated trade unions. At the same time, however, the responsible minister was given the authority to declare any Blacks to be "employees," which allowed him to grant exemptions to some migrants and commuters.

The government's reaction reflects the strategy the previous administration developed for instituting changes. The first moves stake out a limited area of change which do not go beyond the existing consensus within the broad Afrikaner political framework, and avoid anything which would put the precarious unity under strain. As in the case of the "multinational" sports policy instituted in the early 1970s, the responsible minister is granted discretionary power to move beyond the accepted area of change. In the labor field the minister is empowered to grant exemptions to certain workers excluded from trade unions and to authorize mixed unions. But no statutory rights are conferred on these workers—their exemptions depend on ministerial favor. If these exemptions have undesirable consequences, they can be revoked; if on the other hand they create no major problems, the minister can change the status quo piecemeal and eventually present a new order to the caucus and unions as a *fait accompli.*

Despite the fact that key recommendations were watered down, the government's reaction to these two reports still represents a commitment to economic liberalization for a class of urban insiders and an acceptance of their permanence. A new economic framework is emerging which stands in stark contrast to the old policy of regarding all Blacks as temporary sojourners in the White areas—people against whom discrimination was justified by virtue of their being "non-citizens." However, the cabinet does not appear to have grappled as yet with the social and political implications of this new economic framework. There is still no sign that the government is prepared to open up some public schools and residential areas, or to grant urban Blacks a meaningful form of political representation—all of which seem prerequisite for the incorporation of a loyal Black middle class. Any new political dispensation for the urban Blacks is certain to lead to an irrevocable split in the party and its support organizations, and will therefore be delayed as long as possible by the leadership.

THE AFRIKANER BROEDERBOND

Because of their interlocking membership, close ties have always existed between the National party and the Afrikaner Broederbond. Together they mobilized and unified the Afrikaners as a political group, and after power was won in 1948 they closely cooperated in developing and justifying the apartheid policy. In recent years both organizations have been affected by the same ideological cleavages. There can be little doubt that the ultimate fate of the party and the Broederbond will be fundamentally the same.

The Afrikaner Broederbond was founded in 1918 to promote Afrikaner interests and the Afrikaans language. It soon became a secret organization which restricted its membership to male Afrikaners who strove for the ideal of an everlasting and separate Afrikaner nation. It gave preference to Afrikaners and other sympathetic persons and firms in economic, public, and professional life who were *of sound financial standing* and in every respect trustworthy. Its stated aim was the creation of a consciousness among Afrikaners concerning their language, religion, traditions, country, and volk, and the promotion of the interests of the Afrikaner nation.

In the 1930s and 1940s key figures in the political, cultural, and economic elite of the Afrikaners were enlisted. During this period the Bond operated in various spheres. It was the driving force behind a movement to promote Afrikaner private capital and combat the influence of socialist trade unions;[34] it championed mother-tongue instruction in schools; it campaigned against British imperialism. During the war years the Bond was unable to heal the breach within Nationalist Afrikanerdom between the National party and the parapolitical Ossewa Brandwag movement, but it was apparently instrumental in bringing about a coalition between Malan's National party and N.C. Havenga's Afrikaner party, which many Ossewa Brandwag members had joined. It was this coalition which was victorious in the election of 1948 and put the Nationalists in power.

Considerable problems arose after 1948 in establishing a sound relationship between the Bond and the party. J.G. Strijdom, leader of the party from 1954 to 1958, was adamant that the Bond should not interfere with political policy. Apart from consolidating Afrikaner unity, he saw it as the Bond's task to capture for the Afrikaners a greater share of the commercial community and the professions.[35] Towards the end of the 1950s the Bond was reinvigorated by a campaign to persuade the Afrikaner people that the time was ripe for the establishment of a republic. Under Verwoerd there was a marked convergence of the Bond and the party. The Bond then served as the disseminator of the ideology of separate development and, as Verwoerd put it in a letter, "a closed debating forum for rational reflection on the best interests of the Afrikaner people."* The Bond be-

*From personal interview with close confidant of Verwoerd.

came less concerned with economic goals and more concerned with political policy and ideological coherence. Toward the end of the 1960s, tension again arose between the Bond and the party. Influential verkrampte elements in the Bond resisted any modification of the policy of separate development, sniping at the Nasionale Pers newspapers and indirectly at Vorster, and they had a considerable braking effect until some two hundred extreme right-wing members were purged in the early 1970s. In this decade the Bond lost much of its influence*—above all to the bureaucrats, who were in a strategic position to block reforms put forward by the Bond, and to the Afrikaans press.

Over the years the Bond's membership has grown steadily. In 1952 the organization consisted of 3,500 members, of whom 2,039 were teachers, 905 farmers, 357 clergymen, 159 lawyers, and 60 members of Parliament (including the Prime Minister and six cabinet ministers). According to a 1978 report there were 11,190 members, of whom the highest proportion (20.4 percent) were educators. After the 2,424 educators came farmers (2,240), pensioners (1,124), businessmen (1,096), churchmen (848), public servants (518), lawyers (390), bankers (309), municipal employees (198), agriculturalists (265), policemen (212), railwaymen (201), politicians (186), and employees of parastatal organizations (165). In addition, a junior affiliate of the Broederbond—the Ruiterwag ("Mounted Guard")—was estimated to have nearly 12,000 members.

The Broederbond membership is elitist. In 1972 the politicians who were members included the Prime Minister, virtually the entire cabinet, three-quarters of the National party members of Parliament, 28 senators, 69 members of the provincial council, and 13 party organizers. Among the educators were 24 rectors of universities and teachers' training colleges (in effect almost every Afrikaans rector), the directors of education of the four provinces, the chairman of the National Educational Advisory Council, and the head of the Council for Social Research. Besides these educators there were also 171 university professors, 176 lecturers, 468 headmasters, 121 schoolmasters, and 647 teachers. Roughly half the total number of Afrikaans headmasters and inspectors were members. In the newspaper world 16 managers of newspaper groups and all the Nationalist editors (with

*J.H.P. Serfontein, a journalist who in the late 1960s had broad access to Bond documents, argues that in terms of independent political influence the Bond was the main loser and the Afrikaans press the main winner in the verkramp-verlig struggle of the period. See his *Die Verkrampte Aanslag* (Cape Town: Human and Rosseau, 1970), pp. 231-36.

two possible exceptions) belonged to the organization, but only three ordinary journalists were members. With a few exceptions the heads of all the civil service departments were Broeders.[36]

The impetus of the movement comes mainly from the Executive Council, consisting of twelve members, and the secretariat in Johannesburg. From there emanate the newsletters which are discussed at the monthly meetings of the roughly eight hundred branches across the country. Through its "public arm"—the Federasie van Afrikaanse Kultuurverenigings (FAK)—the Bond lays down broad guidelines and coordinates overall strategy for the more than two hundred cultural, religious, and youth bodies affiliated to the FAK. The local branches are not mere passive recipients of head office circulars, however; they are invited to comment on the circulars and can forward criticisms and suggestions to the head office with respect to the conduct of national affairs. These reponses may in turn be circulated by the head office in subsequent newsletters. With leaders drawn from various walks of life, the branches also play an important role in local affairs. They act as counterforces to dissident Afrikaners and to supranational organizations such as Lions International, and they can influence the composition of school and university committees, appointments to important high school and university teaching positions, and the elections of local government bodies, particularly in rural areas. (These are often undertaken on an informal basis and without instructions from the head office.) Local branches also nominate emerging young leaders in their districts as members of the Bond.*

While the Bond has considerable impact as an "ethnic adhesive," its present political significance is usually misinterpreted by the press. It is incorrect to consider it "the secret body which rules South Africa," manipulating the political process. At most it imbues its members with a sense of ethnic discipline while the government tries to reach consensus on political issues. A Bond member who served on the Executive Council explained the role of the Bond as follows in a personal interview:

> Its function is to prevent too wide a range of *public* dissent. We debate issues vigorously in private and then communicate our re-

*To Afrikaners who are not members of the Bond, it is a perennial question whether men rise to positions of power and influence primarily because they are members of the Bond. The answer seems to be that a Nationalist-minded Afrikaner has to show some potential as a leader to become a member. In turn his membership is a boon to his career chances.

flections to the head office. It helps the leadership to feel the pulse of the people and get some indication of the direction it should be moving.

But with the gradual loss of ideological coherence, the Bond is finding it increasingly difficult to establish a national consensus, composed as it is of Verwoerdian ideologues, "pragmatic realists," and "radical" verligtes. In 1972 the influential Afrikaner journalist Schalk Pienaar, a Bond member himself, remarked that "Until recently the Bond could succeed in being a debating community (*gespreksgemeenskap*) which would contain the divergent views in the political life of the Afrikaner and enable collective action to take place. Obviously it is no longer the case."[37] A newspaper editor similarly declared that "the same quarrels, differences of opinion and gradual division which Afrikanerdom is experiencing in public has also permeated the Afrikaner Broederbond."[38]

In the present decision-making process the Bond acts as a secret communication channel between the government and the Afrikaner elite. It is both a generator of ideas which are suggested to the political leadership and a sounding board of government initiatives. Its role can be illustrated by reference to two recent political shifts. (1) In the early 1970s, when the party began to move toward a new sports policy, the Bond brought members serving in sports-controlling bodies from all over the country together for a secret top-level discussion. The proposals emanating from this meeting were discussed by the Executive Council and submitted to the political leadership. With consensus established among the leading sports administrators, the cabinet could move ahead; in the meantime all Bond members were assured that the formulations of the Executive Council "will be reflected in official Government statements."[39] (2) When the government announced in 1976 that it was exploring a constitutional alternative to the Westminster system of government, the Executive Council submitted a memorandum which drew on the political expertise of leading academics. After the proposals for a new constitution were announced, the Executive Council notified members that the "contents of our memorandum are in many respects reflected in the new dispensation for Coloreds and Indians."[40]

It should be stressed that the final decision rests with the cabinet, which can reject or ignore the suggestions of the Bond. Vorster mainly used the Bond as a communication channel. He informed the Executive Council about the progress of the negotiations between South Africa and the West on Rhodesia; the council in turn assured

Bond members in a circular that the interests of South Africa are used as the only yardstick in the negotiations. Vorster also kept the Executive Council informed of developments during the 1975-76 incursion into Angola. Whether P.W. Botha will make similar use of the Bond is not yet clear. A spate of disclosures of the Bond's activities has greatly diminished its value as a secret communication channel. On issues such as political rights for urban Blacks, disagreements within the Bond are so deep-seated that it is unable to offer any suggestions. In this matter its present strategy is to hold wide-ranging discussions (called *dinkskrums*—"think tanks") initiating a process from which some consensus might emerge. There has been one such meeting between Broederbond leaders with the chairman of the Soweto Committee of Ten and several discussions with Colored leaders. By instilling in its members a sense of trust in the political leadership, and as an agency which can legitimize government actions, the Bond is an important asset to the party leadership. However, the Bond at large can clearly no longer produce an ethnic consensus on the complex issues of appropriate strategies for the maintenance of Afrikaner interests. As in the case of the party and the church, a decisive move to the left or to the right will almost certainly precipitate an institutional split. However, such a move is unlikely in the immediate future, and in the meantime the bureaucracy guards over the apartheid structures.

CONCLUSION

The style of Afrikaner politics has changed considerably since the time of an all-embracing national movement in which the party, church, Broederbond, and press moved more or less in step with each other in the realization of distinct political, economic, and cultural goals. The most important development has been the rise of the party as the foundation of ethnic interests and the gradual decline of the autonomous political influence of cultural-political organizations such as the Broederbond. At the same time the ideological coherence of the party, based narrowly on the petty bourgeoisie, farmers, and workers, began to wane by the late 1960s as business interests became predominant and the economy demanded employment of Blacks in positions which could formerly be staffed by Whites only. The Afrikaans press assumed a more independent role in propagating a more flexible implementation of party policy, while the apartheid bureaucracy acted as the guardian of the Verwoerdian blueprint. Class interests have been involved as well. With some 35 percent of the Afrikaners being employed by the state, their economic standing is dependent on a policy which prevents large-scale Africanization of the public and semi-public sector at the expense of the present incumbents.

National party rule has seen the ascendence of the political executive in the state, defined as the broad administrative, legal, bureaucratic, and coercive systems which structure relations within the society. By and large the political executive has ruled in terms of party political priorities and within the constraints of party unity, and it has resisted demands from the business class to give priority to other considerations. When ASSOCOM,* representing English business interests, called for the restructuring of the racial order after the upheavals of 1976, the Prime Minister immediately warned the body against making any proposals for a new socioeconomic order. The political executive has also failed to comply with requests by the military to clearly formulate defensible political goals to assist in preparations for counter-revolutionary war.

There are several reasons why the political executive has not moved more purposefully in terms of broader socioeconomic and strategic considerations. Unlike the autocratic Verwoerd, Vorster had to give much more consideration to establishing consensus before moving ahead. In the absence of clearly asserted authority, "departmentalism" manifested itself in the apartheid bureaucracy and the particularistic concerns of cabinet ministers. Ministers committed to reform have opted for low-profile adaptations rather than boldly spelling out the need for and principles of reform. Finally, there is an overriding political reason. While hostility to apartheid—both external and internal—has slowed down economic growth and weakened South African military efforts, the political opposition has not yet seriously challenged the autonomy of the South African state. For instance, the uprisings of 1976 in Soweto and other Black townships seriously shook the complacency of the ruling group and frightened away some foreign investors, but there were no strikes and industrial production was maintained. The uprisings were eventually put down by the police without the help of the army, and by the middle of 1979 foreign investment was back to its previous levels, although new investments tended to be short-term.

Until the Black opposition, with or without the help of external forces, poses an effective challenge to the political order, the National party leadership considers the costs of gradual change less than

*Associated Chambers of Commerce.

the danger of a political split of Afrikanerdom that would almost inevitably follow significant structural reforms. Similarly, the costs of the present political order are not yet so high that the two new power factors in the White state—the businessmen and the military—will risk a showdown with the political executive.

THE FAILURE OF POLITICAL LIBERALISM IN SOUTH AFRICA

Heribert Adam

> That is why I hold in contempt those young white radicals who sneer at liberals and liberalism. Who were their mentors? If it had not been for the Jabavus, Marquards, Hoernles, they would have been in darkness until now. One cannot measure past labours in terms of present demands. One expects Black power to sneer at White liberals. After all White power has done it for generations. But if Black power meets White power in headlong confrontation, and there are no Black liberals and White liberals around, then God help South Africa. Liberalism is more than politics. It is humanity, tolerance, and love of justice. South Africa has no future without them, least of all White South Africa.
>
> Alan Paton, *On Turning 70*

THE CHANGING FACE OF LIBERALISM [1]

White and Black nationalists alike deeply resent South African liberals. Afrikaner militants view universalistic notions of civil rights and common franchise of all citizens as suicidal for White minority existence, and regard their proponents as naive "promoters of communism" in the guise of majority rule. Contemporary African political activists dismiss as irrelevant the liberal insistence on nonviolent, evolutionary constitutional reforms of a system which excludes the majority from meaningful political participation at their places of birth or permanent residence. Blacks no longer plead for admission into a White system by demonstrating their "civilized standards" at liberal tea parties which have ceased to take place.

This review will be confined to a brief sketch of *political* liberalism without addressing in any detail the complex problem of *economic* liberty as a precondition of liberal democracy. The political history of liberal and radical alternatives in South Africa sheds light on the political success of the anti-liberal nationalist forces.

South African political liberalism has traditionally been associated with the idea of a single South Africa in which all its citizens, regardless of race, enjoyed political rights based on universal suffrage.

Legal equality of opportunities would be supplemented by social security systems for the weaker, noncompetitive citizens. A comprehensive program of education and social welfare would attempt to compensate for the effects of past discrimination. An independent judiciary and bill of rights would protect individuals, not groups. The law would be used to prohibit racially discriminatory practices. Liberals attribute overriding importance to the rule of law, freedom from arbitrary arrest, due process, and freedom of speech, assembly, and association.

The classical liberal tenets of at least legal political equality and a promise of equality of opportunities under the protection of a universal bill of rights have never existed in South Africa. The little support there was for these tenets among the White section has steadily declined since union in 1910. There was initially a nonracial franchise in the Cape,[2] but this system soon eroded under the pressure of other provinces with different traditions and different constellations of interest groups.[3] From the first challenge to the "natives" constitutional rights to stand for Parliament in the Cape to the emergence of franchise qualifications and the manipulation of voting procedures, there was a continuing trend toward the removal of Africans and Coloreds from the common roll: Africans in 1936 and Coloreds in 1955. Their symbolic four White liberal representatives were abolished in 1960 and 1968 respectively.*

The emergence of an interracial Liberal party from 1953 to 1968 with a policy of universal franchise is not inconsistent with this trend. In its heyday in the early 1960s, the party had approximately five thousand members, half of whom were Africans. However, this party of the "left" White and moderate Black spectrum had never won a seat in the all-White elections or more than a fifth of the White votes in its most successful constituency. The liberals were led by some of the most respected men of letters South Africa has produced, but there were divisions in the liberal camp concerning the universal franchise policy as well as the commitment to extra-parliamentary activity after Sharpeville in 1960. With persistent persecution, harassment, and exile of leading liberals, particularly after a few party members became involved in acts of sabotage, organized

*At no point did the exotic liberal import from Britain into the Cape threaten the existing racial power structure. However, the voting behavior of the Cape Blacks served as a constant reminder to the Afrikaner Nationalists of their political rejection as well as the potential force of a liberal English/African/Colored alliance.

political liberalism was long a marginal phenomenon in South Africa before legislation in 1968 made interracial political organizations illegal and led the Liberal party to formally dissolve itself. What continues as the liberal spirit in South Africa today represents either a diluted version of traditional liberalism or is sufficiently adjusted and patriotic to be tolerated by an ever-more powerful Afrikaner nationalism. The pragmatic realism of leading liberals in the 1970s moved them closer to the core policies of the Nationalists.* The Nationalists in turn adopted some of the liberal principles—abolition of social racism, greater economic freedom for the brown and Indian middle class—so that some of the pronouncements on both sides are no longer very far apart. Harry Oppenheimer, for example—not a traditional liberal in the narrow South African sense, but the financial backbone of the "progressive" apartheid opposition—cannot conceive "a surer recipe for disaster" than one man-one vote, but asserts that "power-sharing has to come." While a few dedicated individuals maintain their liberal stance, it would be fair to say that under the pressure of an overwhelming reality many former liberals have quietly jettisoned their earlier idealistic principles in favor of the politics of survival.

This change seems particularly evident in the universities. The English-speaking White students have, on the whole, tended to an apolitical, individual career orientation. The influence and radicalness of their organization, the National Union of South African Students (NUSAS), has frequently been overrated by both the government and its critics. NUSAS, under the constant pressure of harassment by the authorities and rejection by apolitical or conservative students, now confines itself more to service activities than politics, especially since Blacks split off to form their own Black Consciousness groups. Similar trends have developed among faculty, with a high turnover through emigration since the early 1960s. The once outspoken liberal consensus of faculty and administration on the English campuses has

*As early as 1971, in a speech to the alumni at Harvard University, where he had received an honorary doctorate, Alan Paton found himself "hoping that all our people who are not white will make the fullest use of these instruments of power which are being put into their hands by the architects of separate development, no matter how feeble they may be. . . . I stand not for the withdrawal of American investment but for its dramatic improvement on salaries and benefits" (*Knocking on the Door* [Cape Town: David Philip, 1975], p. 231). Paton now urges the U.S. government not "to pressure our rulers to the point they become psychologically impotent to make any changes at all" (quoted in *South African Outlook*, May 1977).

faded into an annual ritual of freedom speeches, reconciling a privileged, segregated existence by celebrating morality. The genuine liberal faculty who show concern about the daily violations of basic freedoms through their public behavior are few and isolated now. Other honored institutions which uphold the liberal spirit, such as the Institute of Race Relations, the Black Sash, and some church groups, have to face similar predicaments. C.W. de Kiewiet, one of the more perspicacious observers of the liberal school, recognized this tendency as early as 1964: "When the intellectual leaders of a country become demoralised and perplexed or feel repudiated, they can become, despite themselves, even without knowing it themselves, converts to the heresies they have battled."[4] In short, thirty years of Nationalist policy have created a segmented society—both as an objective as well as subjective reality—to which some of its foremost critics have adjusted. The conservative implications of the remaining liberal program are evident in the new core principle that forced separation cannot be undone by forced integration, but only through personal choice. Thus Paton now declares, in direct contradiction of earlier Liberal party policy: "Universal suffrage and a unitary state imposed from without is not—for me—compatible with the liberal ideal."[5] Given the predictable outcome of personal choices of White South Africans regarding the maintenance of their advantages at the expense of the underprivileged, the consequences of this classical unequal freedom are readily apparent: the existing distribution of power and privilege will be protected by its beneficiaries, and the challengers will have little institutionalized effective way to counteract them. Without the political clout of a franchise to decide between competing interests for scarce resources, only two outcomes are conceivable: (1) the status quo (save some surface modifications) will remain or (2) ever more costly extra-parliamentary escalation and confrontation will ensue in the absence of mechanisms for the regulation of conflicts. The failure of political liberalism is evidenced by the increasingly entrenched allocation of unequal life chances according to inherited group membership rather than individual merit in the absence of institutionalized redress.

In this situation of polarized camps, the liberal voice of reason has little success. However, it would not do justice to the liberals to blame them for the absence of radical reformist policies when such a stance would mean political suicide or the mere assertion of purist principles with little or no support. The key to an understanding of the hopeless minority position of South African liberals lies in a structural analysis of their specific limitations in South Africa.

INTERPRETATIONS OF FAILURE

The decisive question—namely, why did political liberalism fail in South Africa when it had been so successfully exported into other British settler colonies (North America, Australia, and New Zealand)—needs to be answered. Further, why has formal democracy, a proven regulator of class conflict, not emerged when powerful economic interest groups obviously would have benefited from a stable color-blind arrangement with unrestricted labor supplies and collaborating trade unions instead of overpaid White labor, an artificially restricted domestic market, and international isolation with the prospects of potentially costly future risks of escalating guerrilla war? If it was possible to transplant a liberal system of government from abroad into the nineteenth-century Cape colony, why would similar pressure not succeed 150 years later when the missionaries and philanthropes of London or the "friends of the natives" in South Africa have been joined by much more powerful economic interests? How can it be explained that the U.S. Carter/Mondale administration is now advocating, at least rhetorically, a one man-one vote system for South Africa with hardly a single prominent White South African supporting such a proposal?

A closer analysis of the South African Liberal party, with all its complexities of personal heroism, decency, deficiencies, and shortsightedness, may shed some light on these questions. Without falling into the common trap of personalizing historical forces, let us explore eight possible explanations for the failure of South African liberalism. These eight, partly overlapping explanations can best be distinguished according to crude disciplinary labels. In rough order of explanatory value, starting with the least insightful, they are (1) religious, (2) biological, (3) philosophical, (4) demographic, (5) political, (6) psychological, (7) economic, and (8) historical.

(1) The least useful explanation for the resilience of apartheid against the liberal attack of rationality invokes *religious* barriers of a unique Calvinism. The Calvinist distinction of the elect and the damned might have been used for justification of Afrikaner policies, but cannot explain the exclusion of the "children of Ham" in English South Africa. Notions of the "chosen people" with a "challenge of destiny" which sanctified a collective mentality with a "religious utopianism" did not exist in English South Africa. And yet it evolved similar segregation practices. David Welsh concludes his investigation into the colonial policy of early Natal with the statement that "it is a myth that apartheid is the exclusive product of Afrikaner national-

ism."[6] Some contemporary observers, on the other hand, have pointed out that the broad liberal self-concept of English-speaking South Africa so far has not been tested: "Under the umbrella of Afrikaner control, the conservative colonial settler tradition can be preserved while at the same time the utopia of a future egalitarian South Africa of all races be cherished and preached."[7] Given the history of Natal and Rhodesia, one does not need religious explanations to predict the sympathies of English South Africa in a crunch.

(2) Pierre van den Berghe has asserted that "there must be a *biological* basis to our 'gut reactions' "[8] to explain the persistence and ferociousness with which communal strife is carried out everywhere beyond any rational cause. Sociobiologists stress the evolutionary principle of "kin selection" as the basis for the ethnocentric preference for one's own kind. Individual racial badges of group membership are considered to establish putative "blood" ties with the endurance of close kinship bonds. Against such sociobiological fibers liberal notions of fraternity, regardless of ethnic differences, would have no chance, nor would the universalistic creeds of socialism, with its emphasis on cross-cutting working-class solidarity, and Christianity, with its focus on the God-given equality of all creatures with souls. Not only the history of South Africa but communal strife almost everywhere—from Northern Ireland to Lebanon and many Third World countries—would seem to confirm the sociobiologists' pessimism.

On the other hand, it seems to be the case that resentment between groups almost always needs to be activated and mobilized. Propagandists for ethnocentric communal organizations benefit from it, and their victims react with counter-mobilization. Without such indoctrination from outside, people do not rise in senseless hatred of "others," save in defense against perceived threats to their rights. What accounts for the appeal of the agitator is not biological but cultural factors. It lies in the common socialization experience of members of a distinct culture. In times of anxiety and conflict, this cultural bond offers relief and security, in comparison to which the liberal or socialist brotherhood with the stranger outside the group remains only a doubtful promise.

(3) The persistence of communalism and nationalism reveals a *philosophical* bias of liberalism expressed in its basic assumptions about human nature. Liberalism views human nature as "given" and absolute. Hamish Dickie-Clark has perceptively described this bias:

> The liberal has tended to assume that too much of the world out

> there is fixed, amenable to logic, fundamentally rational and open to persuasion. Moreover, that there are certain truths about people, e.g. that they love and strive after freedom under all circumstances, which are eternal and absolute.[9]

Like their doctrinaire Marxist opponents, liberals incorporate little cultural relativism in their assumptions about people, and fail to take into account that definitions of human nature differ according to historical circumstances. To dismiss divergent ideas about good and evil as "false consciousness" does not make them less real.

In the final analysis, the liberal belief in the power of persuasion rests on the idealistic assumption that people can be convinced by rational argument to abandon their particularistic group interests in favor of a universal truth, morality, or humanity. However, there is little ground to hope for the success of such an appeal when group membership guarantees benefits of power and privilege. This is particularly the case when ethnic chauvinism is reinforced by anxieties about possible or—as in South Africa—certain losses of security, esteem, and general life chances linked with White ethnocentrism. In this situation, ethnic exclusivism offers the psychological rewards of a sense of belonging, and is reinforced by strong group pressures to conform and ostracism of dissenters. In sum, liberals believe that conflicts are caused mainly by prejudice that exists only in the mind, not by antagonistic, incompatible interests.[10] All conflicts appear reconcilable by reasoning, based upon appeals to self-interest, which implies a universally shared common rationality. Leo Kuper contrasts the state of polarization with the "possibility of understanding, of dialogue, of *adjustments of interests*."[11] For the liberal, progress can be defined as the gradual merging of particularisms into a common good-the market of humankind. But what if certain groups progress at the expense of other groups precisely because they reject the liberal notion of the free competition of individuals in the marketplace in favor of the rewards of ethnic monopoly? For such a strategy, the liberal perspective provides no explanation, save the assumption of a deplorable aberration of mankind.

(4) Obvious *demographic* factors militate against the acceptance of liberal principles in South Africa. Unlike in the United States, the South African Whites are correct in their repeated insistence that they would lose all effective political power by granting equal rights to the numerically four-times stronger Black majority. This is particularly true of the Afrikaner subgroup, which, with its relatively recent nationalism and development of a distinct language, has sought

to protect itself against the additional threat of Anglicization. The fear of "becoming a minority in South Africa as helpless as Jews were in Germany" (as one of the leading Afrikaner writers puts it)[12] provides a continuing reinforcement of a corporate identity. The liberals were aware of this obstacle in their path, but considered it a mere Afrikaner paranoia, for which they prescribed an inadequate cure: rather than surrender itself forcibly later, Afrikaner nationalism ought to bury itself voluntarily now. It is naive to expect a ruling group to embrace the liberal principle of self-abdication for moral reasons alone, when it can continue to dominate, albeit as outcasts of a distant humanity.

(5) The *political* reasons for the failure of liberalism are evidenced in the moralistic approach toward a polarized contest of power with high stakes. That the "Liberal Party of South Africa works for a 'change of heart,' on both moral and political grounds"[13] is indicative of its hardly having come to grips with the nature of politics. Nor have the liberals fully understood the character of their Nationalist foe. The rise of Afrikanerdom is seen in terms of "a great historical drama" which could turn into a "tragedy"; the fatal sinners fall because of character deficiencies–"their own arrogance,"[14] which mysteriously traps them in darkness instead of allowing enlightened compromise. One of the leading African members of the Liberal party, Jordan K. Ngubane, explains the root of apartheid as an instinctive habit with a specific birthdate: "The present crisis in South Africa has its origins in the whites' desire to dominate the Africans. This sinister inclination has been predominant among the whites since the formation of the Union of South Africa in 1910."[15] Political persecutions which have been clearly planned and weighed for their impact are denounced as the actions of a "power-mad government in a state of utter panic."[16] In short, the shrewd rationality of a calculating government is underrated. The better educated, upper-class English liberals tend to cling to the stereotyped caricature of the Afrikaner as inept, clumsy, fumbling; in particular they apply it to the lower-class policeman. As Donald Woods puts it: "So many members of the security police seem to be so underequipped to evaluate real subversion that a great deal of time is spent barking up the wrong trees."[17] This culturally nurtured underestimation of the rulers' intelligence would seem one of the more important reasons for the failure of many attempts at resistance in South Africa, carried out frequently with innocuous amateurishness by radical Whites in the early 1960s.[18]

The smug disdain of some sophisticated members of an English world culture for the parochialism of an unenlightened adversary is frequently accompanied by an almost masochistic glorification of "creative suffering"—as if martyrdom would prove the truth of a conviction instead of merely the greater might of the superior power. "I cannot even conceive that life could have meaning without suffering," writes Paton for a U.S. magazine. Creative suffering "changed no laws, it softened no customs, but it made the country [South Africa] a better place to live in."[19] No wonder then that the effectiveness of political action is often ranked lower by liberals than the affirmation of principle. It would seem that the Christian strain in South African liberalism, above all, accounts for this unpolitical approach to political problems. At the same time, this very moral conviction equips leading liberals with staying power and individual courage against all odds which persons with mere pragmatic perspectives can rarely muster.

(6) One of the more important reasons for the failure of liberalism in South Africa relates to the *psychological* obstacles to an interracial alliance in a racially ordered society. Though there have been many impressive examples of African/White resistance and shared victimization,[20] in the end such unequal cooperation proved stifling for Black militancy. White liberals failed to understand that for Blacks a period of separation from their well-meaning brotherhood was essential for the emergence of an independent and self-confident Black movement, just as it was in the civil rights struggles in the U.S. (or, for that matter, in the feminist movement nowadays). Only by cutting the bonds from a dominating mentor can subordinates reach the stage of subjective equality which is a precondition for truly color-blind interaction. Such relationships cannot be decreed or imposed from above by self-appointed allies who do not share the structural inequities, despite all their attempts to identify with their underprivileged counterparts. From the perspective of a Black writer, Ezekiel Mphahlele, who returned to South Africa after two decades of exile, has perhaps best characterized the limitations of White liberal identification with Blacks:

> The liberal white writers like Alan Paton and Nadine Gordimer, who are English-speaking, try to portray African life and character faithfully. But because there is a physical barrier between us, they still have to strain the literary imagination and rely for the most part on their compassion and perception. Somehow along the line African life and character eludes them and they take refuge behind symbolic portrayal. . . . The liberal white still cannot shake off the

> shackles of history by which he is kept prisoner in his own position of exclusive privilege.[21]

Of course there was always a psychological payoff for the White liberal, despite (or because) of his minority position in the White political culture: to the pleasure of belonging to the elite was added the vicarious satisfaction of identification with the underdog. This thrilling experience enhanced his self-image almost like an adventurous tourist who has discovered an exotic new world: "For many members of the Party, inter-racial association has meant entering into a new country, exciting, dangerous and beautiful."[22] Being pampered and celebrated for his courage in supporting the underprivileged, whose elite extended their warm hospitality to the rare guest from the other side, the White liberal enjoyed the benefits of both worlds, and could feel good about his unselfish openmindedness. By accepting such association, subordinates perpetuate their psychologically crippled existence. By going it alone, the colonized have entered a necessary phase of emancipation. It is they who now define the situation. Though the results may well be identical, the effects of the process are essentially different from those of an integrated struggle: the subordinates have acquired a new identity and shed the internalized perception of inferiority. This would seem to be the crucial difference between the new generation of SASO and the earlier Black resistance in the Congress movement, which despite its militant rhetoric was ideologically integrated into a liberal value system. The baffled NUSAS members have now learned this lesson from the Black Consciousness movement, but it is doubtful that the liberal suspicions about "racist rejections" have been dispelled. It would seem the ultimate tragedy for White liberals that, despite their genuine identification with the Black cause and even common suffering, they are likely to be only marginal participants or even excluded from the victory celebration in Azania, if there is one in their lifetime.

(7) A class analysis of South African liberalism and the *economic* basis of its support can shed further light on its failure. Unlike their counterparts in Europe, South African liberals never enjoyed the unambiguous support of the mining and business sections, who in the 1960s supported the more cautious and paternalistic policies of the official opposition parties instead. The "pure" liberals were relegated to "a party of the intelligentsia,"[23] with mainly employed or independent professionals as the decisive supporters and policymakers. As many observers have remarked, these teachers, clergymen,

lawyers, journalists, and university lecturers could, so to speak, afford to be liberals, because they were the least threatened with economic losses or replacement by an African takeover. Moreover, an important reference group for them was the world community of intellectuals with whom they interacted, and whose suspicions they sought to dispel with proof of their virtue. This *Weltbürgertum* of non-parochial intellectuals, engaging in "reasoned interracial appeals"[24] and tempered discourse, was far removed from the labor problems of White farmers, the profit calculations of businessmen, or the racial sentiments of the bulk of blue- and white-collar workers. Elitist philosophizing about human dignity could hardly appeal to a White worker, farmer, or housewife whose own self-esteem was based on having a dependent Black servant to push around.

One of the shortcomings of South African liberals, then, would seem to be that they never descended from the abstract realm of humanity and individual charity to a concrete articulation of economic and political alternatives which would have attempted to reconcile the divergent Black and White interests. Such efforts emerged only in the 1970s in the form of the SPROCAS Reports. But by then the racial polarization together with the decline and political realignment of the English apartheid opposition posed different problems for the survival of liberal principles in South Africa.

(8) The lack of political alternatives for divided societies besides the Westminster model is perhaps the most decisive *historical* reason for the failure of liberalism. This reason is historical in the sense that essential preconditions for political liberalism which were present in the culturally more homogeneous societies of Western Europe are absent in the plural colonial societies of which South Africa is a prime example. As Alfred Hoernle, the most profound analyst of liberalism in South Africa had already pointed out in the 1930s, the classical representatives of liberalism, as a byproduct of the evolution of modern capitalism, "were dealing with social groups the members of which were, substantially, homogeneous in race and culture. . . .[T]hey assumed European models to be capable of export and transfer . . . even to European colonies in which Whites and non-Whites met and clashed and fought for survival and supremacy."[25] This assumption proved incorrect as Hoernle suspected it would, but his liberal colleagues never admitted it.

The fundamental difference between Western political democracy and political procedures in ethnically divided states is the understanding in the former that political power can change from one party to another peacefully according to election results. A defeat is accepted by the incumbent group because its basic rights and privileges will not be affected during the interval of opposition before the next opportunity to regain power arrives. This interchangeability of ruling groups presupposes relative equality in life chances not fundamentally threatened by the opponent's ascendancy to power. Only because the power-holder respects the rules of the game does the defeated party submit temporarily.

In contrast, in power struggles between hostile ethnic segments in so-called divided societies, the explicit policy of the incumbent ruler and the logic of the situation precludes peaceful rotation in office. The rulers unilaterally dictate how much they wish to accede to demands of the subordinates, and only the bargaining power of the latter in conjunction with objective exigencies will influence this process. This situation has developed not because of evil intentions, stubborn prejudices, or special attitudes of ruling groups in power in ethnically divided societies, but because of structural factors not present in Western democracies. Thus, because of a long history of domination by one group, combined with the accumulation of wealth at the expense of the subordinate group(s), a high degree of group cohesion has been created, particularly on the part of the dominant group. In addition, few cross-cutting allegiances exist which transcend the ethnic boundaries. In a hypothetical election based on a common voters roll, the numerically strongest ethnic group would, therefore, almost certainly come out on top. Given the extraordinary privileges which the minority ruling group enjoys, together with the fear of revenge, displacement, and the loss of security generally, the minority clings to power with all its might. This reinforces the group cohesion of each antagonist and makes the democratic system of political decision-making at the most an *intra*-group affair, with scarcely any mechanism for the regulation of *inter*-group relations. At the heart of the problem is the gross inequality of the competing groups, which has to be rectified before majority rule based on the Westminster model of shifting party control can be introduced. And yet, paradoxically, this model of majority rule is seen as the only effective way to achieve the goal of greater equality of life chances for all citizens.

COMPETING RADICAL STRATEGIES

Thus far the liberal forces have been evaluated in comparison with the Afrikaner appeals on the political Right. The assessment of political liberalism would be incomplete, however, without at least a brief reference to the strategies of the Left. Since Black politics is not the topic of this study, it may be justifiable to subsume Black underground resistance since the mid-1960s under this label for the sake of brevity. Up to Luthuli, and including Buthelezi with his powerful Inkatha movement nowadays, Black protest stands clearly in the liberal tradition of evolutionary improvements of the existing economic structure. Measured on the basis of the growing support for Inkatha, Black liberalism remains astonishingly strong in light of its history of failure. Thus, in a 1977 opinion survey of 1020 urban Africans (Freiburg study), 65 percent still expect improvements "through patient negotiations between white and black leaders" and an equally high number favor private (African) ownership of production over state control. Such "liberal" attitudes are increasingly rejected by the politicized urban youth, however.

Among the apartheid opponents left of the liberal critics, a variety of long-established radical positions exist which outline a transformation of South Africa into an alternative socioeconomic system. These spokesmen for different forms of socialism disagree sharply with each other about revolutionary strategies as well as short-term goals. Such bitter recrimination among the Left continues a long tradition of infighting and power-struggles, but in the South African case it also flows from substantial disparities in the assessment of apartheid reality—not just allegiance to different ideological mentors.

Four distinct radical perceptions of change in South Africa can be discerned according to priorities of strategies and delineation of villains among other apartheid opponents. These four perspectives can be labeled (1) Black power, (2) ANC/SACP,* (3) "Marxist-Leninist," and (4) Trotskyite. Their differences are not confined to quibbles about ideological purity and compromise in solidarity against a common enemy, but sometimes lead to such serious charges as criminal behavior and betrayal. A brief description can attempt to unravel the main issues in contention in the world of committed revolutionaries, but neither detailed evaluation of the validity of the different perspectives nor an analysis of their origin can be given here.

The Black power perspective, as elaborated in SASO and Black Consciousness publications, stresses above all the racial humiliation of Blacks, including Coloreds and Indians as members of collectively discriminated groups. In this respect the Black Consciousness approach differs from earlier PAC tactics, which were aimed at the inclusion of Africans only. Contrary to assertions that the ANC or PAC organized

* African National Congress/South African Communist Party.

the township upheavals of 1976-1977, Soweto students maintain that the demonstrations originated from a new political awareness among South Africa's youth. This youth rebellion differed from earlier protests and the industrial action of 1973 in Natal. In Soweto the urban proletariat was mobilized in several solidarity strikes, but they did not push stay-at-home actions to dramatize economic grievances. On the contrary, the economic recession and high unemployment seem to have hampered strike activities and facilitated frictions between migrants and permanent city dwellers. Policy cleavages deepened between urban students and rural Africans, partly as a result of exploitation by the authorities. Inkatha ensured that Natal did not follow the national pattern of uprising despite the earlier strike militancy in Durban.

The ANC/SACP perspective defines the South African conflict as a special kind of colonialism, and as a consequence vacillates in its approach to Buthelezi and the African rural bourgeoisie. In this internal colonialism, national liberation is seen as the first goal to be achieved, with a socialist revolution to take place only after bourgeois democracy has been established. The emerging Black bourgeoisie, or for that matter all "progressive forces" regardless of race, are seen as allies in this struggle because of existing racial restrictions affecting the Black middle class. In contrast to the mass solidarity demonstrations of students, the ANC/SACP leadership now favors tight underground organization and outside training in preparation for guerrilla war and the elimination of African collaborators with the White regime.

The so-called "Marxist-Leninist" line, with a following primarily among academics, also gives first priority to national liberation and equality before the law. However, it places more emphasis than the other perspectives on the revolutionary potential of the peasant sector and the so-called Bantustan contradictions in the system. It is suspicious of the Moscow-oriented orthodoxy and looks at times to Peking as a model for the encirclement of the cities by "red bases" in the Bantustans and the townships.

The Trotskyite perspective advocates translation of "the hatred of apartheid shown during the black youth rebellion of 1976 into the struggle for power within the factories."[26] It loathes the so-called petty-bourgeois leadership of national liberation movements, such as the ANC; nor does it expect the fragmented peasants with their limited vision to lead the revolution. Trotskyites dispute the Communist contention that South Africa does not yet represent a fully developed capitalist economy, as evidenced in the suppression of unions and the racist control of the labor force. They accuse the

Communists of neglecting the organization of the working class, whose interests should not be subordinated to an all-class, national common fight against a colonial power, lest the revolution be sold out to a reactionary Black bourgeoisie, whose emergence the South African government is now said to favor. The Trotskyite analysis detects such a neocolonial sellout to imperialism among the front-line states, particularly in the persons of Kaunda and Nyerere but also in Angola and Mocambique, due to the economic integration of their national economies into the South African center. The path to South African freedom, therefore, is seen in an international working-class struggle against capitalism rather than in the vain pursuit of national liberation. In this vein it is postulated "that the ultimate survival and success of a revolution in South Africa will depend on revolutions in the advanced capitalist countries." A classical description of how such a collapse of Western capitalism will come about is provided:

> It seems highly possible that growing numbers of workers, hard hit by unemployment, may realize the necessity of cementing an alliance with the independence movements of third world countries in general and Africa in particular to achieve the necessary structural changes to advance their own welfare.[27]

These radical strategies may seem to the empirical-minded observer as much flights of fantasy as the liberal belief in the power of reasoning. And yet in the absence of a discredited middle ground, the allegiance to alternatives which may be radically different from both liberal as well as traditional Marxist solutions could grow rapidly indeed.

For all committed socialists it is basically irrelevant whether South Africa is ruled by Afrikaner Nationalists or liberal capitalists; both represent but two faces of the same monster. Any piecemeal reform, it is said, would cheat the subordinates out of their well-earned total victory. In the words of Immanuel Wallerstein: "Liberal interventionism stands forward today as the most dangerous enemy of African liberation movements in South Africa."[28] The advocates of further polarization always assume that the oppressed would inevitably win an escalation. Liberals, on the other hand, point to the many historical reversals of the Hegelian *telos* into much worse forms of misery, from fascism to the Gulag Archipelago. They welcome any improvement in the life of apartheid victims, even if it is undertaken for the wrong motives. Indeed who can predict the unintended consequences of carefully planned designs?

FUNCTIONS OF LIBERALS

The functions of the liberal voice, regardless of its lack of influence, remain to be assessed. Nationalists tolerate the liberal minority because it is no threat and has no power to initiate any change. In their powerlessness the liberal dissenters, albeit unintentionally, fulfill useful functions in the Nationalist design. They demonstrate the "civilized standards" of White democracy to contrast with the totalitarian repression in many societies of South Africa's critics. Even more, the liberals express grievances and point to potential friction points in the system before they become explosive. Their conspicuous deviance from official policy makes them a useful rallying point for internal Nationalist cohesion. The existence of liberal outsiders allows the regimentation of internal dissent by delineating the boundaries of permissible deviation for the insider. To attack and make scapegoats of an outgroup contributes to the solidarity of the Nationalist group.

From an interracial perspective, the presence of liberals has undoubtedly blunted Black militancy and delayed the polarization and confrontation between two exclusive nationalisms. Paton makes a valid point in emphasizing this decisive peacekeeping role of the liberal bridge-builders: "If Black power meets White power, and there are no Black liberals and White liberals around, then God help South Africa."[29] Until very recently liberals have succeeded in instilling hope among Black activists that there is a chance of change from within, that what Leo Kuper calls the "policies of reconciliation"[30] might work after all, and that the channels of peaceful reform are not yet exhausted. It is for this pacifying effect that the apostles of confrontation politics hate the liberals more than their outright opposite adversary.

Few liberals have illusions about their precarious role in the quicksand between the extremes. Many have left the country, which amounts to effective withdrawal from South African politics, although few exiles would admit that they are cut off from the local scene. Those who have stayed and continued with reformist politics in the Progressive party, the press, and some other English institutions have succeeded many times in ameliorating harsh measures and curbing excesses. Without the presence of a Helen Suzman (and now her Progressive party colleagues), the government would not be held publicly accountable for its deeds.[31] In this respect, the White parliament might not be as irrelevant to the South African scene as is often suggested. Those considerations apply even more for the liberal press, which has a sizable Black readership. By providing relatively uncensored information and articulating alternative views of justice, the liberals keep a critical discourse alive. Who could say with certainty that their silence would be more advantageous to Black liberation? Who would advocate that the liberals' concern for better Black education, for the provision of shelter for evicted squatters, for legal aid for the politically prosecuted or advice centers for the victims of the passport laws, or the numerous other activities of morally motivated individuals, working within the system, should be abandoned? Their activities might indeed be palliatives which make the overall system more tolerable, and yet the accumulation of such small-scale reforms at the micro-level may account for more change than the advocates of instant revolution will ever admit. In this respect, liberals have not failed.

The notion of "the failure of political liberalism" may suggest that there was a possibility of success which was not realized because of the shortsightedness of politicians or historical accidents. The narrow Nationalist victory in 1948 (five seats) is frequently cited as a turning point, and other speculations about a different course of South African history revolve around the loss of Hofmeyr as a liberal successor to Smuts. Had he lived longer, Hofmeyr could have extended the Colored franchise to women and redrawn the electoral boundaries (reverse gerrymandering) so as to preclude a Nationalist victory at the polls. Such speculations, however, do not take into account the fact that the entrenched racism of the United party majority would have severely constrained Hofmeyr's liberalism.

South Africa's turning point must be dated much earlier than 1948. The "parting of the ways," in Leonard Thompson's suggestive phrase, started in the nineteenth century with British policy in Natal, later confirmed in the South Africa Act of 1909 granting "responsible government" to the South African colonies. The provision that members of Parliament had to be of European descent and the acceptance of the constitutional color-bars of the Transvaal and the Orange Free State in the Union constitution doomed the nonracial franchise of the Cape. The safeguard of a two-thirds majority of both houses against its removal was finally circumvented in the 1950s. However, constitutional liberalism failed for much deeper structural reasons in South Africa. The ethnic mobilization of backward and defeated Afrikaners as a political class against both the colonial capital and the African competitors in the labor market proved to be stronger in the specific circumstances than the liberal notions of color-blind individual advancement in the capitalist marketplace. Whether in such an illiberal tradition, liberal notions of federalism or consociationalism have any chance of institutionalized conflict resolution in the future polarization, or whether radical geopolitical partition and mindless violent escalation will eventually constitute the "solution" in South Africa, remains to be seen.

CONSOCIATIONALISM AS A POLITICAL ALTERNATIVE?

Among the more farsighted politicians and intellectuals, solutions to conflict regulation in divided societies are now discussed in the framework of consociational democracy. This, they argue, could be a more feasible model than unitary systems, partition, or a confederal solution. However, some crucial preconditions for consociationalism do not exist in South Africa.

According to Arend Lijphart, the consociational model consists of (1) a grand coalition of the political leaders of all population groups, (2) mutual veto power, (3) proportionality, particularly in the allocation of resources and civil service appointments, based (4) on a high degree of internal autonomy for each segment.[32] In theory, there seems nothing objectionable to the principle of *communal* representation as compared with *individual* participation in the political process, independent of communal or ethnic affiliations. Such a normative judgment is based on the empirical evidence that the alternatives are likely worse. As Lijphart says: "Since in a plural society true brotherhood is not a realistic short-term objective, democratic peaceful co-existence is a perfectly honourable goal in itself: It is vastly preferable both to non-democratic peace and to strife-torn democracy."[33] There is no reason to assume that the liberal Westminster model of winner-take-all is the only just, let alone effective, democratic mode of conflict settlement. The export of the British model into the former colonies has (perhaps with the exception of India) proven highly unsuitable for democratic nation-building because the formula disregards the deep persistence of communal loyalties.

However, unlike almost all other plural European or Third World societies, South Africa distinguishes itself by the absence of three related decisive preconditions which make it unsuitable for consociationalism. These are: (1) imposed group membership rather than voluntary association, (2) enforced restriction of segmental leadership, (3) unequal distribution of power and resources between competing groups.

(1) In all other plural or divided societies, with the sole ex-

ception of South Africa, most members of ethnic subgroups voluntarily identify with their cultural kinsmen. It provides their self-concept. They do so primarily in order to lay claims for an equitable share at the power center, or alternatively for secession if they feel they cannot obtain redress for their grievances within the existing political structure (e.g., Quebec, Biafra). This ethnic identification is facilitated by historical disadvantages of culturally different subgroups which desire to seek redress for past inequities. In other instances, they resist state expansion into their domain. If, for example, one language in a multilingual state becomes the official medium of business and government, those raised in any other language find themselves decisively disadvantaged in the competition for jobs and status. Such was the situation of Afrikanerdom at the beginning of the twentieth century before it mobilized linguistically, economically, and politically to capture exclusive state power in South Africa.

In order to preserve their political monopoly, despite their being a numerical minority, the Afrikaners in South Africa disenfranchised Black political competitors at the national level and restricted the opportunities for mobilization and competition of the excluded Black majority. In order to secure this power, they now seek to institutionalize the fragmentation of their challengers in the name of preserving group identities as the "most important dimension of human rights."[34] However, as far as Blacks are concerned, these "cultural identities, life-styles and basic social institutions of historically established groups" exist in South Africa mainly by definition of the ruling group. For example, there are no enthusiastic Coloreds in the self-perceptions of those classified as Coloreds by those in power. The separate life styles they supposedly wish to maintain are those of poverty and anomie, resulting from social exclusion. The unique cultural identities which Cape Coloreds desire to preserve are (or at least were, prior to Black Consciousness) identical with those of White Afrikanerdom from which the ruling group excludes them. Brown people now constitute a "historically differentiated community,"[35] but only as an outcome of racial discrimination. Why would it amount to a "normalisation of inter-group relations"[36] to provide separate parliaments for what are seen as artificial invidious categories of association by their members? It is paradoxical that the more the South African government asserts voluntary ethnic identifiation as the basis of its policy, the more it has to enforce ethnic divisions by legislation.

Similar observations apply to the proposals to assign the urban

Blacks to African homelands. The Xhosa (or Tswana) -speaking inhabitants of Soweto have so far not been given a choice between becoming Transkeian citizens or remaining South Africans. Had they been given the choice, the concept of self-determination would perhaps have been credible. But if the definitions of the groups to be accommodated do not correspond to their self-concepts of identity,* then no well-intentioned constitutional design based on such imposed definitions can satisfy their "social, economic and political aspirations." It seems likely that ethnicity will always be considered a form of racialism by those upon whom it is imposed if it does not correspond with the self-concept of the ethnic group members. Identity is a subjective concept, and genuine identity is bound to the individual's free choice. This presupposes that ultimately no restrictions on boundary crossing exist apart from individual intent. Only when groups are allowed to define themselves through individual voluntary group affiliation can the liberal notion of individual political rights be reconciled with the consociational concept of participation through communal units.

(2) The outstanding characteristic of a consociational democracy is the coalition of elites. This elite cartel presupposes representative leaders who "retain the support and loyalty of their followers."[37] In South Africa this precondition clearly exists for the Afrikaners, and there is still widespread respect for the traditional positions of leadership in Zulu society and in some other rural areas. However, the support which Colored, Indian, or urban Black leaders receive is not due to communal attachments: they are "leaders" because they articulate grievances. They are merely spokesmen of interest groups in the literal sense, and they could hardly guarantee loyal, unquestioned support if they entered into a controversial elite coalition. The only way to establish legitimacy of leadership in non-traditional societies is through an open test in free elections, which means democratic competition between all leaders who claim a following. However, such intrasegmental democracy is lacking among Blacks, as evidenced in the restriction of politicians who advocate alternative

*It has been demonstrated again and again that the great majority of urban Africans with Section 10 rights do not wish to be associated with homelands. (The 5 percent average participation in elections in Soweto is one indication.) The large turnout at urban rallies for a homeland leader such as Buthelezi is no proof of support for homelands. On the contrary, the overwhelming popularity of Buthelezi, whom 44 percent of a sample of urban Africans in the Freiburg study named as their preferred leader, results to a large extent from his rejection of homeland independence.

policies. In this situation, existing "leaders" are always in danger of being considered stooges and collaborators. To avoid losing their public role, they have two choices: (a) to acquiesce in the restriction of their intragroup competitors and rationalize their own position, or (b) move continually in the direction of more radical group demands. Either choice undermines an essential precondition of elite cooperation—legitimacy in the first instance and moderation in the second.

In summary, the consociational model is based on a depoliticized public. As Lijphart puts it: "Both in Africa and elsewhere in the Third World segmental isolation entails a strengthening of the political inertness of the non-elite public and of their deferential attitudes to the segmental leaders."[38] In South Africa the opposite trend can be perceived. Rapid urbanization and geographical mobility in an industrial economy have not only ended group isolation but also weakened deferential attitudes toward political elites. The urbanized Blacks are an atomized and increasingly politicized mass of independently acting individuals. These trends cannot be reversed: they can only be (a) repressed or (b) channelled into legitimate institutions of intergroup bargaining. It is in this latter realm that the liberal tradition of participatory democracy could make a valuable contribution.

CONTEMPORARY AFRICAN POLITICAL ORGANIZATIONS AND MOVEMENTS

Roland Stanbridge

Africans have always been excluded from the main decision-making processes in South Africa, and their desire to be included has been the driving force behind their political activity. Early demands by Africans for power-sharing resulted in a series of massacres of peaceful demonstrators by panicky Whites. As militancy increased among Africans, the government began to legislate against political change and to systematically eliminate African leadership. The history of African political activity shows a vicious circle of hardening attitudes and escalating violence as increased fear and repression by Whites leads to increasing resentment and commitment to violence by Africans. The few concessions the government has made recently are regarded as mere "window dressing" by African leaders, and have done nothing to quell their desire for political power.

The major African political organizations and movements of South Africa—the African National Congress (ANC), the Pan Africanist Congress (PAC), and the Black Consciousness movement—are all working underground after being declared illegal by the government.* In the face of continued reactionary White response, these underground organizations have now embarked on an armed liberation struggle.

There has been a continuing quest for unity among the African peoples of South Africa. It was the need for unity in order to confront the ruling White minority that led to the formation of the ANC in 1912. This need became even more urgent when the Afrikaner government began dividing the African peoples with its Separate De-

*The only African organizations functioning openly outside the homelands are formed by men who operate within government structures. These include Chief Gatsha Buthelezi's Inkatha movement (see article by L. Schlemmer in this volume), the Black United Front, and the Black Alliance. These will be discussed only briefly in this chapter.

velopment policy. However, effective unity has never been achieved. The ANC virtually refuses to recognize the PAC, and the PAC is extremely hostile to the South African Communist Party (SACP). The SACP enjoys close relations with the ANC, but this alliance has caused serious dissension within the ANC. The SACP has always been critical of the Black Consciousness movement. Within the African political movements, one finds a wide spectrum of viewpoints ranging between Black chauvinism and the advocacy of a nonracial democratic revolution.

All the underground organizations and movements had peaceful programs at the time of their formation, but today they are all committed to the liberation of the African people of South Africa through armed revolution. They are all opposed to the Balkanization of South Africa into one White state and a series of Black bantustans; they all believe that foreign investment should be withdrawn from South Africa to hasten the collapse of White rule; and they all believe in some form of socialist revolution.

THE EARLY YEARS OF AFRICAN ORGANIZATION, 1912-1946

When Britain handed political power in South Africa over to the privileged White minority in 1910, Africans throughout the country were faced with the need to unite to protect their rights. A prominent Zulu lawyer, Dr. Pixley ka Izaka Seme, declared in 1911: "The demon of racialism, the aberrations of Xhosa-Fingo feuds, the animosity that exists between the Zulu and the Tongas, between the Basuto and every other native, must be buried and forgotten. . . . We are one people."[1] Other overseas-trained professional men took up the call, and on January 8, 1912 the founding conference of the ANC (at first called the Native National Congress) opened in Bloemfontein. Its purpose, as set forth in Seme's opening address, was to "find ways and means of forming one national union for the purpose of creating national unity and defending our rights and privileges."[2]

From its inception the new organization was faced with a struggle of immense importance to the future of the African people—the fight against the Native Land Act of 1913, described by one observer as a "profoundly illuminating expression of the class interests of the united front of imperialist mine-owners and rich farmers who dominated the newly-formed Union of South Africa."[3] The mine-owners and farmers needed both cheap labor and land, and the Land Act went far to satisfy these demands. Under this law the Whites took 93 percent of the land for themselves, leaving only 7 percent for the African people, who constituted four-fifths of the population. The ANC campaigned vigorously up and down the country against the Land Act, winning widespread popular support. A deputation was sent to London in 1913-14 to plead their cause with the British government, but it was unsuccessful. In 1919 the ANC sent another mission to put pressure on Britain to use her constitutional powers to intervene in favor of the Africans; again, the mission failed.*

In the 1920s South Africa began a period of rapid industrialization, and African workers were drawn into secondary industry by the thousands. African trade union activity was stepped up by the newly formed Industrial and Commercial Union (ICU), and for several years this organization eclipsed the political activities of the ANC. The ANC encouraged its members to work in the ICU. Scores of strikes were attempted by African workers led by the ICU, but they were brutally suppressed by the army and police.

In July 1921 White members of the Industrial Socialist League and the International Socialist League came together to form the Communist Party of South Africa (CPSA). This body was to have a profound influence on subsequent political tactics, and CP activists soon became deeply involved in trade union work.

The main tactic of the ANC continued to be to petition the Union government and to send delegations to discuss African grievances, but these efforts were almost always unsuccessful. During the mid-1930s, exploiting the upsurge of fascist reaction in Western Europe, the White government took the vote away from the Africans of the Cape Province and Natal—the only remaining areas where Africans enjoyed the right to elect White representatives to Parliament. At this time the ANC lost many supporters.[4]

In 1943 a group of young nationalist-minded intellectuals formed a Youth League (ANCYL) in the ANC. They propounded a policy of fighting for African independence, freedom from domination by other national groups, and the establishment of "an African nation." An important dimension of the Youth League outlook was the insistence that the ANC should cease merely making representations to a stubborn government and should engage in more militant action. It rejected the "language of supplication" of the ANC leadership. The constitution of the ANCYL declared its aims to be: "To

*This delegation attended the peace conference at Versailles, where it strongly opposed the handing over of South West Africa as a mandated territory to South Africa. Today the ANC has a close relationship with the South West African People's Organization (SWAPO).

arouse and encourage national consciousness and unity among African youth and to assist, support and reinforce the African National Congress in its struggle for the national liberation of the African people.'"[5] Though the ANC had not managed to regain its initial mass following, the Youth League soon attracted increasingly greater support.

The non-racial independent Unity Movement of South Africa (UMSA) was also created in 1943, by a group of African and Colored intellectuals, many of them teachers. They were avowed Trotskyists who insisted upon an historical materialist analysis which played down the national and racial aspects of the struggle in South Africa. Though it never gained any form of mass following, the movement persisted, and its outspoken analyses of the South African situation earned much respect from Africans. It claimed to have a large peasant following, but this was vehemently denied by the ANC. UMSA based its activities on a "ten-point program" which called for universal franchise, compulsory education, personal liberty, equal rights for all citizens, and revision of the land, criminal, tax, and labor laws. After the Sharpeville massacre in 1961, UMSA formed an "advance political vanguard" called the African People's Democratic Union of South Africa (APDUSA).[6]

In 1945 the ANC drew up a bill of rights based on the Atlantic Charter, which came to be known as "African Claims." It called for, *inter alia*, "one man-one vote," direct representation in Parliament, recognition of African trade unions, abolition of the color bar in industry, abolition of the pass laws, freehold tenure, and equality of opportunity in education. Dr. A.B. Xuma, president-general of the ANC, sent a copy of the "African Claims" to Prime Minister Smuts and asked for an interview. Smuts declined the request, saying: "Your study is evidently a propagandist document intended to propagate views of your Congress. . . . The Prime Minister cannot agree to be drawn into the task by means of an interview with him."[7]

By the end of World War II closer cooperation began to develop between the forces opposed to the White government. In 1944-45 there was a widespread ANC-CP anti-pass campaign which did much to renew widespread support for the ANC. Close fraternal relations developed between the ANC and CP, and today the two organizations continue to work together intimately. In May 1945, when the Allied victory over Nazi Germany was celebrated, the biggest gathering ever seen in Johannesburg met under the combined auspices of the ANC, the CP, and the trade unions.

Militancy was also growing among South Africa's Indian population. The South African Indian Council (SAIC), under the leadership of Dr. Yusuf Dadoo (now leader of the Communist party-in-exile) in the Transvaal and Dr. G.M. Naicker in Natal, proposed that a revolutionary alliance be formed of all oppressed people on the principle of equal rights and opportunities for all. In March 1946 a "Xuma-Naicker-Dadoo" agreement was signed, in which the ANC and SAIC agreed to work together for full franchise rights for all. The Smuts government passed an anti-Indian act (the Ghetto Act) which was interpreted by Indians as a measure designed to ruin the Indian people economically as a prelude to their repatriation to India. Immediately a round of passive resistance struggles was begun by the SAIC, and thousands of demonstrators who defied the new segregation laws went to jail. Many joint ANC-SAIC campaigns were to follow.

A COMMITMENT TO MULTI-RACIALISM

In 1948 the Nationalist party came to power pledged to implement a policy of apartheid. Within five years the following legislation was passed and became effective: Prohibition of Mixed Marriages Act, Immorality Amendment Act, Suppression of Communism Act, Population Registration Act, Separate Representation of Voters Act, Bantu Education Act, Bantu Persons Abolition of Passes and Co-ordination of Documents Act, Native Labour Settlement of Disputes Act, Asiatic Land Tenure Amendment Act, Prevention of Illegal Squatting Act, Native Laws Amendment Act, Native Building Workers Act, Unemployment Insurance Amendment Act, Group Areas Act, Public Safety Act, Bantu Authorities Act, Native Labour Act, and Criminal Law Amendment Act.[8] Under these repressive laws, African, Colored, and Indian people were placed in completely separate categories from White South Africans, deprived of whatever voting rights they may have had, and restricted in areas of residence and choice of profession.

The ANC responded to this wave of racial discrimination with vehement denunciations. The influence of the Youth League had risen sharply since the Nationalist party election victory, and it was responsible for the ANC adopting its militant Program of Action in 1949. This program proclaimed that the principal vehicle of the struggle against the racist regime must be mass action. It set out the demand for national freedom:

> Freedom from white domination and the attainment of political

> independence. This implies the rejection of the concept of segregation, apartheid, trusteeship or white leadership which are all in one way or another motivated by the idea of white domination. Like all other people the African people claim their right to self-determination.[9]

The Program of Action ushered in an era of mass struggles using the methods of passive resistance, non-collaboration, and strike action. But it did not pose the threat of revolution. The ANC was still dominated by its moderate leaders, even though Xuma, who wished to avoid what he saw as premature confrontation, failed to obtain re-election as president-general at the 1949 ANC conference due to pressure by the Youth League. He was succeeded by Dr. J.S. Moroka and then Albert Luthuli.

During this period increasingly closer links were established between the trade unions, the ANC, and the CP. In 1950 a mass rally was held in Durban under the auspices of the ANC, the SAIC, the CP, and the African People's Organization (an organization of Colored people later replaced by the South African Colored People's Organization—SACPO). This was the first time all these organizations had come together to voice their opposition to the racial policies of the government and the bannings of Black leaders. Plans were made for a national strike on May Day and for meetings and rallies all over South Africa. On May 1 there were work stoppages in most cities and peaceful rallies and demonstrations throughout the country. Late in the day, however, eighteen people were killed by police fire and bayonets near Johannesburg.

In reaction to this brutality a joint planning council was set up by the ANC, SAIC, and CP to organize protests. The protests mounted in intensity, and there were a number of clashes in which police shot demonstrators. The council, repudiating violence as a political tactic, strongly condemned police brutality and called for a national day of protest and mourning on June 26—a call supported by the African People's Organization.* A strike took place nationwide in an unprecedented demonstration of unity which was described by the protest leaders as a "first step towards our liberation."†

*Two days before the day of protest the Communist party, which had been outlawed by the Suppression of Communism Act, dissolved itself. Core members met to form the underground South African Communist Party—SACP (*Azania News*, August 1973).

†June 26 is now known internationally as South Africa Freedom Day. Op-

Through 1951 the South African government piled one abuse of freedom upon another. It made the Suppression of Communism Act retroactive, attacked trade unionists, withdrew passports, set up Bantu authorities, and initiated a legal onslaught with the object of removing the Colored people from the voters roll. In December the ANC conference adopted a resolution to rally the people into mass action in defiance of apartheid laws. The resolution was drawn up in conjunction with the SAIC. "It is important to note," wrote Dadoo later, "that when the ANC and SAIC jointly embarked on the Defiance of Unjust Laws Campaign of 1952, it was deliberately not called a passive resistance campaign. It was called a Defiance campaign, although it was non-violent. It expressed a more militant outlook."[10] On April 6, 1952 religious services to pray for freedom and mass meetings of protest against unjust laws were held in a number of cities. The date was deliberately chosen: it marked the tercentenary of Jan van Riebeeck's arrival at the Cape.

In a letter to the ANC, the prime minister warned that if the Congress embarked on a campaign of defiance and disobedience the government would "make full use of the machinery at its disposal to quell any disturbances, and thereafter deal adequately with those responsible for initiating subversive activities."[11] Soon afterwards several leaders of the ANC, SAIC, and the trade union movement were cited for subversion under the Suppression of Communism Act. They were forced to resign from their organizations and were forbidden to attend meetings. Several of these leaders chose Freedom Day to defy this ban, and thus began the defiance campaign. The campaign soon spread widely: from June to December groups of volunteers all over the country defied the law by entering European areas without permits, by entering the European sections of post offices and railway stations, by defying the nightly curfew for Africans in the cities, by leaving their passes at home, and other illegal actions. The prisons became overcrowded and magistrates began sentencing juveniles to whipping. After the number of arrests passed the 8500 mark, the government rushed through emergency measures which were used to suppress the campaign. A decree was proclaimed making defiance of the law a serious criminal offense. This was followed by the Criminal Law Amendment Act and the Public Safety Act, which laid down a maximum penalty of ten years imprisonment and ten lashes with the cane for defiance of the law, and authorized the confiscation of the property of the offenders. The defiance

ponents of apartheid the world over join in protest against racism at public meetings and demonstrations.

campaign petered out, but its purposes had been achieved. Masses of Africans had become politically aroused. There was a sharp rise in ANC membership as people now flocked to join. An "oppositionist" attitude had been inculcated among the African people, and many had overcome their fear of authority. The campaign had also brought the oppressive character of South Africa's discriminatory laws into sharp focus.

African leaders felt that a turning point had to come in their struggle. They were fed up with White intransigence. In October 1952 Luthuli remarked:

> Who will deny that thirty years of my life have been spent knocking in vain, patiently, moderately and modestly at a closed and barred door? What have been the fruits of moderation? The past thirty years have seen the greatest number of laws restricting our rights and progress until today we have reached the stage where we have almost no rights at all.[12]

Moses Kotane, treasurer-general of the ANC, one of many leaders brought to trial for their part in the defiance campaign, voiced similar feelings of frustration in his address to the court:

> The African people are a voiceless and landless people; they are a people without a place in their fatherland to rest or to lay their heads. Their education and development are hampered and retarded as a matter of state policy. . . . Through colour bar laws and administrative measures they are prevented from improving their economic conditions. . . . They are denied freedom of movement in the land of their birth. . . . It is the right of the non-Europeans, as of any other people to have freedom, with full opportunities of development. . . . In the past representations have failed to achieve this object. Nothing is left now . . . but to protest in a way which will make the voters of South Africa realise how great the oppression of my people is and how grave the situation is.[13]

Virtually all means of peaceful protest had been systematically cut off. Persons engaged in non-violent protest against any legislation were subject to long-term imprisonment. However, having mobilized the people and in keeping with its overall strategy to lead a united front of all anti-racist and democratic forces, the ANC planned a Congress of the People, together with SAIC, SACPO, and the South African Congress of Democrats (an organization formed for White sympathizers of the other Congress bodies). These groups came to be known as the Congress Alliance, and were soon joined by the South African Congress of Trade Unions (SACTU), which had been formed in March 1955.*

The historic Congress of the People took place at Kliptown in the Transvaal on June 26, 1955. Delegates came from every center of any size in the country and from the reserves, locations, and farms. (Luthuli and Dadoo were prevented from attending by their banning orders.) Police harassment of delegates was intense. Roadblocks were set up on most national roads, and many hundreds of delegates were stopped, searched, and had their names and addresses taken. At the Congress itself there were scores of policemen with cameras, binoculars, and recording equipment. When the conference was in its final stage, a large force of armed police suddenly arrived, and about fifteen Special Branch detectives mounted the platform. They announced that treason was suspected, and every document in sight was removed. Mounted police sealed off the area, and no one was allowed to leave or enter. Before each delegate left he was interrogated and searched, and documents found on him were retained and sealed in an envelope with his name. Every single White delegate was photographed.[14]

Nonetheless the conference had adopted the now famous Freedom Charter. The importance of this document lies in the fact that it gave the different national organizations of the African, Indian, and Colored people, together with the working class organizations, a common program of national liberation. Among other things the charter states that "South Africa belongs to all who live in it, black and white, and that no government can justly claim authority unless it is based on the will of the people." It specifies the changes which will be necessary to end racial discrimination in South Africa and describes the type of "democratic state" sought. It calls for the land to be divided among those who work it and for the national wealth to be restored to the people: "The mineral wealth of our country, the banks and monopoly industry shall be transferred to the ownership of the people as a whole. All other industry and trade shall be controlled to assist the well-being of the people." It states that all

*SACTU added a new dimension to the struggle of the oppressed in South Africa. It abandoned the slogan "no politics in the trade union movement," which the White trade unions had been trying to foster, and stated in the preamble to its constitution that "Only a truly united working class can serve effectively the interests of the workers; their immediate interests, higher wages, and better conditions of life and labour, as well as the ultimate objective of complete emancipation."

national groups should have equal rights, that all should be equal before the law, that men and women of all races should receive equal pay for equal work, and that education should be free, compulsory, and equal for all children. The basic aims of the ANC today remain those laid out in the Freedom Charter.

In December 1956 the significance of the police activity at the Congress of the People became clear. In the early morning hours of December 5, over a hundred people of all races and occupations were arrested on charges of high treason and flown by military aircraft to Johannesburg. After further arrests the total number of accused came to 156. The evidence brought forward against them concerned their association with the Congress of the People, and much of it consisted of texts of speeches made at Kliptown and documents the police had confiscated there. The prosecution found it extremely difficult to prove treason, however, and toward the end of 1957 charges against nearly a hundred of the accused were withdrawn. After a protracted trial in Pretoria the last of the accused were acquitted in 1961. However, the state had demonstrated its intention to crush what had previously been accepted as legitimate expressions of demands for equality.

A SHIFT TOWARD AFRICAN NATIONALISM

A momentous event occurred while the treason trial was in progress. The militant Africanists in the ANC, led by Robert Sobukwe (a law lecturer at the University of the Witswatersrand), broke away to form the Pan Africanist Congress (PAC). They were disappointed with the lack of achievement of the ANC's policy of cooperation with other anti-apartheid organizations. Their philosophy of Africanism had first been expounded by the Youth League. It called for a political outlook clearly based on African nationalism. According to Sobukwe the PAC rejected apartheid, but it also rejected the ANC's policy of multiracialism. It aimed at "government of the Africans by the Africans, with everybody who owes his only loyalty to Africa and is prepared to accept the democratic rule of an African majority being regarded as an African."[15]

The PAC manifesto defined the party's historic tasks as, *inter alia*, to forge, foster, and consolidate the bonds of African nationhood on a continental basis; to implement effectively the fundamental principle of the right to self-determination for the African people; to work for the creation of a continental union of African states as a concrete institutional form for the African nation and strive for the establishment of an order of society which recognizes the primacy of the material, intellectual and spiritual interests of the individual. Its ultimate objective was defined as the solution of the social question in Africa, that is, "the matter of how man shall live in peace and harmony with his fellowman."[16]

The PAC was thus to be an exclusively Africanist movement. It believed the decisive thrust against apartheid had to come from Africans as the only people without any vested interest in the system. Its stand was condemned as "Black Verwoerdism" by both Black and White opponents, but anyone who took trouble to read Sobukwe's policy speeches would have found a strong commitment to nonracialism once apartheid was destroyed by its "historically defined" enemies. The PAC was also committed to nonviolence. Sobukwe claimed that the ANC was dominated by Whites and Communists. The initial antagonism between the ANC and PAC has never ceased, and today they remain at loggerheads.

On July 30, 1959 Sobukwe announced that the PAC was undertaking a long-term "status campaign." For over three hundred years, he said, the White man had used his power to inculcate into the Africans a feeling of inferiority. "It is our task to exorcise that slave mentality and to impart to the African masses a sense of self-reliance which will make them choose to starve in freedom rather than enjoy plenty in bondage." The first step was to be a campaign for the abolition of the pass laws.*

The ANC had for a year been planning an anti-pass campaign which was to begin on March 31, 1960. The PAC called on its supporters to begin *their* campaign on March 21, 1960. In every city, town, and village men were to leave their passes at home, surrender to the nearest police station, and demand arrest. So long as the campaign was on, nobody was to work. The expressed aim of the campaign was to bring industry to a standstill to force the government to accept the people's terms.[17]

The tragic events of March 21 at Sharpeville and Langa are well

*Agitation over passes had been gathering momentum for some time. Between 1955 and 1959 hundreds of women had burned their pass books, held protest marches, and presented petitions to Native Commissioners. The campaigns of the 1950s had politicized large numbers of people, and several militant actions unconnected with the pass laws had taken place. In May 1958 near civil war occurred in the Sekhukhuni Reserve over the introduction of Bantu Authorities and cattle-culling schemes. In mid-1959 rioting occurred throughout the countryside in Natal because of the extension of influx control to women. In Pondoland in 1959-60 the imposition of Bantu Authorities led to assassinations of chiefs and headmen who were thought to be collaborating with the authorities. These revolts were ruthlessly crushed, and many people died from police gunfire.

known to the world. Sixty-nine Africans were massacred by police gunfire and 178 wounded. Of those killed or wounded, 155 had been shot in the back. By April 19, 83 civilians and three policemen had lost their lives and 365 civilians and 59 policemen had been injured.[18]

A general strike called by the ANC to mourn the massacre began on 28 March and paralyzed the whole country for nearly three weeks. Foreign capital fled. The governor-general declared a state of emergency, and thousands of people were arrested and detained without trial—most of them members of the PAC and the Congress Alliance. On April 8 Parliament passed the Unlawful Organizations Act, banning the ANC and PAC and any organizations that might be formed to replace them.

THE TURN TOWARD VIOLENCE

These events marked a turning point in the struggle of the African people. Half a century of nonviolence had failed. It had consistently been met by police violence, and now the masses were no longer allowed any form of political expression. Both the PAC and the ANC went underground to prepare for violent action. In the middle of the night of December 16, 1961 bombs exploded in buildings in Johannesburg, Port Elizabeth, and Durban. Posters found near the bombings announced that they were the work of a new organization—Umkhonto we Sizwe ("Spear of the Nation"). This was the underground military wing of the ANC, and in the next few years its members performed hundreds of acts of sabotage. Targets were the economic lifelines of the country, such as power pylons, railway lines, and telecommunications, as well as symbols of apartheid, such as the office of the minister of agriculture in Pretoria and the offices of *Die Nataller*, official organ of the Nationalist party in Natal.

The government passed the General Laws Amendment Act, known as the Sabotage Act, empowering the courts to pass the death sentence in cases of sabotage. Alfred Nzo, ANC secretary-general, described the situation as follows:

> The enemy was getting desperate as the effectiveness of its security was beginning to be questioned. . . . The only answer was to ask the white parliament to legalise torture and detention. The 90-Day Detention Law was passed. . . . All the known leading members of the ANC were detained under the 90-Day Detention Law and were put into solitary confinement and tortured.[19]

On June 11, 1963 the police raided the Umkhonto headquarters in Rivonia and arrested the leaders. The very heart of the organization was smashed. The Rivonia trial began in October 1963, and Nelson Mandela, who had been arrested in 1960 and sentenced to three years imprisonment for incitement to strike, was taken from his cell to join those in the dock facing trial for sabotage and conspiracy to overthrow the government by revolution. Mandela opened the case for the defense:

> I admit immediately that I was one of the persons who helped to form Umkhonto we Sizwe. . . . I and the others who started the organisation did so for two reasons. Firstly, we believed that as a result of government policy, violence by the African people had become inevitable, and that unless responsible leadership was given to channel and control the feelings of our people, there would be outbreaks of terrorism which would produce an intensity of bitterness and hostility between the various races of this country which is not produced even by war. Secondly, we felt that without violence there would be no way open to the African people to succeed in their struggle against the principle of white supremacy. All lawful methods of expressing opposition to this principle had been closed by legislation, and we were placed in a position in which we had either to accept a permanent state of inferiority, or to defy the government. . . . We did not want an inter-racial war, and tried to avoid it to the last. But the hard facts were that fifty years of nonviolence had brought the African people nothing but more and more repressive legislation, and fewer and fewer rights. Four forms of violence were considered—sabotage, guerilla warfare, terrorism and open revolution. We chose to adopt the first method and to exhaust it before taking any other decision.[20]

Mandela was sentenced to life imprisonment. Sporadic acts of sabotage occurred in the years following the Rivonia trial, but for the moment the underground movement had been crippled. Its leaders were either in prison or had fled the country.

While Sobukwe was in jail (he was convicted of incitement in 1960), the PAC formed its underground military wing called Poqo—meaning "pure," implying that it was a purely African organization working for the African people. Poqo was primarily a terrorist group. As reported in *Azania News*:

> In that period we were faced with new and advanced tasks and had to organise our work on revolutionary lines in the spirit of revolu-

> tionary struggle for state power. This was the stage of open clashes with the enemy forces, as the people's forces were being mobilised and the field being cleared of enemy agents and informers within the ranks of the people.[21]

During the next few years this "clearing" took the form of a series of murders of policemen, headmen, and chiefs. A number of White civilians were also killed by Poqo members. There were several attacks on police stations and a spate of attempts on the life of Chief Kaiser Matanzima, now prime minister of the Transkei, who was considered to be a collaborator with the government.

By 1964 the police had crushed Poqo. In June 1964 the minister of justice said in Parliament that 202 members of Poqo had been found guilty of murder, 12 of attempted murder, 395 of sabotage, 126 of leaving the country illegally, and 820 of lesser crimes. At this time some 3000 Umkhonto and Poqo members were detained under security laws.[22] Looking back on this period, B. Turok believes that sabotage failed as a political tactic:

> [Sabotage] failed to ignite the prairie fire as many had hoped. While sabotage provided government with every excuse for unleashing a brutal wave of terror, it failed to mobilise the mass of people who were caught by surprise. The black population welcomed the actions but showed little willingness to undertake similar acts spontaneously when called on to do so. . . . Sabotage remained the weapon of an *elite* corps in the liberation movement. As a consequence, sabotage had the effect of isolating the organised movement from the mass. . . . It has been claimed that sabotage lifted the psychological shackles of legalism and of respect for White authority and that if the movement had not taken these steps it would not have survived politically. . . . In the last analysis, however, what is important is that *the sabotage campaign failed on the main count —it did not raise the level of action of the masses themselves.*[23]*

IN EXILE

When the ANC and PAC were banned and forced underground, both decided to establish exile headquarters. Numbers of leaders left the country, and they jointly established a South African United Front with representatives in Dar es Salaam, Cairo, London, Accra, and New York.[24] However, this unity did not last long, and the two

*This is easy to say after the event, but there is no doubt the ANC gained valuable experience from the sabotage campaign—e.g., it learned the value of anonymity, the need for tight security, the advantage of small cells over a central headquarters.

liberation movements had established separate external missions by the end of 1962. The head of the ANC mission was Oliver Tambo, and Potlako Leballo headed the PAC mission.

The ANC. The mandate of the external mission of the ANC was to make preparation for the training of military cadres and their infiltration into the country, and to mobilize democratic and progressive opinion in Africa and the world to support the liberation struggle. In 1972 Nzo summarized its activities:

> Our external mission forged strong links first of all with the All African Peoples' Conference and . . . played an important part in the work of the Afro-Asian solidarity movement. . . . In Europe and America, in the Socialist countries, in Asia and Latin America, at the UN and other international platforms, the ANC resolutely raised the voice and demands of our people. The ANC was one of the founders of the Anti-Apartheid movement which was established in the early sixties in Great Britain and which has now spread to other parts of the world and is one of the major forces which mobilises world opinion against the iniquities of racial oppression and apartheid.[25]

In 1967 the ANC formed a military alliance with the Zimbabwe African People's Union (ZAPU), and jointly they made an attempt to return a force of one hundred guerillas to South Africa via Rhodesia. A battle was fought with Rhodesian armed forces in the Wankie area, and there were heavy losses on both sides. The guerillas retreated. In the following months there were further unsuccessful attempts to get groups of armed men through Rhodesia to South Africa. Turok provides a partial explanation for their failure:

> The populace were not prepared to receive the guerillas beforehand and the political organisation in the villages was lacking. Rhodesian security had terrorised the villagers into refusing to give food and water to the guerillas, and on occasion Rhodesian army men entered villages in the guise of guerillas and if they were not immediately betrayed the village was punished terribly. In the end the villagers could not distinguish between genuine and fake guerillas.[26]

In 1969 the ANC held an important conference at Morogoro (Tanzania), where it was decided to set up a Revolutionary Council charged with mobilizing and accelerating the struggle within South Africa. Another major decision was to expand the ANC by drawing into it all South African revolutionary elements irrespective of their racial origin. This decision, which is still effective, caused serious divisions within the organization. These came to a head in 1975, when an ANC leader, Ambrose Makiwane, charged that "The trouble the African people have at present is that our strategy and tactics are in the hands of, and dominated by, a small clique of non-Africans." He blamed this on "the distastrous Morogoro Consultative Conference which opened ANC membership to non-Africans."[27] Makiwane and seven others were expelled from the ANC. These expellees then made public their disagreements with the ANC leadership in an extensive memorandum released in London on December 11, 1975. They complained that there was an absence of democratic consultation within the organization, that the traditional ANC policies and ideology had been diluted, and that the SACP, whose leaders were White, had effective control of the ANC.

Inside South Africa the ANC achieved very little during the 1960s after the Rivonia headquarters were destroyed. In the early 1970s, when the Black Consciousness movement was spreading through the country, the ANC became more active internally—clandestinely printing and distributing newspapers and leaflets, forming new cells, recruiting young men for military training, and infiltrating armed guerillas into the country.

The PAC. The PAC had more difficulty in establishing itself in exile. A major problem was continuing internal dissension and power struggles. At a press conference at Maseru in Lesotho in March 1963, Leballo claimed that Poqo (the PAC's terrorist wing) had 150,000 members.[28] The following month the police raided his office and removed a membership list said to contain about 15,000 names, and soon after there were mass arrests of Poqo sympathizers in South Africa. This was a severe blow to Leballo's prestige. By 1964 Leballo had become very unpopular with other PAC refugees in Lesotho, who, among other things, considered him too dictatorial. Leballo moved to Ghana. He managed to hold on to the deputy-presidency, but could not quell the internal strife.

The PAC's image became tarnished internationally when it was found that senior members were appropriating funds. In mid-1968 the eleven-nation Liberation Committee of the OAU, meeting in Algiers, decided to increase its aid to the ANC, but to suspend aid to the PAC until unity had been restored. Representations had been made to the OAU by members of the PAC's National Executive

Committee who had recently been expelled for "counter-revolutionary activities."[29] They told the liberation committee that the PAC was pursuing a policy which was a complete departure from its original policy and principles. Soon thereafter large numbers of PAC men were deported from Zambia: a Zambian government spokesmen said the PAC had engaged in futile activities which had dissipated efforts against the enemies of freedom.[30] (The following year, the PAC again received funds from the OAU.)

The PAC was scarcely noticed by the White population after Poqo was crushed, and like the ANC it provided no real political leadership inside the country.

The UMSA. As noted earlier, at about the time Umkhonto and Poqo were formed, the nonracial Unity Movement of South Africa (UMSA) established an "advance political vanguard"—the African People's Democratic Union of South Africa (APDUSA). APDUSA set up headquarters in Lusaka and opened a branch office in Dar es Salaam, but was unable to get wide support or funds from the OAU. In early 1970 the leaders decided to revitalize UMSA and APDUSA, and sent secret agents into South Africa to recruit people for political and military training in countries to the north.

In 1971 APDUSA was involved in an incident in East Pondoland where the people in a community were resisting compulsory removal to a point ten miles away from the coast. They had twice before been forcibly moved, and when a third attempt was made to move them they stood their ground. When police arrived to remove the community, the people resisted, and sixty-two were shot. This event was followed by a countrywide investigation of APDUSA, and there were mass arrests of African, Colored, and Indian men at various centers—Cape Town, Port Elizabeth, Natal and Transvaal towns, in the Transkei, in Welkom in the Orange Free State province, and near the Botswana border. Some were released after being held for more than nine months, while others appeared as state witnesses in a trial that began in June 1971. Fourteen men were charged with being members or active supporters of UMSA or APDUSA, and conspiring with fellow members in Zambia to recruit people for military training with the object of overthrowing the South African government by force.[31] The trial ended on April 4, 1972. One of the men was acquitted, but the rest were found guilty and sentenced to terms of five to eight years in prison.

In 1975 UMSA's external leader B.A. Honono met with PAC leader Leballo and a faction of the ANC. In Kampala on November 3 they announced the formation of the United Liberation Front for Azania (ULFA). Their belief, said Leballo, was that peace "must be brought about by gunfire just like it was in South Vietnam."

Since 1967 the PAC has been unceasing in its call for unity of the liberation forces, and it has often been joined in this call by the OAU. It holds that

> no invading army of political fighters or political organisation or even groups of political organisations is capable of achieving a military victory against [South Africa's] military might. Only the united action of our united people acting in unison can achieve such a victory. . . . For this reason we feel that all those who claim to be "freedom fighters," no matter what organisation they belong to, should be told that they are no longer welcome to remain in independent Africa, and be given an opportunity to mould themselves into an independent army whose leadership, decided upon by themselves, will take part in exploratory talks leading to the formation of a United Front.[32]

UMSA joined in this call, but the ANC in an editorial printed in 1967 in two of its publications—*Mayibuye* and *Sechaba*—replied:

> We agree that united action by all sectors of the oppressed in South Africa can only hasten our liberation. . . . But a United Front demands a high level of discipline and integrity from its participants. It calls for absolute honesty and frankness, for unity in action and for the maintenance of maximum security of organisation. . . . These criteria are met neither by the Pan Africanist Congress nor by the Unity Movement.[33]

The PAC believes that the CPSA is behind the ANC refusal to join forces. In 1973 the editor of *Azania News* observed: "The ANC wants unity with us but the Communist Party of South Africa is irretrievably and irrevocably opposed to any such move. The ANC finds itself in a hopeless minority in the highest councils of its own army, while the CPSA is in unassailable control."[34] It seems unlikely that a United Front will be formed in the foreseeable future.[35]

THE RISE OF BLACK CONSCIOUSNESS

Inside South Africa the political aspirations of the African and other oppressed peoples appeared to have been totally crushed by the mid-1960s. The charismatic leaders of the 1960s were all in detention or exile, and the ANC and PAC were apparently ineffective. Revival waited on a new generation. This leadership vacuum was to be partially filled in the late 1960s by a new impetus that came initially from Black students.

In 1960 the new ethnic university colleges for Blacks had been born into a tradition of restriction. The student representative councils were under strict surveillance, the National Union of South African Students (NUSAS) was not allowed to operate on campuses, and Black students were not allowed to publish student newspapers. The formation of the multiracial University Christian Movement (UCM) in 1967, which adopted a radical stance, attracted many Black students to its conferences and gave them opportunities to debate issues. But soon Black students began to feel that both NUSAS and UCM were White-dominated, and that they paid little attention to problems of the Black student community. It was felt that the time had come for Blacks to develop their own thinking, unpolluted by ideas from Whites who had a big stake in the status quo. At the 1968 UCM conference about forty Blacks from university colleges, teacher training colleges, and theological seminaries resolved themselves into a Black caucus and debated the question of forming a Black students' organization. This led to the formation of the all-Black South African Students' Organization (SASO), which was inaugurated in 1969 at Turfloop. Its first president was Steve Biko, a leading exponent of the new philosophy of Black Consciousness.

Biko defined Black Consciousness as "an attitude of mind and a way of life":

> It is the most positive call to emanate from the black world for a long time. Its unadulterated quintessence is the realisation by the black man of the need to rally together with his brothers around the cause of their oppression—the blackness of their skin—and to operate as a group in order to rid themselves of the shackles that bind them to perpetual servitude. It is based on a self-examination which has ultimately led them to believe that by seeking to run away from themselves and to emulate the white man they are insulting the intelligence of whoever created them black.[36]

SASO soon withdrew its recognition of NUSAS, stating that the role of White liberals was to fight for their own freedom. SASO membership spread rapidly, as did the ideas of Black Consciousness. By 1970 Indian students in Durban and Colored students in Cape Town were referring to themselves as "Black." SASO defined Black people as "those who are by law or tradition, politically, economically, and socially discriminated against as a group in the South African society and identifying themselves as a unit in the struggle towards the realisation of their aspirations."[37] According to Donald Woods, "The idea behind Black Consciousness was to break away almost entirely from past Black attitudes to the liberation struggle and to set a new style of self-reliance and dignity for blacks as a psychological attitude leading to new initiatives."[38]

SASO declared itself to be working for the liberation of the Black man from the psychological oppression that resulted from living in a White racist society. In its manifesto it called for Whites to be excluded "in all matters relating to the struggle towards our aspirations" and said that personal contacts with Whites should be discouraged. The manifesto also rejected foreign investment because it gave stability to South Africa's exploitative regime, rejected the concept of separate universities, rejected all attempts at dialogue between African states and South Africa "at a time when the true leaders of the people are kept rotting in life imprisonment,"* asserted the indisputable right of the people of Namibia to conduct their own affairs without any interference from South Africa, and promoted the concept of Black consciousness and the drive toward Black awareness as "the most logical and significant means of ridding ourselves of the shackles that bind us to perpetual servitude." SASO also vehemently denounced South Africa's Bantustan policy.[39]

Though ostensibly a student organization, SASO soon took on a leadership role among Black intellectuals. At the 1970 SASO conference it was decided that the philosophy of Black Consciousness should be spread beyond the main centers. Together with other SASO leaders, Biko travelled throughout the country, holding discussions with Black organizations and visiting Black campuses, and expounding their ideas. The result was the formation of an umbrella political movement for all groups sharing the ideas of Black Consciousness—the Black People's Convention (BPC). It was the first Black political party since the banning of the Congresses in 1960.

*The ANC and PAC were also attacking South Africa's policy of 'dialogue,' in addresses to international forums.

More than one hundred delegates from African, Colored, and Indian organizations attended the launching conference at which the BPC declared its aims:

> To unite and solidify the Black people of South Africa with a view to liberating and emancipating them from both psychological and physical oppression; to preach, popularise and implement the philosophy of Black Consciousness and Black solidarity; to formulate and implement an educational policy by Blacks and for Blacks; to create and maintain an egalitarian society where justice is meted equally to all; to formulate, apply and implement the principles of Black communalism—the philosophy of sharing; to create and maintain an equitable economic system based on the principle and philosophy of Black communalism; to cooperate with existing agencies to reorientate the theological system to make religion relevant to the needs, aspirations, ideals, and goals of the Black people; to operate outside the White government-created institutions such as Bantustans, Indian Councils and Coloured Representative Councils.[40]

Soon after the formation of the BPC, the UCM disbanded. One reason was continuous security police harassment of its leaders, but the main reason, according to the president Winkie Direko, was the growth of Black Consciousness among the members, and their consequent unwillingness to work within a multiracial organization.[41]

From its inception the BPC worked intimately with SASO. Together they were responsible for stimulating the development of several Black self-help, legal aid, medical aid, self-education, and community programs. They also gave birth to a host of new "Black" organizations—e.g., Black Arts Theatre, Black Press Project, Black Workers' Project, and Black Theology Project. By 1975 some seventy Black organizations were affiliated with the BPC.

Black Consciousness leaders were closely watched by security police from the time the movement began, and in the years to follow they were banned, detained, and tortured by the hundreds. Several were to die while being interrogated. Black Consciousness took South Africa's White liberals by surprise, and the movement soon came under attack from some of the foremost liberal spokesmen. They regarded it as anti-White, and many tried to equate it with the Black Power movement in the United States. Said Alan Paton:

> Black consciousness is, or certainly appears to be, anxious not to get mixed up with Black Power. How long can this pretence be

> kept up? Black consciousness wants to change the order of things and rightly so. But you can't change the order of things without power. How long will the young zealots be satisfied with a mush of culture, mysticism, lyricism, and going round saying "Haven't I a lovely skin?"[42]

There was also hostility to Black Consciousness from the exiled political movements. *Azania News* said in August 1972: "We specifically want to warn against the promotion of black consciousness which seems to be gaining foot in our country today. Black consciousness is a racial reaction to white racism and white liberal paternalism. It is not a solution to either." But as the movement gathered momentum, the PAC changed its attitude, and began to acclaim Black Consciousness as "the ideology with which the PAC burst forth upon the Azanian political scene and rallied the African masses."[43]

On the other hand, the CPSA was consistently critical of Black Consciousness. A typical comment is this one from the *African Communist* in 1973:

> In order to become a more positive and dynamic force in uniting the various strata of the oppressed people, the concept of Black consciousness needs the reinforcement of the scientific and enlightening ideology of the working class, Marxism-Leninism, and to be integrated within the hard-won common programme of the liberation alliance: The Freedom Charter.[44]

SASO's critical analyses of the Bantu education system helped to engender intense dissatisfaction with the system, and students around the country began speaking out against it. Matters came to a head in April 1972 when Abraham Tiro, a student leader at the University College of the North, delivered a scathing attack on Black education. He said that the tribal universities, by virtue of their links with the government departments of Bantu, Indian, and Colored education, were intended to educate Blacks for a subservient role in society. Tiro was immediately expelled. The students pledged to boycott all lectures until he was recalled. The authorities responded by closing down the university, after which the SASO executive committee met and decided that the general grievance with the education system should be escalated into a major confrontation with the authorities. They called on all Black universities and educational institutions to boycott lectures; the boycott was extremely effective. Police intimidation was severe, but by the end of the year many hundreds of Black students were still refusing to attend lectures. Tiro fled the country in 1973 to escape a banning order. He obtained political asylum in Botswana, where he was subsequently assassinated by a parcel bomb.

In 1973 there were wholesale bannings and arrests of critics of the government. At least fifty prominent Black Consciousness leaders were banned, including almost the total leadership of SASO and the BPC. Nevertheless, the following year SASO and the BPC found enough strength to jointly organize two rallies to celebrate FRELIMO's victory in Mocambique. Despite a ban imposed under the Riotous Assemblies Act, hundreds of demonstrators gathered for a rally at Curries Fountain in Durban on September 25. The peaceful crowd was set upon by police dogs and three hundred police wielding batons, and was forcibly disbanded. The other rally was at the University College of the North, which police broke up using teargas; several students were arrested. In the following weeks all SASO and BPC leaders were arrested, as well as organizers of other Black organizations such as the Black Allied Workers' Union, the Theatre Council of Natal, and the People's Experimental Theatre.

The longest trial that had yet been heard under the Terrorism Act began on January 31, 1975. Twelve BPC and SASO members appeared on charges that included conspiracy to transform the state by unconstitutional means, conspiracy to condition Blacks for violent revolution and to create and foster feelings of racial hatred toward Whites, publication of subversive and anti-White literature and plays, holding of subversive gatherings, and discouraging of foreign investment and cooperation with the South African authorities. In effect it was the trial of Black Consciousness itself.

The issue in the trial was whether Black Consciousness as a philosophy, and as promoted by the two organizations, constituted terrorism. The judge found the indictment vague, and after six months new charges were brought against nine of the accused: conspiracy to bring about violent revolutionary change, fostering of racial hatred, and preparation to recruit Black people into a power bloc hostile to the state and the White population. Most of the accused refused to plead. One, Zitulele Cindi, former BPC secretary-general, said:

> We are charged with plotting violent revolution but it is we who have been the victims of institutional violence. If building schools throughout the country and trying to instil a feeling of self-reliance among blacks is terrorism then I would plead guilty to the charges, but I do not believe it is terrorism.

The trial ended in December 1976. The nine convicted were sentenced to terms of imprisonment of five to six years. The South African judicial system had extended "terrorism" to include the expression of thoughts, ideas, and desires for liberation.

THE OFFSPRING OF BLACK CONSCIOUSNESS

Soon after the pro-FRELIMO rallies, the Black Renaissance Convention (BRC) was formed. It held its first meeting at Hammanskraal in December 1974. All Whites were barred from attending on the grounds that their presence would inhibit free discussion and because of possible misrepresentation in the White press. By an overwhelming vote the delegates also prevented a prominent homeland leader, C. Ramusi of Lebowa, from addressing the conference. Sponsors of the BRC were the multiracial SA Council of Churches, the Roman Catholic Church of SA, the Christian Institute, the Association for Education and Cultural Advancement of Africans, and the Dutch Reformed Church of Africa. Organizing secretary Rev. Smangaliso Mkhatshwa said the BRC's purpose was to enable Africans, Coloreds, and Indians to discuss their "existential experience in South Africa." The BRC conference was broadly devoted to the themes of Black Consciousness.

After the conference Rev. Mkhatshwa said the BRC showed that Blacks needed to galvanize into concerted action because of "the political leadership vacuum which was left by the demise of the ANC and PAC. . . . None of the existing ethnically based organizations have bridged the gap. Instead, they have absolutely thrown the black people into political confusion."[45] The importance of the BRC was that it showed that Black Consciousness was successfully bringing together Blacks who held widely divergent views. Represented at the BRC conference had been SASO and BPC radicals, representatives of Black sports bodies, academics, and moderate churchmen. The conference made it clear that they were unanimous in their abhorrence of apartheid.

A new movement of political importance became prominent in 1976—the South African Students' Movement (SASM), which had been formed in 1970-71. SASM was an important part of the Black Consciousness movement, and it was born as a result of discussions by high-school students at youth clubs in Soweto. They first formed the African Student Movement (ASM) at three Soweto schools. ASM spread quickly, and when it became national in 1972 it was renamed the South African Students' Movement.

At SASM's first congress in March 1972, it was charged that Bantu education was designed "to domesticate us rather than educate us. It was designed to prepare us for the labour policies of the government and the ruling class it represented."[46] The possibility of rejecting Bantu education was discussed. The second SASM congress attracted security police attention, and in 1973 SASM leaders began fleeing the country because of police terror tactics. (Most went to Botswana.) In 1974 several SASM members were detained; some were charged under the Suppression of Communism Act and some under the Terrorism Act. The leaders began to meet secretly and established underground cells in such centers as Soweto and Durban.

In March 1976 the government began to implement its decision that Africans should be taught certain subjects in the Afrikaans language. The Afrikaans requirement was first imposed in a school in Soweto. Students there protested immediately, and students at other schools boycotted classes in a demonstration of solidarity. Despite threats by the Bantu Education department that the schools would be closed, the protest actions spread, and by May 1976 were quite general. After a few confrontations in which police tried to force pupils back to classes, an SASM branch called a meeting which five hundred pupils representing all of Soweto attended. It was decided that all high schools and secondary schools in Soweto should take sympathetic action. An Action Committee was formed which planned peaceful demonstrations. One such demonstration on June 16 led to a massacre in which hundreds of schoolchildren were killed by police and many hundreds more injured. (The newly formed Black Parents Association conducted an investigation which accounted for 238 deaths in the Baragwanath area alone.)[47] This was the flashpoint which set off countrywide demonstrations, the burning down of schools, and rioting. Hundreds more were to die from police gunfire.

After the tragic events of June 16, the Action Committee changed its name to the Soweto Students' Representative Council (SSRC). At its first meeting the council adopted the slogan "The blood of the martyrs will nurture the tree of liberation." From the outset the SSRC concerned itself with broad issues relevant to the whole community. Among its first actions were two calls for three-day general strikes in Johannesburg, both of which were very successful. Tsietsi Mashinini, the first president of SSRC, had to go into hiding almost immediately; he fled the country on August 23.

Under Mashinini's successor—Khotso Seathlolo (only 18 years old)—the SSRC organized a massive examination boycott and a mass march into Johannesburg to voice their demands for the release of students and the abolition of Bantu education. Three hundred were arrested. One of them—16-year-old Dumisane Mbatha—died in detention soon after his arrest. Thousands attended his funeral. Police began breaking up the funeral crowd, and in some cases mourners were shot. Seathlolo was wounded in a car chase in mid-January 1977, but managed to escape to Botswana. Under its next leader—Daniel Sechaba Montsitsi—the SSRC organized massive protests against proposed rent rises for Soweto; the protests were successful. It called on Soweto's government-appointed Urban Bantu Council to resign, and within a week the council had collapsed. Montsitsi and seventeen SSRC leaders were then arrested. Trofomo Sono, the next president, led the SSRC in pressuring Black teachers to resign, and on September 27, 311 teachers, including ten school principals, resigned in protest against Bantu education. Security police had begun rounding up all SSRC leaders in August, at which time Sono fled to Botswana.[48]

In the aftermath of the June 1976 revolt in Soweto, the chief minister of Gazankulu homeland, Hudson Ntsanwisi, called an emergency meeting of homeland leaders. Identifying themselves as "part and parcel of the liberation movement," the leaders sought a realignment of Black political forces operating outside the Black Consciousness movement. The leaders of KwaZulu, Gazankulu, and Lebowa met in secret with the new mayor of Soweto, David Thebahali, and officials of Inkatha. They decided to unite across tribal lines and across the urban-rural division, denouncing the idea of independent homelands. They called their new movement the Black Unity Front, and in early 1977 the chairman announced that the organization had set itself a five-year target for majority rule in South Africa.[49]

SASO and the BPC continued to operate after their leaders were convicted in the Black Consciousness trial, albeit less actively. At BPC's 1976 conference Steve Biko was elected honorary president for life, but he was unable to attend because of his banning orders. In February 1977 the BPC held an extraordinary congress in Durban at which it established a secretariat for external affairs with a mandate to attend to housing and educating young Black refugees from South Africa. In May SASO and the BPC formed a joint action committee to operate while the majority of executives of both organizations remained in detention. Thousands of religious services were held throughout the Republic in response to the call. In June the BPC convened a meeting attended by representatives of several Black organizations to discuss the question of homeland independence. Among the groups represented were SASO, the Black Parents' Association, the Union of Black Journalists, the African Social, Educational and Cultural Association (ASSECA), SASM, and the Black Priests' Solidarity Group. In a statement to the press the organizers announced a nationwide campaign against the bantustans because "Independent bantustans are merely an extension of divide and rule and are intended to preoccupy and misdirect the vast creative energies of the people away from the true goal of liberation."[50]

On September 12, 1977 Steve Biko died in detention at the hands of the security police—the forty-sixth African to die in detention without being brought to trial. At this time violence was erupting around the country; schools and government buildings were being burned down; in QwaQwa the homeland minister of justice, a school principal, and a school inspector were stoned by school students.

The following month every major Black Consciousness organization was banned: BPC, SASO, SASM, SSRC, Union of Black Journalists, Black Community Programs, Black Parents' Association, the Eastern Province Youth Organization, the Medupe Writers' Association, Natal Youth Association, National Youth Association, Transvaal Youth Organization, Western Cape Youth Organization, Zimele Trust Fund (founded by Steve Biko in 1975 to help political prisoners and their families), and the Siyazinceda Trust Fund. Leaders of most of these organizations were detained by the security police, and many have not been heard of since.

The Soweto Committee of Ten, formed by prominent people in Soweto after the collapse of the Urban Bantu Council, was also banned. After the Committee of Ten was banned, the Azania People's Organization was formed to continue the work of propagating the ideas of Black Consciousness. Its principal leaders were detained in May 1978 by the security police.

RENEWED STRENGTH FOR THE ANC

Sharpeville 1960 marked the turning point for African liberation movements from struggle through peaceful channels to a commitment to violence. Soweto 1976 probably marked the real beginning of armed struggle. Since then the ANC and PAC have had to do little recruiting for guerillas. In July 1977 it was reported that since Soweto more than four thousand young people had fled through Botswana, Swaziland, and Mocambique to join the liberation movements. In October 1977 the UN Deputy High Commissioner for Refugees reported that in the southern African states about three thousand refugees were being accommodated.

In a policy statement made in December 1977, the banned SASO declared that "the structures and activities of the Black Consciousness Movement will now join those of the National Liberation Movement in underground politicization and mobilisation work among the oppressed masses. . . . The National Liberation Movement in South Africa is now stronger than ever before and encompasses all individuals and organisations striving for the liberation of the oppressed masses and for the establishment of a non-racial and just society."[51] However, some of the BPC and SASO leaders who fled South Africa appeared to be trying to find a way to create a "third force" to project the Black Consciousness movement as an alternative to the ANC and PAC.

Since June 1976 the liberation movements have received vastly increased financial assistance from their supporters. The OAU recently resolved to "extend maximum political, economic and military assistance to the liberation movements in South Africa to enable them to execute the armed struggle."[52] Both the ANC and PAC have been more active inside South Africa since 1976 than at any time since the early 1960s. Scores of trials, most of which implicated the ANC, bear testimony to the heightened underground activity. Evidence presented at these trials indicates the existence of a nationwide network of cells for recruiting guerillas. Through this network many hundreds of young men are sent out of the country each year for guerilla training, and arsenals of arms, ammunition, and explosives have been built up at various points within the country. Guerillas have been trained as far afield as Libya (PAC) and the USSR (ANC). Further evidence of increased ANC activity is the large number of "pamphlet bombs"* exploded in the country in the last three years, and the increased "Freedom Radio" ANC broadcasts from countries bordering South Africa. At least four new clandestine newspapers are now published inside the Republic.

In March 1977 a Defence Force white paper was presented in Parliament warning that the terrorist war might spread to the northern and eastern Transvaal and northern Natal. It called for a total national strategy for defense because South Africa was at war "whether we wish to accept it or not."[53] Defense spending went up by 21 percent to R1,654 million. The period for continuous national service

*Pamphlet bombs are usually concealed in trash cans. A charge of explosive, armed with a simple timing device, is used to eject thousands of lightweight pamphlets into the air which contain political statements usually attributed to the ANC.

for White youths was increased to two years. Deputy Commissioner of Police General Kriel announced in July that heavily armed police were carrying out a paramilitary function patrolling the country's borders with Botswana, Rhodesia, Mocambique, and Swaziland to intercept trained insurgents trying to enter South Africa and to prevent youths from leaving the country for military training.

In August 1978 ANC secretary-general Alfred Nzo released a dramatic communique stating that

> On August 1, 1978 a small detachment unit of the gallant sons and daughters of South Africa, Umkhonto we Sizwe—the military wing of the African National Congress—was forced into combat engagement with large contingents of the South African Defence Force in the Rustenburg area, Western Transvaal. . . . The enemy . . . initiated an intensive terrorist campaign against the ANC guerillas and the local population. Ceaseless and aimless gunfire from low flying helicopters ploughed the area. They sprayed the battlefield with chemicals: napalm, defoliants and teargas from canisters.[54]

South Africa has thus far been silent concerning this claim by the ANC. But however true the communique, it is obvious that preparations for armed struggle are at an advanced stage in South Africa. The ANC now enjoys support from Frelimo and the MPLA and has training camps in the former Portuguese colonies. Were SWAPO to come to power in Namibia, or the Patriotic Front in Zimbabwe, the ANC's position would become much stronger because it enjoys a good relationship with both these liberation movements.

DECLINE OF THE PAC

Although the PAC improved its image abroad during the early 1970s, it has recently suffered several reverses, and is even in danger of losing recognition by the OAU. At a Soviet-oriented international "solidarity conference" held in Lisbon in 1977, a resolution was passed naming the ANC the "sole authentic representative of the South African people." This was the first major international gathering to choose between the ANC and PAC. In February 1978 quiet moves were made by some progressive states inside the OAU Liberation Committee to withdraw recognition from the PAC. Among those arguing against the PAC were Angola and Algeria.[55]

PAC president Robert Sobukwe died of cancer in February

1978. He had spent the last eighteen years of his life as a prisoner on Robben Island and as a banned person in Kimberley. Soon after Sobukwe's death a power struggle began between supporters of Leballo and members who were dissatisfied with the old style leadership. The problems erupted in the open when PAC members were detained in Swaziland in April. Wrote the Johannesburg *Star*: "It is an open secret that the detention of prominent PAC officials followed a visit to the country by acting PAC president Potlako Leballo, who alerted the Swazi government to the fact that the Swazi faction of the PAC was opposing his leadership."[56] Thirty PAC members were rounded up and deported from Swaziland. It was also reported that Botswana had been expelling PAC men.

At the end of June 1978 PAC members met in Dar es Salaam to clarify the position of the dissidents within the PAC and to settle quarrels. Those who opposed the leadership of Leballo were outmaneuvered, and seven members of the central committee were expelled. Sixty other delegates were told that if they continued to support the expelled members they too would face expulsion. If it were not for the recent injection of Sowetan youths attracted to the PAC's slogan "Africa for the Africans," the PAC would be in a very shaky position today.[57]

With the successive major Black political movements—ANC, PAC, and Black Consciousness movement—having been banned and forced underground, the new initiative for overt political activity has come from homeland governments and government-created institutions. Buthelezi's Inkatha movement is under close police surveillance, and the authorities are not very happy with its colors—green, gold, and black—which are the same as the ANC's. On one occasion Inkatha's publicity secretary Gibson Thula remarked: "We would not be looking at reality if we did not admit the legitimacy of the ANC in the struggle for liberation."[58] Buthelezi himself was once a member of the ANC Youth League, and he has met with Oliver Tambo a few times during recent visits abroad.

At a meeting at the Zulu royal capital of Ulundi in January 1978 Buthelezi was elected chairman of a new national political movement, the South African Black Alliance (SABA), to represent Africans, Indians, and Coloreds. Associated with the formation of the party was the Colored Labor Party, the Indian Reform Party, and the homeland leaders of QwaQwa. Buthelezi knows that if the South African government wants to try to avoid a full-scale guerilla war, it will have to negotiate with him. What organizations like SABA or the Black United Front could possibly achieve in the way of concessions from the government would be some form of federalism. But this would not be acceptable to the ANC, which, strengthened by the explosion of Black Consciousness, seems to be the most significant Black political force in South Africa today. However, the South African government would only grant such concessions if it had been driven into a corner by guerilla warfare, and at such a stage the influence of men like Buthelezi would have been eclipsed by the guerilla leaders. The guerilla war would be continued with the full backing of Black Africa's progressive states and the socialist countries.

CONCLUSION

The elaboration of a theory of revolution for South Africa has proved to be extremely difficult. The peaceful resistance methods of the early years of the ANC failed to bring any changes in repressive legislation, but in retrospect the ANC believes that this was a necessary stage, since one of the requirements for effective armed struggle is "disillusionment with the prospect of achieving liberation by traditional peaceful processes."[59] The ANC's policy is against flamboyant revolutionary gestures in which lives are unnecessarily lost. Planning is essential: "Untimely, ill-planned or premature manifestations of violence impede and do not advance the prospect for revolutionary change, and are therefore clearly counter-revolutionary."[60] Nevertheless (says the ANC), it is not necessary to wait for a deep crisis in the enemy camp or for a "revolutionary situation" to exist before armed struggle can begin (as the PAC claims): "The actual beginning of guerilla warfare can be made, and having begun, can steadily develop conditions for the future all-out war."[61]

When talking of revolutionary armed struggle, the ANC is careful to point out that it is talking about political struggle, which includes the use of force. "Our movement must reject all manifestations of militarism which separate armed peoples' struggle from its political context. [In our movement] the primacy of the political leadership is unchallenged and supreme and all revolutionary formations and levels are subordinate to this leadership." Emphasis is put on politicizing the masses. "We must ensure that what is brought to power is not an army but the masses, at the head of which stands its organised political leadership."[62]

One of the issues for continuing debate within and among the African political movements is whether the liberation struggle is a class or a national struggle. There has been controversy between those who urge an immediate socialist program and those who insist that national liberation should be the first stage of revolution. The socialists fear that nationalism would lead to directionless race war, and possibly to a Black bourgeois solution instead of a progressive one, while the nationalists are opposed to the dilution of mass Black fervor by White Communists. Before 1959 the ANC had the extremes of Black chauvinism (the Africanists) and nonracial democracy within its ranks, but the African exclusivists could not prevail under the shadow of the Afrikaner government, and when the ANC allied itself with the SACP, it adopted the principle of "one man-one vote" rather than "Africa for the Africans." When the Africanists broke away to form the PAC, they claimed to represent the voices of genuine African nationalism and adopted an overt anti-White and anti-Communist stance. (Nowadays the PAC describes itself as a Marxist-Leninist vanguard party!)

By the time of Sharpeville White opinion had hardened against Blacks. The ANC came to the conclusion that all-out confrontation was the only solution, and that the line had been drawn sharply between Black and White.* As the sabotage campaign progressed and Whites coalesced more densely into the laager, the whiteness of the enemy was no longer minimized in ANC policy documents. It was acknowledged that the class contradictions in South Africa were largely racial. Thus even the White working class, through legal artifice and union exclusiveness, had been drawn into the privileged capitalist class, while the majority of Blacks were kept in a state of economic deprivation. Nevertheless, though the ANC spoke more and more in terms of the whiteness of the oppressor and the blackness of the oppressed, it still kept the door open for radical Whites as well as Indians and Coloreds, allowing for the possibility of a nonracial progressive solution in the end. "Strategy and Tactics," the policy document adopted by the ANC at the 1969 Morogoro conference, states that

> confrontation on the lines of colour—at least in the early stages of the conflict, is not of our choosing. It is not altogether impossible

*In the 1970s the Black Consciousness movement used the increasing polarization in the country to bring together the Africans, Coloreds, and Indians as *those oppressed by Whites*—a concept of Blackness with immense mobilizing power.

> that the white working class, or a substantial section of it, may come to see that its true long-term interests coincide with that of the non-white workers. We must miss no opportunity to try to make them aware of this truth. Our policy must continually stress that there is room in South Africa for all who live in it, but only on the basis of democracy.[63]

The ANC stresses that it does not want an elite Black group to gain ascendancy:

> Victory must embrace more than formal political democracy. There must be a return of the wealth of the land to the people. . . . The perspective of a speedy progression from formal liberation to genuine and lasting emancipation is made more real by the existence in our country of a large and growing working class whose class consciousness complements national consciousness.[64]

The PAC remains less accommodating toward Whites: "We have stated clearly that we have no spare black skins or black souls to give to white revolutionaries, but we shall deny no one the right to liberate himself or to link himself with those of like mind. We cannot reconcile ourselves to neo-colonialism within the liberation movement." However, the PAC states that its ultimate goal is "the establishment of an Africanist socialist democracy in a non-racial society. PAC believes in one race—the human race—with everybody who owes his only allegiance to Azania being regarded as an African."[65] The PAC has not made it clear how the difficult change from a nationalist revolution to a socialist solution can be made. Because the PAC might allow a bourgeois solution (and because it is backed by Peking rather than Moscow), the PAC is perhaps more likely to get Western support in the future than is the ANC.

The Freedom Charter and the SACP program do not expect socialism to follow immediately upon a national democratic revolution. A private sector, controlled so as "to assist the well-being of the people," will still be tolerated, says Joe Slovo. "Rural policy involves confiscation, redistribution and redivision of the land amongst the people, implying an extension of private ownership." This policy is not pandering to more conservative elements in Black politics, says Slovo, but is a recognition that the private sector has a vital role to play in the interim phase experienced by every socialist country.[66]

THE STIRRING GIANT: OBSERVATIONS ON THE INKATHA AND OTHER BLACK POLITICAL MOVEMENTS IN SOUTH AFRICA

Lawrence Schlemmer

BACKGROUND TO THE SEVENTIES

Prior to 1960, the African National Congress (ANC), formed in 1912, stood alone as the voice of politically active Africans in South Africa; in 1959, however, an ANC Youth League breakaway led to the formation of the Pan African Congress (PAC). At the peak of its popular mobilization, the ANC claimed a membership of approximately 100,000. At *its* peak the PAC claimed approximately 30,000, mainly drawn away from the ANC. These membership figures are questioned as registers of formal enrollment, but they may indicate the extent of committed public interest. In the ANC "Defiance Campaign" of 1952, nearly 8,600 "pass-law resisters" were arrested, there were fairly successful boycott campaigns of selected businesses in the Transvaal, and certain Black residential areas staged well-supported "stay-at-home" strikes among workers. The PAC also demonstrated a capacity to mobilize when shortly after its formation it organized a march by some 30,000 Africans in Cape Town and numerous other collective acts of political protest. After the Sharpeville disaster (1960), when 69 Africans were fatally shot after a crowd of tens of thousands had marched to a police station in protest against pass laws, over 18,000 arrests were made in raids all over the country. These figures clearly show that political activism was not limited to small cliques or factions in the community.

On April 8, 1960 both the ANC and the PAC were declared unlawful organizations under the terms of the "Suppression of Communism Act." Both organizations went underground: the PAC in the form of the secret organization Poqo (meaning "pure") and the ANC under the name Umkhonto we Sizwe ("Spear of the Nation"). There were fairly extensive Poqo riots in the Cape, leading to some 3,000 arrests, but an ANC-organized strike in the Transvaal was largely unsuccessful. For some three years Umkhonto we Sizwe engaged in limited and sporadic acts of sabotage, but political resistance was clearly on the wane.[1]

In the period from 1963 to 1968, on the surface at least, there was a lull in African political organization inside South Africa. Clearly the collapse of organizational activity was in large measure a reflection of the removal of activist African leadership by arrest, conviction, and bannings and other security measures directed against the more activist rank-and-file followers. The destruction of these organizations was accomplished very rapidly with little popular reaction. Widespread though their support was, they had failed to gain the protection which would have been offered had they been truly mass organizations with large committed followings.

From the 1950s onward, when mass membership was actively sought, the problem of attracting rank-and-file support was endemic.[2] Perhaps the goals, almost always stated in political terms, were too remote from the realities of everyday life. Albert Luthuli, one-time president of the ANC, suggests this in his autobiography when he advises activists to consider the implications of their actions on the consciousness of ordinary Africans. There was perhaps too much faith that campaigns would gather momentum of their own accord. The economic and security interests of ordinary people were neglected in the emphasis on the necessity for self-sacrifice in the pursuit of long-range objectives. Self-sacrifice requires ideologies of commitment—ideologies found more often among the young and the well-educated than among the rank and file. There was not sufficient concern with what was most pressing in the eyes of the man and woman in the street. Were the pass laws, for example, of high priority for the factory workers who had the right to work in town? Then, virtually throughout the history of the ANC, for the ordinary member there were demoralizing cross-currents of opinion about the desirability of collaborating with White liberals, with White Marxists, with Indians and Coloreds. Should not a clearer "African-South African" image of leadership have been maintained? Finally, there was the great weakness of most opposition movements in South Africa of underestimating the strength of the White Nationalist government and its control systems. On numerous occasions a massive turnout of police was interpreted as panic on the part of the authorities or as a "moral victory" for the movement, when in fact the coercive apparatus of the state was not even remotely strained.[3]

These observations should not detract, however, from the fact that the history of the ANC and related movements is one of great courage, commitment, and endurance in the face of well-nigh overwhelming odds. For all their strategic setbacks, the ANC and PAC have left a legacy of pride and an example of leadership for many Africans which lives on today.

THE BLACK CONSCIOUSNESS MOVEMENT

The years of quiescence from 1963 to 1968 were for many Black students a period of ferment. African students sympathetic to the ANC formed the African Students' Association, while those sympathetic to the PAC formed the African Students' Union of South Africa. There was also a third group—the Progressive National Students' Organization. The latter two organizations opposed all cooperation with the multiracial National Union of South African Students (NUSAS), which they saw as dominated by White liberals. There was intense rivalry between these groups, and their membership, which was never large, steadily declined.

In 1968, Black students who had become disillusioned with NUSAS, including some who had been influenced by American Black theology introduced by the nonracial University Christian Movement, formed the South African Students' Organization (SASO). In a sense the founder of the organization was Steve Biko (who died in police detention in 1977). SASO excluded Whites, and as such enjoyed a brief period of acceptance by the segregation-minded South African government authorities.

SASO soon established a strong following on the Black university campuses. It was to become one of the most influential elements on the South African Black political scene and constituted, with currents of Black theology in the churches, the genesis of the "Black Consciousness" movement. In 1971 SASO convened a national conference involving a wide range of Black organizations to discuss a common strategy. Out of this conference the Black People's Convention was born in 1972. Also established in 1972, under the umbrella of the Black Consciousness movement, was the Black and Allied Workers' Union.

SASO and the Black Consciousness movement were founded on the principles of Black solidarity, pride, self-confidence, and self-help, and on the need for psychological emancipation from the sense of inferiority which centuries of White domination and paternalism have inculcated in Blacks. An important aim was to discover sources of Black identity in the indigenous cultures of South Africa's Black people, which was complicated by the fact that some Black people in South Africa derive from cultures other than the southern African

Bantu group. Close cooperation with liberal or even radical Whites was firmly rejected. The liberals were seen as an influence which had traditionally weakened the revolutionary zeal of Black movements, and cooperation with White radicals was avoided because of a desire not to become involved in the dissemination of foreign Marxist ideologies in a context where they were seen as inappropriate. The mode of operation of the movement involved broad "conscientization" and community self-help projects, which would instill a sense of self-reliance and community solidarity. The movement embraced not only university students, but also secondary-school students and adults. The adults involved were mainly the "intelligentsia" in the Black communities—ministers, teachers, professionals, and some Black businessmen.

In addition to the principles of Black unity, solidarity, and self-help, the Black Consciousness movement was dedicated to the liberation of South African Blacks and, as such, to Black majority rule. In its search for a policy for the future, it adopted a range of economic principles broadly typical of African Socialism. As Hanf and Vierdag put it, if one takes both political and economic ideology into account, the Black Consciousness movement seems to stand midway between the ANC and the PAC positions of the late 1950s.[4] The stance of SASO as regards the ANC-PAC rivalry was one of "positive neutrality."[5]

The major impact of the Black Consciousness movement has been to raise the level of "consciousness" of the Black people of South Africa, and in this it achieved remarkable success among the youth and the urban intelligentsia. Fundamental to the type of consciousness the movement espoused was its definition of "Black." Black people were defined as "those who are by law or tradition, politically, economically and socially discriminated against as a group in South African society, identifying themselves as a unit in the struggle toward the realization of their aspirations."[6] The older inclusive term for Africans, Indians, and Coloreds—"non-white"—was vehemently rejected because it was seen to imply a negation of identity and dignity: a "non-being" or a residual status. (It is often used now as a derogatory term for Blacks who still aspire to be like Whites.) An obvious question that arises is whether the Black Consciousness ideology is racist. Bennie Khoapa has described it as "going to the very gate of racism in order to destroy racism."[7] The movement's views on White identity (as reported by Thomas Ross) suggest that in a new South Africa Whites would be encouraged to remain, but that there would be no designated minority rights for Whites. The ideal is a nonracial society, but one created by Blacks, in which Whites would not be allowed any group exclusivity.[8] No doubt the Black Consciousness movement is characterized by a considerable measure of anti-White hostility, but as Biko so often said, that hostility was a response to White racism. In a society where racial status had been completely reordered, Blacks would not necessarily display the deep-seated negative stereotyping of people of different colors that has been so typical of White behavior in South Africa.

In less than ten years the organizations making up the Black Consciousness movement had become very influential among well-educated urban Blacks; then in October 1977 they were all banned by the South African government. No specific reasons for the banning were given, but it can be assumed that the government, *inter alia*, was attempting to break down the widespread resistance to "Bantu education" among African youth which had persisted since the Soweto disturbances of June 1976. Black Consciousness as an ideology has undoubtedly survived the bannings, however, and no African political organization can ignore the principles which have emerged from it. Yet for all its eloquence and the sophistication of its thinking, Black Consciousness remains an ideology of *reaction*: a reaction against White racism.

As already noted, Blacks in South Africa are drawn from a diversity of ethnic backgrounds: Nguni- and Sotho-speaking Africans, Hindu and Muslim Indians, Malay Muslims, Christian Coloreds,* etc. It is highly problematic that a sense of unity can be created among these groups which lies deeper than that born of reaction to White racism or pragmatic strategy. In 1972 Philip Mayer and this author found little evidence of an inclusive "Black" consciousness among non-intellectual, non-student African populations.[9] A recent detailed political survey among urban Africans in the Transvaal and Natal has shown that no more than about 6 percent of a cross-section of African adults could be regarded as clearly defined supporters of the Black Consciousness movement.[10] But the political significance of Black Consciousness is much greater than these estimates suggest—perhaps primarily because it has taken root among the educated elite from which leadership is typically drawn. An illustration of its significance can be seen in the township disturbances of 1976.

*To an outside observer the Christian Coloreds are simply dark-skinned Afrikaners.

LAWRENCE SCHLEMMER

YOUTH REBELLION IN THE TOWNSHIPS

For many months prior to June 16, 1976, African school boards, parents' associations, school principals, and other bodies like the South African Institute of Race Relations had warned the Bantu Educational authorities that attempts in the Transvaal to enforce the use of Afrikaans as a medium of instruction was unacceptable to African pupils.* Afrikaans was unacceptable to African pupils partly because it symbolized the system of Nationalist rule and Separate Development, and partly because their teachers and they were not proficient in Afrikaans. Instruction in it would constitute yet another handicap to scholars already suffering great disadvantages. The students had demonstrated their opposition earlier in the year by effectively boycotting schools in Soweto, but the authorities ignored all pleas and enforced the policy.

On June 16 a crowd of over ten thousand school children between the ages of seven and twenty gathered and marched in protest. They carried placards reading "Down with Afrikaans," "To Hell with Afrikaans," "Afrikaans Stinks," "Afrikaans Is a Tribal Language," etc. Perhaps a foolish display in a country with strong language loyalties, but certainly not a revolutionary uprising. Their mood was jovial and noisy: they were enjoying their defiance of the system. As cars passed they shouted "Power" and raised fists—not so much a demonstration of violent intent as an expression of solidarity and determination. These were children imbued with the spirit of Black Consciousness, however indirect their contact with the movement might have been.

The procession continued with no harm to property or passers-by until stopped by the police, who were fully armed and perhaps uncertain about the intentions of the demonstrators. The police ordered the marchers to disperse. When they did not obey, the police fired into the air. The demonstrators, infuriated and frightened, retaliated with stones, injuring two policemen. The police then fired into the crowd, killing four students—one only thirteen years old. The crowd fled, but violence erupted throughout the township, and two White officials were killed. Initially only government buildings or other symbols of white authority were affected, but then beer-

*It has been official policy since 1955 that English and Afrikaans are to be used on a 50/50 basis in African secondary schools, but the policy had not been enforced. From the beginning of 1976, however, Bantu Education officials in some areas of the Transvaal began to enforce the regulation.

halls and bottle stores were destroyed, with many of the rioters shouting slogans like "Less beer, more education," and "More schools, not bottle stores."*

In the days following, the demonstrations became increasingly focused on political issues. In addition to the systematic destruction of government and White-owned property, the burning of liquor outlets, etc., the demonstrators stoned vehicles on roads outside the township. They began calling upon adults to join their campaign. There was one attempted march toward Johannesburg and one demonstration in the streets of central Johannesburg, which was quickly stifled. There were calls for general strikes by all Black workers. The calls for strikes were accompanied by pickets to discourage workers from catching trains, and workers returning from work were subject to harassment. Workers were told that their houses would be burned if they went to work, and indeed some workers' homes were attacked. The first one-day strike was about 50-60 percent successful, the second somewhat more successful, but the fourth (in November) completely unsuccessful, partly because the police were better prepared to protect transportation and because employers threatened strikers with dismissal.

By now the demonstrations had spread to over 160 other parts of the country—Pretoria, and other areas on the Witwatersrand, the northern Transvaal, the eastern Cape, and even to Colored youth in the western Cape, who staged massive demonstrations in the center of Cape Town despite formidable police retaliation and many deaths. As the demonstrations progressed, there were signs of effective ad hoc underground organization, and as police detained the leaders, new figures emerged to lead the students. The group primarily responsible for the coordination was the Soweto Students' Representative Council.

Throughout the country, hundreds of lives were being lost. The police could quite easily prevent destruction of property outside the townships, but in the townships the unrest continued for some months, with intermittent lulls. The death toll approached the 700 mark, with over 1000 injured, and many hundreds arrested. But the demonstrators appeared to have lost their fear of bullets. They seemed inspired by a sense of mission, with wave after wave of new vanguards emerging to lead the action. The demonstrations seemed

*Since a large proportion of the revenue for administering townships like Soweto is derived from the sale of liquor to Africans, these townships have been well-serviced with liquor outlets. The demonstrators were fully aware of the connection.

to be sustained more by inner commitment than by any sense of practical strategy. In group discussions with participants conducted by the author, some references were made to help from other African countries, but this was clearly not a general expectation. Some participants took encouragement from the very violence they had encountered; they interpreted the police response as fear and panic. More generally, the struggle was seen as self-vindicating and cumulative, bound to succeed in the long run.

The consequences of the demonstrations have been diverse. First, the point should be made that at no stage was "law and order" throughout the country threatened. Many people were killed, but the South African police used only a small part of their coercive potential. If mass demonstrations had really threatened the police on a large scale, the death toll would have been much greater.

The demonstrations did evoke some positive response from the authorities. A commission of enquiry was appointed, an announcement of improvements in the system of education was hastened (including a decision to drop the label "Bantu" before "Education"), and the authorities backed down on the issue of instruction in Afrikaans. Furthermore, the government announced that Africans would be allowed long-term leasehold purchase of houses without the requirement of homeland citizenship, offering them greater security of tenure in the townships.* In addition, the Urban Bantu Councils were to be replaced by a form of elected representation giving urban Africans a measure of increased responsibility for their own local affairs in the so-called "Community Councils."† (It should be noted that Africans have still not been granted full freehold ownership rights in the townships in "White" areas, nor have they been given full powers of local government.)

How should these demonstrations be understood? Quite obviously the issue of instruction in Afrikaans was merely the precipitating factor. The issue of fundamental importance is the quality of Bantu Education, and the general view among youth that it is designed to prepare them for second-class status in the society. For the

*Several years earlier the government had terminated the system of leasehold purchase on the grounds that Africans in "White" urban areas were temporary sojourners. Recently leasehold purchase was reinstated, subject to the condition that the purchaser accept homeland citizenship. This condition was now withdrawn.

†The Urban Bantu Councils were purely advisory bodies and never enjoyed much legitimacy among Africans. They were elected, but the percentage turnouts were usually very low: 15-25 percent.

youth, Bantu Education is symbolic of the social system as a whole. As Hanf and Vierdag point out, young blacks are more or less completely segregated from the wider society.[11] Their parents at least have contact with Whites through working in White areas, but young students and unemployed young people move in a world limited to the ghetto-like existence of urban Blacks. Their only contact with the wider system of apartheid is in their dealings with the township administration and their experience of the school system. Their frustrations become focused particularly on the educational system, because it is the most intimately associated with their life-chances and their possible escape from the poverty of township life.

There are other factors which help to explain the township disturbances and why the demonstrations were more or less limited to teenagers and young adults. Mid-1976 was a time of rising unemployment, particularly for Black youth. The impact of this on young people's views and expectations was probably aggravated by the fact that the rise in unemployment came after a period of economic prosperity, when Black wages and job opportunities had improved as never before (1970-1975). Another factor which probably contributed to the discontent was the homeland citizenship clauses introduced by the government with regard to the right to home ownership on leasehold. Most young urban Africans had never even seen the homelands, and a law which coerced their parents (and themselves, if under-age) to assume homeland citizenship must have been seen as very ominous in its implications. On the other hand, events in southern Africa, like the withdrawal of Portugal from Mozambique and Angola and the talk of settlements in Rhodesia and South West Africa, may have raised political hopes—or at least produced a climate of optimism, a sense of new opportunities for change. Finally, the school system itself certainly heightened tensions. It had been notoriously overcrowded for years, and there was a large increase in enrollment in secondary schools in Soweto in 1975. Considering the generally poor performance of the system for Africans, and the intense anxiety and strain it must have caused them, an increase in pressure on the system could easily raise their frustrations to critical levels.*

These factors must be considered in any assessment of why the disturbances occurred in 1976, but they operated against a background of more general frustrations. Particularly noteworthy is the fact that conditions in the townships allow little opportunity for

*According to 1975 enrollment figures, only 0.75 percent of pupils in Bantu Education were in Forms 4 or 5, and only 4.6 percent were in Forms 2, 3, 4, and 5 combined (*Financial Mail*, June 25, 1976, p. 1112).

young people to develop the kind of leisure and play subculture which in other societies tends to depoliticize them. In South African townships young people have most of the frustrations their elders have without the counterbalancing and stabilizing influence of jobs to keep and families to maintain. Finally, it should be noted that the way ad hoc informal leadership emerged during the disturbances suggests that the Black Consciousness movement and in particular the South African Students' Movement had succeeded in creating a sense of cohesion at least among certain elements of the young.[12]

The student resistance continued for a long time after the initial violence. There was an almost complete boycott of certain key schools in Soweto, Pretoria, and elsewhere, which broke down only at the end of 1977. Many hundreds of youngsters have fled the country to seek a future (or military training) elsewhere, a process that continues. The youth in the demonstrations displayed an almost puritanical fervor (opposing the use of alcohol, opposing consumerism among their parents, etc.), and while perhaps most of them were not highly politically motivated at the outset of the disturbances, the confrontations with the police and the attendant publicity have no doubt had a very significant politicizing effect.

BLACK LABOR ON THE MOVE

Another Black movement with possible political implications is the African trade union movement. Until late 1979 Africans were not regarded as employees in terms of the Industrial Conciliation Act governing labor relations in South Africa, and as a consequence they could not be members of registered trade unions, nor could they negotiate within the Industrial Council system of negotiation and dispute-settlement. Labor relations affecting Africans were governed by the system of "Works" and "Liaison" committees which operated within individual industrial firms; however, Africans were not prohibited from forming nonregistered, informal unions.*

African labor activity has a long history. Major strikes occurred as early as 1918 and 1919. (In 1920, for example, approximately 70,000 Black mineworkers went on strike.) In 1919 Clements Kadalie formed the Industrial and Commercial Workers' Union (ICU), which initially was successful in negotiating improvements in wages at government level. By 1928 the ICU had nearly 30,000 members, but or-

*Following the first report of a commission of enquiry into labor legislation under Professor Nie Wiehahn, the government in 1979 first allowed permanently resident urban Africans to form registerable trade unions and subsequently relaxed the provisions to allow all non-foreign migrant workers to belong to registered unions.

ganizational problems and lack of recognition by the registered unions, employers, and government authorities led to its disintegration.

After the decline of the ICU, a number of African unions and union coordination bodies continued to exist, and the movement underwent a resurgence after the Great Depression, despite great difficulties. Some African unions received assistance from registered unions, and the government wage boards were not always unsympathetic, but the union movement had little chance of success without sufficient recognition from employers to have at least stop-order facilities for union dues.[13] There were also severe problems of factionalism and ideological cleavage. The South African Council of Trade Unions (SACTU) emerged as a non-racial body coordinating both some registered and some African unions; by 1961 it had forty-six affiliated unions and a membership of over 50,000. It took a political stance, which had the inevitable consequence of large-scale bannings of leaders, and the council disintegrated. Government action, lack of recognition by employers, the hostility of most White unions, and differences about strategy with the friendly White unions led to a further decline in African union strength and cohesion, and by 1970 only two African unions remained.

In 1972 African wages in industry were lagging badly behind increases in the cost-of-living. The so-called Poverty Datum Line* had become a popular concept. The Urban Training Project, a moderate labor education body, had started to operate in the Transvaal, and a resurgence of labor consciousness appeared to have taken place among African workers, with sporadic informal strikes occurring at an increased rate. In 1973, a spate of strikes occurred in Durban and surrounding areas which left industry crippled for almost two weeks. Over 70,000 Africans went on strike, occasionally joined by Indian workers. This combined strike action proved to be a signal event; significant concessions were granted across the board by most employers, and the government ordered a review of minimum wage levels for unskilled workers. The strikes were motivated by economic rather than political considerations, and the strikers displayed remarkable cohesion and self-discipline.[14]

Both the ANC abroad and the Black Consciousness movement sought to take some of the credit for these strikes, but the weight of evidence suggests that the strike leadership emerged from within and that the strikes were the outcome of a groundswell of popular grievances. After the strikes new incentives existed for the establishment

*An amount calculated by the universities as the minimum required to maintain health and decency.

of African unions. White and other non-African assistance was forthcoming from the Urban Training Project, the University Wages Commissions, and from two or three registered unions. In Natal a coordinating body, the Trade Union Advisory Committee, was formed. By mid-1974 twenty African unions were in existence, with a claimed membership of almost 40,000.

Since 1974 some by now traditional impediments to African union success have been restored.* Except for a very small number of foreign firms, employers are unwilling to recognize the unions, and some degree of recognition is essential for union success. From 1973 onward employers have been strongly encouraged by the government to base their labor relations policies on "Liaison" or "Works" committees, which are at best "house" or company organizations and at worst little more than consultative bodies. Both forms of committees, although they are elected and undoubtedly offer possibilities for improved communication in industry, fragment an industrywide labor force, are vulnerable to manipulation by management, and inasmuch as they discourage the recognition of unions, impede the development of labor bargaining strength. In addition, there has been persistent surveillance by the security police. In particular, non-African trade union educators and union leaders have been banned, including individuals who were striving to establish a practical basis of understanding between unions and management—e.g., the chairman and secretary of the Urban Training Project. Furthermore, ideological differences have made cooperation between sections of the African trade union movement difficult. There has been some internal dissent in the African trade union movement in Durban. The Black Consciousness labor movement—the Black and Allied Workers' Union—has at times created difficulties by accusing White personnel in the Black unions of paternalism and exploitation. Some unions have become unduly committee-dominated, with little popular participation, but most important of all, the confidence of African workers has been weakened by the economic recession since 1975 and the consequent mounting unemployment. Despite considerable encouragement and concrete assistance from abroad, the African unions appear to be struggling to maintain present levels of activity and organization. At the time of writing, it seems that there is sufficient organizational skill available within the African unions and

*From late 1973 to 1977 the author was on the council of the Institute for Industrial Education—a trade union education body within the structure of unregistered unions in Natal. The material presented here is based on this experience and on discussions with African trade unionists.

enough interest among workers to make it likely they will survive and be important if and when economic recovery commences. Now that African unions can become registered it seems likely that the Black labor movement will prosper. Government controls on political activity will be very strict, but Black workers' rights and privileges will be enhanced.

CHIEF GATSHA BUTHELEZI AND "INKATHA"

Another development of major significance has been the emergence of Inkatha yeNkululeko yeSiswe—the "National Cultural Liberation Movement"—under the leadership of Chief Mangosutho Gatsha Buthelezi. Originally brought into existence by the Zulu king Dinizulu in 1928, it aimed at promoting the cultural traditions and national solidarity of the Zulu people as well as a wider unity of African people in South Africa. Chief Buthelezi had revived the organization before 1973, but in 1975 he and other leaders reshaped its goals to make it more relevant to the political and social challenges of the day. Inkatha is clearly a mobilization organization with a very strong political flavor. Its colors, songs, and slogans are the same as those of the ANC. (Chief Buthelezi is an ex-member of the ANC: he served in the Youth League, and was expelled from Fort Hare University for his activities in connection with the ANC. He was a lieutenant of Chief Albert Luthuli, former president of the ANC.)

The aims of Inkatha are (1) to promote cultural liberation—i.e., to overcome dependency and to instill a sense of pride and independence in Africans (a prominent representative in the Transvaal says, "Call it 'Black Consciousness' if you like"); (2) to promote community development along lines of self-help and self-reliance in order to combat problems of underdevelopment and poor morale; (3) to work toward a change in the educational system for Blacks in South Africa; (4) to abolish race discrimination; and—most importantly—(5) to achieve the full incorporation of Blacks into political decision-making in South Africa (in other words, majority rule).

The strategy of Inkatha is reflected in a statement by Chief Buthelezi (who regards his role in Inkatha as more important than his position as chief minister in the KwaZulu cabinet) that "Before we do anything, we need to organise ourselves into a disciplined body. We need to come together to support each other, plan with each other and act with each other."[15] Thus there should be mobilization and solidarity at the grass roots before any specific political activity is undertaken. The model for political development is one of the formation of interest-based organizations as a means of achieving political articulation, because government

> does not relate to the masses directly as it does to the organisations and associations which are important to the people. . . . The governability of a society which has emerged from . . . rapid and radical social change could easily depend on the kind of organisations and associations which were developed prior to and during the transition period.[16]*

With regard to the political goals of Inkatha, the picture is confused at this stage, and it is probably premature to draw any final conclusions. Certain basic principles are becoming clear, however. First, there is an awareness that grass-roots interests should prevail: "It is not the role of political leadership to impose on a people a political system which that leadership considers to be an ideal."[17] Second, there is a discernible trend in favor of a "one-party democracy" as the basis of policy goals. On the issue of opposition parties in KwaZulu, Buthelezi has expressed doubts, arguing *inter alia* that "poverty is too near the bone,"[18] implying that in situations of underdevelopment and inequality, opposition parties can exploit deprivations felt by the people in an irresponsible way. A former secretary-general of Inkatha, S.M. Bengu, has questioned the applicability of a multiparty democracy in a nonracial South Africa, implying that the by now virtually traditional African one-party democracy is a more appropriate political form.[19]

For Buthelezi, however, "there is in South Africa no blueprint for the society we are striving to establish," and "there is a very real need for a Pan Africanist conference in which the nature of South Africa of the future is debated."[20] The range of options entertained by Buthelezi has tended to narrow over the past few years. In 1974 he offered a fairly detailed set of proposals, with a nonproportional form of federalism as an intermediate stage in a gradualist transition to majority rule.[21] This "offer," not surprisingly, was ignored by the present government, despite calls for a response from government-supporting newspapers.[22] Since then the climate in southern Africa

*A problem common in the Third World, which has contributed to the lack of accountability of politicians throughout Africa, has been the absence of organizations at the middle range which both sanction the actions of politicians and provide feedback from the population (see S.N. Eisenstadt, *Modernization, Protest and Change* [Englewood Cliffs, 1966]). Clearly, Buthelezi aims at encouraging a balanced development of interest and influence groups.

has become even less favorable for concessions. As Buthelezi put it in early 1976: "I must say now, and I must say with considerable emphasis, that such reconciliatory offers as were contained in my federal formula will be increasingly difficult to offer in the Southern Africa that is now emerging."[23] And a few months later: "Whether we like it or not, and for good or evil, the generic force of politics in South Africa today is the movement toward majority rule. The rejection of this option is in fact nothing other than the election to solve the country's political ills by violence."[24] Majority rule, then, is clearly the designated goal. Very recently Buthelezi has again suggested the possibility of a federal arrangement, but without the gradualism proposed in 1974; however, he maintains that the final form of government in an open South Africa can only be determined at a national convention.

The economic ideology emerging in Inkatha is reflected in Buthelezi's statement that a requirement for a political system in a transitional situation in South Africa

> is that it makes radical redistribution of wealth possible, while it facilitates increased productivity. . . . [S]tate control is essential in both the productive process and in the distribution of wealth. . . . Experience has taught us that when a classical free enterprise model is tampered with to give *selective* state control, this is no more than political manipulation of the underprivileged by the privileged.[25]

And a few months later: "Nowhere in Southern Africa has a capitalist free enterprise system been able to distribute wealth and power in such a way that political stability has been assured."[26] Buthelezi suggests that not only industry, but also other bodies relevant to class relations (e.g., trade unions) should be subject to state control:

> Black unions could well be instrumental in establishing an elitist class of skilled workers who have a vested interest in maintaining the status quo. . . . Trade unionism needs to have a broadly-based responsibility towards the community it serves and it needs to develop a sense of commitment within the overall strategy which has been adopted by a wide range of organisations.[27]

There is a welcome absence of the superficial Marxist sloganeering which one encounters elsewhere in southern Africa, but nonetheless the analysis tends toward the one-party state socialist model. In one of Buthelezi's very recent speeches, however, there is clearly a prescription for an economy based on a mixed socialist and capitalist model, but with considerable state control. In enunciating the principles of Inkatha, Buthelezi said:

> We believe it essential that all men join hands and enter into a partnership with the state to effect the greatest possible redistribution of wealth commensurate with maximising the productivity of commerce, trade and industry *whether state controlled or privately owned*. . . . [S]tate control . . . [is] essential for the utilisation of land, water and power in the interests of the economy and in the interests of developing underdeveloped areas and populations.[28]

It would seem that he envisages state control of basic resources while privately owned industry would be allowed or encouraged, subject to the state's exercising considerable control, particularly in order to achieve an optimal redistribution of wealth. There is a good deal of pragmatism in his stance, including an acceptance, albeit critical and selective, of the need for Western investment in South Africa and KwaZulu because the creation of employment is a high priority: "In these circumstances I cannot bring myself to be an ideological puritan."[29]

Buthelezi is not racist in outlook, but he has strong elements of a Black [African] Consciousness orientation. Inkatha is not open to non-Africans at this stage, but he envisages an open membership in the future when circumstances are more appropriate. There appears to be total acceptance by him of a role for Whites in a new South Africa:

> Blacks in South Africa will have to accept my commitment to whites, just as whites will have to accept my commitment to blacks. . . . I do not view whites as expendable expatriots. They come from the very soil of South Africa. This is the land of their birth and they have a right to be here. There will be no political solution in which they are not active partners.[30]

Along with this noteworthy idealism, there is pragmatism: "Whites are not dispensable. Commerce and industry could not come to a near-standstill even for a short period of time."[31]

Inkatha has been effectively operating for only about three-and-a-half years, and during this period has experienced rapid growth.[32] Its current membership is well over 200,000, which makes it the largest Black political organization in South African history. It is also a remarkably heterogeneous organization: some 29 percent of its members are under eighteen years of age, based mainly on the recruitment of groups at secondary schools; it has a growing number of women's brigades, and half of its present membership is female; and a wide range of occupational groups are represented—subsistence farmers, workers, white-collar employees, civil servants, professionals, and businessmen. Its rapid spread is reflected in the fact that in February 1977 it consisted of 300 branches, but by mid-1978 had expanded to no less than 946 branches.

Inkatha is a predominantly Natal-based organization; only thirty-six of its branches are located outside Natal. The areas outside Natal where it is a strong movement are likely to be places where large numbers of Zulu-speaking people or people of Zulu origin are concentrated, like Soweto and the Witswatersrand, for example. Although specific data on tribal affiliations of members are not available, it appears that over 95 percent of its membership is Zulu-speaking. It is mainly a rural-based organization; only 203 of its 946 branches appear to be located in urban areas. However, its recent growth has been concentrated in urban areas, and the organization may ultimately have a balanced rural-urban distribution. Another positive trend in the organization is a rapidly increasing involvement of youth. In mid-1976 only 26 students attended the annual Inkatha youth-training course, while in 1977, 400 young people attended, and in 1978, approximately 1,000.

The structure of Inkatha is in some respects fairly typical of party-political organizations throughout the world. The lowest level of organization is the branch (or in the case of young people and women, the "brigade"). A branch must have more than thirty members and is related to local political boundaries, township wards, or headmen's wards in rural areas. Branches and brigades are organized into constituencies (in rural areas, coinciding with a chief's area of authority), which are in turn combined in a regional body. At the head of the organization is the Central Committee, comprising not less than twenty-five members, including the President, the secretary-general, twenty members elected at the annual general conference, and three members nominated by the President.

Inkatha differs from purely party-political organizations in two significant ways. First, the activities of branches and brigades are not confined to political mobilization; they are encouraged to undertake self-help development projects and organize community education programs in family affairs, nutrition, health, etc., thereby combining politics and community development. Second, Inkatha is formally interlocked with the government of KwaZulu; ultimate decisions on policy both for Inkatha and (in certain respects) for the KwaZulu

Legislative Assembly are formulated by the "National Council."* This is the supreme body in KwaZulu, and it comprises the Central Committee of Inkatha, the Legislative Assembly of KwaZulu, and representatives of specialized functions within Inkatha. Another feature of this interlocking of structures is that the King of the Zulu nation—His Majesty Paramount Chief Goodwill Zwelethini, titular head of the self-governing Zulu region—is Patron of Inkatha. KwaZulu civil servants and teachers are encouraged to become members of Inkatha. For a while there was uncertainty among civil servants and teachers about this since South African civil servants are not formally allowed to be members of political parties, but in KwaZulu the policy of civil servant participation has been formally adopted.

As has already been noted, Inkatha has experienced spectacular growth. Its rapid "take-off" appears to have been due in large measure to the active cooperation of tribal chiefs, who established branches within their own constituencies. The chiefs, being ex-officio members of the KwaZulu Legislative Assembly, could fairly readily be persuaded to mobilize their constituents. There have been suggestions that some chiefs felt threatened by the movement, but on the other hand the organization provides them with a way of becoming involved as key figures in a modern political organization.

This initial tribal take-off accounts for the strong rural base of Inkatha. Subsequent support appears to have been won on the basis of popular appeal, particularly among women, and on the enthusiasm of some teachers in enrolling youth. There is less enthusiasm to join among men, but there is considerable support among rank-and-file African workers for the cause of Inkatha. Buthelezi's own popularity spearheads the appeal of the organization. For some years he has been drawing huge audiences of over 10,000 people at a time when speaking in urban areas, both in Natal and Soweto.[33] In one Inkatha rally in Kwa Mashu on April 24, 1978, Buthelezi drew a crowd of 80,000.† A recent study in Soweto, Pretoria, and Durban revealed that Buthelezi had more support in these three areas combined than any other Black leader or political grouping, free or imprisoned. Some 44 percent named Buthelezi as the political figure they most admired, and an additional 7 percent cited him as a homeland leader who was also a genuine political leader. Compared with this roughly

*As most readers probably know, KwaZulu is a partly self-governing "homeland" established by the South African government in pursuance of its policy of Separate Development.

†The *lowest* newspaper estimate of the crowd has been taken.

50 percent support, imprisoned or exiled ANC leaders were named by 22 percent*, other homeland leaders by 18 percent, Pan African Congress leaders by 7 percent, and Black Consciousness figures by 6 percent.[34]†

The study by Hanf et al. also explored responses to Inkatha. Among the respondents of higher socioeconomic status, positive and negative attitudes toward Inkatha were in a ratio of 2:3 in Soweto, but roughly 2:1 in Durban, with Pretoria evenly balanced. Among the rank and file, the ratios of positive to negative responses were 2:1 in Soweto and 6:1 in Durban. (An insufficient number of rank-and-file respondents in Pretoria knew of Inkatha at that stage to provide a stable pattern.) Obviously Buthelezi supporters are overwhelmingly in favor of Inkatha, but what is most noteworthy in the results is that roughly half the ANC supporters are also in favor of Inkatha. This seems to suggest that Inkatha has managed successfully to establish some continuity with the ANC in the minds of ordinary urban Africans, due no doubt to Buthelezi's former membership in the ANC and the symbolism of a uniform resembling that of the ANC.

In 1974 the South African government rejected a request by the KwaZulu Legislative Assembly for powers to control opposition parties, but no publicly organized opposition to Inkatha had yet emerged, and therefore Inkatha was the only party in the elections. It was opposed by twenty-three independent candidates in fourteen of the fifty-five constituencies. In these constituencies Inkatha candidates polled an average of 90 percent of the votes—overwhelming what opposition there was. The victory has to be seen in context, however. Only some 50 percent of the eligible KwaZulu citizens registered for the elections, and for the contested seats roughly 38 per-

*Notwithstanding the dominant position of Buthelezi, the degree of support for the ANC is remarkable, since the organization has been banned for 17 years.

†These results need some qualification. The selection of Pretoria, Soweto, and Durban underrepresented Xhosa-speaking people, who seem to support Buthelezi and ANC/PAC leaders in roughly equal measure. Had the Cape urban areas been included, Buthelezi's relative position would have fallen somewhat, but he would still have emerged ahead of other groupings in overall terms. Another qualification is that the study, conducted in early 1977, preceded the rise to prominence of the leaders in Soweto known as the "Committee of Ten." However, since this group's predecessor group—the "Black Parents Association" —did not receive significant mention in the survey question about the "most admired leader," the inclusion of the Committee of Ten would probably not have dramatically altered the results concerning rank-and-file support for a national leader. In Soweto itself, however, support for the Committee of Ten is dominant (see Schlemmer, "Change in South Africa," in this volume).

cent of the registered voters turned out to vote. Since registration of voters was probably higher in the contested constituencies, the results do not suggest an overwhelmingly active electoral response to Inkatha. On the other hand, for most people the results of the election were probably a foregone conclusion, lessening the popular enthusiasm. Also, a 38 percent poll among poorly educated people, many of whom are not able to be influenced by the mass media, is not insubstantial. On balance, in the context of *official* Black homeland and local authority politics in South Africa, the results should be taken as a demonstration of the powerfully dominant position of Inkatha in the political affairs of the Zulus.

Inkatha demonstrated its capacity to exert political control at the local level in other ways as well during the elections. Most of the independent candidates were constrained to declare their loyalty to Inkatha, one prominent candidate in Durban loudly protested his mistake in standing as an independent, and others seemed to withdraw from the elections at the last moment under informal Inkatha pressure. There were rumors of other kinds of pressures being brought to bear on independent candidates, all of which seem to demonstrate Inkatha's capacity to exert influence.

Inkatha's control over local level political action is demonstrated in still other ways. It has imposed sanctions on teachers who do not mobilize Inkatha youth groups or encourage what is seen as the appropriate orientation among the young.[35] Inkatha and the KwaZulu government were partly responsible for preventing Soweto-type youth disturbances from spreading to Natal in 1976—disturbances viewed by Inkatha as inappropriate and premature.[36] Inkatha members form a security screen around their leader at public meetings to discourage any repetition of an incident on March 12, 1978 in which Buthelezi was stoned by some members of the Black Consciousness movement at the funeral of Robert Sobukwe, the PAC leader.[37]

Broadly then, it seems that Inkatha has gained very substantial support and recognition, even though not all the enrolled members are independently motivated. (As noted, teachers are expected to join.) It is beginning to show a capacity to control local level leadership and political action, particularly in KwaZulu. Increasingly it seems able to impose sanctions.

A major point of criticism of Buthelezi and Inkatha is that the chief and his political movement are divisive in Black politics, introducing an ethnic element into a struggle which for decades has been waged by the ANC, the PAC, and recently the Black Consciousness movement in the name of interethnic solidarity. Another criticism is that by operating from a base of homeland politics, Buthelezi and Inkatha—no matter how critical they may be of South African government policy—lend credibility to that policy, and the more they criticize, the more they give the policy legitimacy. Most homeland leaders are frequently referred to as "stooges," and Buthelezi, because he is relatively more successful than the others, is regarded by some Africans as the greatest traitor of all.[38]

Does Buthelezi's stance ultimately strengthen Separate Development, and is the Inkatha movement divisive? Buthelezi takes great pains to distance himself from the policy of the government and is certainly no stooge, as quotations from his speeches clearly attest. Colin Legum has commented on the rationale for operating within the framework of Separate Development:

> Whereas the Congresses (ANC, PAC, NIC [Natal Indian Congress]) had little effective grass-roots support in the reserves and only a precarious base in the urban areas, they [African homeland politicians] now operate legally from substantial political bases within a constitutional framework. Leaders can now legally be deprived of their right to act as spokesmen for their designated constituencies only by an abrogation of the laws designed to establish Separate Development. Therefore, despite their lack of effective political power, they have been given unprecedented opportunities for political manoeuvre in their confrontation with the white establishment.[39]

The fact remains, however, that Buthelezi, through his critical and at times militant stance, must to some extent have made the homeland program seem to promise the beginning of a devolution of power, and may even have created the impression in some minds that the government is outwitting itself—that given time it would fall victim to its own policies. This would be dangerous complacency for opponents of the government, and this aspect of Buthelezi's strategy should be assessed very carefully.

An assessment depends to a large extent on whether or not the "opportunities for political manoeuvre" that Legum refers to will be used to achieve meaningful change rather than merely improve the image of the homelands. Judgment can in part be based on the assessment of the likely medium- and long-range effects of mass mobilization. Here the criticism that Inkatha is essentially sectional or tribal in character, being based in KwaZulu, is relevant. According to this criticism, Inkatha is at best limited in its capacity to mobilize, and at worst divisive and a threat to African solidarity. To this Buthelezi replies that

> In character and spirit, Inkatha is not peculiarly Zulu or even peculiarly Natal. . . . There is nothing to stop us having a number of Inkathas which, because their structure . . . and their constitution is similar, can join together in a movement towards liberation. . . . There is no Zulu freedom that is distinct from the Black man's freedom.[40]

Inkatha is open to membership by all Africans, and it is claimed that support among non-Zulus is growing.[41] There are three possible paths of development for Inkatha: (1) other groups may join the movement and transform it into a completely nonsectional program; (2) it could spawn other similar movements which could unite or cooperate with it; and (3) it alone can spearhead the struggle and achieve wider support once success is attained.

Prior to an assessment of possibilities, perhaps some comment on the issue of "tribalism" is needed. Obviously inward-looking, linguistic group loyalties or chauvinistic communal identifications are divisive and counterproductive to Black aspirations outside certain homelands in South Africa. However, there are undeniably group feelings among sections of the South African population which are closely akin to nationalism. Afrikaner nationalism is one, Zulu communal feeling is another, and few people are likely to dispute that a Swazi or Lesotho "nationalism" exists. The nature of group feeling between, say, the Tswana-speaking people of Botswana and the Zulus in Natal is not very different.[42]* If a "national" cohesion exists among the Zulus, and if the entry of Whites into South Africa blocked expansion of that cohesion, a powerful Zulu-based mobilization organization like Inkatha could renew the process today.†

An alternative possibility rooted in "tribal" feeling is a "two-step" process whereby an immediate ethnic identification (Zulu group feeling, say) provides a sense of pride and mission while broad political goals, like African or Black nationalism, provide the focus of mobilization. This is what Buthelezi appears to be suggesting when

*Looking back in history, it seems obvious that the "Mfecane" of Shaka was a process of nation-building—a process whereby small units were assimilated into a larger group, leading to a wider unity. It is typical of historical processes of conquest leading to "enlarged areas of cohesion" (Barbara Ward, *Five Ideas That Change the World* [New York, 1959]).

†The South-West Africa People's Organization (SWAPO) in Namibia owes much to the initial impetus it enjoyed among the Ovambo group, and today it is perhaps the dominant focus of political identification among all Black Namibians.

he calls for other Inkathas which could "join together." This is perhaps a more likely alternative. We should remember that African nationalism is largely the result of reaction to White domination. It is a racial or political phenomenon without the deep-seated emotional appeal which springs from feelings of in-group identity and affinity. The Zulus have this more "primordial" in-group feeling; as B.G.M. Sundkler says of them: "Their history is an ever-present fact in their lives, moulding their outlook."[43] But in earlier research, conducted in 1972, the author found among Africans in Durban no clash between strong Zulu pride and an identification with African nationalism; in fact, the former may have added fuel to the latter.[44]

These observations on "tribalism" suggest that those who insist that all forms of ethnic identification among Africans in South Africa weaken the cause of Black opposition are oversimplifying the matter. Black identity which is more than a reaction to White domination, even though it may differ from region to region, may be very important for mass mobilization in opposition to the present order in South Africa.

At a more pragmatic level the danger of disunity and divisiveness appears to be somewhat reduced by attempts by Buthelezi and others to forge unity across ethnic lines. In 1976 Buthelezi, Ntsanwisi (chief minister of Gazankulu), and Dr. Cedric Phatudi (chief minister of Lebowa) met about fifty leading Black politicians and leaders in Soweto to establish the Black Unity Front aimed, *inter alia*, at achieving a disciplined Black community with effective Black leadership. The township disturbances and subsequent government action against urban Black leadership undermined this initiative, but Buthelezi has recently entered into a pact with the Colored Labor Party and the Indian Reform Party to strive for unity of purpose among all unenfranchised people. The new movement, called the Black Alliance, has since been joined by leaders of the Swazi, Basotho, Qwa Qwa, and Gazankulu homelands.

Because Blacks lack power in key decision-making, alliances among Black groups are usually little more than symbolic gestures of solidarity. Unity fronts can achieve little that is concrete, but some tangible gains are essential to the continued solidarity of such movements. In addition, for Black unity movements there is the ever-present danger that key homelands like Lebowa or Gazankulu may opt for independence. The promotion of Black unity, however important, should not be the only criterion by which Black political movements in South Africa are judged. Effectiveness in political bargaining is as important—if not more important. No unity front can survive a long period of political ineffectiveness because the leadership will not command resources with which to dispense the patronage and power to impose the discipline which will maintain cohesion.

It is in terms of this perspective that Inkatha should be judged. The notion of bargaining power is certainly prominent in the formulation of ideas at the leadership level. As Buthelezi has put it: "The machinery of Inkatha has provision for discipline. With discipline we can stall this whole country for a couple of days."[45] The notion of "stalling" is a guarded reference to the potential power inherent in African domination of the labor force. Recently Inkatha has involved itself in the affairs of industry and labor by encouraging the observance of codes of progressive employment practices in South African industry (the U.S. "Sullivan Code," the EEC Code, and the Urban Foundation/Saccola Code).[46] This type of involvement is likely to bear fruit in the current climate of industrial reform and may win very substantial support for Inkatha among the African working class, which means bargaining power without necessarily implying confrontations or strategies of disruption.

In summing up, perhaps one can say that the history of Black political movements and actions in the 1970s repeats the lessons of the early 1960s, the 1950s, and earlier decades. Movements and programs with a high-key political tone and flavor or confrontational approach have not survived the forces of order and constraint. They have had to move underground, or the activists have had to flee the country, leaving the more cautious members to subsist on political nostalgia. This is not to deny the importance of underground movements—the succession of political trials is tangible evidence of the threat posed by the ANC and other underground groups—but their power to disrupt a well-protected political and economic system seems to be very limited, and their effect on rank-and-file action, despite widespread sentiment in their favor, also appears to be quite limited. The action of refugees operating as guerillas along the borders of the country, in an international climate which offers sympathy and support for such movements, would be a more serious threat to the system. However, no such action has yet begun because South Africa, through a variety of linkages, exercises a powerful influence on even the borders of those countries which are most hostile and would otherwise play host to guerilla movements.

The type of internal action which has had an impact, albeit far short of threatening the system (e.g., the 1973 strikes, the township disturbances), while not wholly without prior planning and organization, has appeared to erupt in response to "sociopolitical factors"

—i.e., critical levels of grievance or anxiety among the groups affected. Both the government and industry have recently taken cognizance of these causal factors, and a period of strategic but limited reform seems to have begun.

In a situation of inequality and political alienation such as that in South Africa, the unexpected can always occur, and the specter of the mass political uprising is ever-present. But the stage has been set for the entrance of this specter (or salvation) for decades without its making an appearance. If the political analyst wants to avoid making the mistake of prematurely predicting internal upheaval, urban terror, etc., he must avoid the tendency to anticipate the intensity of Black reaction by projecting the objective dimensions of racial inequality. It is with cautious wisdom that the strategy and consequences of a movement like Inkatha have to be assessed.

If Inkatha lives up to its aims (always problematic in a situation of constraint), it could, for the first time in Black politics, reap the benefits of a strategy proposed by Dr. A.B. Xuma of the ANC in the 1940s—a strategy never fully implemented. It is a strategy of enrollment and mobilization aimed at a long-term goal without political activism or calculated political risk-taking. Before discussing the goal, there are two procedural questions to be considered. First, is it possible to mobilize and enroll members on a large scale without political dramatics? It may be possible if there is a measure of enforced enrollment. It would seem that Inkatha has already adopted such an approach by using the sanctioning power of the KwaZulu administration to nudge teachers, civil servants, and others into cooperating. The second question is: Will Inkatha survive? Will not the strategies outlined or hinted at by Buthelezi alert the South African government to the long-term dangers for the system and result in Inkatha's being banned? This seems unlikely. Inkatha offers the South African government a substantial return for allowing its continued existence. Thus Inkatha has prevented the township disturbances from spreading to Natal, and counterbalances the influence of confrontation-minded Black leaders; Buthelezi has opposed calls for disinvestment in South Africa, and KwaZulu confuses the critics of Separate Development. This is a necessary tradeoff for Inkatha and should not be hastily condemned by opponents of the South African government.

Nevertheless, this tradeoff situation is likely to continue to earn for Inkatha and Buthelezi the bitter resentment of the radically oriented Black intelligentsia, a group which is self-consciously modern and anti-tribal (its Africanism would be more appropriately termed "Neo-Africanism"), is informed by the unitary state democratic ideal (the reverse side of the coin of British colonial and neocolonial domination), seeks to acquire legitimacy as a leader-group through spokesmen adopting an unambiguously anti-government stance, and experiences status anxieties as a well-educated group denied social recognition. These Black "radicals" will inevitably feel ill at ease about a leader like Buthelezi because he contrasts with them in many ways: he is a Zulu aristocrat with traditional legitimacy, and as such experiences none of their status anxieties as a new intelligentsia; he acts through government-created institutions, and does not have to be a spokesman-leader whose standing is dependent only on the quality and consistency of his criticism of apartheid;* he is both a spokesman and a strategist, blending principle and pragmatic planning. The conflict between Inkatha and elements of the Black intelligentsia is unlikely to abate,† and Buthelezi will probably continue his strategy of attempting to win their cooperation, but where this fails he will simply stake his support against theirs. Support for Buthelezi does not appear to fall below 20 percent in any non-Zulu ethnic group, and his overall support among the emergent African "middle class" in Soweto, Durban, and Pretoria is only about 10 percent less than his support among all Africans in these areas;[47] hence his political base in the population-at-large is extensive.

Finally, however, the viability of Inkatha must be assessed in the light of the possible outcomes of its strategy. The outcome most feared by those who see Inkatha as radical and dangerous is a mass strike, concentrated perhaps in Natal. This would have far-reaching political implications, but it could not be sustained for more than a week or two—workers have to feed their families, and the reaction of the government would probably be to destroy the organization by force if necessary. Inkatha may develop a confrontationist strategy along those lines, but it would not be the optimal course.

The strategy which is perhaps most congruent with the current stance of the organization is that which has been called the "groundswell" strategy by Buthelezi, which can alternatively be termed the "demonstration effect" strategy. Mass mobilization in itself, if sufficiently extensive, can be a powerful incentive to a government to make fundamental policy changes and even to negotiate with representatives of the mobilized masses. In South Africa this is perhaps

*This concept is derived from Heribert Adam.

†A recent manifestation of this conflict has even occurred inside Inkatha, with an apparent rift between the former secretary-general (Bengu) and the Inkatha leadership (*Daily News*, October 17, 1978).

the only *peaceful* strategy likely to achieve significant results. What might these be, at a minimum?

The South African Minister of African Affairs has indicated that the government is prepared to accommodate a homeland which does not wish to be independent,[48] and there have been various government proposals for a "confederal" link between such homelands and the South African core area. The degree and type of power-sharing in a system of overarching political linkage would be dependent upon the relative bargaining strength of the contending units. Buthelezi now firmly rejects independence, but on the other hand he is building the "identity" of a power-center in KwaZulu alternative to that of Pretoria. Currently, for example, a prestige parliament building is due to be built at Ulundi, and KwaZulu has its own flag. Many critics of Buthelezi see these moves as an indication that he would accept independence if offered a reasonable consolidation of the KwaZulu territory. This is perhaps possible, but in view of all Buthelezi's policy statements and the goals and scope of Inkatha, it is hardly probable.

On the basis of these observations, it seems likely that Buthelezi would seek to take Inkatha into any future negotiating situation with a *fall-back* position of accepting a federal state, with an enlarged KwaZulu being the political "center" of a federal "segment." This segment, however, would extend well beyond the geographic confines of KwaZulu, and almost certainly beyond the ethnic confines of the Zulu language group. This strategy might seem like a mere extension of separate development to some, but given the bargaining power of a mobilized working class, could have a fairly substantial influence on government policy.

The South African government, on the other hand, probably would press for a confederal arrangement with as little power-sharing as possible, but its reluctance to share power could be counterbalanced by the advantages of having a powerful, legitimate Black partner in central government to help stave off external and internal pressures, provided White political identity could be maintained. Furthermore, a loose confederacy might be a security threat, while a federation could provide a basis for further progressive developments.

To the extent that popular mobilization could ensure Black influence on central policies, ultimately formalized in a constitution and perhaps even symbolized by a joint presidency, the kind of scenario outlined—essentially a consociational devolution of power—must be seen as qualitatively very different from separate development. Above all it is a peaceful strategy, and this consideration must not be made light of in a situation where an armed struggle would be much more destructive and drawn out than any violence hitherto seen in southern Africa, with the destruction of an economy of utmost importance to the whole region as but one of its costs. Inkatha may hold out for a more favorable settlement, but as a possible minimum the outcome of its present strategy holds considerable promise for the interests of everyday Africans in South Africa.

THE "APEX OF SUBORDINATION": THE URBAN AFRICAN POPULATION OF SOUTH AFRICA[1]

Martin E. West

South Africa's burgeoning African* urban population is often portrayed as holding the key to political change within the country. Because of the size and complexity of this population and the difficulties of doing research in South Africa, relatively little information about it is available.[2] In this paper the growth of the urban African population and the crucial legislation affecting it will be discussed; social differentiation in the cities will be examined (Soweto is particularly important for a number of reasons and will be examined in some detail); and finally an attempt will be made to assess the political importance of the urban African population.

BACKGROUND

The African people of South Africa are part of the large Bantu-speaking group of people spread over much of Africa south of the equator. Through recent archaeological research it is known that ancestors of the present African population of southern Africa entered the region from the north, and in all probability were living in what is now the Transvaal during the first few centuries A.D. From there they spread over the central and eastern parts of the country long before Europeans made their first incursions in the south.[3] The people then living in southern Africa shared a common cultural, linguistic, and racial heritage, and although differentiation occurred, giving rise to the various ethnic groups in South Africa today, it should be stressed that the traditional societies that emerged in South Africa retained a great deal in common.[4]

*In this paper the term *African* is used to refer to all persons classifed as "African" by the South African government—i.e., those who belong to the Bantu-speaking groups. "Black" is used to refer to all persons who are not white. (This usage is becoming increasingly common in contemporary South Africa.)

The great changes which resulted from European settlement and colonization led to an increasing movement of Africans from country to town. The Whites have attempted to control this flow, but the proportion of the African population living in towns in South Africa has increased steadily from 10 percent in 1900 to 35 percent in 1975. While the growth of the African urban population is important in itself, it is instructive to consider some comparative figures:

Table 1

COMPARATIVE URBAN POPULATION PERCENTAGES (Est.)

	Years		
	1904	1960	1975
Proportion of White population living in town	53%	84%	88%
Proportion of African population living in town	13	32	35
African urban population as proportion of total urban population	30	46	50

Sources: D. Welsh, "The Growth of Towns," in *Oxford History of South Africa*, eds. M. Wilson and L. Thompson (Oxford: Clarendon Press, 1971), vol. 2, p. 173; *Survey of Race Relations* (Johannesburg: S.A. Institute of Race Relations, 1977), p. 51.

These figures are conservative, as it is generally assumed that official statistics underestimate the de facto African urban population—in part because of the large number of illegal townsmen who avoid enumeration. M. Lipton suggests that Soweto's population may be underreported by as much as 50 percent.[5] Mdantsane (near East London) is estimated to have a total African population between 33 and 69 percent larger than the official legal population, and the African population of Cape Town is said to be close to double the official figure.[6] Another factor influencing the statistics is that some substantial African urban populations—notably those living adjacent to Pretoria, East London, and Durban—are now enumerated as living in "homelands," even though their actual position alongside the "White" cities has not substantially changed.

The picture is clear: the majority of the African population lives outside the so-called homelands, outnumbering Whites in all "White areas" by at least two to one. The six million or more urban Africans at present outnumber White urban-dwellers by nearly three million, and based on current projections will increase to fifteen million by the year 2000, compared with the estimated White urban population at that time of just over five million.[7]

THE LEGISLATIVE FRAMEWORK

The entry of Africans into urban areas has been encouraged by White authorities at some points and discouraged at others, but it has always been controlled by legislation.[8] As F. Wilson points out:

> Having devoted the first half century of industrialization to finding ways of getting Blacks to go to work in the industrial centers, the Whites with political power devoted the second half of the century to finding ways of preventing Blacks from taking root as human communities in these same areas.[9]

While Africans have been induced into working in industry and on White-owned farms by such measures as the imposition of taxes and the 1913 Land Act, there is a long history of efforts to control their influx into urban areas. The Report of the South African Native Affairs Commission, 1903-5, recommended "the formation of labour locations, where the Native could reside with his family near his employment"; the commission held that urban Africans who were employed "should be encouraged to stay as useful members of the community," but that "surplus or idle Natives should be expelled."[10] The idea that Africans could be expelled to rural areas was attractive to White authorities, and D. Welsh notes that "by the turn of the century it was officially held in most parts of South Africa that urban Africans were not permanent members of urban communities but migrants whose domiciles were in the rural areas."[11]

This view of the temporary nature of the urban African population was forcefully spelled out in the Report of the Native Affairs Commission of 1921:

> It should be understood that the town is a European area in which there is no place for the redundant Native, who neither works nor serves his or her people, but forms the class from which the professional agitators, the slum landlords, the liquor sellers, the prostitutes and other undesirable classes spring.[12]

This report was a prelude to an important piece of legislation—the 1923 Natives (Urban Areas) Act—which required local authorities, under government control, to establish segregated African areas,* set

*Welsh suggests that the emphasis on segregation during this period "was a response to rapid African urbanization and the assumed threat to the white worker. . . . Politicians, both black and white, were aware of the revolutionary possibilities presented by the urban African masses who could be mobilised for action

up advisory boards, register service contracts, control the influx of Africans, remove 'surplus' Africans, and establish curfew regulations where deemed necessary.[13]

Despite the various efforts to control the movement of Africans to town, their numbers grew steadily with the demands of the economy. With this growth came an increasing official acceptance of the permanence of much of the urban African population. As Welsh notes, recognition of this permanence came with the publication of the report of the 1946-48 Natives Laws Commission, commonly called the Fagan Commission, which stated that [first]

> the idea of total segregation is utterly impracticable; secondly, that the movement from country to town has a background of economic necessity—that it may, so one hopes, be guided and regulated, and may also perhaps be limited, but that it cannot be stopped or be turned around in the opposite direction; and thirdly, that in our urban areas there are not only Native migrant labourers, but there is also a settled, permanent Native population.[14]

Just when it appeared that some formal recognition might be given to African urban residents, the Nationalist party came to power (1948) and rejected the findings of the Fagan Commission in favor of those of a 1920s commission which had determined that permanent urban residence was the exclusive right of the White population.[15] This was the beginning of the policy, still in effect today, that insists that there is no permanent urban African population in South Africa.

Since 1948, the Nationalist party has introduced a considerable amount of legislation restricting African urban residence and the right to seek work. M. Horrell, for example, cites twenty-one such pieces of legislation for the period 1951-71,[16] and P. Lewis refers to no fewer than ninety acts of Parliament passed between 1945 and 1966 that affect the administration of Soweto and other African townships.[17] This legislation affects most aspects of life, including mobility, education, land tenure, housing, transport, building, trespassing, brewing of beer, marriage, and the settlement of labor disputes, but the key legislation refers to urban residence per se.

The Native Laws Amendment Act of 1952 extended influx control to all urban areas. It included women in its provisions, extended the power to remove Africans deemed to be undesirable, and introduced a "concession" allowing Africans to visit an urban area for up

against a social order that denied them equality" (The Growth of Towns," p. 188.

to seventy-two hours before having to acquire official permission.[18] In the same year all Africans were required to carry passes (reference books) to be produced on demand. The legislation granting rights of urban residence to Africans is contained in the oft-quoted Section 10 of the Natives (Urban Areas) Consolidation Act of 1945, summarized by Horrell as follows:

> It provided that no African may remain for more than 72 hours in an urban or proclaimed area unless he or she:
> (a) has resided there continuously since birth;
> (b) has worked there continuously for one employer for not less than 10 years; or has resided there lawfully and continuously for not less than 15 years; and has thereafter continued to reside there and is not employed outside; and has not while in the area been sentenced to a fine exceeding R100 [$115] or to imprisonment for a period exceeding six months;
> (c) is the wife, unmarried daughter, or son under the age of 18 years, of an African in one of the categories mentioned above and ordinarily resides with him;
> (d) has been granted special permission to be in the area.[19]

It is worthwhile to examine briefly the "rights" conveyed in this legislation. Throughout the onus is on the individual to prove qualification for residence—not for the state to prove disqualification—and such terms as "continuously" are strictly interpreted. However, the Bantu Laws Amendment Act of 1964 includes people qualified under this section of the Urban Areas Act among those who can be deemed idle or undesirable and ordered out of an urban area.[20] Thus, even satisfying the provisions of Section 10 does not guarantee security of urban tenure, and no urban African in South Africa can be sure of being allowed to remain in town.

African political representation has also been the subject of much legislation. The small number of Africans who had the franchise were placed on a separate voter's roll in 1936, allowing them three White Members of Parliament, two provincial councillors in the Cape, and four elected White senators representing Africans all over the country. At the same time an advisory Natives' Representative Council was established.[21] This council, which was never effective, was abolished in 1951 with the passing of the Bantu Authorities Act, which sought to establish "tribal, regional, and territorial authorities" and thereby enhance rural, traditional authority.[22] The Promotion of Bantu Self-Government Act of 1959 laid the blueprint for the homelands policy. It abolished all parliamentary representation for Africans and provided that urban representatives of rural territorial authorities be appointed.[23] The 1968 Prohibition of Political Interference Act made racially mixed political parties illegal and prevented any further African participation—however marginal—in the parliamentary process.

As noted earlier, provision was made for Advisory Boards in the African urban areas under the 1923 Urban Areas legislation. The Urban Bantu Councils Act of 1961 allowed local authorities to establish Urban Bantu Councils (UBC's) in their areas in place of Advisory Boards. UBC's were to include elected and appointed members, but by 1970 all members were to be elected. Some local government powers could be assigned to these councils, but they were to have advisory roles only in the crucial area of finance. By 1975 only twenty-four UBC's were operating, however.[24] In 1977 the Community Councils Act was passed, empowering the government to constitute Community Councils in urban areas to replace Advisory Boards or UBC's. The new councils were granted a wide range of administrative powers, but their actions remained subject to approval by the responsible minister of the government, who was empowered to withdraw any power or duty assigned to a council.[25]

Advisory Boards, UBC's, and Community Councils have not enjoyed widespread community support, and there has often been active opposition to them. Councillors are often viewed (especially by the young) as "sellouts," and a UBC member is reported as saying that young people "call us the Useless Boys' Club and lack confidence in us because they know we have no power."[26] In Soweto a Community Council was established despite opposition from local leaders, and elections were held in 1978. There were only two contested wards (out of eleven), and the proportion of eligible voters participating was 5.6 percent. The elected council did not constitute a quorum, and a by-election was held later in the year for nineteen additional seats. In the fourteen contested wards a 6 percent turnout was recorded, and only ten of the thirty-three candidates polled more than 100 votes.[27]

Control over African urban areas was vested in (White) local authorities until 1972. They had to administer their areas in accordance with the mass of urban African legislation, but in the early stages they had some flexibility, and in some cases were empowered but not required to act. This latitude was eroded by subsequent legislation which inter alia tightened up the provisions of Section 10 of the Urban Areas Act. In 1972-73, control over African urban areas passed from local authorities to a system of twenty-two Bantu Affairs Administration Boards, whose members are appointed by and directly responsible to the Minister of Bantu Administration and Development.[28]

Bantu Affairs Administration Boards are expected to be self-supporting, but they have encountered financial difficulties. They have been expected to provide the various services formerly provided by the local authorities, and have tried to make ends meet through rental increases and through profits derived from their monopoly control of official liquor sales. Local authorities had long depended on profits from liquor sales, but in July 1975 the boards were empowered to keep 80 percent of the liquor sales profits to bolster their deteriorating financial position. Figures available for nine boards for the year ending March 1977 show that income from beer and liquor sales constituted between 40 and 66 percent of their total income. The West Rand board (which includes Soweto) made a profit of $4 million on sales totaling approximately $24 million.[29]*

Liquor outlets were almost totally destroyed in Soweto and Cape Town in the 1976 uprising, and were widely attacked elsewhere. M. Savage has commented as follows:

> Given the fiscal importance of liquor in providing revenue to build housing, pay for services and so forth, and consequently by the fact that the more a particular community drinks the liquor sold by the government the potentially better are its facilities, it is hardly surprising that beer halls and liquor stores formed one of the first targets for attack in the recent urban uprising. . . . The student critique of liquor was not limited to its role in the financing of the urban administration, but went further in objecting to the havoc caused by alcohol in communities where meagre pay packets are drowned in drink, where alcoholism contributes to crime and family break-ups, and where liquor is used by many as a political anaesthetic.[30]

The tenders for new liquor facilities include requirements that walls be fireproof with no windows, that bullet-proof glass separate employees from customers, and that steel security doors and direct police radio links be provided.

*It has recently been established that the boards also receive the incomes from fines paid by employers found guilty of illegally employing Black workers. The Cape Town Peninsula board, for example, received $438,000 from this source during 1978 (*Hansard* [South Africa], v. 6, 1979, col. 458).

It is likely that services and standards have declined in many urban areas following the introduction of the administrative board system. A revealing statistic is that in 1978-79 the Cape Peninsula Board spent only about $104,000 on new housing while spending $723,000 on the provision of liquor facilities.[31] At the same time, the boards are widely considered to be more harsh in their administration of policy than were the previous local authorities, and Wilson suggests that permanent residents feel even more insecure under the new regime.[32]

Mention should be made of the impact of legislation on two particularly well-established urban African communities—in Cape Town and Johannesburg. Early legislation, while providing for segregation, did not prevent Africans from acquiring freehold, except in the Orange Free State.[33] The Natives Resettlement Act of 1954, however, allowed the government to remove more than ten thousand families from the western parts of Johannesburg and settle them in areas adjacent to the municipal townships. Subsequently other African families were removed from areas north of Johannesburg. These resettlements were made under the pretext of slum clearance, but many African families lost freehold rights in the process.[34]

Some African families also lost freehold rights in the Cape Town area following the Group Areas legislation. In 1955 it was announced that the Western Cape was to be a labor preference area for people classified as Colored, and that the government planned to remove all Africans from this area. This plan has been dropped. Some five thousand African migrants were brought into the area by the Railways and Harbors Administration at the time of the announcement, causing some interdepartmental friction: nationalist ideology required a reduction in the number of African workers while the policy of economic growth required an increase. But the overall effect was to freeze the erection of African family housing (not even allowing for the natural increase of qualified urban residents) and to ensure the enforcement of influx control regulations more rigorously in the Western Cape than in probably any other area of the country. Despite the great disparity in population (the Johannesburg area has an African population of something under two million, Cape Town about two hundred thousand), the Langa (Cape Town) influx control court tried 23,954 cases (105 daily average) in 1975 compared to the Fordsburg (Johannesburg) record of 20,110 (95 daily) in the same period.[35] Given the countrywide decrease in prosecutions under the various influx control regulations from 475,920 in 1973-74 to 386,414 in 1974-75, it is noteworthy that there was an *increase* in arrests in the Cape Peninsula area from 20,219 in 1974 to 34,495 in 1975.[36]

The emphasis in the Cape Peninsula has been on migrant labor at the expense of urban residents. The severe restrictions on urban residence have led to the development of an illegal African population of an estimated one hundred thousand.[37] The freeze on family housing in favor of migrant compounds has been partly to blame for the rise of squatter settlements; the other key factor has been an increase in the number of women and children who have defied the law and moved to the squatter areas. They have come mainly because of the increasing difficulty of subsisting in the homelands, and also because of an apparent increasing unwillingness to accept broken family life as an inevitable part of the migrant labor system. The response of the government has been to destroy the squatter communities and deport all those living in them illegally, whether or not they are employed. (In the squatter area of Modderdam, where a community of some ten thousand people was recently destroyed, a survey found that 71% of the households had a breadwinner who was legally employed either as a migrant laborer or a permanent resident.)[38] There is no evidence to indicate that the destruction of African squatter communities in Cape Town has significantly reduced the number of Africans living there illegally; most return following deportation or simply move their possessions to another site. Despite their inefficacy, the harsh measures continue, as can be seen in the record of prosecutions under influx control regulations. The assault on women in the Cape Peninsula is particularly noticeable: the number of women arrested under these regulations rose from 8,422 in 1974 to 13,665 in 1975. (The latter figure represents 39.7 percent of all arrests of women under influx control measures reported from the major urban centers in 1975.)[39]

The harsh action in the Western Cape was taken under existing legislation, with the assistance of the Prevention of Illegal Squatting Amendment Act of 1976.[40] However, an act of legislation passed in 1970 was to have an even more lasting effect on the entire urban African population. This was the Bantu Homelands Citizenship Act of 1970, which provided that every African who was not a citizen of a self-governing territory was to become a citizen of a territorial authority area. Such persons would retain South African citizenship only in terms of international relations, and would still be required to hold South African reference books (passes). The new citizens of the territorial authority areas were to be given certificates of citizenship issued either by their authority or by the South African government acting on its behalf.[41] This was the beginning of the implementation of the Nationalist policy for making all urban Africans citizens of homelands.

This homelands policy became more clearly defined with the Status of the Transkei Act of 1976, in which the South African government designated the Transkei a sovereign and independent state. Under the terms of this act, all Transkei citizens lost their citizenship. Transkei citizens included all children of Transkei citizens (whether born inside or outside the territory), lawful residents of five-years standing who applied for citizenship, any South African citizen not included in some other provision who speaks "a language used by the Xhosa- or Sotho-speaking sections of the Transkeian population, including a dialect of such language," and "every South African citizen who was related to any member of the Transkeian population, or had identified himself with any part of such population, or was culturally or otherwise associated with any member or part of such population."[42] Thus a great many Xhosa-speaking urban dwellers, and some Sotho-speakers, were automatically stripped of South African citizenship. The citizenship issue was disputed by both the Transkei and Bophuthatswana authorities without success. This was not surprising since the cornerstone of Nationalist urban policy is to justify the absence of political rights for Africans in "White South Africa" by such external citizenship. The policymakers believe that homeland citizenship will have almost magical qualities. The former Minister of Bantu Administration and Development said in the Senate in 1976 that "the identification of the Black man with his nation will put the so-called privileges of Section 10 . . . in the shade. Section 10 . . . will possibly not need to be repealed because the nations concept will overshadow it."[43]

The same minister—Mr. M.C. Botha—made the basis of the homelands policy even more clear. He is reported to have said:

> It is irrefutably true and ethnologically correct that each Black nation remains one entity even if its people happen to be in their homeland and in the White area of South Africa. . . . Bantu persons in the White areas, even if they are to be there always, remain secondary to White persons (whose homeland it is), in the same way that the Whites are secondary to Blacks in the Black homelands.[44]

He announced that preferential treatment in urban areas would be given to those who "sought a healthy relationship with their homelands," while others would be "less welcome" in White areas. He then reiterated the core of the homelands policy and its underpinning: "All Bantu persons in the White area, whether they were born there or not, remain members of their respective nations. . . . The basis on which the Bantu is present in the White area is to sell their labour here and for nothing else."[45]

The South African government thus embarked on a "carrot and stick" policy designed to implement homeland citizenship. A widely advertised lifting of restrictions on leasing plots and owning houses was reported to apply only to homeland citizens, as was a removal of restrictions on trader licenses and the use of professional offices, but following widespread violence in 1976, these concessions were made applicable to all urban residents.[46] However, it is very likely that homeland citizens will receive the preferential treatment promised by the minister at the expense of those who reject such citizenship ties. It is, of course, theoretically possible that independent homelands would withdraw citizenship rights from people living outside their borders, but it is unlikely that the South African government would allow this to happen because the basis for its urban policy would collapse as a result. A Minister of Bantu Administration has warned that

> If, after independence, a Bantu homeland deprives its own people living in the Republic of South Africa of their own citizenship, the Government of the Republic will be forced to consider very seriously whether people in such a homeland are welcome to be in or come to our country.[47]

The framework of Nationalist policy is clear. Given the Nationalists' faith in the homeland citizenship "solution," all that remains to be done is to work out the details of urban African local government. The local government powers allocated to the Community Councils do not significantly exceed those of local White municipalities. At the same time there are plans to strengthen the ties beween Community Councils and homeland governments, which is not likely to make them more attractive to urban residents.[48]

In conclusion, the government has no political plans for the growing urban African population other than to impose external citizenship at the same time as it increases the powers of local government—to be exercised, it should be noted, by persons who will technically be foreigners.[49] Despite the uprisings in 1976 and general opposition to much of this policy, Nationalist spokesmen have consistently rejected any thought of modifying their approach. For example, the former South African Prime Minister, Mr. B.J. Vorster, stated in late 1976 that he "completely rejected the view that urban

Blacks should be considered separately from homeland Blacks, and ruled out any new political dispensation for urban dwellers."[50]

URBAN AFRICAN SOCIAL DIFFERENTIATION

As we have noted, the South African government's population policy is based fundamentally on a belief in the separate unity and identity of interests of Black ethnic groups. I contend that the "immutable differences" ascribed by the Nationalist government to the various African ethnic groups, to the extent that they can be documented, are no more significant than, say, the differences between English- and Afrikaans-speaking Whites—differences which do not prevent their forming a common political front. While proponents of government policy see the urban African population as irrevocably split along ethnic lines, many opponents tend to talk about Africans as if there were no differences at all among them. Of course, neither view is correct, but a dearth of up-to-date material complicates matters, and in particular makes it difficult to assess the impact during the last three years of the rise of the "Black Consciousness movement" and of the tensions between old and young, townsmen and migrants.

The South African government divides the African population into nine ethnic groups: Zulu, Xhosa, Swazi, Southern Sotho, Northern Sotho, Tswana, Venda, Tsonga, and Ndebele. All these groups have been assigned one or more homelands each. Anthropologists classify the Zulu, Xhosa, and Swazi as Nguni; the Nguni constellation shares certain cultural features, and their languages are mutually intelligible. The Southern and Northern Sotho and Tswana are all Sotho and resemble each other in the same ways as do the Nguni. The Ndebele, although of Nguni stock, have long lived among Sotho people and can almost be classified as Sotho. The Tsonga and Venda are neither Nguni nor Sotho.[51] As previously noted, all these groups have a common origin and much else in common. In many cases there are no clearly defined boundaries between groups. It is not easy to say where to draw the line between Xhosa and Zulu, or where Northern Sotho shades into Tswana, for example; the Transkei has both Xhosa- and Sotho-speaking residents, and so on. Even in a traditional situation, differences were not as clear-cut as has been suggested, and more than three centuries of change, both rural and urban, have not clarified matters.

This is not to say that cultural differences do not exist, but that they have to be put in perspective. In a political context it is essential to distinguish between cultural and political ethnicity. The South African government sees these two aspects as inextricably intertwined, which as Mayer points out is "supportive to White domination."[52] However, material from Soweto and elsewhere in South Africa suggests that acceptance of cultural ethnicity does not prevent a rejection of political ethnicity. Mayer reports a renewal of cultural ethnicity in Soweto coupled with a clear-cut rejection of ethnic divisions in a political context.[53]

But what of cultural ethnicity? To what extent are traditional African beliefs and customs important in town? There are some published data available on the subject, but they are liable to misinterpretation.[54] The bulk of the material comes from Mayer's study of East London and M. Wilson and A. Mafeje's study of Langa, near Cape Town. Mayer's classic work is particularly important because it introduces certain ideas which have gained wide currency. First, it has given impetus to the distinction between the so-called "Red" and "School" people in rural Cape areas (the "Reds" being conservative traditionalists and the "School" people being at least nominally Christian and Western-oriented).[55] Mayer reports that Red migrants "encapsulated" themselves in town and tried to reject as much as they could of a Western way of life. The image of the encapsulated migrant yearning for his homeland is one the South African government would very much like to believe in, but Mayer's model has some basic flaws. The "homeboy" encapsulating group is an *urban* phenomenon, for example, and the basis for cooperation is likely to be as much common rural background or class factors as ethnic ties. The inevitable changes brought about by this way of life have not been sufficiently examined,[56] and in any case encapsulation has declined with the passage of time.*

Mayer's discussion is about migrants and not about established townspeople. In town the evidence is that class divisions transcend ethnic factors.[57] Mayer says of Soweto:

> Exclusive tribal patriotism seems to have almost died in Soweto. . . . Ideologically it is race and class oppositions that are claimed

*The second edition of Mayer's *Townsmen or Tribesmen* includes a final chapter which reviews changes over nearly a decade since the original research. It shows clearly how the Red organization was breaking down—partly through the blurring of the Red/School division, partly through the change in the rural areas which had provided support for traditional orientations, and partly through a program of re-housing where the migrants lost the right to choose their neighbors and became less dependent on rural kith and kin (*Townsmen*, pp. 299ff.).

> to matter, while ethnic oppositions are denied or simply shrugged off. This was one of the most clear cut findings in the whole mass of research material.[58]

The Soweto findings are particularly important because they come from a polyglot community where ethnic cleavages might be expected in various aspects of social life. The importance of class factors in virtually unilingual communities such as those in Durban, East London, Port Elizabeth, and Cape Town is not unexpected.

The basic line of cleavage in African urban society in South Africa is that between migrant and townsman.[59] This division has been fostered by the enforced migrant labor system, particularly in the Western Cape, where the demographic imbalance is acute. (In Langa the masculinity ratio is nearly 11:1, while it is 3:1 for the official population over all areas.)[60] F. Wilson suggests that the tensions between "urban insiders" and migrants in certain areas "may be so great as to inhibit any political solidarity amongst [them]."[61] It was these tensions (reportedly inflamed by the police) which led to violence between migrants and townsmen in Soweto and Capetown in 1976. The cleavage between these two groups is intensified by economic disparity—migrants tend to be worse off than townsmen both because they are largely unskilled and because they have extra expenses as a result of their migrant status. They are therefore less able to afford to strike than are townsmen, which was a point of friction in the student-led strikes in 1976.

More recently a cleavage appears to have developed between young and old. Thus the Black Consciousness movement arose mainly among the younger generation, and a breakdown in communication between the generations was reported during the 1976 uprising. (However, the events of that period may have done much to produce a common solidarity subsequently.) The Black Consciousness movement—particularly in Soweto—emerged from the ashes of the townships, and it fostered links across boundaries—most notably with younger Colored and Indian people who accept a common Black political identity.

It is possible that a common experience of domination can increase social differentiation in the subordinate group rather than lessen it, as Kuper suggests in his study *An African Bourgeoisie*:

> A common subjection has not stifled class differentiation within the African community, nor has the low ceiling placed on their achievements prevented Africans from drawing distinctions among themselves. . . . Perhaps the rejection by the dominant group, the

> strength of pressures towards an equal subordination, and the limited scope for achievement stimulate, under certain conditions, differentiating tendencies rather than the reverse.[62]

Kuper further observes that

> There is no unity for Africans, either, no solid identity of interests, whether defined objectively or from an African point of view. . . . Only in the very general sense of freedom or emancipation can the objective interests of Africans be described as identical, and even then it is by no means clear what proportion so perceive their interests. Certainly there is divergence in the interpretation of ends and in the selection of means.[63]

These words were written over a decade ago. Today it might be argued that the Black Consciousness movement has provided an important unifying force for Africans which allows them a common expression of identity.

To understand this, it is useful to examine Mayer's use of Weber's concept of a pariah as applied to urban Africans in South Africa. Mayer uses it to refer to the stigma experienced by people who have a "sense of total subordination" within the South African social system.[64] Government policy has been instrumental in fostering this negative identity, but in doing so it has contributed to the demise of political ethnicities. To stress ethnic loyalties is perceived as playing into the government's hands, and this has been an important factor in the history of the African nationalist movement. The banning of nationalist movements and the outlawing of interracial political organizations (along with the lack of enthusiasm for government-provided alternatives) has left a vacuum which may well be increasingly filled by the Black Consciousness movement.

But whatever degree of political unity may have been engendered by the Black Consciousness movement and the events following the June 1976 uprising, it is clear that the urban African communities exhibit important cleavages and increasing differentiation. Mayer describes it thus:

> In common with other Black town populations in South Africa, the people of Soweto are becoming increasingly diversified by income and occupation, but unlike most others, they are polyglot, drawn from many different Black ethnic groups. Two themes interweave from a Black viewpoint—the theme of White domination and that of class versus ethnicity. . . . [I]t appears that most urban

> Blacks would for most purposes place . . . ethnicities second to class or status considerations, or they would substitute a single Black ethnicity.[65]

Mayer has discerned two models perceived by Soweto residents: a "pariah" or race domination model, held particularly by elites, which attributes Blacks' subordinate position primarily to discrimination based on race, and a class model, held particularly by the masses, which attributes Black subjection primarily to economic factors.[66] These models (which are not mutually exclusive) put the social differences in a wider perspective, but do not affect internal stratification.

In summary: there is increasing diversification in the urban African population involving such factors as income, occupation, religion, age, residential status, and so on. After many years of urban residence, most African townspeople rate these factors as more important than ethnic divisions. The government, on the other hand, has tried to strengthen ethnic divisions through its homeland policy and its efforts to segregate town dwellers along ethnic lines—particularly in residence and schooling. It seeks thereby to encourage separate political ethnicities and stronger ties with the homelands and their governments. All the available evidence tends to point to the failure of this policy—not only because non-ethnic factors are preeminent in urban social organization, but also because even where existing cultural ethnicity is being renewed, it does not support political ethnicities. As Mayer observes about Soweto: "The most common alternatives perceived as replacing cultural ethnicity among urban Africans are either identification with a new common Black culture or with Western culture."[67]

It is of course theoretically possible that there will be a renewal of political ethnicity, and if this were to occur it would most likely be in those urban areas that are in close proximity to homelands or—like Umlazi near Durban or Mdantsane near East London—are actually part of them. However, it should be pointed out that there is no apparent trend in this direction. In the early 1970s Mayer stated that it was "likely" that many town dwellers would "welcome the idea of Bantustan citizenship . . . as an alternative to their present pariah status, and in the hope of the political belonging and political self-expression which are being denied to them in the wider South African framework."[68] Since then there have been the 1976 uprising, widespread strikes, and the independence of Mocambique and Angola, as well as signs of change in Rhodesia and Namibia. Roughly five years after making the statement quoted above, Mayer's assessment was that "The evidence suggests that it is too late for [homeland] political ethnicity; its place is likely to be taken more and more by Black ethnicity."[69]

SOWETO: A CASE STUDY [70]

In the last few years Soweto has become almost synonymous with urban Black protest. Soweto is important not only as a symbol, but also as an indicator of the direction of development of the African urban community in South Africa; it has "the most highly industrialised Black population in Africa"[71] and at the same time the broadest cross-section of population of any African urban area in South Africa. And not least, it provided the spark for the wave of rebellion that spread throughout the country in 1976.

Soweto (the name is derived from the first letters of "southwestern townships") is a sprawling area of some thirty-four miles—at its closest point some eight miles from Johannesburg's city center, and at its farthest some twenty miles away. Soweto meets most of the specifications for a community of its type:[72] it is a convenient distance from the centers of employment, with which it is connected by rail; it is separated from White residential areas by buffer industrial zones, and is so situated that expanding White residential areas will not encroach upon it; it is separate and therefore isolable, its links with the city consisting of only two or three roads and one railway line; and there are two large military bases close by—Diepkloof on the eastern border of Soweto, and Lenz a few miles south. Soweto's only real drawback, from the government's point of view, is that it is not in a homeland (and some Soweto leaders as well as an occasional *verligte* Nationalist have proposed that even this be remedied).

The growth of Soweto has been governed by the growth of industry. Civic authorities accepted no responsibility for the welfare of African workers until 1917-18, when high mortality rates following an epidemic of influenza led to the development of the first housing schemes. The area grew rapidly during World War II as thousands of Africans moved to town to satisfy the demands of the war economy. After the war, it was found that fifty thousand families were living in slum conditions; housing schemes were expanded, but never fast enough to keep pace with the growing demand.[73] In 1975 there were officially 17,725 families (representing nearly ninety thousand people) on the waiting list for housing, and plans were announced to build four thousand houses, less than a quarter of the number needed.[74] In 1976 there were officially 9,892 families on the waiting list for housing (the "primary waiting list"), which accounted for nearly one quarter of the 42,614 families reported to be on waiting lists in fourteen different Bantu Affairs Administration areas reports recorded in the 1976 *Survey of Race Relations* (reports from nine other boards were not available at the time).[75] Soweto is thus extremely crowded.

As is the case with most other African urban areas, it is not possible to give even a reasonably close estimate of the population of Soweto. In 1975 Mayer, while noting the problems of under-enumeration, estimated the population at 800,000.[76] When I worked in Soweto (1969-71), it was the reasoned estimate of some officials that the population was not less than one million,[77] and it is not likely to be less today. Soweto is therefore the third largest city in South Africa and has a population larger than some of the neighboring independent territories.

The Soweto population comes from all areas of South Africa, and virtually all language groups are represented. The following table, adapted from Mayer, gives the percentages for each group (estimated):

LANGUAGE GROUPS IN SOWETO: 1973

Language Group	Percent of Total Population	
Zulu	29.8%	
Xhosa	10.0	
Swazi	6.8	
Total Nguni-speakers		46.6
Tswana	16.2	
South Sotho	14.2	
North Sotho	9.9	
Total Sotho speakers		40.3
Tsonga	7.2	
Venda	4.4	
Others	1.4	
Total "others"		13.0

Source: Mayer, "Class, Status and Ethnicity," p. 142.

Eight of the groups with designated homelands are represented in Soweto, but no attempt has been made to segregate it into eight different sections. Ethnic segregation became compulsory only in 1955, by which time a number of Soweto's twenty-two townships were already inextricably mixed. All townships are now officially zoned by language groups—Nguni, Sotho, and "other"—and available housing is allocated on this basis. I was told in 1971 that only about half the townships had any sort of effective zoning, and that was only on the basis of the classification of the head of the household. Estimates of "interethnic" marriages in Soweto range from one-third to one-half of recorded cases.[78] An attempt to segregate children by forcing them to attend separate schools for different language groups has been more effective, but, if anything, has contributed to student political unity.

The Soweto population is polyglot, comprising mainly ordinary working people, most of whom view themselves as permanent residents, whether legally in town or not. About 79% are in family accommodations while the remainder are "single" people living in hostels.[79] The great majority are poor: in 1967 an official survey of Soweto found that 68 percent of the families interviewed were living on incomes below the estimated minimum monthly income for a family of five.[80] The situation has not significantly improved, despite recent wage increases. In 1976 the Household Subsistence Level for a family of six was calculated for Johannesburg at about $156 (R135) per month. At the same time the average monthly income of African workers in Johannesburg was estimated to be approximately $60 (R52); the estimated average monthly income for single households was $109 (R95) and for multiple households, $217 (R189).[81] While these figures are only estimated averages, they give an indication of conditions in what is probably the most prosperous African urban area in South Africa. There is a small but growing middle class in Soweto, represented by skilled employees, white-collar workers, and professionals, but the *Financial Mail* suggested in 1977 that fewer than 2 percent of Soweto's population were likely to be earning the estimated $575 (R500) per month required for the most modest middle-class lifestyle. (*Financial Mail* examined the proposition that a growing Black urban middle class with material assets to lose might help deter violence. Its finding was that the growing Black middle class will press for major political change—not show restraint.)[82]

The Soweto population is thus predominantly poor and overcrowded. The facilities are somewhat better than in many other African urban areas, but they are inadequate given the population. Despite the activities of a national and local police force, the area is one of the most dangerous in the country. According to a survey made in 1969, 30 percent of those interviewed had been assaulted on the street at some time, 22 percent had been robbed on the street, 15 percent had been robbed on trains, and 14 percent had had their homes burgled, [83] while figures for 1974 show 854 murders, 92 cases of culpable homicide, 1,282 reported cases of rape, and 7,682 assaults with intent to commit grievous bodily harm.[84]

When I worked in Soweto a number of outsiders acquainted with the area expressed the feeling that the situation was potentially explosive, and that any number of things could trigger violence. At the time I believed that the overburdened transport system might provide the spark. More than a quarter of a million people rode daily at peak hours on a single railway line, and there had been a number of accidents in which people were seriously injured and the reaction of the crowds that gathered verged on open violence. In the event, it was the educational system that provided the spark. (Some commentators have downplayed the role of the educational system in the uprising in favor of a broader explanation, but the educational system should not be overlooked.)

It is important to note that the system of Bantu education was designed to educate Black children to fit into the apartheid system. Children were not to be educated beyond their assigned station in life. The education was not compulsory; the authorities said that compulsory education would cost too much. (It was pointed out recently that the $117 million being budgeted for the introduction of a Black television service would completely cover the cost of compulsory Black education.) Bantu education was introduced by the Nationalist government following a report of the Commission on Native Education, 1949-51. Perhaps the most important recommendation in this report was that mother-tongue instruction be introduced for the first years, followed by dual instruction in English and Afrikaans. Dual medium instruction in the official languages was to be introduced "in such a way that the Bantu child will be able to find his way in European communities;to follow oral written instructions; and to carry on a simple conversation with Europeans about his work and other subjects of common interest."[85] Welsh suggests that this provision was an attempt to downgrade the extensive use of English in schools: "Afrikaner nationalists criticised the widespread use of English in African schools for spreading English culture and making the total environment more English in character, thereby handicapping Afrikaners in their struggle against anglicization."[86]

In any event, this policy put African pupils at a further disadvantage relative to White pupils. Other disadvantages are related to finance (an average of $700 per capita is spent on White pupils by the state, compared with an average of $60 for African pupils) and class-size (the average teacher-pupil ratio for White children is 1:20;

for Africans it is 1:54).[87] The stated goal is compulsory education for all, but it is a long way from being achieved. There is a very serious shortage of African schools (in 1976 some seventy were needed in Soweto alone), and pupils are often turned away as a result. Thus in 1970, for example, five thousand children in Soweto were denied schooling owing to a lack of facilities.[88] Despite the help subsequently provided by private enterprise to erect more buildings, the shortage is still chronic.

Because of the deficiencies of this system, plus the lack of opportunities in employment, there is an extremely high dropout rate: only 2 percent of the estimated 4.5 million pupils complete nine years of schooling and only 0.2 percent finish high school. As the *Financial Mail* puts it: "After a quarter of a century of Bantu Education, there are less than 400 doctors and 100 lawyers in a population of almost 20 million."[89] It was against this background that young Sowetans began their protest in 1976, triggered by a requirement that social studies and mathematics should be taught in Afrikaans, despite a clear indication of student opposition reflected in a survey of high school pupils in Soweto in 1971. This survey, conducted by Dr. M.L. Edelstein, had shown that 88.5 percent of the students wished to be instructed in English, 9.5 percent in an African language, and only 2 percent in Afrikaans.[90]

The demonstrations, which ironically led to the death of Dr. Edelstein outside a Soweto school, were met by police gunfire, and the rash of disturbances spread to 160 Black townships within seven months (according to Savage), resulting in the deaths of some 660 people.[91] There followed a lengthy boycott of schools, mass resignations of teachers, the detention of many students and other leaders, the banning of most organizations of any political import, and the moving into exile of numerous young Blacks.[92] Government action was clearly designed to remove leadership at a crucial time, and thereby buy some respite—as was the policy in the 1960s. It is likely that this tactic will again prove reasonably effective as a short-term measure.

SOME CONCLUSIONS

The last decade has seen a growing urban African population becoming increasingly Westernized and industrialized, and moving more and more into a position of confrontation with government policy. This policy has remained essentially rigid, allowing only moderate changes within the specified framework. The Soweto confrontation of 1976 was met with a Sharpeville-like overreaction, and was thus escalated by Whites—a point which is not usually made clear when talking about these events. The violence that ensued was controlled by only part of the force available, and—widespread as it was—was nowhere near sufficient to threaten the stability of the government.

The events described here have not led to any lessening of the problems of political strategy for the urban Black population, and the banning of so many Black organizations has added enormously to these problems. Urban residents have rejected government-sponsored community councils, and the only organizational alternatives appear to be underground movements, the weak and unrecognized trade unions, and possibly the Inkatha movement founded by Chief Buthelezi. These represent what R.W. Johnson has referred to as the "new wave" of African political movements of the 1970s, which owe little or nothing to the political movements of the past.[93] In fact, there is likely to be conflict between the Black Consciousness leaders and the older nationalist movements, which will work against a common unity—at least in the short term.[94]

The young Black political leaders are faced with the problem that the Black Consciousness movement has provided an ideology but not a strategy. Some have chosen to go into exile and continue their struggle as guerillas, thereby being lost for the foreseeable future to internal political organization. It is not clear what tack the remainder (at least those out of detention) will take. Johnson suggests that the Black Consciousness movement may not recover from the blows it has received, and that in any case it will lose something of its thrust.[95] I maintain, however, that its ideology will remain extremely important in formulating attitudes and assisting in "psychic liberation," which is basically all it has claimed to do.

Another important problem area is the condition of the urban African workers. The government is clearly very sensitive to strikes, as the events of 1972-73 showed, when African workers won pay increases and other concessions through a series of illegal strikes. These were treated with far more caution than were the student-led demonstrations of later years.[96] Strikes have continued, but on a smaller scale. There were 374 strikes involving African labor (some 57,656 workers) in 1974 and 119 strikes in 1975.[97] South Africa's largest strike of Black labor occurred in September 1976, but lasted less than three days. However, one would have to agree with Johnson's analysis that, although it possesses a crippling weapon in strike action, African labor

> lacks trade union organisation and what organisations it has are

> weak and penetrated by police informers. It is deeply divided between urban resident workers and the single migrants from the homelands. . . . It is, moreover, conscious . . . of its relatively privileged position and of the fact that it has something to lose.[98]

Johnson contends that fear of unemployment was more important as a motivating factor in the 1976 strike than unemployment itself, and notes that student calls for another strike in November of the same year failed.[99]

The government is attempting to meet the problem of rising African unemployment. A bill was submitted to Parliament in 1978 to increase the power of the authorities to remove out-of-work Africans to the homelands.[100] Implementation of this policy, along with the existing migrant labor policy, is designed to take the pressure off the South African government to keep order in the urban areas, but at the same time it will have the effect of providing further links between Africans in urban and rural areas. As Johnson has observed: "Thus the government has, foolishly perhaps, guaranteed that the heightened political consciousness of urban blacks will not stay dammed up in the townships but will lap into the homelands fairly quickly. The potential consequences of such a process have not yet become visible, and are indeed, incalculable."[101] This factor may increase the possibilities of urban worker action being stimulated from the homelands.[102]

Grave difficulties must be overcome to achieve urban Black political mobilization, but it seems that Black workers—if their organization grows and their skills increase, as seem likely—pose more of a threat to the South African government than does the student movement. Internally and in the short term, as we have seen, this threat is not yet significant; as Johnson says: "The laager is intact and can be defended."[103] At the same time, urban Blacks have the power to affect the South African economy through its external links. Thus Johnson contends that

> To date the greatest power of the urban Africans has, as we have noted, been felt in the international money markets. Black protestors may not be able to stop factories and mines for long, if at all, but they can interdict the flow of foreign capital into South Africa on which the economy depends.[104]

The South African government has faced the challenge of the urban Black population in a number of ways. It has tightened its legislative restraint, harshly suppressed protest, and attempted to cripple Black organization by banning groups and detaining individuals. At the same time, it has tried to project a more positive image, allowing certain concessions, and replacing the former hard-line Minister of Bantu Administration with more pragmatic ministers —Dr. C.P. Mulder and then Dr. P. Koornhof. Some of the changes were of style rather than substance—for example, the renaming of the Bantu Administration Department as the Department of Plural Relations (under Mulder) and later the Department of Cooperation and Development (under Koornhof). In early 1979, however, two developments occurred which were heralded as constituting definite changes in policy. One of these involved the squatter community of Crossroads, and the other, the report of the Commission of Inquiry into Legislation Affecting the Utilisation of Manpower (the Riekert Commission).

Crossroads, an illegal African squatter community near Cape Town of some twenty thousand people, was scheduled for destruction by the South African authorities, which attracted considerable international attention. The newly appointed Minister of Bantu Administration, Dr. Koornhof, visited the area, and in one of his first official acts forestalled the demolition. After protracted negotiations, a decision was made to build a new African township in Cape Town to house Crossroads families whose breadwinners either were legal Cape Town residents or could show that they were gainfully employed. Excluded were those who had been sentenced to a fine of $550 (or six months in jail) or more, vagrants, and people who had housing and employment available in the Transkei. This was a radical departure from previous government policy, and meant that the South African government was prepared to condone illegal residence and employment. However, the decision was specific to Crossroads, and was made under considerable internal and international pressure; at the same time the government announced its intention to tighten up influx control regulations to prevent a recurrence of such a situation by publishing its White Paper on the Riekert Commission, in which it rejected proposed reforms.[105]

The Riekert Commission had recommended the abolition of the provision that unauthorized Africans could not remain in urban areas for longer than seventy-two hours. It also recommended that influx control regulations be changed to allow entry of African workers with approved jobs and housing in the urban areas. Enforcement of the regulations was to be in terms of jobs and housing requirements, with increased fines for employers found with illegal employees. One of the aims was to reduce the large number of arrests under the pass laws; another was to punish employers rather than employees. The state rejected the proposal to abolish the 72-hour rule, and while it accepted the principle of heavier fines for employers (now up to $550 per illegal employee), it decided to retain the various measures to punish employees.[106] The overall result will be a harsher system of control which will make it more difficult for employers to hire those who are not qualified to be in the urban areas.

The government accepted a number of the Riekert Commission's recommendations regarding qualified African residents. Those qualifying under Section 10 of the Natives (Urban Areas) Consolidation Act (see page 131 above) would be able to change employers without obtaining official permission, to have their wives and families with them in town (whether or not the dependents were qualified themselves) provided approved housing was available, and to transfer their Section 10 rights to other urban areas—again provided that housing and work were available.[107] One effect of this will be to create a labor elite of permanent urban residents who will have considerable mobility; at the same time it will exacerbate the cleavage between urban residents and migrants. Permission to transfer Section 10 rights to other urban areas will benefit the authorities by allowing the transfer of the urban unemployed in the smaller towns of South Africa to areas where work is available (at the expense of the migrants).

Thus there is no really significant change in policy. Permanent urban dwellers with Section 10 rights will probably find their lives somewhat easier, but the outlook for all other Africans in the towns is bleak.* No further political rights are envisaged for urban Africans outside the framework of existing policy, and there is no reason to suppose that revolts will not continue. The loss of life in Soweto is remembered, and the uprising in Soweto and elsewhere in 1976 may yet turn out to be a turning point in the history of South Africa. Urban guerilla activity is increasing, despite many logistical problems, with the support of a new generation of post-Soweto exiles. This will not bring about change of itself, but the urban Black population is likely to play an important role, both inside and outside the country, in contributing to the destabilization of the present situation which is a prerequisite for the transformation of South African society.

*It should be noted that the Riekert Commission made no findings regarding the position of urban Blacks in the Western Cape because policy there "was based on other than economic grounds." It is not clear to what extent the new provisions for Section 10 people will apply in the Western Cape. It is not clear how long these provisions will apply in any case, since children of Section 10 residents lose these rights when they are forced to take homeland citizenship. Whether the new concessions will apply to them in the future has not been determined.

CURRENT LABOR ISSUES IN SOUTH AFRICA

Francis Wilson

My purpose in this paper is to report and analyze what seems to be happening in the field of labor in southern Africa at present. It is important to recognize that this area is one where economic and political boundaries do not always coincide. I shall start by considering labor in the gold mines, where there have been substantial changes over the last five or six years, and then examine, in turn, farm labor, aspects of labor in the manufacturing sector, the specter of unemployment, and finally what one might call the "blotting paper function" of the South African political economy. Discussion of trade unionism is in general excluded because it is dealt with in a separate chapter (pp. 174-93 below).

LABOR IN THE GOLD MINES

What has been happening in the gold mines? Despite the reports of the Wiehahn and Riekert Commissions,[1] there is an underlying stability and absence of fundamental change in the power structure in South Africa. Nevertheless there have been some fairly surprising developments in the mining industry during the 1970s. For example, Black wages, after being static if not actually declining in real terms over a period of sixty years or more, suddenly trebled between 1971 and 1976. In addition, there has been an outbreak of "compound confrontations." The compounds of the gold, coal, and other mines of South Africa, where up to 8,000 men are housed in barracks as "bachelors," living there for twelve or sometimes eighteen months at a time, are surely unique in the contemporary world. These institutions have been blowing apart with great frequency since 1973. There were some sixty-six incidents between September 1973 and June 1976 in which some 178 men were killed and over a thousand injured.[2*] It is important to note that there has been little

*Since that time there have been a number of further confrontations, including a major riot on the eve of the opening of the Anglo-American Corporation's Elandsrand gold mine (April 9, 1979), involving several hundred workers and

inside research: very few people able to speak any of the African languages have been allowed into the compounds for any length of time.[3] We can say with some assurance, however, that one of the reasons for the compound confrontations has been wage grievances. An important aspect of these were shifts in wage differentials within the Black labor structure which were not thought through carefully and were transmitted to the workers casually.

A second reason for the confrontations is the increasing anxiety and tension in the mines as they are sunk deeper and deeper.[4] Mining is very treacherous. Two miles down it is hot and exhausting, and there is danger at all times of rock bursts or methane gas explosions. As the level of mining sinks deeper into the earth, the work place becomes even more dangerous. This has a psychological effect on the workers which contributes to the social explosions within the compounds. A third reason for the confrontations is political interference—most notably from the government of Lesotho, which imposed a compulsory deferred pay scheme on all mine workers without consulting them. There is little doubt that this interference was a major cause of some of the conflict in the gold mines in the Orange Free State, where miners went on strike to express their dissatisfaction with the Lesotho government.

Ethnic tension has been played up in the South African press as one of the reasons why Black mine workers fight each other. Ethnic tensions do exist, but why? It seems obvious that if any ethnically diverse groups of 8,000 people—for example, Afrikaners and English or Transvaalers and Cape people—are put together under the conditions that exist in the mine compounds of South Africa, there will be conflicts between them. Under the circumstances prevailing in these compounds, the differences between, say, Xhosa and Sotho can assume major importance, while under other circumstances, as is evident from the fact that there have been hundreds—even thousands—of marriages across the Xhosa-Sotho line within South Africa, the differences are seen as insignificant.

In my judgment the two most important causes of compound confrontations are the compound system and the lack of worker-management communication.[5] As previously noted, the compound system consists of "labor batteries" of up to 8,000 men living in highly unnatural social conditions. This system is the focal point

causing considerable damage. The unexpectedness of the riot and management's puzzlement concerning its causes serve to emphasize the absence of channels of communication and the brittleness of the social structure within the compound system.

of the migrant labor pattern in South Africa, and it seems certain that such a pattern cannot continue indefinitely without some kind of breakdown. With respect to communication between workers and management, management has for many years thought that if it could communicate clearly to workers, it would get clear messages in return. However, there is considerable evidence that what management thinks it is communicating to workers is not the message the workers are receiving, and there is even more evidence that workers feel unable to get their messages through to top management. Thus a major weakness of the present system is a lack of effective communication between management and workers.

The Changing Wage Structure. Over the past five years there has been a significant shift in the wage structure in the mining industry. Average wages of Black mine workers remained static, and may even have fallen in real terms, between 1911 and 1971, but between 1971 and 1976 there was a dramatic trebling of Black wages, and the gap between average White and average Black wages closed sharply. Expressed as a ratio the White-Black wage gap in 1911 and 1936 was approximately 11:1; as wages of Whites rose substantially beginning in the mid-1930s, it widened to a ratio of 21:1 in 1971. Five years later (1976) the ratio had fallen to 8:1. (It should be noted that if the gap between White and Black wages is measured as the difference in real cash terms, then the gap continued to increase for some time after 1971.)[6] Why should there have been this sudden change between 1971 and 1976?

To some the obvious reason was that the price of gold had risen substantially during this period; to others the reason was that there had been a wave of strikes, centered in Durban, which rippled through the economy. The first group, notably on the side of management, argued that mine wages had been as high as they could possibly be given the constraints of the gold price, but that once these constraints were lifted, wages naturally increased. The second group, primarily on the side of worker organizations, argued that wages had remained static because of the absence of worker power, and that once worker muscles could be flexed, as they had been in Durban, change was inevitable. All this sounds very plausible until one refers back to the period in South African history just after World War II, when similar developments occurred. In 1946 there was a huge strike of Black workers in the mines, which gave the industry a considerable scare;[7] then in 1949 there was a sudden increase in the price of gold received by South African producers when Britain devalued its currency. If either or both of the arguments above are valid, Black wages should have increased substantially during this period. What really happened was that between 1946 and 1951 the wages of White mine workers rose by 12 percent, while the wages of Blacks *declined* by 7 percent.[8]

While I am *not* arguing that the rise in the price of gold and the wave of strikes were irrelevant to what occurred, it seems necessary to dig deeper to explain why wages shifted as they did during the 1970s. What was happening structurally in the mining industry to cause this change? By the end of the 1960s the mining industry was faced, not for the first time, with a shortage of Black labor. The number of Black South Africans in the gold mines fell below 100,000 for the first time since before World War II, and the mining industry began to analyze what was happening with some care. They realized that the number of Black South Africans working in the mines had been falling rapidly since the early 1960s and might approach zero in the not-too-distant future. The reason for this sharp decline was that Black South Africans were changing to jobs in manufacturing.

Since the mid-1930s the mining industry had been able to draw on labor from a wide area north of latitude 22° south which included, at one time or another, Northern Rhodesia, Tanganyika, Angola, South West Africa, Northern Bechuanaland, and above all, Nyasaland. This broad access to labor had enabled the South African mining industry to go on developing while keeping real wages fairly constant. The expanding manufacturing sector, on the other hand, did not have access to this labor supply. As a consequence, wages for Blacks in manufacturing had been rising since the beginning of World War II, and the gap between Black wages in the manufacturing and mining sectors was becoming greater and greater.

From the point of view of a Black South African it was becoming less and less desirable to work in the mines if there were jobs in manufacturing, where wages were better and conditions less arduous. The mining industry realized that it soon might find itself in a situation where 100 percent of its Black labor force was drawn from outside South Africa. A lively debate ensued. Some favored raising wages, arguing that it was necessary in order to compete with the manufacturing sector, so that some South Africans could be drawn back to the mines. Others in the industry argued that such a strategy would be foolish. The mines had always drawn labor from far afield, so why should they pay more for labor than they needed to? They pointed out that it would be perfectly feasible for the industry to get all the labor it needed from Ruanda or further afield in Africa by flying everyone in.

While the debate was in full spate, a number of interrelated events took place which affected the mining industry. First, in the summer of 1972/73 there were the Durban strikes, which sparked international interest in the whole South African wage structure through a campaign led by the *Guardian* in Great Britain. This enormous interest (both local and international) in wages had a ripple effect through the whole South African community. Manufacturers became aware that they were going to have to do something about wages, and in the mining industry there was apprehension that the events in Durban might spark worker protests in the mines. Meanwhile the price of gold, which had been stable for many years, started to rise. In December 1971 the U.S. government devalued the dollar, which raised the official price of gold from $35 per fine oz. to $38 per fine oz.; a further devaluation in February 1973 raised the official price to $42 per fine oz. In November 1973 the gold pool was created, and government reserves were sold on the free market; by December 1974 the free market price of gold had risen to $198 per fine oz. (Between 1971 and 1974 the average price received by the Chamber of Mines quadrupled from R28,6 to R107,4 per fine oz.)

In April 1974 two events occurred which had a profound effect on the mining industry. First, there was an air crash in Francistown, Botswana, in which seventy-two Malawian mine workers were killed. The President of Malawi immediately announced that he was stopping all further recruiting to the South African mines, and that when Malawians in South Africa finished their contracts they would come home and not be allowed to return to the mines. At this stage there were some 120,000 or more Malawi men working in the South African mines. No one had for a moment expected such a drastic step. For an impoverished third world country which had been heavily dependent on outside employment for thirty years or more suddenly to call all its workers home seemed to defy the laws of economics—but Malawi did it.

Later in April 1974 came the coup in Lisbon. For the South African mining industry, the immediate implication was that the Portuguese were no longer going to be in charge of Mozambique, but that Frelimo was likely to come to power. In 1974 Mozambique was, after Malawi, the second major source of labor for the industry, and seen in historical perspective Mozambique has been perhaps its most important supplier of labor. For the thirty years after World War II an average of 100,000 men a year from Mozambique worked in the South African mines, and as far back as the 1890s, 60 percent of the labor force in the South African mines was drawn from Mozambique. Mozambique has thus been part and parcel of the South African economy during its century of industrialization.

It is in the light of all these developments—the Durban strikes, the rise in the price of gold, the abrupt cutting off of the supply of labor from Malawi, and the uncertainty regarding labor from Mozambique as a result of the fall of the Portuguese empire—that the sharp increase in Black wages in the mines can best be understood. These events taken together strengthened the arguments of those within the industry pushing for an increase in wages in order to draw more Black South Africans into the mines. In assessing how far wages should rise, it seems likely that the mine managers pursued some sort of "minimax" strategy to ensure that labor came from a number of different areas. Clearly they did not want to find themselves ever again in a situation where too many of their eggs were in one basket—particularly if that basket was outside the political control of South Africa. At the same time there were considerable benefits to the industry of maintaining recruitment offices in as many countries as possible.

While these changes were taking place, a further event occurred which dovetailed neatly into the emerging pattern. The Rhodesian government requested permission to supply some labor to the gold mines, and as a result the Chamber of Mines began recruiting in Rhodesia in December 1974. Since 1912, recruiting by the gold mines had been banned in Rhodesia on the grounds that local employers should not have to compete with the South African mines for their labor. Due to a combination of circumstances, including the Unilateral Declaration of Independence in 1965, the economic boycott imposed by the United Nations, population growth, and other factors, Rhodesia had moved in a twenty-year period from being a major labor importer (particularly from Mozambique, Malawi, and Zambia) to a steady state labor society (which neither imported nor exported labor) to a country that sought to export its growing problem of unemployment.[9]

Table 1, which shows the recruitment to the South African mines from different countries over the period 1973-1978, gives some idea of the abrupt changes in the labor supply pattern. Between 1973 and 1976 the number of Black workers in the mines as a whole fell from 422,000 to 361,000, while the number of South Africans almost doubled, from 86,000 to 158,000; the proportion of Black South Africans rose from one fifth to almost one half. (For purposes of this analysis Transkei is included as part of South

Table 1

GEOGRAPHIC ORIGINS OF BLACK WORKERS EMPLOYED BY SOUTH AFRICAN GOLD MINES AND BY TRANSVAAL COAL MINES AS OF 31 DECEMBER 1973, 1976, AND 1978

	1973		1976		1978	
Area of Origin	Number *(000's)*	Percent	Number *(000's)*	Percent	Number *(000's)*	Percent
South Africa[a]	86.2	20.5%	158.5	43.8%	250.3	54.9%
Lesotho	87.2	20.7	96.4	26.7	104.1	22.9
Swaziland	4.5	1.1	8.6	2.4	8.4	1.8
Botswana	16.8	4.0	15.5	4.3	18.1	4.0
Mozambique	99.4	23.6	48.6	13.4	45.2	9.9
Tropicals	128.0	30.3	33.8	9.4	29.6	6.5
TOTALS	422.2	100	361.3	100	455.7	100

Sources: Mine Labour Organisation (Wenela) Ltd., *Annual Report*, 1973; The Employment Bureau of Africa Ltd. (formerly Wenela), *Annual Reports*, 1976 and 1978.

[a]Figures for South Africa include Transkei and Bophutatswana.

Note: Totals also include workers employed by two platinum mines. Figures do not add up exactly due to rounding.

Africa.) The number of mine workers from Lesotho increased from 87,000 in 1973 to 96,000 in 1976, while the proportion rose from 21 to 27 percent. By 1976 the two major suppliers of labor were South Africa and Lesotho. Both the number and proportion from Swaziland also increased during this period, but its overall contribution to the labor supply has always been fairly small. The number and proportion from Botswana remained fairly static. But with regard to Mozambique and the "tropical" areas north of South Africa's most northern point, the change was dramatic. In 1973 the number of mine workers from Mozambique was 99,400 men,* but in 1975, the year after Frelimo came to power, the number of Mozambicans in the mines rose to 120,000. By 1976, however, the number was down to 48,000, and it continued to fall in subsequent years. Thus the Mozambique share of the mine labor market fell from 23.5 percent to 13.4 percent within three years. The num-

*The annual average between 1946 and 1974 was almost exactly 100,000.

ber of "tropicals"—mainly Malawians—fell from 128,000 in 1973 to 34,000 in 1976, but these numbers mask the fact that Malawians fell from some 120,000 to almost zero while the number of workers from Rhodesia rose from zero to between 20,000 and 25,000.* In 1977, however, recruiting was once again allowed in Malawi, and in that year the number of Malawian mine workers rose from under 200 to almost 12,000. Overall the situation changed between 1973 and 1976 from one where the mines were primarily dependent upon Malawi, Mozambique, Lesotho, and South Africa (in descending order of importance) to one where South Africa provided almost half the labor to the mines, Lesotho supplied about one quarter, and the next most important source was Mozambique, with a share of 13 percent.

The mines did not deal with the labor supply crisis simply by raising wages: they were also able to develop new sources of labor, which meant that wages did not rise as high as they might otherwise have. In particular, the opening up of the Rhodesian labor market was an important breakthrough. Similarly, the emergence in the mid-1970s of the tip of the iceberg of Black unemployment within South Africa made the mines aware of a potential for recruiting in the White farming areas.

Before moving on to look at labor in the agricultural sector of the South African economy, one other major recent event in the history of the gold mines should be noted. In March 1979 a long-simmering dispute between mine management and the White mine workers' union came into the open when the union went on strike against plans to shift the color bar within the mines. The proximate cause of the strike was the appointment at O'Kiep copper mine of a Colored man, qualified as a diesel mechanic, to fill a long advertised vacancy. White mine workers at O'Kiep went on strike, and the mine workers' union immediately brought out some 90,000 men on strike around the country. This move was interpreted by observers as primarily a warning to the government not to abolish statutory job reservation within the mining industry. The strike took place shortly before the Wiehahn report of the Commission of Inquiry into Labour Legislation was due to be released, and the mine workers' union was understood to be seeking to ensure that the color bar remained legally intact.

*Between January 1975 and May 1977 the total number of men brought in under contract from Rhodesia was approximately 50,000 (*Financial Mail*, 13.5.1977; *Daily Dispatch*, 16.1.1978).

There is not space enough here to go into the details of the long saga of attempts by management over fifteen or twenty years to shift a rigid color bar within the mining industry and the determined resistance by White workers not to allow themselves to be undercut by Blacks.[10] The dispute extends back into the history of the mines to the Rand rebellion in 1922, when White mine workers went on strike (leading eventually to full-scale rebellion) against plans by management to save labor costs by replacing Whites with Blacks at a much lower rate of pay. Since then an important dispute within South African White politics has been between those Whites who have been prepared to adopt a flexible color bar which shifts in response to changes in the economic structure, but which leaves most Whites in managerial and supervisory positions above Blacks, and those Whites—particularly within the working class in the mining industry—who have argued that any shift at all in the color bar was the thin end of a wedge which would lead to Whites being phased out of the industry. By taking a hard line the White miners have been able to extract enormous concessions from mine management, so that over the years White mine workers have become a highly paid elite whose earnings have been derived in some measure from work the Blacks have been graciously permitted to do provided the Whites were paid for the increase in productivity.

The 1979 strike is significant because the mining industry has stood firm for the first time when threatened with the specter of 1922, which has haunted it for two generations. When the mine workers' union declared a strike, it got very little support either from other Whites within the mining industry or, more importantly, from the National Party government. The party which originally derived much of its power from its championing of White worker rights had by 1979 moved to a position where it was backing the Chamber of Mines and opposing the workers whose political support had for so long been a vital component of its constituency. In response to Part 1 of the Wiehahn report the government accepted the recommendations to abolish the principle (though in the mining industry not yet the practice) of *statutory* work reservation.[11] From both the Wiehahn report and the government response, it was clear that the aim was to remove the legal rigidities in the color bar, but the continued existence of the color bar, flexibly administered, remained unchallenged.

LABOR IN AGRICULTURE

At present most political analysis of South Africa focuses either on Bantustans or on the urban areas (or both). Yet the White-owned farming area of South Africa (including state-run forestry) constitutes no less than three quarters of the total land area. One quarter of all Black South Africans live there. Although it is now relatively dormant, it is nevertheless a key to future developments within the country. Consider the following points. First, the number of Blacks employed in agriculture in South Africa increased steadily through the past generation until the late 1960s. By the early 1970s a turning point seems to have been reached (allowing for the possible inaccuracy of the statistics), and the number of Blacks in agriculture is now declining. This follows a worldwide pattern. As urbanization proceeds, the stage is reached where not only the relative but also the absolute number of people on the land starts to decrease. For Whites in South Africa the turning point came in the early 1930s, and a good deal of South African politics has revolved around this fact. For Black South Africans, however, the turning point did not come until forty years later. The underlying causes—changing techniques of production and mechanization—need not be spelled out in detail, but it is perhaps worth noting that at a recent conference on farm labor in South Africa a farmer owning a larger amount of land pointed out that if he was unable to get casual laborers it would be necessary for him to move to monoculture and to use chemical weed killers, which he estimated could reduce his labor demand by two thirds.[12]

Any analysis of present-day South Africa, political or economic, has to take into account the pressure arising from the movement of Black people from the White farms. Related to this is a process which might be called "leap-frog urbanization." In South Africa, if farm laborers decide to go to town, or if the farmer evicts some of those living on the farm because there are no jobs for them, then the laborer and his family must move, but legally they cannot move directly to town. Indeed neither the farm worker nor his family have rights to be anywhere at all—least of all in the urban areas. As a consequence people are moving off the farms into resettlement areas in Kwazulu, the eastern and western Transvaal, or the eastern Cape. From one perspective the resettlement camps are awful places: they are densely populated areas, indeed rural ghettos; for women they are places from which there is no escape; there is little land to cultivate or on which to build some other kind of economic base. However, from the perspective of a farm laborer these resettlement camps (which have been mushrooming throughout rural South Africa since the mid-1960s) function as escape valves. A farm laborer can take his family from a farm in, say, the Orange Free State and move to Witsieshoek, just north of Lesotho. In this small rural area, the population has risen from approximately 20,000 in 1970 to over 120,000 in 1978. Witsieshoek is a rural area 200 miles from the southern Transvaal and more than 50 miles from a town of any size, but it is possible for a farm laborer to get a house there, settle his family, and then go off to town as a migrant worker.

In Witsieshoek and other resettlement areas Blacks can build houses for themselves (which they cannot do in town) and can feel fairly certain that they will be able to leave their homes to their children. Thus, because of the constraints within the social structure, a process of urbanization-at-a-distance is emerging where suburbs are developing in rural ghettos miles from the economic bases which sustain them. The extent to which such resettlement areas will continue to function as escape valves from the farms may be severely restricted given the report of the Riekert Commission,[13] whose recommendations are likely, if not radically altered by the government, to make it increasingly difficult for people living in the "homelands" to get jobs in the cities. The Riekert recommendation that African men be allowed to move into the cities with their families provided there is both a job and accommodation available to them applies only to people coming from other "prescribed" (urban) areas, including smaller towns where Black population growth has in many instances outstripped the creation of new jobs. The increase in poverty and unemployment—and consequently petty pilfering—in many of these areas during the 1970s is perhaps one reason for the proposal to shift the emphasis from recruiting labor in the "homelands" to drawing workers from the smaller towns. Such a change in policy, if effectively executed, would imply a further consolidation of the boundary between the White-controlled core of the South African economy and the reserves, which the South African government is seeking to transform into independent countries.

Another important aspect of agricultural labor in South Africa is the enormous diversity in both wages and working conditions. Perhaps the most striking example reported at the Saldru farm labor conference was a small farming community in the northwestern Cape where cash wages for Black farm laborers varied by a ratio on the order of 8:1.[14] This is an evidence of the barriers to mobility in South African agriculture which make it impossible to talk about a single labor market in South Africa. There is considerable insulation between segments of labor within the country, and it is possible to be encapsulated on a farm or encapsulated in a particular region. However, paradoxically, there are also substantial degrees of interconnectedness, which stem mainly from the migrant labor system. There are two main areas in the economy to which agricultural workers migrate: the sugar farms of Natal and the fruit farms of the western Cape. Much of the labor for both of these areas comes from the eastern part of southern Africa lying between the Fish river near Grahamstown and the Umzimkulu river on the north eastern boundary of the Transkei. This area is also a source of much of the labor for the gold mines and for industry on the Witwatersrand and in the western Cape. Given this situation, it is easy to understand how a decision by the President of Malawi to cut off the supply of labor to the Witwatersrand mines or a coup in Lisbon, for example, can have repercussions affecting farm laborers in the western Cape. Because of the migrant labor system, there is an international labor market in southern Africa, and a potential worker at home in the Transkei does not have to go to a farm in the western Cape if he does not choose to: he can go to the mines instead. Thus if mine wages increase dramatically—if he hears that it is possible to earn R2,50 per shift, say, where only a few years previously the wage was 40 cents a shift—then he may decide to go to the mines rather than to some farm. This leads to pressure on the farming communities which draw heavily on migrants to raise wages. (This connection has been graphically demonstrated by Tony Ardington in an article dealing with wages in the sugar industry.)[15] Thus the paradox persists. Side by side with insulation in places like the northwestern Cape, where wages vary by as much as a factor of eight between a few farmers, there are broad linkages which can mean that a decision by the President of Malawi restricting mine workers from Malawi from going to the South African gold mines can have a direct impact on the wages paid to fruit farm workers near Cape Town—some two thousand miles away.

When looking at South African agriculture, it is helpful to analyze the labor ecology of the area. First, there are what might be called "labor reserve" farms, which are to be found primarily in the eastern part of the country, but also elsewhere near Bantustans. These are farms which have considerably more people living on them than the farmers want. These provide labor for industry and for the mines, often in the form of migrants who leave their families behind. In this situation farmers complain bitterly about the barriers to mobility and argue that they are "the incubators of labor" in South Africa. In truth they do have to bear much of the social cost because, paternalistic as they often are, many feel obliged to look after the people living on their farms. And on some farms populations have unduly high proportions of dependents, both old and young. (These "labor reserve" farms are found in the eastern Cape, Natal, and parts of the Transvaal region.) Second, there are what might be called "steady state" labor farms—that is, farms where the number of people (families included) living on them is roughly the number required by the farmer. Third, there are what might be called "labor mining" farms. These are farms which draw heavily on labor from elsewhere but which, like the mines, bring in only "labor units"—that is, working men—as migrants. (These are found particularly in the western Cape and parts of Natal.)

In addition to the various aspects already mentioned, there is one further matter regarding agriculture which should not be overlooked in this context. It relates in particular to master-servant relations on the farms and, more generally, to the political future of all those living in agricultural areas. There are reports of crop burnings and other forms of arson which point to the possibility of widespread worker resistance in the agricultural sector. These developments, embryonic at present, may yet emerge as more significant than changes elsewhere in the economy.

LABOR IN MANUFACTURING

There is not sufficient space to deal with all aspects of the labor market in manufacturing, and the focus here will be primarily on migration. There has been an enormous expansion of the migrant labor system in South African manufacturing over the past fifteen years. It is widely known that there is extensive migrant labor in the mining sector and that there is a good deal of migrant labor in the agricultural sector, but the dramatic shift over the past decade and a half has been the increase in the proportion of oscillating migration within the manufacturing labor market.

This shift seems to arise from an apparent contradiction within the South African political economy. The two main goals being pursued within South Africa are (1) economic growth, one consequence of which is urbanization, with more and more people being pulled into the expanding urban areas in Johannesburg, Cape Town, and Durban, and (2) "separate development," which is based on the idea of creating politically independent and (hopefully) economically viable "Black states" or "countries," such as the Transkei, Bophuthatswana, Kwazulu, or the Ciskei.

In order to pursue both goals, it is necessary that every Black in South Africa be a citizen of one of these "Black states," while at the same time Black men are employed in the "White" urban areas as workers. In the 1960s the implications of this policy became explicit first in the western Cape, which was used as the trial area for the policy; it was then applied more generally with the promulgation of general labor regulations in 1968. In the early 1960s government spokesmen made it clear that their policy was to try to clear the western Cape of Africans. This was to be done for a number of reasons, including the overall requirements of apartheid policy that the flow of Black labor to the cities should gradually be slowed down, halted, and then (by 1978) reversed. Also, with particular reference to the western Cape, it was felt that the apartheid policy could best begin there since Africans could be replaced by Coloreds if the government pursued an active Colored-labor-preference policy. Thus at the end of 1966 it was announced that the number of workers allowed in the western Cape was to be frozen, and that from the beginning of 1967 employers would be encouraged to reduce their employment of African workers by 5 percent per annum. Within the western Cape the immediate consequence of the announcement of the policy was a slowdown and ultimately a freeze on the building of new houses. In the first half of the 1960s approximately three thousand houses were built for African families in the western Cape and the Cape Town area; in the first half of the 1970s less than three hundred were built. Yet in terms of natural population growth of those African families already permanently established with rights to live in Cape Town, there was need for at least 280 to 300 new houses *each year*, apart from the increased demand for housing resulting from the continuing process of urbanization.

While the policy of driving the Black population into the Bantustans was being pursued relentlessly, the goal of economic growth was being sought no less arduously. During the 1960s and 1970s the economy of the western Cape grew substantially: the docks were expanded, large buildings were erected, new roads were laid, and the University of Cape Town embarked on an ambitious physical development program. As a consequence, more African workers were drawn into the area. Some planners had projected that the increased demand for labor could be met entirely from within the Colored community living around Cape Town, but in fact the needed labor could not be obtained from that source, and African contract workers were brought in on a temporary basis. In order to house these workers, employers were permitted to put up temporary hostels; built at the end of the 1960s, they were still in use a decade later. Between 1968 and 1974 the employment of African contract workers in Cape Town more than doubled. Within the construction industry alone, employment of such workers trebled, and within the government sector, where Colored labor-preference area policy was likely to have been most rigorously applied, the number of such workers more than quadrupled. Even allowing for the recent depression in the South African economy (particularly in the construction sector, where the number of African contract workers in Cape Town has fallen from 33,000 to 19,000 since 1975), the number of African contract workers in Cape Town seems to have increased substantially over the years 1966-1978. Parallel with this, the number of hostel beds has increased—first on a temporary basis, and then more permanently, with hostels being built by government, government employers, and private entrepreneurs and employers. But during the mid-1970s virtually no *family* housing was built for occupation by Africans. As a consequence many Black workers whose families had rights to be in town had as much difficulty finding accommodations as did the far greater number of workers whose families did not have such rights (despite the fact that the head of household was working in Cape Town).

It is against this background that the emergence during the mid-1970s of squatter settlements around Cape Town, such as Modderdam, Unibel, and Crossroads, can best be understood. These placed the government in a difficult position because of the conflict between Cape Town's need for African workers to develop its economy and the government policy that the families of such people should not be in or near the city. Indeed government policy was that the number of African workers themselves should have been substantially reduced rather than increased over the previous decade. According to the most reliable survey available, the average man living in Crossroads in 1977 had been working in Cape Town for approximately eighteen years, and the average housewife living in Crossroads had been in Cape Town for more than eleven years.[16]

Crossroads and other African squatter townships around Cape Town can be seen as serving three main functions. First, they enable contract workers who are supposed to be living in single-sex barracks to move to a place where they can build a shelter and live with their families. (In 1977 it was estimated that almost one quarter—23 percent—of the heads of household living in Crossroads were contract workers who were paying rent in the hostels or other single quarters in Cape Town. Twenty-two percent of these household heads living in Crossroads qualified to live permanently in Cape Town under Section 10(1)(b) of the Urban Areas Act, but their wives—with a few exceptions—did not qualify.) Second, they provide homes for those few families who qualify for housing but for whom, due to the freeze on housing development during the past decade, nothing is available. Third (and increasingly important), they provide employment for those who do not have jobs in the formal sector of the economy. It has been estimated that in South Africa it requires a capital investment of some R10,000 to create one job.[17] With the growing specter of unemployment and the rate of population growth considerably in excess of the rate of growth in employment, the importance of finding ways of creating jobs more cheaply becomes apparent. Evidence from Crossroads suggests that the squatter community is particularly successful in providing a base on which people can build jobs for themselves, whether as sellers of vegetables or second-hand clothes or as craftsmen of one sort or another—e.g., repairing motor cars, making tin trunks, knitting jerseys. It is obvious, but worth reemphasizing, that it is far easier for an unemployed person to create a job for himself in a squatter community such as Crossroads, where money is coming in from the nearby city, than in an isolated rural area where there is almost no cash flow at all.

The contradictions inherent in government policy became most apparent in Cape Town because the Colored-labor-preference-area policy had caused the government to pursue its policy of driving Africans out of the city more vigorously there than in other parts of the country even though Cape Town was five hundred miles from the nearest "homeland." The "homelands" are only a few miles distant from Pretoria and Durban, on the other hand, and it is possible for squatter communities to mushroom nearby without any apparent conflict with policy. As regards Johannesburg, the picture is by no means clear. How Soweto has been able to contain the population growth of the past decade without expansion of new housing is difficult to understand. The overcrowding in the cities is by all accounts horrific. Is it not likely that this was one of the factors behind the explosion of Soweto in 1976?

Within Cape Town the population pressures led to the mushrooming of squatter communities, to which the government response was force. In 1977 and early 1978 the squatter settlements of Modderdam and Unibel, which housed 25,000 people, were bulldozed flat, leaving behind an area that looked as though it had been bombed. During 1978 threats were repeatedly made both by officials and leading government spokesmen that Crossroads would also have to go. The implications were clear: without a change in policy, bulldozers or some equally destructive (though possibly less visible) form of force would be used against the settlements.

Even though the migrant labor system was deeply embedded in the South African political economy, it had become apparent by 1974 that there was intense debate within the National party about the possibility of adjusting government policy to allow a worker to bring his nuclear family to town with him, provided there was work for him in the city and that a house was available either from the government or from the employer; such a worker would be considered a foreigner whether he came from a country like Malawi or from one of the Bantustans.[18] This debate about the possibility of allowing the worker's family to come to town on a temporary basis while the breadwinner was at work came to a head over Crossroads, and with the appointment of Dr. Piet Koornhof as Minister of Plural Relations in October 1978, it seemed that there might be a shift in government policy in this area. After six months of intensive negotiations and due to a unique combination of grass-roots resistance and considerable international pressure, Koornhof early in April 1979 announced a plan for Crossroads which included the building of a new township in Cape Town and acceptance of the fact that not only contract workers would be allowed to settle in town with their families (so long as they had work), but also that self-employed craftsmen in the informal sector (and others providing services to the community) would be allowed to stay with their families.

It is too early to tell whether the new plan for Crossroads was merely an ad hoc grasping of a thorny international nettle or whether it marks the beginning of a fundamental shift in government policy away from a system of migrant labor "units" to one of migrant labor families allowed to live in the cities but classified as foreigners. However, the recommendations of the Riekert Commission of Inquiry suggest that the government is *not* about to embark on a new policy for migrants throughout the economy. The Riekert proposal that workers be allowed to bring their families to live with them near their place of work provided accommodation is available applies only to those men who possess rights of permanent residence in some other urban ("prescribed") area* and who wish to move, say, from Cradock to Port Elizabeth. Workers from the reserves will continue to have to live separate from their families.

THE SPECTER OF UNEMPLOYMENT

The specter of unemployment has grown larger and larger within southern Africa during the 1970s, particularly in the rural areas from which the industrializing South African economy has drawn so much labor for so long. A good deal of research has been undertaken into this matter.[19] It would be impossible to summarize here the mass of data provided in these studies, but it is perhaps useful to draw out some of the more salient features. At the macro level, bearing in mind all the difficulties involved in obtaining

*In terms of the Blacks (Urban Areas) Consolidation Act, 1945, as amended (Section 10(1)):

No Black shall remain for more than 72 hours in a prescribed area unless he produces proof in the manner prescribed that—

(a) he has, since birth, resided continuously in such area; or
(b) he has worked continuously in such area for one employer for a period of not less than 10 years or has lawfully resided continuously in such area for a period of not less than 15 years, and has thereafter continued to reside in such area and is not employed outside such area and has not during either period or thereafter been sentenced to a fine exceeding R500 or to imprisonment for a period exceeding six months; or
(c) such Black is the wife, unmarried daughter or son under the age at which he would become liable for the payment of general tax under the Black Taxation Act, 1969 (Act 92 of 1969), of any Black mentioned in paragraph (a) or (b) of this subsection and after lawful entry into such prescribed area, ordinarily resides with that Black in such area; or
(d) in the case of any other Black, permission so to remain has been granted by an officer appointed to manage a labour bureau in terms of the provisions of subsection (6) of section 22 of the Black Labour Act, 1964 (Act 67 of 1964), due regard being had to the availability of accommodation in a Black residential area.

The Riekert report is referring to men with rights in terms of Section 10(1) (a) or (b). In this connection it is not irrelevant to note that in terms of the Bantu Laws Amendment Act, No. 12 of 1978, the birthright to permanent urban residence in terms of Section 10(1)(a) of the Urban Areas Act will no longer be granted to any person who after the date of independence of a particular homeland was born of parents who are regarded as citizens of that homeland, irrespective of whether they live there or not (S.A. Institute of Race Relations, *Survey of Race Relations in South Africa 1978* [Johannesburg, 1979], p. 320).

accurate statistics, the estimates of unemployment and underemployment vary enormously. Charles Simkins estimated that in 1977 approximately 2.3 million people (or 22 percent of the labor force) were underemployed, while P.J. van der Merwe estimated that approximately 1.1 million were underemployed in 1976—less than one half of Simkins's estimate.[20] While it can be argued that Simkins's figure is too high, it is relatively easy to show that van der Merwe's figure is probably too low.

Despite these not inconsiderable differences, there is agreement that unemployment has increased and is increasing. For Simkins the unemployment picture has been a steady rising secular trend. All observers agree that unemployment has increased significantly during the past five or six years, but Simkins goes further than others in arguing that Black unemployment was running at approximately 19 percent even through the 1960s. Van der Merwe disputes this finding. In January 1978 the South African Department of Statistics estimated African unemployment to be 634,000—i.e., 12.4 percent of the labor force. Most observers argue that this is too low a figure, not least because it excludes the Transkei and Bophuthatswana.[21]

It seems generally agreed that, at this stage, there is little further research that can be done at a macro level to get a clearer picture of unemployment. What is now needed are better sample surveys (it is hoped that the current population survey now being conducted at regular intervals by the Department of Statistics in Pretoria will provide a wealth of new information)[22] and in-depth micro studies to provide a more detailed picture of the nature and implications of the unemployment. Probably the best of the micro studies so far is one by Lieb Loots which was carried out in two areas—one urban (Pretoria) and one rural (some 200 kms. from Pretoria).[23] In his sample Loots found that unemployment among urban African men was running at 19 percent while for women in the Pretoria township it was no less than 35 percent. In the rural areas unemployment among African men was approximately 15 percent and among women, 21 percent. Thus Loots found unemployment rates in the rural areas were slightly lower for both men and women than in the urban areas, but that in both areas unemployment for women was much worse than it was for men. It appears that the unemployed are generally young and, among women, highly educated. Relatively low unemployment was found among technical and professional men.

Two points should be emphasized here. First, from the statistics it is apparent that unemployment is not a new phenomenon, although it increased markedly during the 1970s. If this is so, then there is need to explain the paradox of substantial unemployment side by side with acute shortages of South African labor in some sectors which forced the mines to choose between recruiting further afield and raising wages. The most likely explanation is that many of the unemployed are not eligible to work in the mines because they are women, or are too old, or cannot pass the various health tests, or for a variety of other reasons, including fear of working underground. Nevertheless, the paradox points to the need for more detailed research in order for us to understand better what is happening.

The second point relates to the fact that the political boundaries of the region do not correspond with the economic ones. For a hundred years of industrial revolution, labor has been drawn to the mines and the economic core of southern Africa from a "labor catchment area" that extends far beyond the boundaries of the Republic of South Africa. This has resulted in what Duncan Clarke has called the "International Division of the Labour Reserve."[24] Power in the southern African region is now structured in such a way that much of the growing unemployment in the mining and industrial urban areas can be dealt with by the simple expedient of drafting the unfortunate unemployed out of the cities to the rural areas (excluding the "White" farms) whence they came. It is politically easier for this to be done where the rural areas lie beyond some political boundary, as is the case with men coming from Mozambique, Lesotho, Botswana, Swaziland, Malawi, Zimbabwe-Rhodesia, and elsewhere. But these are not the only political boundaries in the region. Not the least of the consequences of the implementation of the Bantustan policy over the past two decades—in Pretoria's eyes at least—has been that it makes it easier to send unemployed Africans from the urban areas back to rural areas within South Africa on the grounds that these rural areas are (or are fast becoming) politically independent countries.

Some idea of the political complexity of a situation where political and economic boundaries do not correspond can be seen in the consequences of the downturn in employment in South Africa during the early 1970s. Because of the fall in employment, particularly in the construction sector, Africans in Cape Town were willing to take jobs in the gold mines. This was a major social change. For generations Cape Town had been a relatively high wage area to which many Blacks migrated after working during their youth in the mines, and before this there had almost never been a movement of workers from Cape Town toward the mines. In the early 1970s, however, the mines actively recruited labor in Cape Town. This not only helped to alleviate the problem of Black unemployment in South Africa (and also in Lesotho and Swaziland), but also made South Africa less dependent on countries further afield. There is some evidence that the pressure to reduce the number of Mozambicans in the mines came primarily from the South African side. The reduction in employment of Mozambicans from 100,000 to 45,000 (see Table 1 above) was useful to South Africa in that it reduced African unemployment within South Africa by 55,000 and also reduced the political risks inherent in employing so large a proportion of the mine labor force from an area now ruled by a revolutionary government. For Mozambique's new Frelimo government, however, pressure to reduce the flow of labor into South Africa placed it in an extremely difficult position. On the one hand, such a restriction was entirely consistent with Frelimo's well-articulated policy to reduce economic links with apartheid; on the other hand, for a government desperately in need of foreign exchange and with an economy weakened by the sudden withdrawal of large numbers of managerial and technical personnel, the loss of employment opportunities within South Africa, relatively well paid by Mozambique standards, would be seriously damaging.

In this context, when assessing the political economy of southern Africa it is important to understand the bias in capital accumulation in the region during the past century as a consequence of the oscillating pattern of labor migration. For example, labor has been supplied from Lesotho to the diamond mines of Kimberley and the gold mines of the Witwatersrand and the Orange Free State which has helped to generate growth in these areas. The mines have been developed, factories and shops have been established, and tax revenue has been generated which has been used to build schools, roads, and other basic infrastructure. However, because they were migrant laborers, the workers who contributed to this growth did not settle with their families in the areas where the growth was taking place. Thus when during the 1960s the mineowners decided to abolish the migrant labor system in the diamond mines, and the government permitted only South African Blacks with rights to permanent residence in Kimberley to remain with their families, the people of Lesotho suddenly lost the right of access to an area which they, their fathers, and their grandfathers helped to develop. Similarly, reducing to a minimum the links between Mozambique and South Africa would be against the trend of an historical development which has bound the two areas together as part and parcel of the same economy. In the long run it might be correct for Frelimo to reduce labor links with South Africa, but is it the best policy in the short run? Certainly it would be very painful.

Another way of examining this problem is to consider what policy would be most advisable for a future government of Zimbabwe regarding labor being supplied to the South African gold mines. Should a new government halt recruiting and refuse to supply labor to the Witwatersrand, or should it allow current practice to continue? Among the arguments for permitting mine workers to continue to go to South Africa would be that they help to earn valuable foreign exchange, that the wage rates there are likely to be three or four times what could be earned in Zimbabwe, and that it would help to reduce unemployment in Zimbabwe. But one of the long-term consequences of such migration is that Zimbabwe would develop a dependency on South Africa which would be likely to increase Zimbabwe's vulnerability to South African pressure.

The one country in southern Africa that could be reasonably independent of South Africa is Namibia, which does not have the symbiotic labor relationship with South Africa that Lesotho, Botswana, Swaziland, Mozambique, and (increasingly) Zimbabwe have. A fundamental dimension of the politics of southern Africa in the last two decades, as the students of Soweto have so acutely noted, is that the South African government has been developing a strategy to rob Black South Africans of their access to the accumulated wealth of South Africa—not least in the form of employment opportunities and tax revenue—by turning the Transkei and other labor reserves into independent countries.

I am not one of those who believe that fundamental reform is inevitable in South Africa over the next five or ten years. There seems to be an immense stability (perhaps "durability" is a better word) of the South African system provided the area does not become the locus of international conflict. Nevertheless, within the framework of apartheid there have been a number of changes in the labor market and in the field of labor relations. The purpose of this paper has been to highlight some of the more important of these on the assumption that to understand what is happening in southern Africa it is important to analyze the underlying labor structure. In my attempts to contribute to that understanding I am only too conscious of the fact that I can do no more than "peer through a glass darkly."

BLACK TRADE UNIONS IN SOUTH AFRICA SINCE WORLD WAR II

Philip Bonner

In mid-1976 only about 75,000 of the well over a million South African Africans employed in industry were dues-paying members of trade unions.[1] African trade unions thus represented only a tiny fraction of the African work force, and to all outward appearances were puny and weak. Yet, paradoxically, it was at this time that the South African government chose to announce the establishment of a commission of enquiry into labor legislation—the Wiehahn Commission—to recommend reforms in South Africa's industrial relations structure, including (by implication) the possibility of recognition of African trade unions. Why, after so many years, has the government chosen to relent on its much publicized opposition to Black trade unions,[2] and what purpose is recently proposed labor legislation designed to fulfill? This paper will seek to answer these questions by way of an historical review of labor relations in South Africa since World War II, beginning with an outline of the country's industrial relations structure.

The basic structure of South Africa's industrial relations was established by the Industrial Conciliation Act of 1924 and the Wage Act of 1925. With relatively minor modifications, this structure remains in place today.[3*] Both pieces of legislation were passed in the wake of the 1922 White Mineworkers Strike, which reached almost insurrectionary proportions before being bloodily put down, and both have been widely interpreted as a victory for White labor of an order similar to the electoral victory which swept the Nationalist/Labour Pact government to power in 1924.[4] In reality they were not. It is true that the Industrial Conciliation Act granted full recognition to White unions and set up industrial councils of trade union-

*Alterations have included the Bantu Labour Act of 1953, which allowed for the establishment of works committees and specifically denied Black workers the right to strike, and the Industrial Conciliation Act of 1956, which split racially mixed trade unions—i.e., those composed of Indians, Coloreds, and Whites—into separate racial groupings and imposed job reservation (i.e., reserved certain job categories for Whites). (See M. Horrell, *South African Trade Unionism* [Johannesburg, 1961], pp. 27-33, 93-95.)

ists and employers which could negotiate industry-wide agreements—clear gains for the White trade union movement. On the other hand, the elaborate negotiation and conciliation machinery set up by these acts was firmly biased in favor of employers and severely restricted the unions' right to strike, which is after all the only real sanction a union can employ. Worse still, the practice of settling disputes of all kinds within industrial councils led to a bureaucratization of trade union leadership, increasing the distance between officials and union rank and file.[5] As a result, White trade union membership declined, and many trade unions degenerated into little more than benefit societies, to the extent that management began to encourage trade union membership as a means of securing a better disciplined work force and wider adherence to the agreements the trade union leadership had signed.[6] All these factors have a bearing on the thinking of the Wiehahn Commission.

Black workers gained nothing from the legislation. They were denied participation in recognized trade unions—more specifically, they were excluded from the category of "employee" as defined in the Industrial Conciliation Act. At best their wages and working conditions were set by industrial councils or wage boards, where they might obtain some indirect representation; at worst they were set by individual employers or by the state, with whom they had no say at all. Moreover, while African trade unions were not made illegal, their ability to act was severely curtailed by Masters and Servants legislation which laid down criminal penalties for the breaking of a contract, by pass laws which forced people to take work under unfavorable conditions and provided machinery for prosecuting and deporting those who would not work, and by the migrant labor system.[7] The combination of these and other related structural factors made African trade unions next to impossible to organize in mining and agriculture.

It is in the context of this labor relations structure that African trade unions have painfully emerged. The earliest significant African labor organization was the Industrial and Commercial Workers Union (ICU). Founded in 1919, the ICU grew by leaps and bounds until, by 1927, it was one hundred thousand strong and had branches stretching from the Cape to Southern Rhodesia. For all its numerical strength, however, the ICU was a weak, unstructured, and—in any one area—ephemeral body. Organized as a general rather than an industrial union—that is, recruiting members at random rather than systematically by industrial sector—and operating as much as a political as an industrial body, it reflected not so much increasing industrialization and urbanization as mounting distress in the African reserves.[8] In the 1920s, secondary industry had not yet been established on any appreciable scale in South Africa, which meant that the ICU had no significant industrial base.[9] On the other hand, the underdevelopment and impoverishment of the reserves was becoming gradually more acute, and the position of the labor tenantry on the farms was becoming increasingly depressed.[10] It was to this constituency that the ICU primarily appealed, assuming the character of a composite populist movement that bound together a wide range of disparate elements subject to these strains. Like the adherents of populist movements generally, these were groups who were basically losers in the process of economic change—people who were being squeezed off the land but could find no permanent place in an industrial milieu.[11] Given this situation they were, not surprisingly, extremely difficult to protect, and posed problems the ICU was never able to resolve. Instead it tended to take the easy way out by making vague populist appeals—often with a pronounced millenarian flavor. It is no accident that their most effective leader was A.W.G. Champion of Natal, who excelled in this respect. Champion pulled off his first major political coup in 1926 by successfully opposing the "dipping" of Africans in Durban.[12]*

As the experience of the ICU shows, there was no real social base for Black industrial trade unionism in the 1920s, and this continued to be the case until early in the following decade. Then in 1932 South Africa followed Britain off the gold standard, the price of gold went up, and a large part of the increased profits accruing went either directly or indirectly to stimulate manufacturing growth. As a result, the manufacturing sector, which in terms of the gross national product had already overtaken agriculture two years before, began to catch up with mining as well, finally exceeding it in 1943. In two bursts of growth—1933 to 1939 and 1940 to 1946 (the latter promoted by the protection from foreign competition and increased production arising from the war)—national income almost trebled, with the number of manufacturing establishments rising from 6,543 in 1933 to 8,505 in 1939 and 9,999 in 1946, and gross value of output increasing by 140 percent in the first period and 141 percent during the second.[13]

At the same time there was a shift of emphasis within manufacturing itself. Even before World War II, the industrial group

*"Dipping" was the compulsory disinfection of Africans arriving from rural areas by immersing them in a tank filled with an antiseptic solution—similar to the procedure used for cattle.

comprising metal products, machinery, and transport had become the largest segment of the manufacturing sector, and this was reflected in the increased capital intensity of manufacturing as a whole: capital/labor ratios rose from £794 to £981 per worker between 1932 and 1939, and reached £1,156 per worker in 1946. The implications for Black labor and for Black trade union organization were far-reaching and profound. The growth of manufacturing required both a much larger reservoir of labor and a reservoir of labor of a quite different kind. Between 1933 and 1939, for example, an additional 240,000 Africans entered the industrial work force (if trade and commerce are included, the increase was in the order of 400,000), almost doubling the size of the urban African labor force.[14] What growing capital intensity of manufacturing represented, moreover, was increased mechanization of production and the collapse of the skilled/unskilled division of labor, which had largely coincided with the racial division of labor, into a single category of semiskilled operatives or machine-minders.[15] The significance of this change for African labor should not be exaggerated —even in the industrial sector the vast bulk of African labor remained unskilled.[16] But where it took place, the increased mechanization had far-reaching repercussions. Semiskilled work required a much tighter work discipline than was deemed compatible with continued migrant labor, and it opened up opportunities for African women's labor, which had previously been confined to domestic service. Between them these changes resulted in greater stabilization and urbanization of the African population.[17] The urban African population trebled between 1921 and 1946 (by which time one in four Africans were located in urban areas), and the masculinity ratio shifted from 5:1 in 1921 to 3:1 in 1946—a key indicator of growing permanent urbanization.[18]

These enormous changes in the structure of the labor market and economy ushered in a new era of African trade unionism. African workers were more stabilized, more committed to an urban milieu, and more likely to seek improvements in conditions within it rather than without. At the same time they had the determination and muscle to press their demands. Greater stabilization and proletarianization bred a heightened working class consciousness and weakened so-called tribal divisions sustained by migrant labor and the structure of traditional controls. Equally, increased skill and training brought increased bargaining power. Laborers were no longer simply interchangeable units; money had been invested in their job training, and they had the capacity to disrupt production because they could not be instantly replaced. For much of World War II they were also regularly in short supply, both in an absolute sense (this was one of the few times in South African history when there was more or less full employment) and in relation to the available pool of skills. As industry expanded and large numbers of skilled Whites were drained off by the war, there was a massive shortage of skilled and semiskilled workers in South Africa[19] which could only be made up by the wholesale introduction of Blacks. In this environment African trade unions flourished.

In the mid-1930s a Trotskyite named Max Gordon helped establish a group of African unions on the Witwatersrand, and these grew in power and popularity during the war. By 1940 Gordon and his lieutenants had successfully organized about twenty African unions, claiming a total membership of between 23,000 and 26,000. These were joined in 1942 by a largely Communist-organized group of trade unions in the combined Congress of Non-European Trade Unions (CNETU) so that by 1945, at the peak of its influence and numbers, CNETU would claim a membership of 158,000, grouped in 119 unions and embracing 40 percent of the 390,000 employed in commerce and manufacturing.[20] Accompanying these changes there was a dramatic rise in worker militancy and wages. In the ten years 1930-1939, 71,078 man-days were lost in the African labor force, averaging 2.7 days per striker, while in the six years 1940-1945, 220,205 man-days were lost at an average of 4.2 days per striker. At the same time, real wages of African workers soared as trade unions demanded improvements and a measure of recognition. Between 1930/31 and 1939/40 real earnings rose by 9.8 percent, while in the next six years they leaped by a staggering 51.8 percent—so much so indeed that World War II was one of the few periods in South African history in which the Black/White wage gap narrowed.[21]

In retrospect, the war years and the period immediately after provided the best chance that African trade unionism had in South Africa. The unions' bargaining position was strong, as is reflected in the increases in wages and de facto recognition they secured; there was a broad working class ferment in South Africa, as is evidenced by the bus boycotts and anti-pass law demonstrations which punctuated the period, as well as by the extraordinarily militant squatter movement that developed on the Rand; and the unions were faced by a state that was prepared to make certain adjustments in industrial relations because of the particular circumstances of the war.[22] First, wartime production was booming, and the government was anxious not to disrupt either this or the South African contribution to the war effort; second, there were divisions within the government between those representing broadly the industrial and the agricultural sectors (agriculture at this point was suffering desperately from a shortage of labor); and third, there was a general Afrikaner opposition to the war effort as reflected in the often violent reaction of the *Ossewa Brandwag.*[23] Weakened as it was, the state was in no position to oppose a determined campaign for recognition by the African trade unions, as is indicated by various concessions made during this period, such as a relaxation in the pass laws and the withdrawal of fare increases on transport, and by various proposals made to recognize African trade unions. The Native Affairs Commission of 1939/40, for example, while regretting the growth of African trade unions concluded that

> the existence of a number of Native trade unions demands some form of recognition. The Commission has accordingly advised that this should be given: but, such recognition should be in a form which will prevent the native unions concerned from becoming the dupes of Europeans who seek to exploit their grievances for their own profit. What is necessary is that some official channel shall be established through which native trade unions can bring into official cognisance any grievances they are labouring under, and, if well founded, have them remedied, rather than leave them to adopt the dangerous advice of some unbalanced semi-educated natives who batten on native ignorance and cupidity.[24]

For neither industry nor Black trade unions was this going far enough. In 1943 both the Witwatersrand Mine Labour Commission and the Transvaal Chamber of Industry recommended recognition of African trade unions, while a survey of the attitudes of industrialists conducted in the same year went so far as to assert that

> Whatever progress has been made in the efficiency of our labour in this country it has been greater where management has had a unified and organised body of workers to deal with. And if the natives are to enter industry in ever-increasing numbers, it is clear that their being organised and disciplined in proper unions is an indispensable prerequisite to their development as stable and efficient workers.[25]

This probably represents the high water mark of pressure for recognition of African trade unions, and the reason no further concessions were elicited may well lie with the union movement itself. Many militant African trade unions were led or strongly influenced by South African Communist Party (SACP) activists, and from the time of the Soviet Union's entry into the war these had a special interest in sustaining the war effort. This is not to say that they took up a mindlessly collaborationist position toward the South African state; on the contrary, they were prominent in leading anti-pass law and other anti-government campaigns during this period.[26] Nevertheless, on the crucial issue of the disruption of industrial production and African trade union recognition they hung back, and an historic opportunity may have been lost.[27]

For some while after the war the African trade unions remained relatively influential and strong, even though membership was declining from its 1944-45 levels.[28] It was in somewhat belated recognition of this that the government drafted the Industrial Council (Natives) Bill of 1947, which provided for limited African trade union recognition. And when this proved unacceptable to both the unions and much of manufacturing, the government appointed the Industrial Legislation Commission of Enquiry—the Botha Commission.[29] The Botha Commission went even further than the Industrial Council Bill in the direction of trade union recognition. It recognized the "danger" that trade union recognition might ultimately give African workers the power to make political demands, but responded with the argument that "If political demands could be enforced through the medium of trade unions recognised and controlled by the government, this is far more likely in the case of unrecognised and uncontrolled unions as confirmed by the activities of the I.C.U." With this in mind the commission recommended a two-stage process of recognition whereby every union would be certified but not necessarily recognized—the key advantage of this proposal being that it "eliminates the necessity of prohibiting trade union activities in certain circumstances." Finally the commission recommended the prohibition of general unions and trade union coordinating bodies like the CNETU, which might take on a political complexion, and suggested that unions for agricultural workers, domestics, and mine workers should be certified but never recognized.[30]

The United party and Labour party supported these recommendations, but in the meantime the political scene had been radically transformed. In 1948 the Nationalists had come to power and set their face firmly against African trade union recognition. In 1950 the Suppression of Communism Act, which was directed primarily against the trade unions, was enacted. Under its terms a trade union official deemed to be a Communist (within an extraordinarily broad definition) could be ordered to resign. This was followed by even more draconian legislation under which people engaged in activities frowned upon by the state could be arbitrarily banned or detained. In this way, by 1956 fifty-six trade union officials had been ordered to resign, and at the height of Black political agitation in 1960, two-thirds of the Witwatersrand local committee of the South African Congress of Trade Unions (SACTU) were detained.[31] At the same time, African trade unionism was assailed on a number of other fronts. In 1953 the Bantu Labour (Settlement of Disputes) Act made strikes by Africans illegal and set up a works committee system as the only recognized organ of African industrial representation. In 1955, representatives of African trade unions were denied access to wage board hearings, thereby losing the important right to call for and influence wage determinations, which was one of the weapons used by Gordon's unions in the 1930s. And in 1959 the Bantu Labour Act was amended to make stop orders for African trade unions illegal.[32] In addition, throughout this period the position of the African working class was being weakened by a panoply of apartheid legislation which entrenched migrant labor and undercut African urban rights, exposing Africans to deportation to "homeland" areas and to the prospect of permanent unemployment if they involved themselves in trade unions or any other form of worker agitation.[33]

As the effect of these measures began to tell, industry's demands for African trade union recognition began to fade. In 1953, manufacturing representatives who only three years before had attacked the government's industrial relations policy because it did not provide for adequate union recognition were prepared to accept the Native Labour Bill of the Nationalists, which merely provided for a works committee system. Similarly, while uncertainty and alarm flickered briefly concerning the state's ability to contain industrial conflict after SACTU appeared to gather strength in the late 1950s, this subsided as soon as SACTU was effectively repressed.[34] This remained industry's attitude toward African labor until the Durban strikes of 1973.

In the interim the main representatives of African labor were the Trade Union Council of South Africa (TUCSA) and SACTU. Both of these trade union confederations came into being in the mid-1950s in the course of a general realignment of the trade union movement in response to the government's industrial legislation—particularly the amended Industrial Conciliation Act of 1956, which segregated registered trade unions into racial groupings. The need for unity in the face of what was perceived by many to be an attack on the whole trade union movement, White as well as Black, led to the exclusion of African trade unions from TUCSA and the setting up of a rival Black trade union federation—SACTU.[35] It should be noted, however, that SACTU was not merely a response to exclusion. From the beginning SACTU thought that industrial relations and politics in South Africa could not be divorced, and they worked closely with the African National Congress (ANC)—the chief African nationalist organization—and the Congress Alliance (a broad front of African, Indian, Colored, and White congresses) for political change. As the statement of policy submitted to the first annual conference of SACTU pointed out:

> The SA Congress of Trade Unions is conscious of the fact that the organising of the mass of the workers for these demands [i.e., basic worker rights] . . . is inextricably bound up with a determined struggle for political rights and for liberation from all oppressive laws and practices. Every move of the workers for their basic rights in South Africa is hampered by general legislation affecting their right of movement, their right of domicile, their lack of political representation. Every struggle of the workers for higher wages, for better working conditions, even for the smallest advance in factory conditions . . . is immediately met by the full force of the Police State organised to restrict every civil human right.[36]

These were sentiments with which one could hardly take issue, and once translated into political action they met with the full repressive arsenal of the state. Trade union leaders were banned and later detained in the hundreds—especially in the aftermath of the shootings at Sharpeville and the formation of Umkhonto we Sizwe—the military wing of the ANC—in which SACTU militants were involved. Between 1960 and 1966, 160 SACTU officials were arrested or detained, and by 1965 SACTU had virtually ceased to exist.[37] SACTU itself was never officially banned, however, even though the ANC and the Pan African Congress (PAC), which split off from the ANC in 1959, were proscribed in 1961, and SACTU continued to be closely associated with the exile liberation struggle. This provides an important insight into the South African government's current political predicament. In order to curry favor with the outside world and to avoid sanctions from international organized labor, they feel obliged to respect the right of freedom of association for workers—at least formally. The emergence of nonpolitical trade unionism in the 1970s has presented them with a major political problem, since these unions represent a powerful force operating outside the constraints of the existing industrial relations structure which cannot be attacked in the same way as before.

SACTU's virtual extinction then can be attributed to its participation in the liberation struggle and the consequent repressive action of the state. This raises serious questions for current African trade unionism. In particular, could such an outcome have been avoided, and does a similar fate await African worker organizations today? To the first question, Edward Feit's recent study on SACTU seems to give the answer "Yes," and to suggest fundamental weaknesses in the SACTU leadership's thinking and strategy.[38] Here we must consider the factors underlying Feit's analysis if we are to assess the validity of his conclusions. In the thinking of SACTU's leaders, it seems possible that two ideological currents combined: one was the idea of national revolution and the other the notion of the limits of trade union consciousness. Wedded to the idea of a proletarian revolution, the SACTU leadership, like that of the SACP, believed that it could take place only after a national bourgeois revolution; consequently the trade unions were to be incorporated in that struggle and subordinated to national revolutionary ends.[39] A second strand in their thinking may have reinforced the first (admittedly a highly speculative suggestion). Since Lenin, there has been a tendency in socialist thinking to be skeptical of the limits of trade union consciousness even for limited national revolutionary ends. Trade union consciousness, as Lenin argued in *What Is to Be Done?*, tends to be sectional and economistic in character, being capable only of pressing for minor improvements in conditions—that is, incorporation within capitalism on slightly better terms rather than overthrow of the structure of exploitation as a whole.[40] This idea seems to have been transferred to SACTU's analysis of the national struggle, leading them to subordinate the trade union movement to the national liberation struggle, and—if one accepts Feit's account—the consequences were catastrophic.[41] Organizers' energies were continually diverted to political causes, and vast amounts of energy and credibility were expended on political stay-aways (from work)—like the ones in protest against the non-enfranchisement of Blacks in the 1958 election and against the 1961 referendum to decide if the Union should become a republic. These had negligible chances of success and tended to neutralize or dissipate such wider consciousness as had developed in the unions' struggle to improve conditions. Again, while formal adherence was expressed to the notion of concentrating union organization energies on strategic sectors of the economy (especially transport and metal), this was never in practice carried out (or when tried was too late). Instead there was a tendency to bring as many workers into the movement as possible, no matter how inadequately or incoherently they were organized—even to the point of sanctioning general unions which were subject to many of the same weaknesses as the ill-fated ICU. The results were predictable: the new unions were often ill-organized and sometimes corrupt; workers in them got negligible support in their struggle for better working conditions; and their support fell away.[42] Thus rather than SACTU providing the disciplined battalions of workers for the national struggle, its prior concentration on politics threw this constituency away.

There is obviously some substance to these charges. SACTU did divert resources to political causes; it did neglect strategic areas of the economy; it did dissipate its energies in too many directions. But to dwell on the alleged failures of SACTU is to read history backwards and to uproot SACTU's struggle from its historical context; restored to its political context SACTU appears in a more favorable light. The mid-1950s in South Africa was a period of economic recession, which in the prevailing political climate made protection of African workers' material conditions a difficult task. The enactment of job reservation in 1956, which gravely weakened Black workers' industrial leverage, was one consequence, as the state sought to protect the White working class from the effects of the economic downturn. So too was a 5 percent drop in the real earnings of Black workers which occurred at this time.[43] Indeed this 5 percent figure may well understate the real drop in African earnings, for the Black working class during this period was faced with a veritable total assault on its institutions and material conditions. Forced removals from urban housing, increased bus and train fares, increased taxes, and increased rents were all heaped on Black workers, and there is no indication that Black wages in any way kept up. The Black workers' response presented SACTU with a further dilemma. A groundswell of popular resistance to these measures developed, which was only partly directed through existing political and trade union channels. The question now became whether SACTU (and the ANC) should let this wave of opposition sweep past them and perhaps expend itself in diffuse and fruitless resistance against the state, or whether they should seek to direct the popular movement into a more effective and sustained form of resistance. Not surprisingly they chose the latter course of action, with SACTU attempting to capture the spirit of the 1957 Alexandra bus boycott in a mass organizational drive. Here is at least part of the genesis of SACTU's populist position.[44]*

The SACTU unions did not seriously neglect the interests of previously organized workers during this period. SACTU, it should be remembered, was a trade union *confederation*, and its appropriate sphere of action was matters of concern to all affiliates, which were often political, and the organization of the unorganized. Affiliate unions, on the other hand, catered more directly to the interests of their own members in conventional trade union ways. It is presumably some testimony to their success that they achieved an increase in membership from about 20,000 in 1955 to 53,323 in 1961.[45]

It would be a mistake, however, to underestimate the difficulties the SACTU unions faced. In addition to the economic recession, there was anti-union legislation enacted by the state. It can be argued that without some access to recognized industrial relations machinery, it is next to impossible for workers to secure even minimal benefits and improvements of conditions. All independent access of this kind was removed by the state in the late 1940s and early 1950s. The only alternative to confrontation with individual employers was to secure the support of registered unions, which was the strategy of one group of unregistered unions. First they operated through a liaison committee with TUCSA; then with the help of TUCSA and the International Confederation of Free Trade Unions (ICFTU), they constituted themselves into the Federation of Free African Trade Unions of South Africa (FOFATUSA). When TUCSA opened its doors to Africans, FOFATUSA became directly affiliated with it, but only after agreeing to meet certain conditions—namely, not to jeopardize the interests of the parent

*For SACTU's response to this wave of militancy, see the Presidential Address to the Second Annual Conference of SACTU, where he refers to "the heroic unity of the bus boycotters in the Transvaal" and argues that "failure on our part to act as the spearhead of the working class in its fight for immediate wage increases and a happier life can only lead to the defeat of the workers and the disintegration of the magnificent unity that exists today," and the Report of the General Secretary to the Fourth Annual Conference of SACTU, where he admits that "the organising of more workers into effective new trade unions has not kept pace with the degree of consciousness prevalent among workers."

union (TUCSA), especially in regard to job allocation, and to be satisfied with only minimal gains.

The dilemma of the African trade union movement at this point (and to some extent today) could therefore be expressed as follows: only the unions which accept control and a subordinate relationship to parent registered trade unions can obtain gains for their members and hence retain the support of their membership. Militant unions not prepared to accept control are driven into the realm of politics, but their lack of recognition ensures that they cannot secure the gains for their members that will enable them to become a strong organized force, which means that their political activity can be readily contained by the repressive apparatus of the state.[46]

With the crushing of SACTU in the early 1960s, there was a period of relative quiescence in South Africa's industrial relations. Whereas between 1955 and 1960 there had been an average of seventy-six strikes a year, there were only sixteen strikes in 1962 and seventeen in 1963. The level of strike activity increased between 1965 and 1970, but worker militancy remained appreciably damped down.[47] In part this can be attributed to extreme government repression, but other factors were an average increase in real income for Blacks in manufacturing of 2.4 percent a year between 1960 and 1971 as a result of economic recovery, and the government's policy of pushing higher wage determinations to disarm economic discontents.[48] In 1973, however, the pattern of labor relations dramatically changed. In the interim the differential between White and Black wages had steadily widened, and the wage increases that had been given in 1972 were rapidly being eroded by galloping inflation. The upshot was a classic crisis of rising expectations, reinforced by a fading of the memory of government repression. A wave of strikes rolled across Natal involving upwards of 60,000 workers.[49]

These strikes proved extraordinarily successful. They were illegal, but there was no way in which the police could imprison 60,000 workers. Nor could they arrest the so-called agitators or ring leaders, because the workers consistently refused to elect bargaining committees whose members could be singled out for arrest.[50] Consequently, workers were able to extract increased wages from employers, and their earnings were raised throughout South Africa by as much as 20 percent.[51] The successful confrontation, moreover, gave a boost to working class militancy and union organization. During 1973 and 1974 there were more than 200 strikes a year involving Africans, reaching a peak of 374 in 1974—the second highest strike total for one year in Africa at the time.[52] In addition, all but a handful of the approximately twenty-five African trade unions now in existence were organized in the three-year period 1973-1975.[53]

At present these unregistered African trade unions break down into five distinct groups:

1. Parallel unions.
2. The Black Allied Workers Union (BAWU).
3. Urban Training Project unions on the Witwatersrand.
4. Trade Union Advisory and Coordinating Council (TUACC) unions in Natal and the Council of Industrial Workers of the Witwatersrand.
5. The Western Province Workers Advice Bureau in Cape Town.

To what extent have these unions confronted or escaped the dilemma of African trade unions pointed to earlier? The parallel unions we have already discussed. BAWU bears a family resemblance to its predecessor organizations—the ICU and SACTU. Like the ICU it is organized on a communal rather than a factory basis, and is essentially a populist movement; like SACTU it is characterized by militant rhetoric, has a strong political orientation, and is closely affiliated with the "Black Consciousness" movement; like both (but particularly like SACTU), it has been hounded out of existence by the authorities for its political activities, with the possible exception of a small center at Newcastle in Natal.[54]

The other three union groups follow what they consider to be a more sophisticated strategy. Each as a cardinal point of policy eschews party political connections and confines itself to trade union problems. Within these limits, however, deep-seated differences of policy have arisen. The Urban Training Project unions, for example, place a heavy emphasis on approaches to management, sometimes even before organizing workers from their factories. They appeal to management's enlightened self-interest, believing that it is sometimes a failure of communication which leads to management's hostile attitude toward African trade unions.[55] Their vision of the role of trade unions is comparable to that of the registered trade unions, emphasizing a relatively specialized and bureaucratized leadership, little mobilization of workers from below, and the benefit functions (e.g., funeral benefits) of trade unions—all of which is consistent with their strategy of emphasis on approaches to management.[56] Even this low-profile approach, however, has not let them escape the banning of three White officials at the end of 1976.[57]

The TUACC group, with associated unions on the Witwatersrand, employs what has been described as a mobilizing approach—i.e., they help workers to mobilize before approaching management to bargain or request recognition, and they help them to mobilize over factory issues to develop a sense of solidarity and strength and to maintain a high degree of participation in the union. This requires regular meetings and training of shop stewards to ensure against the amorphousness of the ICU and some of the more feeble SACTU unions. Hence a strategy of disciplined growth aimed at recognition from management rather than registration by the state is adopted, whatever the enthusiasm for unionization among the Black working class or the immediate political climate (as, for example, after Soweto). In this way they hope to escape the "dilemma" of the African trade union movement referred to earlier.

Finally, there is the Western Province Workers Advice Bureau (now the Western Province General Workers Union), which shares certain features with TUACC, but is distinguished by one crucial difference—it facilitates the establishment of factory committees which are connected to each other via a coordinating committee, but it does not organize industrial trade unions per se.[58]

Between them these union groups have fostered a sense of working class power among Africans which has presented a serious problem to the South African government. The government's first response after 1973 was to attempt to resuscitate the works committee system, a measure of whose uselessness was that by 1972 only twenty-four such committees were functioning.[59] In new legislation it added a liaison committee machinery to the works committee system, and embarked on a vigorous campaign with employers to ensure that new committees were formed. As a result, by August 1977 2503 liaison committees and 301 works committees had been set up.[60] That these were no substitute for African trade unions is attested by the number of strikes that have broken out in establishments where such committees have been formed, and by a glance at the structures of the committees themselves. Liaison committees are constituted at the instance of management, who organize the elections and who nominate up to 50 percent of the members; obviously they cannot be a forum for frank discussions among workers. Works committees, on the other hand, consist solely of workers, but like liaison committees have no provision for reporting back to workers or for regular elections. Moreover, despite victimization provisions, all workers on these committees are acutely conscious of their vulnerability vis-à-vis management, and so are rarely prepared to ventilate the grievances of the shop floor.[61] In short, as several years of experience have now shown, works committees do not work as channels of communication or machinery for bargaining.

A second response simultaneously introduced by the government was a limited right to strike. However, this was so bound up with restrictive provisions that it was extremely difficult to make use of. Even limited picketing was outside the law, as the only legal strike of African workers to take place subsequently in South Africa (at Armourplate) was to show.[62] Finally, in 1976 the government tried to extend the liaison/works committee system by allowing for industry-wide bargaining by the nonrepresentative representatives of these committees—the first fruits of which were the derisory increases awarded to Black workers in the recent Engineering Industrial Council Agreement.[63]* Employers took a different tack. First, they raised wages, as has been noted. Second, they identified lack of communication as one of their problems, with the result that since 1973 the personnel management industry has boomed and the Black personnel manager has become an increasingly familiar part of the industrial relations scene.[64]

None of these measures achieved what the government and employers hoped for. Despite the bannings of union officials at the end of 1976 and continued harassment since, the African trade unions continue to expand, and some multinational employers have granted limited recognition to them in defiance of the government's express wishes, which has exacerbated the African trade union problem for the government. Thus, although African trade unions are small and the level of strike activity has declined since the onset of the 1975-76 depression, the unions are still growing, and the government has enough historical perspective to know that there is the potential for virtually unlimited growth. One possible response to the situation is repression, but this is ruled out by two considerations. The first is that the unions are clearly nonpolitical and cannot easily be attacked on political grounds; the second is

*An additional clause was a secrecy provision relating to these agreements, which was designed to exclude African trade unions, but which when strictly interpreted seemed to outlaw the reporting back of works/liaison committees to the groups they represented. (See Metal and Allied Workers Union [Transvaal]. "Report on the Period July-December 1977," *Financial Mail*, 6 May 1977.)

that strong international pressures would be likely to ensue from any such repression.

South Africa has never been particularly afraid of the sanctions Western governments might bring to bear, since these have always been half-hearted and tempered by the knowledge of the profits that investments and trade with South Africa would continue to yield. Organized labor, on the other hand, is a different matter, and pressures from this quarter have continued to grow. Perhaps the most striking example is the boycott of South African coal undertaken in 1974 by the American Mineworkers Union and the dock workers of Mobile, Alabama, on the grounds that it was produced under indentured labor conditions. South Africa is supposed to react to such pressures by retreating deeper into the *laager*, according to the conventional wisdom, but in this case it moved with remarkable speed to abolish the penal provisions in its Masters and Servants legislation, which had been in its law books for 120 years.[65]* Other pressure from organized labor has also been felt—demands by Swedish trade unions that Swedish companies in South Africa grant recognition to African trade unions, an international campaign against the bannings of trade union officials at the end of 1976 orchestrated by the ICFTU, mounting pressure on British Leyland to deal with the Black Metal and Allied Workers Union, and so on.[66] None has had the dramatic effects of the American mineworkers' action, but taken together they have made the South African government feel increasingly boxed in.

To some extent the situation has also been taken out of the government's control by the actions of multinational employers. The multinationals' dominance of the South African economy has become increasingly pronounced in the last decade and a half, and these companies have been disposed toward African trade union recognition on the basis of their experience in other African countries.[67] At the same time, they are sensitive to international pressures and, in particular, the growing demand that they disinvest. In these circumstances the recognition of African trade unions has become an increasingly attractive option in that it helps deflect international

*It has been suggested that this involved no great sacrifice on the part of the South African government because these laws were redundant except for a small minority of farmers, and that the objective had already been achieved by other legislation (C. Bundy, "The Abolition of the Masters and Servants Act," *SALB* 2, 1 [May-June 1975]: 37-46). However, recent off-the-record statements by mining representatives indicate that in mining, at any rate, the impact has been profound.

pressure upon them to completely disengage from the South African economy. As a result, Ford and S.K.F. (a Swedish ball-bearing manufacturer) have granted limited recognition to African trade unions,[68] and the South African government has begun to worry that the situation is slipping out of its control.

It was this problem Nik Wiehahn was brought in by the government to resolve. Professor of Industrial Relations at the University of South Africa and advisor to the government, he was charged with the task of restructuring South Africa's industrial relations with a view to the incorporation and control of African industrial workers. A glance at the composition of the Wiehahn Commission suggests that it is less concerned with incorporation than control. Trumpeted abroad as a multiracial investigatory body, the commission includes only one Black on its panel—a Business Administration lecturer from UNISA—even though the main object of its investigations is Black trade unions and the African worker.[69] Leaks to the press have provided a preview of its likely recommendations, and these have largely borne out the impression that it is primarily concerned with control of Black trade unions.

What the commission is suggesting essentially boils down to four major proposals: first, that African workers should be granted trade union rights; second, that works councils should be established in each factory as a forum for multiracial, in-plant employer-employee liaison; third, that job reservation should be abolished; and fourth, that legal restrictions on striking should be continued, with a labor court established as the final arbitrator in industrial disputes.[70]

It might be asked: What is so objectionable about the Wiehahn proposals? After all, isn't union recognition what was desired all along? Closer examination, however, reveals a sinister intent. While African trade unions will gain recognition, which is a major step forward in anyone's terms, they will be locked into the same industrial council system which has emasculated White trade unions in the past. Their right to strike will be restricted even more thoroughly than under the 1924 Industrial Conciliation Act, they will have no control over job allocation (apprenticeship ratios, closed shop agreements), and they will be limited to periodic industry-wide negotiations and the operation of union benefit schemes.[71] In this way their officials will risk becoming bureaucratized and professionalized, tending to resolve every issue across the boardroom table with management and losing touch with the members they represent.

This tendency will be reinforced by the works council structure. In outward appearance the works council represents a significant advance, particularly when taken together with the provision to abolish job reservation. Works councils will be multiracial, legislative job reservation will be eliminated, and customary job reservation will be difficult to maintain. However, these works councils will almost certainly be dominated by White workers, because of their greater bargaining power and skills, and representation may even be weighted in their favor, as in the Rhodesian trade unions after 1963.[72] In addition, works councils are likely to operate in such a way as to restrict trade union participation, and will be able to enter into plant-based agreements with managements at the expense of such agreements as independent unions might seek to reach.

Finally, union registration will impose restrictions and may be selectively conferred. The procedure for recognition of African trade unions will involve some kind of certification, along the lines proposed at the end of World War II. Trade unions will be forbidden to take up political affiliation, and the militant unions will run the risk of either being left out in the cold or having their organizers banned or imprisoned should they refuse to toe the official line. In any case, the unions' position will be assailed under the terms of the new Fund Raising Act (1978), which redefines welfare organizations so as to include present-day African trade union organizations, and will therefore subject them to various new controls, among which may be the curtailment of financial assistance from outside (e.g., from international trade union organizations).[73]

In terms of the Wiehahn proposals, the future of independent African trade unionism looks problematical. Of course, there is the possibility that the Nationalist party caucus will find these proposals unacceptable, or that other pressure groups may succeed in getting them rejected or watered down, in the same way small Afrikaner businesses and White trade unions secured the modification of the draft Bantu Relations Regulations Amendment Act of 1975.[74] There is every indication, however, that the government would like to push them through. Should the government succeed, foreign business will give the legislation a rapturous response. It will, after all, provide a heaven-sent opportunity for them to escape from political and labor pressures at home. But while this may offer an interim solution, it is unlikely that it will help them for long. South Africa's migratory labor system persists, and criticism of it will continue. More important, African workers' aspirations will not be stifled by a system which is no co-option and all control. In the long run, foreign businesses would be better advised to espouse the cause of independent African trade unions as the only intermediary institution which offers hope of a nonviolent outcome to the South African industrial and political situation.

SOME IMPLICATIONS OF AFRICAN "HOMELANDS" IN SOUTH AFRICA

Newell M. Stultz

The term *homelands* in the context of the contemporary Republic of South Africa refers to ten African reserve areas—rural territories inhabited almost entirely by Africans following traditional patterns of life. The combined area of the homelands is nearly 60,500 square miles, which is only 12.4 percent of the total area of South Africa in 1975, but is about as large as Nicaragua, Tunisia, or the state of Michigan in the U.S. In 1970 the de facto population of the homelands was just over seven million persons, or 32.5 percent of the total South African population.[1]

According to the republican government in Pretoria, all ten homelands are incipient nation-states. Two of them have already been declared sovereign—Transkei on October 26, 1976, and Bophuthatswana on December 6, 1977. This "independence" has been roundly condemned at the United Nations and elsewhere; indeed the whole homelands concept has been rejected by most of the nations of the world for several years. But on a continent where implausible colonial boundaries have been sanctified by post-independence governments, there is something intriguing about a state that purports to have relinquished control over territory the size of South Carolina. The overall purpose of the White regime prompting this divestiture may be reprehensible, but it is possible that the homelands scheme will have results different from what Pretoria intends, perhaps even opposite to those intentions.

BACKGROUND

The official Pretoria contention that there are African homelands within the borders of the Republic of South Africa which can and should evolve into individual nation-states is a fairly recent one, dating from the early 1960s and the Verwoerd government. The

Some of the research on which this paper is based was made possible by a fellowship in conflict in international relations awarded in 1976 by the Rockefeller Foundation, whose support I gratefully acknowledge.

roots of the idea are much older, however, going back nearly a century and a half. During this period there have been six steps contributing to the emergence of the homelands. These steps include (i) territorial demarcation, (ii) definition of land rights by race, (iii) ethnic specification, (iv) political separation, (v) extra-territorial citizenship, and, finally, (vi) homeland independence. We shall consider each of these steps briefly.

The first step—territorial demarcation—was the setting aside of lands exclusively for the occupation and use of the "natives," which was begun even before the middle of the nineteenth century. In 1949 Howard Rogers of the Department of Native Affairs described the policy as follows:

> As various tracts of land in the [present] Union of South Africa from time to time came under European [i.e., White] domination and extensive areas were appropriated for European settlement, some provision had to be made for the large Native population which remained subsequent to annexation and this naturally took the form of the reservation for their occupation of definite areas styled Native locations or reserves.[2]

The first such "reservation" was made in Natal in 1846-47, soon after the colony was brought under British control. (It is interesting to note that two American missionaries were among the five members of the commission that made this demarcation.) In later decades other territories were annexed by neighboring White governments as "Native lands"—in Rogers's words, "in the interests of peace, order and good government and, as regards certain of them, at the request of the Natives themselves."[3] In view of Pretoria's current contention that the homelands are the traditional and only true African lands in South Africa, it is noteworthy that in the nineteenth century government confiscations of these areas and boundary adjustments at the expense of the natives were not uncommon. Quoting Rogers again:

> After each of the numerous Kaffir wars fresh dispositions of land were made, loyal tribes being rewarded by the allocation of additional lands to them, rebellious tribes having their holdings very much reduced, if not altogether taken away, and additional areas, after each conflict, being thrown open for European occupation.[4]

The most active period in this process of creating African territories commenced exactly one hundred years ago (1879) with the annexation to the Cape Colony of Fingloland and the Idutywa Reserve (known together as "the Transkei"). When the Union of South Africa was established in 1910 it included scattered African "reserves" in the form of a wide horseshoe stretching from the northwestern Cape Province through the western, northern, and eastern Transvaal into Natal, and down the eastern Cape to the Fish River near Grahamstown. In area these reserves comprised some 22.7 million acres, or 7.8 percent of the total area of the Union. (They make up nearly 60 percent of the combined territories of the homelands—including Transkei and Bophuthatswana—today.)

The second step—the definition of land rights by race—was effected by the declaration in the Natives Land Act of 1913 that Africans could not acquire title to land outside the reserves (designated the "scheduled areas") and that non-Africans could not acquire title to land within them. This principle of territorial segregation of land rights by race had been advocated before union by the South African Native Affairs Commission (1903-5). The Natives Land Act anticipated additions to the reserves looking toward a general land settlement, but this part of the 1913 legislation was not carried out. The proposal to enlarge the reserves was not acted upon until 1936, when Parliament passed a sequel law—the Native Trust and Land Act—which provided for an increase in the size of the reserves by 15.3 million acres, thereafter known as "quota" land. When this land had been added, the reserves would comprise 38 million acres and represent just over 13 percent of the total area of the Union (before Transkei independence). By early 1972, thirty-six years after the enactment of the aforementioned law, 85.7 percent of the stipulated quota land had been acquired and added to the African areas.

The third step—ethnic specification—was the enunciation of the principle that development of the reserves would follow ethnic lines and build upon tribal structures. This began with the enactment of the Bantu Authorities Act in 1951, which shifted political power in the reserves away from elected councils, whose jurisdiction sometimes crisscrossed tribal boundaries, to a hierarchy of "Bantu authorities" following tribal lines, within which ex officio chiefs predominated. The principle was elaborated in the Promotion of Bantu Self-Government Act of 1959, where it was made clear that, in Pretoria's view, the Africans in the Union of South Africa did not constitute a single, homogeneous people, but rather a number of territorially separate "national units" defined on the basis of language and culture. The act recognized eight such units—the North

Sotho, South Sotho, Tswana, Zulu, Swazi, Tsonga, Venda, and Xhosa. In time the Xhosa would be divided in two to reflect the division between the Ciskei and Transkei territories, and a tenth unit would be created for the South Ndebele. (See Table 1.)

The fourth step—political separation—extended to the political sphere the principle of racial segregation that applied to land ownership. In particular, all representation of Africans in the central Parliament in Cape Town was ended, and increased powers of local autonomy were devolved upon African governments within the national units. Thirty years into the era of apartheid, it is easy to forget that before 1930, at least in the Cape Province, the franchise was theoretically color blind: males of whatever race meeting certain educational and property qualifications could qualify for the vote.* In fact, Colored and African men were 20 percent of the electorate in the Cape Province by 1929. A year later the vote was granted to White women but not to other women, and a year after that all

Table 1

THE AFRICAN HOMELANDS

Designation	Ethnic Group	Area, 1973 (sq. mi.)	De facto Population, 1970 ('000)
Transkei	Xhosa	14,946	1,727
Ciskei	Xhosa	3,637	526
KwaZulu	Zulu	12,638	2,106
Bophuthatswana	Tswana	14,669	877
Lebowa	North Sotho	8,677	1,086
Venda	Venda	2,386	269
Gazankulu	Tsonga	2,444	269
Basotho Qwa Qwa	South Sotho	186	26
Swazi	Swazi	804	117
Ndebele	South Ndebele	78	a

Sources: A Survey of Race Relations in South Africa, 1976 (Johannesburg: S.A. Institute of Race Relations, 1977), p. 220; *Black Development in South Africa* (Pretoria: Benbo, 1976), p. 200.

[a]Included in the populations of other homelands in 1970; estimated to be 55,000 persons.

*In the Transvaal and the Orange Free State the vote was always limited to Whites, and this was practically the case in Natal as well.

educational and property qualifications were eliminated for White men. As a result, by the mid-1930s Colored and African voters together made up only 8.5 percent of the electorate in the Cape Province. Then in 1936 the Representation of Natives Act removed all Africans from the common voters roll in the Cape and substituted three communal seats for Africans from the Cape in the lower house of Parliament and four senators in the upper house to represent Africans throughout the Union. (The three MP's and the four senators had to be Whites.) In 1959 the Promotion of Bantu Self-Government Act ended all African representation in Parliament.

As a counterbalance to the loss of parliamentary representation, there was a strengthening of representative and responsible African "self-government" in the reserves. Under the new Transkei Constitution Act, the first "one man, one vote" election among Africans in the Transkei territory was held in November 1963 to elect forty-five members to the Transkei Legislative Assembly. (Sixty-four other Assembly members were chiefs sitting ex officio.) A few weeks later, the first Transkei cabinet was formed under Chief Minister Kaiser Matanzima. African ministers in Transkei assumed responsibility in the fields of finance, justice, education, interior, agriculture and forestry, and roads and public works.[5] Eight years later, enactment in Cape Town of the Bantu Homelands Constitution Act (1971) anticipated Transkei-like political evolutions elsewhere, and indeed over the next four years seven other "territorial authorities" followed in the path broken by Umtata (capital of Transkei). At the beginning of 1977 only the Swazi and the South Ndebele homelands were not self-governing.

The fifth step—extra-territorial citizenship, or the linking, as citizens, of every African in the Republic to one or another of the national units (excluding, of course, Africans from outside the borders of South Africa—e.g., gold miners from Mozambique and Malawi)—was critical for the success of the homelands program. The key group was Africans resident in the so-called "White areas" of South Africa (estimated to be 53.5 percent of the total African population in 1970), most of whom are permanent residents rather than migrants. Such linking had been accomplished for the so-called "urban" Transkeian Xhosa under the terms of the Transkei Constitution Act of 1963. At the time of Transkei independence in 1976, one-third of its statutory citizens were persons permanently residing beyond its borders (author's calculation). The Bantu Homelands Citizenship Act of 1970 extended a similar homeland citizenship to every African in the Republic who was not already a citizen of a self-governing area. The act expressly stated that citizens of the homelands would continue to be citizens of South Africa under international law, although clearly the framers of the act looked forward to the day when the two citizenships would be exclusive. (It is interesting that the 1970 act appears to be the first time the term *homelands* was used in the title of legislation.)

The sixth step, of course, is homeland independence. To this writing only two of the ten territories have opted for independence —Transkei and Bophuthatswana, as noted. However, press reports from South Africa suggest that three others—Venda, Lebowa, and the Ciskei—are thought likely to follow suit. Under South African law, at independence all the citizens of Transkei and Bophuthatswana ceased to be South African citizens, although over two million of them remain in South Africa. Their status has become that of legal aliens, which is of course the objective of the whole exercise from the standpoint of the White government in Pretoria—namely, to establish a White "homeland" in southern Africa wherein, in international law, all Africans are temporary visitors away from their true "homes," which are elsewhere. (The status of the 2.3 million Coloreds and 70,000 Asians in South Africa is ignored in this scheme.)

"DECOLONIZATION"

As prospective independent states, the South African homelands (or "Bantustans," as they are sometimes referred to) have been almost universally condemned. On Transkei Independence Day, for example, the United Nations General Assembly in New York voted 134 to 0, with only the United States abstaining, to declare Transkei independence "invalid" and to request member governments "to prohibit all individuals, corporations and other institutions from having any dealings with either the Transkei or any other future bantustan."[6] This action was not unexpected, given earlier declarations of the General Assembly on the topic, but in official Pretoria's view the rejection of Transkei is strikingly unfair and shows malicious prejudice toward the Whites of South Africa. Prime Minister Vorster remarked cynically that Transkei would have been more acceptable to the UN had it been born violently with considerable loss of lives. South Africa believes the world community is applying a double standard in its case. "If Lesotho or the Seychelles or Equatorial Guinea or Costa Rica can be independent, why not Transkei?," asks Dennis Austin in a recent paper.[7] Pretoria believes its homelands policy should be understood as a process of "decolonization" of South Africa no less thorough or legitimate than British or French decolonization in the past.

In support of this view, a comparison of Transkei with the Kingdom of Lesotho is often made by South African Whites, as well as by Transkei's elite. Lesotho is Transkei's immediate neighbor on the northwest, and its independence in October 1966 was warmly welcomed by the world community. Yet on almost every objective dimension of comparison between the two states, the circumstances of Transkei would appear more propitious for independence. Transkei is half again as large as Lesotho, and in fact is larger than six other independent Black African states.[8] It has a larger population than Lesotho, a coastline, a more prosperous economy, a higher level of government services, a better educated populace, more and larger towns, and a more comprehensive physical infrastructure. If Transkei is more culturally and ethnically homogeneous than most other African states, it is no more so than Lesotho, except in one respect. Half of the membership of the Transkei National Assembly at independence were ex officio chiefs, while in the case of the bicameral Lesotho parliament at independence, twenty-two of the thirty-three members of the upper house, or Senate, were ex officio chiefs, but this chamber had limited powers of delay and review. Lest my purpose here be misunderstood, let me emphasize that both Transkei and Lesotho are among the poorest and least capable countries of the world, and their existence as states mocks the idea of sovereign independence. But one cannot logically reject Transkei for this reason without also rejecting Lesotho, and this few are prepared to do. The rejection of Transkei must rest, therefore, on grounds other than its lacking the conventional "attributes of statehood." Many Whites in South Africa have already concluded that the true cause is unreasoning international hostility to them and *any* efforts they may make to resolve the difficulties of South Africa that fall short of complete political capitulation to the Blacks. There are, however, at least four other reasons for rejecting Transkei which White South Africans typically ignore.

First, even if Transkei is as credible an independent state as Lesotho, this can be said of perhaps none of the other homelands. Destitute as Transkei is, it is overall the "best case" of the homelands concept, and is thus unrepresentative. Since world acceptance of Transkei would strongly imply acceptance of the homelands policy as a whole, it can be argued that in this larger context the "attributes of statehood" criteria are appropriate. Two of these attributes are particularly noteworthy in this context: territorial size and territorial fragmentation.

Size. Three homelands are larger than Lesotho: Transkei, Bophuthatswana, and KwaZulu. Another—Lebowa—is smaller than Lesotho but larger than Swaziland. The remaining six homelands, however, would be ministates among ministates. By no stretch of the imagination can the Qwa Qwa or Swazi homelands of 186 square miles and 804 square miles respectively be seen as prospective sovereign states. Indeed the preposterousness of this idea prompts speculation that Pretoria has another purpose in mind in these two cases (to be discussed below). But from the standpoint of their size, the Ciskei, Venda, Gazankulu, and South Ndebele homelands are no more conceivable as states. Thus most of the homelands are clearly too small to be taken seriously as future sovereign entities.

Fragmentation. Except for islands and island nations, the territory of nearly every nation-state is continuous, if not compact. The separation of Alaska from the "lower 48" is an interesting example of the contrary, but at least one need not pass through Canada to travel between these two parts of the United States. The principle of sovereignty here would seem to be that an independent country should not be dependent upon another for communication between or among its several parts. Most of the homelands would fail to pass this test. Independent Transkei consists of three parts, but two of them are small and peripheral to the large central core of the country. However, at independence in 1977 Bophuthatswana had seven noncontiguous parts, and even when the 1975 proposals for the consolidation of KwaZulu are implemented, it will still have ten parts. Indeed, only the three smallest homelands and the Ciskei are projected to be single-piece states after current consolidation plans are completed. Of course, fragmentation of the homelands into thirty-five or so pieces makes so-called "White South Africa" also oddly shaped, but it is worth noting that save for Walvis Bay in Southwest Africa/Namibia, no part of the White homeland is projected to be cut off from the remainder.

2. A second factor that distinguishes Lesotho from both Transkei and Bophuthatswana (and potentially from every other homeland) relates to citizenship. As previously noted, at the time of Transkei independence some 1,155,000 persons acquired exclusive Transkei citizenship involuntarily, notwithstanding their *permanent* residence outside the boundaries of the new state. Pretoria has denied that this is a highly anomalous situation. On November 7, 1976, for example, Prime Minister Vorster, appearing on the Ameri-

can television program "Face the Nation," likened these persons to the citizens of Lesotho who are also at any time away working in the Republic. But this analogy is faulty. The Lesotho citizens—perhaps 200,000 persons—are migrants who are away from Lesotho only temporarily; they are equivalent to Transkeian migrants in the Republic, who number approximately 350,000 altogether. But these are not the same individuals as the permanent residents. There is in fact no equivalent in the case of Lesotho to the 1,155,000 Transkei citizens who are permanently settled in the Republic. Basotho who might have constituted such a population were left in the Republic as citizens of South Africa when Lesotho became independent in 1966. Similarly, Tswana and Swazi in the Republic remained South African citizens after the independence of Botswana and Swaziland. What became of these people? It appears that they were administratively assigned by Pretoria to homelands of like ethnic character, for we find that these homelands have a high percentage of their populations living in the "White areas" of South Africa—64.5 percent for the Tswana (Bophuthatswana), 77.5 percent for the Swazi, and 90.1 percent for the Basotho (Qwa Qwa). It is clear that international recognition of Transkei and Bophuthatswana would tend to legitimize the denial of the rights of citizenship to millions of Africans permanently resident in White-claimed South Africa; recognition of Lesotho in 1966 carried with it no such implication.

Indeed, the particularly blatant absurdity of the Swazi and Qwa Qwa homelands as prospective sovereign states suggests, as noted earlier, that Pretoria may have another purpose in mind for them. It is speculation, of course, but I suspect that Pretoria hopes to offer the Swazi territory for annexation to Swaziland and the Qwa Qwa territory to Lesotho. The price South Africa would hope to extract would doubtless be the willingness of these independent governments to accept responsibility for the *total* populations of these homelands as defined by Pretoria—especially those persons in the White-claimed areas. Were this done, Pretoria would have established at last an exact parallel, demographically speaking, between the independence of Swaziland and Lesotho and the independence of the homelands. It may be that a similar strategy is contemplated with respect to Botswana, although the independence of Bophuthatswana is clearly a complicating factor. It goes without saying that it is difficult to imagine any of the independent Botswana/Lesotho/Swaziland governments being willing to pay such a price, however much they may covet the territories in question.

3. The third difference between Lesotho and the homelands is a matter of perception. It is doubtless the case that many South African Whites imagine that if the Africans of Lesotho could be satisfied with political independence in their tiny and impoverished mountain kingdom, the Africans of South Africa should be similarly assuaged with no more than equivalent opportunities. However, this conclusion is likely erroneous—especially for Africans outside the homelands. The current citizens of Lesotho, as well as of Swaziland and Botswana, excepting perhaps some naturalized persons, were never South African citizens, as the homeland citizens were and in many cases still are. Because of this and their determined resistance over half a century to their territories being incorporated into South Africa, which was anticipated in the South Africa Act of 1909, the idea did not take root among them, as it obviously did among Africans and other victims of discrimination within South Africa's borders, that they no less than the Whites had a rightful claim to a democratic share of the wealth and promise of South Africa. Thus homeland independence involves "opportunity costs" for South African Africans that were not perceived to exist by the populations of the High Commission territories as those areas approached independence in the mid-1960s. In short, many Africans within South Africa (as much of world opinion) have come to believe that they are entitled to a more generous share of what I have called the "common South African estate" than merely the right to be citizens of one of the world's powerless and impoverished ministates. (Obviously, these differences in perception revolve around different views concerning the relative past contributions of the Whites and Africans to the making of the contemporary Republic.)

4. A fourth reason for rejecting Transkei independence relates to the issue of obtaining African consent for homeland independence, which usually is given precedence over the logically prior question of the right of a homeland to opt out of South Africa. We will digress briefly to consider this second issue first.

When Lesotho became independent in 1966, no voices were heard claiming that the step was improper or illegitimate, although earlier in the century it was widely assumed that all three High Commission territories would eventually be incorporated into the Union of South Africa. By the 1960s, much of the world appeared to welcome Lesotho's independence (indeed perhaps even insisted upon it) as a means of keeping the territory out of Pretoria's hands and free of apartheid. Yet a decade later, when Transkei claimed independence for ostensibly the same purpose, some held it had no right to do so. Their view, similar to that of Lincoln toward South Carolina in 1860, was that it could not secede. The implication would seem to be that in the history of southern Africa there was at some point a critical "fork in the road": the inhabitants of Basutoland (as Lesotho was then known) and the other High Commission territories went down one path toward eventual national sovereignty, while Transkeians and other Africans in what became the Union of South Africa went down the other toward indissoluble union with the people (or at least the African people) of that country. The fact that the Africans themselves had nothing to do with this choice is easily dismissed. "History," it is said, "has committed the homelands to South Africa." And the fact that (for quite independent reasons—namely, the vulnerability of many of its members to their own secessionist movements) the Organization of African Unity has sanctified the former colonial boundaries as inviolable gives added international respectability to this view. For their part, Transkei's leaders counter with the claim that their country was conquered by the British a century ago and has now merely regained its lost sovereignty—like Ghana in 1957 and Kenya in 1963.

This is an argument with no prospect of resolution; it is also perhaps not a very important argument. That is, if Black South Africans were to accept in an open and fair vote a racial partition of their country that was not demonstrably against their interests, I have little doubt that most important powers among the Western nations would accept it, the views of the OAU notwithstanding. But in fact the prevailing view is that in the case of both Transkei and Bophuthatswana, Pretoria connived with a small group of unrepresentative traditionalists to press independence upon populations that did not want it. Several different types of evidence are commonly cited to support this contention. In both homelands public opinion on the independence issue was tested at general elections contested along party lines, and the pleas of many individuals for the question to be put in the form of a public referendum were ignored. But by the time these elections were held, both territories had become virtual one-party states. Thus the overwhelming victories of the Transkei National Independence party in September 1976 (71 of 75 seats) and of the Bophuthatswana Democratic party nearly a year later (43 of 48 seats) failed to convey the sense of electoral mandate that the leaders of the two parties—Paramount Chief Matanzima and Chief Lucas Mangope, respectively—subsequently claimed. Moreover, objections were raised concerning the low turnout of voters (about 42 percent in both instances), the particular indifference shown by voters in the urban areas, the use of security measures to stifle opposition groups, and the fact that in the end elected members constituted only half the total memberships of the two new assemblies. My own view is that Roger Southall was correct when he concluded in 1977 that Matanzima "had little claim to a popular mandate for leading the Transkei to independence," but that he has not demonstrated his more sweeping contention that in 1976 a majority of Transkei citizens either "strongly opposed" Transkei independence or were "pressurized" (presumably against their wishes) to accept it.[9] Certainly since 1968 there has been no mandate *not* to seek independence—that is, to keep Transkei part of South Africa—which was Paramount Chief Victor Poto's position in 1963, but because the meaningfulness of the Transkei and Bophuthatswana election results can be questioned by fair-minded persons, the political separation of these two areas from South Africa lacks the legitimacy a more democratic decision-making process, especially a public referendum, might have provided.

There is another "measure" which is commonly cited to distinguish Lesotho from all the homelands—namely, the overwhelming financial dependence of the latter upon the Republic of South Africa. In discussions of homeland economic "viability," this dependence is often related to the manifest need of the homelands to export labor to the Republic, but in this respect Transkei and Lesotho are very similar, although some of the other homelands, being much closer than Transkei to the industrial centers of South Africa, earn appreciably more of their gross national income in the Republic.[10] It is argued that because of these financial ties none of the homelands can be truly independent of Pretoria's wishes, and the implication is left that this is not the case with Lesotho because it gets little direct assistance from South Africa. It seems appropriate to deal with this issue here.

The empirical evidence for the contention that the homeland governments are financially dependent upon Pretoria is substantial and incontestable; moreover, this dependence appears to be growing as development proceeds. In the year 1974/75, for example, Pretoria provided 77.4 percent or more of the incomes available to the homeland governments in Transkei, Bophuthatswana, and KwaZulu, and in the first "post-independence" budget prepared in Transkei (1977-78), Pretoria's contribution rose to 84 percent. But Lesotho is even poorer than these homelands, and indeed the World Bank has reported that up to 1968/69, several years after its independence, British grants-in-aid still financed about half of

Lesotho's current budget.[11] The difference between Lesotho and the homelands in this matter is that since 1967/68 Maseru (capital of Lesotho) has tried to hold its recurrent expenditures steady in real terms so as to reduce the country's dependence on British budget support, while an opposite strategy has been followed in South Africa. As a result, even before the Transkei independence the per capita expenditures of its government were three times the level in Lesotho, placing Transkei in the upper third of twenty-one African countries whose expenditures were surveyed. The point is that the homelands *in principle* could reduce or eliminate their budget dependence upon Pretoria too if their governments were prepared to curtail drastically their expenditures *and* if other nations were to step in and help. But while the General Assembly has urged the nations of the world to come to Lesotho's assistance to help it reduce its dependence on South Africa, it has insisted that no help be extended to any of the homelands.[12]

Partition. As a process, then, South African official "decolonization" fails to impress not only because it is not an exact parallel with the process that resulted in the independence of Lesotho, but also because there is a strong feeling among many observers of the region that if political separatism is to have any hope of success, what is called for is not a string of new southern African Black mini-republics, but a forthright racial partition of the subcontinent. There are many and varied definitions of partition, but it is possible to identify several key conceptions that recur frequently.[13] Most observers appear to believe that to succeed a racial partition of South Africa should produce one (or at most two or three) African-controlled state which covers at least half the surface area of the Republic before Transkei independence. For convenience we shall refer to such a state as "Azania." (In fact this is the name suggested by the banned Pan-Africanist Congress for the Republic of South Africa as a whole after it has been "liberated" from White minority rule.) The consensus is, then, that Azania should be a large state possessing substantial industry, a diversified economy, abundant natural resources, extensive areas of farm land, numerous cities, a coastline, modern port facilities, reasonable boundaries, compact territory, and well-developed internal communications. Further it is supposed that Azania's economy should be minimally dependent upon White South Africa, implying a virtual cessation in the practice of migratory labor. Politically, Azania might be a federal or a unitary system, but it should not be dominated by African traditionalists—i.e., chiefs. What is envisaged is an African nationalist regime on the pattern of Zambia or Kenya, but probably not the more radical Tanzania or Mozambique. Whether or not such a regime would be democratic in the liberal Western sense, it is regarded as critical that the initial founding of Azania should be an undeniably popular step among Africans. Hence it is usually contemplated that some sort of referendum will be held on the partition question.

Obviously there is a vast difference between Azania, as we have described it, and Transkei and Bophuthatswana as they now exist. But what if Transkei were to join with the neighboring Xhosa-speaking Ciskei, and the intervening port city of East London (population 120,000), with White farm lands included? Would not the resulting "Greater Xhosaland" be a credible nation-state and likely to elicit broad African interest and support? Can we not conceive of Transkei and Bophuthatswana independence as merely early steps toward an eventual federation of Black states in southern Africa? The presumption of course is that a similar process of consolidation, expansion, and strengthening of the other homelands would occur concurrently. It is possible that the deficiencies of the current homelands policy which Transkei and Bophuthatswana independence serve to highlight (e.g., the need for territorial consolidation) could prompt a new round of thinking on the part of policymakers, assisting in the formulation of a more far-reaching partition policy. Indeed, a renewed discussion of the idea of partition in the White South African press in the middle of 1977 suggested this was already occurring. On the other hand, there are at least five ways in which the independence of the first two homelands could *lessen* the chances for a more viable partition in southern Africa. Let us briefly consider each of these.

1. Independence creates vested interests which may be difficult to dislodge. Specifically, it is likely that present or future office-holders who would lose status or power as a result of Transkei or Bophuthatswana becoming part of some larger political entity would oppose such a step.

2. Similarly, the entrenchment in office of two African homeland prime ministers, by increasing the difficulty of coordinating African views and commitments, inevitably reduces (as the phrase "divide and rule" has it) the pressure they can mount on Pretoria, lessening the chances for greater White concessions of land and resources.

3. Independence tends to legitimize and permanently fix territorial boundaries; thus the time for boundary adjustments is before independence.

4. To the extent that the present homelands policy, culminating in Transkei and Bophuthatswana independence, has been understood by Africans and others as, in the words of Austin Turk, "a cover for continuation of white domination," it has stigmatized *any* separatist plan as fraudulent.[14] Indeed, it is probable that any plan emanating now from Pretoria that does not represent outright capitulation of the regime to Black interests will evoke great suspicion.

5. Finally, given the variety of interests that would have to be accommodated through processes of compromise and concession in any plan for real partition, there would seem to be an advantage in dealing with all of these interests at once in a single, overarching settlement. To approach each of these issues separately would make the negotiations much more difficult.

In sum, it is difficult to imagine South Africa incrementally "easing into" a successful race partition of its territory. Does this mean the end of partition as a future possibility? Perhaps not. I share Heribert Adam's view that, short of military intervention by a major world power, the violent overthrow of the present South African regime is highly unlikely.[15] Yet it seems clear to me that efforts at revolution will continue and intensify and that these, with the regime's inevitable responses, will gradually lead to anarchy in South Africa, in which the quality of life for everyone, White and Black, will be destroyed. Then, in a context of protracted political and military stalemate, combined with fatigue and desperation among all parties, it seems possible that the idea of a negotiated racial partition of the country could emerge as a "last way out"—a partition far more generous to African interests than any now contemplated, and one legitimized for Africans by the intensity of sacrifice and suffering (including White sacrifice and suffering) that had advanced the struggle to this point.

In such an eventuality, could there be any role for the homelands? Those that had become independent might be used as "safe havens" by guerrilla groups, but Pretoria would doubtless exploit the dependence of these states on South Africa to try to prevent this from happening. Or the homeland leaders might try to mediate between the warring parties, but it seems doubtful that they would be acceptable to the full African population in this role. I can foresee only one contribution of the homelands (and particularly of those that have chosen independence) to this scenario should it occur, and that is a passive contribution—namely, the vague presumption they create in the thinking of many Whites of partition as a "last resort" in the South African conflict. Although *Sechaba*, the quarterly periodical of the African National Congress, has predicted only a brief Transkei independence ("Transkei's spurious independence will meet its end together with the 'white South Africa' which gave it birth"),[16] most observers see homeland independence as an irreversible step—certainly so long as the Whites retain significant power. In this sense, then, Transkei and Bophuthatswana independence has narrowed somewhat the range of options available to South Africa as a whole. It seems probable that in the future an increasing number of Whites will be inclined to believe that by accepting some partition they have become committed to partition as the only alternative to revolution or endless civil war.

POWER-SHARING

If the tensions in contemporary South Africa do not produce either racial partition of the country or revolution, many observers feel that they might be contained by some form of "power-sharing." On the one hand, it is assumed that it is very unrealistic to expect the White electorate of South Africa under any foreseeable conditions to accept a political structure based on the principles of "one man, one vote" and "majority rule," because most Whites are convinced that this would mean their permanent political subordination to an African majority whose material and cultural interests, if not necessarily hostile to those of the Whites, at least substantially diverge from them. Attainment of democratic majority rule in South Africa would thus be synonymous with revolution. On the other hand, it is assumed that White supremacy in its present form cannot be maintained in South Africa. Power-sharing refers to the political incorporation by White South Africa of currently excluded and oppressed populations by means and to a degree that it is believed will lower social tensions to manageable levels without seriously jeopardizing the material or cultural interests of the Whites. The concept of power-sharing can be extended to cover a great variety of specific possibilities. Although the words are on the lips of many people today who are concerned with the future of South Africa, there is almost no agreement about what power-sharing means. The only point of consensus is that the previous total exclusion of Africans, Coloreds, and Indians from effective decision-making roles in the country must end, and that Whites have the right to insist that their interests be protected.

Yet notwithstanding the impreciseness of the concept, it seems clear that the homelands policy is producing limited power-sharing in the homelands themselves. Thus Transkei and Bophuthatswana fairly well approximate constituent elements in many of the federal plans for South Africa that have been devised for politically incorporating previously excluded groups.[17] In this perspective, the financial dependence of the homeland governments on Pretoria can be seen as merely the transfer of wealth in a federation from the richer to the poorer units.[18]

To be sure, the tangible benefits of this power-sharing are skewed in favor of a small elite. Within each of the homelands new classes of African civil servants, businessmen, and politicians are being formed with unprecedented power and a definite material self-interest in the homeland experiment. The "beneficiaries" of the policy (as Roger Southall has referred to them in the case of Transkei) are a very small group—perhaps as few as 1.5 percent of the total population of the homeland. And even within this group there is in each homeland a much smaller number of chiefs, high-level civil servants, politicians, economic managers, and entrepreneurs whose material benefits have been far greater than the rest. For example, according to the 1976-77 "Estimates" for Transkei, there were 175 civil service positions in the territory occupied by Africans, not including the cabinet ministers, for which the minimum salary was $5,451 or more. Considering that the annual per capita income in Transkei only a few years ago was $201, these are princely incomes, and the stake the individuals drawing them have in the survival of the Transkei state cannot be doubted. Observers on the scene believe that these new elites will succeed in holding their territories to politically conservative ways for the foreseeable future. Thus as far as the homelands themselves are concerned, the power-sharing that has occurred may turn aside pressures on the larger political system for more sweeping accommodations. Or in the words of Southall: "In so far as the Transkei is a 'model' for the other Homelands, a ring of other satellite, quasi-independent states can be expected to emerge which, because of the privileged nature of their elites, will be committed to opposing revolutionary change."[19]

But African pressures for radical change in South Africa have seldom originated in the countryside. A more important question would appear to be whether the grant of power to Africans in the homelands promotes power-sharing in the cities, where the Soweto school children demonstrated that the explosive potential is far greater. It is often suggested that the real purpose of Pretoria's

Bantustan program is to reduce dramatically the African proportion of the total South African population by discarding the African reserve areas, after which it will be safe (from the White man's point of view) to "integrate" the remaining Africans. But if we were to make the improbable assumption that the Indians and Coloreds would side with the Whites against the Africans in any future democratic political structure, the number of Africans left in South Africa after all the homelands became independent would still constitute 55 percent of the total population. The only way Africans could be reduced to less than a majority of the South African population would be for the regime to relinquish control of all but the cities of South Africa. Even then the Whites would still make up less than one-third of all the inhabitants, and the Africans 48 percent. Thus no simple hiving off of rural African populations can alter fundamentally the minority position of the Whites. It is probably the case that the power-sharing possibilities of any situation increase as the differences between the sizes of the contending groups decrease, but it may be that power-sharing is most difficult in situations where one of the contending groups constitutes a decisive majority. In this context, the reduction in the size of the African population of South Africa from 70 percent to 55 percent of the total population might be of little significance.

There are, however, at least three other ways in which the homelands can promote power-sharing outside their boundaries. One has to do with race relations at the individual level—or the elimination of what Pierre van den Berghe has called "micro-segregation."[20] The most immediate and obvious result of independence for Transkei and Bophuthatswana was the ending of so-called "petty" apartheid in these territories, and the freeing at the grass-roots level of millions of Africans from the control of the South African police. Schedule 11 of the Transkei Constitution Act lists 122 laws of South Africa that it repeals fully or in part, including such landmark pieces of apartheid legislation as the Reservation of Separate Amenities Acts, the Group Areas Act, and the Prohibition of Political Interference Act. Other measures not listed have simply not been enforced. There is as yet no clear evidence, but it is possible that the ending of petty apartheid in these two territories undermines petty apartheid throughout the region by the power of example. Transkei and Bophuthatswana are not, of course, the only nonracial or African-controlled states in southern Africa, but they are the only such societies that were previously subject to apartheid. They are thus an interesting case study, albeit in rural and tribal areas, of what can happen when apartheid is abandoned by a society.

A second way that the homelands have promoted power-sharing in the region generally is by exposing Whites in South Africa, and particularly members of the White elite, to the unfamiliar sight of Africans exercising independent political power. Traditionally in South Africa White political leaders at the pinnacle of state power have had no need to deal directly with Africans in any political capacity. This has now changed—an important milestone being the first meeting between Prime Minister Vorster and all the homeland leaders together in Pretoria on March 6, 1974. The long-run effect is unclear, but it must be acknowledged that contemporary relations between Pretoria, on the one hand, and Umtata and Mmabatho, on the other, require bargaining from independent power bases. Obviously the willingness of White leaders to deal with and take seriously African political leaders is a necessary condition for the resolution of the political tensions of South Africa.

A third way homelands can promote power-sharing is by exerting political pressure on the White regime. No one argues that power-sharing, as we have defined it, is presently the goal of the White government—certainly not as far as the urban African population is concerned—or that Pretoria would embrace power-sharing without extraordinary pressures being applied first. In some measure the homelands provide an arena for such pressures. Indeed it is frequently observed that the homeland leaders are as outspoken in their criticism of White supremacy in South Africa as were the leaders of the African National Congress and the Pan Africanist Congress at the time those two organizations were banned (April 1960). Moreover, their official positions give them resources and relative immunity from political harassment and repression that African leaders in the past did not have. On the other hand, with the exception of Chief Buthelezi of KwaZulu, none of the homeland leaders has seemed able to extend his influence into the cities, although some limited attempts have been made. Not surprisingly, urban Africans in the aggregate have shown striking lack of interest in the affairs of the distant homelands. While some homeland leaders have tried to address urban problems during their infrequent visits to the cities, their role as Bantustan officials has undermined their influence, causing them to be perceived as accomplices of apartheid. To a degree the charisma of Buthelezi coupled with Zulu group-pride has enabled him to override objections to his participation in the government of KwaZulu. It is reported that in early 1976 a speech of his drew a crowd of sixteen thousand persons in Soweto, and the alliance between Inkatha YakaZulu, ostensibly a Zulu cultural organization of which Buthelezi is president, and the Coloured Labour party and the Indian Reform party suggests an organizational base for "Black" unity (i.e., the unity of the oppressed) that has been unknown since the days of the "Congress of the People" in the late 1950s.

The brief unity of the homeland leaders—particularly their agreement to refuse independence for their homelands (until March 12, 1974, when Matanzima declared unconditionally for Transkei independence)—was a source of potential pressure on the regime to abandon "separate development." The high-water mark of this resolve was the first summit conference of six homeland leaders in Umtata on November 8, 1973. At this meeting the six pledged themselves to joint action in the future and endorsed the idea of a federation of the homelands as "a long-term policy." Later, Buthelezi reported that they "decided in future to request, not separate meetings with the Prime Minister, but one conference where they would all deal with black problems, not on an ethnic basis."[21] Several such conferences have been held since, but as a practical matter, Transkei and Bophuthatswana independence has seemed to end the idea of a homeland united front against apartheid.

Yet the overall effect of homeland independence so far has been to move South Africa away from power-sharing in the core. We refer here to the involuntary loss of South African citizenship by Transkeian Xhosa and Tswana in the urban areas of the country. The social justice and political accommodation implicit in power-sharing cannot be approached by stripping people of their citizenship in the areas of their de facto permanent residence. If this is a step toward anything, in 1978 it is a step toward revolution.

A NOTE ON HOMELAND ECONOMICS

In his introduction to *Change in Contemporary South Africa*, Leonard Thompson states that as a matter of definition, change in the Republic to be accepted as "significant" should involve "radical redistribution of power and wealth" among the races.[22] Whatever one may think of the powers that have devolved upon the homeland governments, it is obvious that no great wealth has changed hands in the process. Only a brief summary of the major points of that process is possible here.

While economic conditions vary somewhat, generally all the homelands are exceptionally poor and woefully undeveloped. After a survey in 1968 of 2,185 households in the Bizana and Kentani districts of Transkei, for example, Johann Maree and P.J. de Vos estimated that 85.1 percent of these households had incomes below the poverty line, defined as the "theoretical absolute minimum requirements of a family to stay alive in the short run." Not surprisingly, many fail to "stay alive." In 1973 Maree reported estimates that in five Transkei districts as many as 40 percent of all African children die before the age of ten as a direct or indirect result of malnutrition.[23] Many conditions contribute to this result, but among the most important is the very limited work opportunities apart from subsistence agriculture, which has long been saturated in terms of employment. In 1976 in Transkei, for example, when there were only about fifty thousand paying jobs in all of the territory, it was estimated that the labor force increased by 26,300 persons.[24] In recent decades at least three-quarters of new work-seekers in Transkei have had to leave the territory to find work or remain unemployed, and for this reason Transkei and the other homelands have often been referred to as a "reservoir of cheap labor" for South African industry.

Because unrestrained migration of Africans from the homelands into the White-claimed industrial core of the country runs counter to the social goals of the central government, a high priority of its economic plans for these areas has been the generation of local employment, even at the expense of comprehensive development. Until 1968, however, little had been accomplished because policy forbade the introduction of White-owned capital into the homelands and the local populations were entirely without capital. But in that year the policy was changed: White capitalists can now invest in homelands if they agree to collaborate with one of the official development corporations. To offset the lack of economic incentives to encourage industry to locate in the homelands, Pretoria has introduced a number of special incentives, known as "concessions." For example, an industrialist investing in Transkei can receive a 40 percent rebate on the cost of shipping his manufactured goods out of the territory by rail. During the first several years of operations he is allowed tax concessions on 10 percent of the value of manufacturing machinery and equipment and on 50 percent of the wages paid to African employees. There are parallel programs which are designed to turn over existing small businesses in the homelands to African managers and owners, but in terms of scale, so-called "agency agreements" with private White capitalists based elsewhere have become the primary motor of economic change.

In sum, while the rate of capital investment in the homelands has grown in recent years, which in turn has increased the rate of job creation in these areas, the number of new jobs falls far short of the number needed to accommodate the new work-seekers each year. In consequence, the dependence of the homelands on labor migration to the "White areas" not only continues but intensifies. Most of the new jobs are very low-paying, so that the material benefits they provide are limited. Indeed the low wages paid to African workers in the homelands are an important incentive to external investment not included on the official listings of "concessions." Thus, though new wealth is appearing in the homelands and is especially visible at the geographic "growth points" designated in them, it is not yet African-owned wealth. In particular, Africans have not gained ownership of means of production. Even the few small businesses in the homelands Africans have taken ownership of are typically commercial outlets for goods produced elsewhere by White-owned factories. To be sure, a condition of the agency agreements negotiated with the development corporations is that they must result in eventual Black ownership of industry in the homelands.* But given the limited African capital available, there can be little doubt that short of outright expropriation by the homeland governments (against which the White agents are protected by guarantees of compensation from Pretoria), most of the new factories in the homelands will continue to be owned by White capitalists in the Republic and elsewhere.

CONCLUSIONS

Pretoria's contention that the development of the homelands as "homelands" can divert African nationalism in the region and thereby resolve the race tensions of the country is unquestionably wrong, and it is interesting to speculate concerning how responsible officials can hold so tenaciously to this illusion. To some degree it must reflect their lack of exposure to contemporary Africa beyond their own borders, as well as traditional Afrikaner prejudice that Black Africans are not capable of very much acting on their own.

*In view of the importance of development to the homelands, it is interesting to note that until recently the development corporations were not accountable to their local homeland governments. Structurally this has changed in Transkei with independence: the Matanzima government now appoints half of the directors of the Transkei Development Corporation, but it remains to be seen whether Umtata will attempt to impose its development priorities on the TDC.

However, the wholesale rejection of the homelands scheme in the United Nations and elsewhere is similarly unrealistic, and suggests a simplistic understanding of the dynamics of social change in the area. Moreover, the dogged refusal of most members of the world community to see any parallels between the situations of Lesotho and at least Transkei clearly suggests the use of a double standard.

The populations of Lesotho, Swaziland, Botswana, Transkei, and Bophuthatswana are, in a manner of speaking, all refugees from apartheid. The status of each of these five territories gives similar elites essentially equivalent opportunities and imposes upon their populations much the same costs in continuing poverty and overall powerlessness. The implications of the independence of the homelands, then, are much the same as the implications of the existence of the BLS countries, except that as long as the world ignores the homelands, they are necessarily thrown back on Pretoria if they are not to become completely isolated.

Independence of the homelands has meant subtle movements away from the status quo, such as the abolition of "petty" apartheid in the rural areas, somewhat greater transfers of wealth and capital to these rural districts (under very controlled conditions), and the emergence of a small class of African administrators and an even smaller African petite-bourgeoisie. In education primarily, homelands have permitted African self-expression culturally in ways unprecedented in southern Africa in this century. But as yet there is no evidence that these changes are accumulating to produce something profound. In particular, the homelands have not yet contributed to the industrial organization of African workers that Heribert Adam sees as the most promising "leverage" on the overall system at the present time.[25] Past speculations that independent homelands might join with other Black states in the region to withhold their vast supplies of labor from the South African economic core, and thereby bring powerful pressures on their White neighbors, have not been borne out by the facts. Nor have the homeland governments, independent or otherwise, tried to organize work stoppages among their "citizens" in the economic core areas.[26] Compared with what is going on politically around South Africa at the present time in Namibia, Zimbabwe-Rhodesia, and Mozambique, the implications for Pretoria of changes in the homelands have been decidedly nonthreatening to date. But perhaps the hour is still early.

STRUCTURAL INEQUALITY AND MINORITY ANXIETY: RESPONSES OF MIDDLE GROUPS IN SOUTH AFRICA

Kogila A. Moodley

INDIANS AND COLOREDS AS MIDDLE GROUPS

In the social science literature on South Africa, Indian and Colored South Africans are frequently lumped together by virtue of their common intermediate situation between the numerical majority of Africans, on the one hand, and the politically dominant Whites on the other. The 733,800 Indians constituted 2.9 percent and the 2,432,000 Coloreds, 9.6 percent of the country's population in 1975.[1]

The historical origin of the Coloreds in South Africa dates back to the landing of van Riebeeck at the Cape in 1652.* The more endogamous Indian presence in South Africa can be described in three phases. The first phase began with their entry in the mid-nineteenth century as indentured laborers on the sugar plantations of Natal. The second phase, beginning in the 1960s, was marked by the official recognition of Indians as permanent citizens of South Africa. Prior to this they had been considered an unassimilable element who were encouraged to repatriate. In the third phase attempts have been made to differentially incorporate Indians—together with Coloreds—into the White political process. Initially this took the form of separate councils for each group, but more recently new constitutional proposals have extended this idea further into plans for group sovereignty in matters pertaining exclusively to group concerns (e.g., education, housing).

*Even among some race-conscious Whites, it has become acceptable—almost fashionable—of late to speculate about their genetic "roots" and the degree of slave blood in their veins. See for example the much publicized study by A.J. Boeseken, *Slaves and Free Blacks at the Cape 1658-1700* (Cape Town: Tafelberg, 1977), and its prominent reviews in the daily press under the heading "Roots" (*Star Weekly*, February 25, 1978, p. 12).

According to the Nationalist design, the White, Colored, and Indian groups will each have its own elected parliament, cabinet, and prime minister. An electoral college, composed of representatives of the three groups according to rough population ratios (White 50; Colored 25; Indian 13), will choose a state President who will head a "Council of Cabinets." This liaison body will be expected to deal with all national issues by trying to reach consensus; failing this, the President will decide policy.

The crucial feature of this blueprint from the Nationalist viewpoint is the impossibility of creating a Colored-"English" opposition alliance. The threat of such an alliance has always been a concern for Afrikanerdom, and was largely instrumental in the removal of Coloreds from the common voting roles in the 1950s and 1960s. Such an interracial liberal political coalition will be prevented by having the majority party in each ethnic group elect all of that group's delegates to the electoral college—i.e., all fifty White representatives will be Nationalist party members. Thus, neither Indians nor Coloreds can be decisive elements in the likelihood of a confrontation between Whites and Blacks. Afrikaners take for granted that they can be accommodated into a facade of power-sharing without altering the real power balance.

From the African perspective, both intermediate groups are relatively privileged in apartheid society; they now share even less the African life situation. Africans therefore generally assume that Coloreds and Indians cannot be expected to identify with the aims and aspirations of the majority. But while it is frequently assumed that the middle groups do not desire to cooperate in a common Black front against White supremacy, there is probably an equally strong suspicion of or even sentiments of rejection against a genuine Black coalition among the African grass roots.

This analysis will focus on two interrelated questions. The first question is: How significant is the role of Indians and Coloreds in the conflict beween Afrikaner and African nationalism? A review of past and present political actions will emphasize the *common* resistance of subordinate groups and its underlying unifying tendencies.* The second question is: What are the obstacles for intersubordinate al-

*In any discussion of South African life, labels are of immense importance. Among more politicized Africans, Indians, and Coloreds, the term "Black" is the preferred label. But given the political realities of apartheid and the differential application of legislation, color labels such as Black and Brown cannot be used consistently.(Indians could also be considered brown, for example.) Hence in this paper labels will be used interchangeably. Where all three subordinate groups

liances, in particular through a broadening Black Consciousness movement? A counter-review will pay special attention to the *cleavages*, and the origin of mutually suspicious and hostile perceptions, particularly between Africans and Indians, will be traced in (a) the socioeconomic realm and (b) cultural discontinuities. Finally, an analysis of past conflicts, particularly the Durban riots, will lead to an assessment of the prospects for a Black alliance.

The limited scope of this article does not allow detailed treatment of both Indians and Coloreds. Hence, the focus will be on Indians and, wherever appropriate, comparative data and perspectives on Coloreds will be incorporated to illuminate the main similarities and differences between the two middle groups.

COMMON RESISTANCE

In an article on "The Future of South Africa," sociologist Austin Turk expressed a widely held view by describing Indians and Coloreds as being politically peripheral to the "real 'core' parties."[2] Indians and Coloreds are usually ignored in South African conflict scenarios, but this perspective can be challenged in several ways.

The view that Indians and Coloreds are only incidental in the struggle between the two major antagonists in South Africa can be challenged *historically*. In the past both groups have allied themselves with Africans at various stages, although the political organizations of Indians, Coloreds, and Africans have remained separate for tactical reasons. Indians started to draw international attention to apartheid as a total system in the United Nations when India complained on their behalf.[3] As early as 1946, South African Indians rejected the offer of communal representation in the government of South Africa on the grounds that it would be an inequitable and unacceptable arrangement because it was confined to them only. In 1977 the argument that such differential "privileges" would jeopardize race relations figured prominently in the cautious stance of the largely appointed Indian Council, which resolved to neither endorse nor reject the government's constitutional proposals for the time being.* Other

are involved, they will be referred to as Blacks, but where there is need to distinguish between the subordinate groups, Indians, Coloreds, and Africans will be used. It should be understood that such group labels always refer to the actions of the politically active minority of each group, which may be at variance with the largely unknown sentiments of the inactive, apathetic, or resigned majority.

*As one Afrikaner paper observed: "In the eyes of many Indians and Coloured people the power struggle is between whites and blacks . . . . And in the outstanding milestones in a common Black political history were the 1947 joint declaration of cooperation between Indians and Africans insisting on extension of the franchise to all sections of the population; the 1952 Defiance Campaign utilizing the experience of earlier passive resistance campaigns to address African and Indian grievances; and the 1955 Freedom Charter, which Indians were instrumental in formulating, incorporating the concerns of all three Black groups. These efforts represented unified articulations of common deprivation and inequitable treatment, when Black groups pooled their resources of Gandhian discipline and political technique with courage and a combined commitment to change social conditions through peaceful means.

More recently, a notable role has been played by various Black voluntary associations with significant Indian and Colored membership. Though initially established on the basis of specific homogeneous interests, voluntary associations have changed from their previous socializing role to a confrontational one in the pursuit of their members' interests. Sports associations, for instance, have assumed some political importance, and the role of Indians and Coloreds in the pressure for multiracial sports associations has been noticeable. The South African Soccer Federation, for instance, was successful in influencing the Federation of International Football Associations to withdraw its previous special dispensation to stage international soccer tournaments in South Africa. Such instances demonstrate the decisive role intermediate groups can play at crucial historical and strategic junctures.

One has only to look at the involvement of intermediate group members in exile politics, and the overrepresentation of Indians among the banned, detained, and imprisoned political activists, to recognize the importance of the contribution which both Indians and Coloreds make to organized resistance. Although neither Indians nor Coloreds are sufficiently numerous to rock the boat at a national level, their impact on regional organizational structures can be quite substantial. The concentration of Coloreds in the Cape Province (especially in Cape Town, where they constitute 54 percent of the pop-

view of many of them it will be the numerically stronger blacks who, in present world conditions, will be able to count on international support" (*Die Transvaler*, February 18, 1978). Reasoning along less opportunistic lines, a member of the Lenasia Indian Management Committee, which rejected the constitutional proposals, pointed to "the guilt we will have to endure," and stated further that "It is frightfully painful that we can contemplate schemes to defraud the indigenous population of its inalienable rights and establish White, Coloured, and Indian parliaments" (*Race Relations News*, October 1977).

ulation) and of Indians in Natal means that both groups could be of crucial significance were there to be a strike situation. Job reservation, the obstacles to African trade union activity, the restrictions on African ownership of land in urban areas, and Africans' limited access to specialized training have all contributed to a higher concentration of skilled workers among Coloreds and Indians than among Africans. In the case of Indians this was accentuated historically by the entry of "passenger" Indians, who came as independent traders, rather than on contracts of indenture, and were largely successful in the commercial sector. While such differentiation among subordinate groups may deepen cleavages, it can also complement a common organizational effort. Initially, the more resourceful "passenger" Indians acted as spokesmen to articulate the group's grievances.

The government's attempts at accommodating the Indian and Colored middle class in new constitutional proposals would seem to point to the necessity for some acquiescence from even the relatively small intermediate groups, as well as internal consistency and legitimation of the overall apartheid design. As a White commentator put it in the late 1960s: "A close affinity between the Whites, Coloured and Indians can only strengthen the ranks of the Whites and increase the confidence with which they can work for a peaceful solution of the 'Bantu problem.' "[4] And *Die Transvaler* commented on the constitutional proposals as follows: "A very wide measure of agreement among different peoples and groups will be necessary to introduce a new state structure to make it endure."[5] Indians and Coloreds constitute significant referent groups whose approval must be sought in order to market the new political package.

In January 1978 Y.S. Chinsamy of the Reform party, which had earlier dissociated itself from participation in the "Council of Cabinets" because urban Africans had been denied representation on it, launched Black alliance talks under the aegis of the Inkatha movement. It incorporated Indians, Coloreds, and Africans in what has been described as "the broadest based 'political alliance' South Africa has yet seen."[6] It raises the same question as the Black Consciousness movement—i.e., what are its chances of transcending established contact at the leadership level and gaining mass support from the three groups involved?

When the impact of structural inequality is experienced across racial lines, certain cross-cutting alliances may be formed on the basis of economic interests, regardless of race. The 1973 strikes, though generally described as "African strikes," included a sizable number of Indian participants. This was contrary to the general assumption that there existed an unbridgeable rift between the two groups. The rapid unionization of Indian workers in comparison to Africans, the higher proportion of Indians in skilled positions, and their higher average level of education were said to separate the interests of the two groups.[7] Hence, the behavior of Indian strikers was explained by many employers as based on fear of African retaliation. In a subsequent investigation of these factors by the Durban Institute for Industrial Education, it was found that 80 percent of the Indian participants interviewed had Standard 6 or less education, and almost a half earned below the poverty datum line figure of R18* per week. Indian workers were therefore neither better-educated nor better-paid than their African fellow-workers.[8] With respect to fear as the motivating factor in the strike-participation of Indians, 60 percent of the sample (N=120) expressed solidarity with Africans as the reason for participation.[9]

Evidence of Indian-African working-class unity was also noticeable in the 1974 dispute about increases in bus fares by Indian bus owners in Chatsworth. The (African) Black Allied Workers' Union supported the (Indian) Southern Durban Civic Federation in rejecting the planned increases. The secretary of the union, Mr. Menziwe Mbeo, complained that "Bus owners do not seem to realize that the majority of Indian and African workers in Durban earn far less than the standard poverty datum line."[10] The workers' cause was further dramatized by comparing the situation of South African Blacks with conditions under Western systems. Mbeo continued:

> The bus association should ponder on the fact that when purely business interests threaten to supersede the welfare of the whole Black community, then our community is rapidly getting as decadent as the West because over-commercialization for its own sake is foreign to the very spirit of this continent.[11]

The increasing identification of Indian and African students has been noticeable in spite of separate education. Indian students at Durban-Westville strongly supported their fellow African students at Turfloop in May 1972 when 1146 of the latter were expelled for protesting the expulsion of their past Students' Representative Council president.[12] In proposing the boycott motion to a meeting of a thousand students, one speaker said: "We are not voting as Indians but as Blacks. We need solidarity to eradicate this repugnant

*R (Rand) = US$1.18 (1978).

system."[13] Similar stands were taken by Indian students at the M.L. Sultan Technical College and at Springfield Indian Teachers' Training College. The aftermath of the Soweto riots in June 1976 brought forth much the same response; of the Black students arrested by the police for distributing pamphlets, well over half were Indians.

In addition to this type of collaboration, Indians have always been engaged in philanthropic activities outside their group, especially with Africans. These range from Indian doctors offering low-cost medical attention to African patients, to Indian businessmen raising bursaries for African university students, to building a school in Kwazulu, to Indian manufacturers helping to set up factories to be run by Africans.

Given the general racially structured inequality in South Africa, however, these charitable activities are unlikely to have much impact on the perceptions of a more privileged group by a less privileged one (or vice versa). Efforts to create goodwill, particularly when they appear paternalistic and opportunistic to recipients, are likely to fail under conditions of enforced unequal separatism. This is even more likely where a middle group lends itself to being the convenient buffer or shock absorber for the privileged minority and vulnerable scapegoat for the poor majority at the other end. It is hardly surprising that the Indian response in such a predicament is ambiguous and wavering according to circumstances. In this respect, the oft-cited "unity of the oppressed" in their common plight would seem to remain only a slogan.[14]

Indeed all three groups—Indians, Coloreds, and Africans—are disenfranchised at the power center, suffer economically and politically inequitable treatment daily, and face to all intents and purposes a future of greater fragmentation, continued denial of meaningful political rights, and great economic uncertainty. That deep cleavages prevail among the oppressed ought to be explicable through a detailed analysis of (a) the socioeconomic realm, (b) the cultural discontinuities which give rise to mutually suspicious and hostile perceptions, and (c) the continuing significance of previous encounters of conflict.

SOCIOECONOMIC CLEAVAGES

Differential political constraints serve to separate Blacks from one another and influence their identifications. Unlike Africans, Indians and Coloreds may own land in urban areas, notwithstanding numerous restrictions and the impact of the Group Areas Act. Without understating the difficulties involved in obtaining trading licenses even for Indians and Coloreds, their petty bourgeoisie is allowed a much greater scope than its African counterpart. Indians have therefore been seen as in the position of blocking African aspirations. As middleman the Indian has been considered the exploiter who is in a position to take money from poor Africans. Even Coloreds have at various points expressed dissatisfaction with the "encroachment" of Indian traders on their areas and have from time to time called for protective exclusion. At one point in Durban there was a tirade against Indian men marrying Colored women so as to gain trading privileges in the Colored areas. There are few, if any, positions in which Africans hold supervisory positions over Indians or Coloreds. This had its roots in the post-indenture period when Indians moved into competitive urban life, and Africans were considered more "adept" at heavier manual work. As the demands of an expanding secondary industry created more semiskilled and supervisory positions, filled first by Coloreds and Indians, these prejudices became more entrenched. In the Western Cape, labor policy took an openly preferential line in favor of Coloreds and froze African labor at a given limit. Nonrecognition of African trade unions (until recently) in contrast to mixed White/Colored/Indian unions has also impeded African mobility. On the other hand, there are tendencies to replace unionized Indians with their "cheaper" African counterparts. However, the occupational mobility of both Coloreds and Indians is clearly related to their comparatively privileged status. This is particularly evident in areas such as Durban, East London, and Port Elizabeth, where the presence of sizable concentrations of Indians and Coloreds heightens the sense of relative deprivation of Africans.[15]

These differences are being perpetuated in the low priorities given to African education, aimed at meeting the needs of the "homelands." By contrast, Indian and Colored education is geared increasingly toward the demands of industrial society. Separate education, especially at the university level, has eliminated one of the best opportunities for aspiring elites to get to know each other across ethnic lines. Contacts of Black students outside the formalized university structure have not been facilitated by the Group Areas Act, which restricts ethnics to their own areas. The need for urban Africans to adhere to curfew regulations combined with the ruling that non-Africans need to obtain permits to enter African areas have compounded the mutual isolation. Moreover, Indians and Coloreds on the whole live in better homes in better developed urban environments. The Group Areas Act, which displaced large numbers of Indians and Coloreds at great cost, created an artificial need for new and better, heavily mortgaged homes. This accentuated even further the differences between the life situations of Africans and other Blacks. When Africans do not see members of their own group living in similar circumstances, ethnic cleavages are intensified. Such situations are hardly conducive to bridge-building among the fragmented and differentially oppressed.

The gradations of political inequality among Blacks are reflected in all areas of employment in differential salary scales. In the motor industry, for instance, the 1976 average monthly wages for Whites was R552, Coloreds R168, Indians R234, and Africans R132, while in the textile industry, the corresponding figures were Whites R561.39, Coloreds R129.15, Indians R189.45, and Africans R101.36.[16]

The similar position of Coloreds and Indians in the racial hierarchy—legal and customary—is not reflected in their similar economic placement, however. Indians have a larger middle class than the Coloreds, even though incomes of most Indians are very low. The 1970 census estimates that 76 percent of all working Indians have incomes of less than R100 per month, compared with 89 percent for Coloreds, and 26 percent for Whites.[17] This means that a considerable percentage of Indians live below the poverty datum line, but their incomes have risen steadily, especially during the 1970-75 period. Of all three Black groups, Indian incomes have come closest to White incomes; in 1975, Indians earned approximately half the average White household income, as compared with a third by Coloreds and one-eighth by the average African household.[18]

The greater upward mobility of Indians in comparison with subordinate groups is not unrelated to their high degree of group integration, which is evidenced in comparatively high educational attainment and health standards, with low crime rates, divorce rates, and illegitimate birth rates. Unlike Africans and Coloreds, Indians have managed to maintain a close-knit family and community structure in an essentially hostile environment. The Group Areas Act, however, has had a very deleterious effect on Indians on the whole, and has resulted in a noticeable increase in crime, divorce rates, and other indicators of traditional disorganization. Notwithstanding these anomic tendencies, Indians are still by far the most cohesive of Black groups. Of all the non-White groups, Indians place the highest priority on formal Western education, and despite their overall low income, they have a disproportionately high number of students enrolled at universities. For instance, the only Black faculty of medicine—at the

University of Natal—reported that from 1957 to 1974, 308 Indians had graduated as medical doctors, compared to 41 Coloreds and 207 Africans.[19] Like the Jews and Palestinians in the diaspora, Indians as an insecure minority view higher education as a crucial portable asset and the best insurance for a potential crisis.

CULTURAL DISCONTINUITIES

In general, Indians are more resented by most Africans than are Whites. The isolationist character of the Indian community, which Africans perceive for the most part as arrogance, is frequently cited as one explanation for this paradox.

There is indeed ample evidence for this exclusivism that is generally attributed to the group. Africans or Coloreds are, comparatively speaking, seldom included at equal status level at Indian social gatherings, beyond the appearance of African leaders such as the late Chief Luthuli and more recently Gatsha Buthelezi. Indeed, much the same can be said of Indian-White contact, although contact with Whites is certainly considered more prestigious by Indians than contact with Africans. This is of course hardly surprising for South African society. The Theron report pointed out that in similar fashion Coloreds are more inclined to associate socially with Whites than with Indians and Africans. While African antagonism toward Whites is probably more deep-seated than their resentment of Indians, because of the political peculiarities of South African society, open expression of such animosity is frequently suppressed for fear of retaliation from the more powerful Whites.

Indians appear to evoke resentment for other reasons as well as their exclusivism. First, despite the Indians' shared position of political powerlessness, they are (as already shown) in a more privileged position in the economic hierarchy; second, there is close contact between the African and Indian proletariat in shared inadequate and overcrowded public transport, at work, and in common business and shopping areas. Under these conditions, contact often gives rise to scapegoating and envy utilizing ethnic differences. The frustrations Africans experience in their daily struggle for survival in apartheid society would seem to be compensated more effectively through making the passivist Indian minority the prime target of their resentment.*

*The scapegoating of Indians has not been practiced by Africans alone, but has a long history in South Africa. The anti-Indian campaigns of the 1940s,

Above all, Indian-African perceptions of each other have to be understood in their historical phases. In the 1950s and early 1960s, the influence of the Indian Congress elite was noticeable in including some Africans, Coloreds, and liberal Whites as significant participants in Indian social life. Since then, the tendency among the Indian elite has been for greater exclusivism. Among the more conservative bourgeoisie, religious exclusivism has had a long tradition, since the focus was on the sacredness of rituals in which only group members were relevant. Later on, however, the more politicized elite tended increasingly to use exclusivism as a way of expressing group pride and retaliating against White nonreciprocation. On a symbolic level, it represented a form of rejecting White political domination. Most social contact with Whites, regardless of whether they are government supporters or opponents, is now generally viewed as contaminating. This Indian ideological isolationism inevitably has carried over to African relationships as well and even produced an accentuated sectionalism *within* the Indian group. Whereas in the 1950s and 1960s, concomitant with greater intergroup contacts—albeit at the formal level—there was a tendency toward all-Indian inclusiveness, cutting across intragroup religious and linguistic differences, there now seems to be a greater intragroup differentiation along linguistic and religious lines. Ethnic origins are delved into and revival of ethnic traditions sought. Giving "Tamil" names as distinct from North Indian names, for example, is considered important by some former political activists.

A marked contrast is represented by a few younger Indian members of the Black People's Congress who downplay and even debunk cultural origins, engage in a wide range of contact with other Blacks, and embrace aspects of African culture as evidence of their bona fide intentions of becoming one with the majority of oppressed Africans. Their grass-roots contact with Africans and other Blacks differs sharply from the elite-based contact of the Indian Congress, which was more formal and did not include the embracing of African cultural symbols.* Although officially the Black People's Congress, prior to its banning, could not show significant numbers of Indians as mem-

which won many votes for the Nationalists in the 1948 election, exacerbated racial tensions and provocatively singled out Indians as prime justification for racial separation.

*Even when Indian Congress leaders did come into contact with rank-and-file Africans, to whom they frequently gave free medical or legal services, there was still a status gap which made for qualitatively different relationships from those the BPC seeks to foster.

bers for fear of political repercussions, the essential message of this movement has penetrated the minds of a significant number of university students and, to an even greater extent, high school students. Even those who react against the philosophy of Black Consciousness are influenced insofar as they are uncomfortable in their usage of traditional labels such as "non-Whites." Hence they either desist from using these labels or take pains to explain why the term *Indians* is being used rather than *Blacks*.

Among the older generation and the vast majority of the unpoliticized Indians, however, the obsession with maintaining the "purity" of the group is still noticeable. Hence all types of intermarriage, ranging from interlinguisitic to interreligious to interracial, are considered undesirable, and yet—paradoxically—exogamous marriages have never been more common than they are at present. The strictest taboo would seem to be on interracial marriage, followed by interreligious and interlinguistic.* The supposed desire of Africans and Whites to marry Indian women is, as in the White racist folklore, a prevalent theme which recurs when discussing prospects for the group's future. In subjective importance it exceeds concern for prospects of the group's economic well-being and political freedom. "Will we be able to maintain our identity?" becomes the crucial focus. It would be relatively simple to dismiss such behavior as racism which has been internalized by subordinate groups, but there is a wider background which must be understood. First, there is the deeply rooted tradition of endo-

*Indian-African marriages rarely take place even though there are no legal proscriptions. (Intermarriage between Whites and Blacks is illegal, but not among the three Black groups.) The complexities of the situation are illustrated by the following story, which is frequently told with varying emphases and has virtually become part of the folklore:

> A wealthy merchant in East Africa answered his door one evening to find two young Africans. Upon enquiring the purpose of their visit, he was told that one of them had come to ask for the hand of the merchant's daughter in marriage. With due decorum and considered coolness, the merchant called the visitors into the livingroom, offered them a drink, and called in his daughter. The proposition was then put to her. Respectfully she replied that she had nothing against it if the gentleman would take care of her and if she were to have her parents' permission. The merchant then told the young man that, in accordance with tradition, it would only be correct for him to bring his parents to make a formal approach. That night, after the guests had left, the family packed its belongings and fled the country.

This story, in its numerous variations, is used to underline the need for presence of mind and tact in dealing with such situations, as well as to emphasize the chances that this could occur close to home.

gamy among Indians, which is highly discriminatory and based not only on racial and religious groupings but also on linguistic differences and in some instances regional origin in India. Various dietary rules and differing ideas of purity and pollution made interdining among Indians of different religious backgrounds a rare phenomenon in the past, and at present it takes place, if at all, only at the elite level. Second, the relevance of racial classification in South African society from birth to death creates problems for the progeny of mixed racial ancestry, as it has in the few instances of Indian-African unions. Hence the fear of "loss of identity" under such circumstances is real indeed.

An analogous situation has developed in the case of Coloreds. There is correlation between the increase in racially discriminatory legislation and the accentuation of emphasis on Colored "identity." This was reflected in the concern about the label *Colored* in light of its Afrikaans translation *kleurlinge*, which was seen as lumping together all non-Whites. The more conservative "Coloredists" distanced themselves from Africans and sought to emphasize their cultural and biological links with Whites.[20] In some instances they sought also to restrict the trading rights of Indians and Africans in their areas. Added to this was a desire to extend the application of the Immorality Act to proscribe sexual relations between Coloreds and Africans to safeguard their "Colored identity."

Among the politicized Colored intellectuals, on the other hand, the Trotskyite "Unity Movement" found some support. Its policy of rigid noncollaboration with the "enemy" and rejection of all deals smacking of compromise reinforced Colored separateness from the ruling group, without necessarily forging the desired links with African nationalists at the grassroots level.

ENCOUNTERS OF CONFLICT

Underlying Indian-African relations, especially among the older generation of Indians, is the trauma of the 1949 Durban communal riots. The Durban riots began on January 13, 1949, near a crowded bus depot frequented by Indians and Africans. The commission that reported on the disturbance described it as follows:

> The spark which caused this tragic explosion was almost ludicrous in its insignificance. If one sifts the obviously perjured evidence, the probable facts appear to be these. A Native boy, 14 years of age, had words with an Indian shop assistant, 16 years of age, and

> slapped the latter's face. The Indian youth lodged a complaint with his employer, also an Indian, who came out of the Indian Market into Victoria Street and assaulted the Native boy. In the tussle the Native's head accidentally crashed through the glass of the shop window, and in withdrawing it the boy received cuts behind the ears, which caused the blood to flow. Unfortunately this happened at a time when . . . a mass of Natives and Indians had congregated in quest of conveyance to their homes. The Natives saw an adult Indian assaulting a Native child and they saw blood. That was enough. They went berserk and attacked every Indian within sight.[21]

On the other hand, the historian Eric Walker refers to retaliatory action from another perspective: "Some of the wealthier Indians . . . whose arrogance had offended many of their humbler co-religionists fired at Zulus from the windows of their swiftly moving cars."[22] While Indians may have owned "swiftly moving cars," their possession of firearms was illegal, and hence it is highly unlikely they were displayed publicly, if at all. In reporting the occurrence the next morning, the newspapers devoted less space to the riot than to a storm at Mossel Bay. But the racial tension flared up again in violence, and over the next two days there were widespread attacks in the Durban area on Indians and their property. The District Commandant of Police, whose force had been conspicuously passive during the riot, reported to the commission that

> Houses were now being burned by the score, all in the vicinity of Booth Road. Almost all the Indians not evacuated from this area were either killed, burned to death or left dying. While the men were clubbed to death, Indian women and young girls were raped by the infuriated Natives. This state of arson and looting continued throughout the night and when further military and naval reinforcements arrived many instances occurred where the forces had to resort to the use of firearms to protect life and property.[23]

It should be pointed out that the poorest sectors of the Indian community, whose economic position was not much better than most Africans, were worst hit by the upheaval because of their greater vulnerability in outlying slum areas, which are more accessible and less protected than the city core. This suggests that looting figured lower in the motivation of participants than the outlet of long accumulated frustrations expressed in animosity toward Indians.

In spite of what still figures in the contemporary mythology of

Indians as proof of the "unpredictable" character of Africans, the Durban riots were never a clear-cut racial conflict. Ironically, in the political arena at the time the Indian-African Congress leadership had been forging bonds since 1946. During the riots a joint statement pledging support for Indian-African unity was issued, and the riot-affected areas were jointly patrolled by Indian and African leaders. The writer's own memory of the riots, and the experiences of various other individuals, is that many Africans gave assistance to Indians at risk to themselves by shielding them from activists.

Official estimates of the destruction were 142 deaths—one European, 50 Indians, 87 Africans (caused mainly by police action), and four of undetermined racial origin. Those injured numbered 1,087 (32 Whites, 11 Coloreds, 541 Africans, and 503 Indians). One factory, 58 stores, and 247 dwellings owned by Indians were destroyed, and two factories, 652 stores, and 1,285 dwellings were damaged. Thousands of Indians became refugees overnight. Eight months after the riots, 770 refugees were still in camps.[24]

The attitudes of the public toward the events differed according to racial groups. Indians complained about the behavior of the police, alleging that stronger and prompter action would have minimized and arrested the riots. Many considered the official estimates of injuries and damages too low. Little regret was expressed by African public spokesmen. Whites are reported to have generally reacted with statements such as "Indians had it coming to them," or "The trouble was that they got the wrong Indians."[25] Webb and Kirkwood comment on the noticeable absence of any rallying together of all groups to the defense of law and order, for whatever group, in the interest of upholding the rule of law.

Although the riots were spontaneous, it can be argued that they were structurally predetermined by the nature of South African society. The differential incorporation of the various racial groups, enjoying different levels of rewards, set the stage for seeking a scapegoat and revenge for long-suffered misery. Indians were perceived by Africans as most obviously benefitting from this situation precisely because they occupied a "middleman" role. These stereotypes provided a focal point for quick mobilization of Africans.

The significance for contemporary race relations of the Durban riots some thirty years ago—particularly for Indian attitudes toward Africans—results from the cultivation of the image of Africans as mercilessly antagonistic toward them. The repetition of exaggerated stories of rape and looting, common in the folk history of Indians but reported with the authenticity of personal experience, creates a climate of fear and apprehension concerning Africans. This is abetted almost weekly by reports of break-ins of Africans into Indian homes, and by stories of terrorization of Indians by Africans. This has not led to a reduction of African servants in Indian middle-class homes, however, but rather to a shift from male servants to females and younger boys, who are considered "controllable." Since most of these servants work illegally in the Indian households* and are subject to frequent police raids, their dependency and consequent exploitation has also increased. On the other hand, many Indian households function as private social welfare stations and minimal shelter for border cases (orphans, unemployed, handicapped, alcoholics) who would otherwise face even greater misery in their own areas.

That Indian-African relations in the 1970s still display considerable mistrust is evidenced by the near-occurrence of a riot in the predominantly Indian North Coast town of Stanger in 1974, after a twelve-year-old African employee in an Indian greengrocery died suddenly. Although post-mortem results revealed that he had died of "natural causes," the Africans present interpreted the situation in racial terms. The stereotype of the Indian exploiter who treats his employee poorly, overworks and underfeeds him, was evoked, and rioting spread to the neighboring areas, where Indians were attacked at random by angry Africans.[26]

An improvement in Indian-African relationships at the important level of personal contacts is virtually impossible as long as gross structural inequalities persist. The grassroots distrust is occasionally fanned by public squabbling of Indian and African leaders who, for reasons of their own, engage in needless disputes instead of striving in the interest of a common cause. Such an incident took place in 1976 when Indian sociologist Fatima Meer suggested publicly that the real Black leaders in South Africa are on Robben Island. The matter was raised in the Kwazulu legislature as an instance of Indians insulting African leaders, and threatening references were made to the 1949 race riots by a member of the Kwazulu legislative assembly.[27] A year later, when Buthelezi was invited to address a meeting at the University of Durban-Westville, some Indian students protested on the grounds that he was not their real leader but a government stooge. Buthelezi's response was that if they continued along these lines, he

*Africans are not allowed to live in Indian areas unless they are registered with the Bantu Affairs Department. Furthermore, only one servant per household is legally permissible. Since the registration procedure is time-consuming and obstructive, it is not uncommon to succumb to the temptation to hire those who offer themselves for employment without the necessary papers.

could not promise them that the 1949 race riots would not happen again.

CONCLUSION: PROSPECTS FOR INTERSUBORDINATE ALLIANCES

With the decolonization of Mozambique, the challenged change to majority rule in Rhodesia, and the Cuban presence in Angola, South African Whites have been forced to ask themselves what potential support they can reasonably expect from their Black fellow citizens. As can be expected from the incumbents of power in polarized conflicts, they express confidence in the support of the majority in order to boost morale and suppress doubts about the strength of the opposing camps.

There is apparently greater unanimity of opposition to and noncollaboration with the government on the part of the Colored minority than among the Indians. Although there are no systematic data here, the Colored leadership may be assumed to have greater credibility on the basis of its elected status and the rapport of the Colored Council with its people who support a confrontation stance.

In contrast, the Indian community reflects a wide range of opinion. The response is far from unequivocal and is complicated further by the need to choose between the policies of the White opponent and the alternative, as they see it, of communism. While the internalization of the Afrikaner propaganda concerning the Communist threat, together with fears of violating South Africa's strict legal sanctions on this issue, might explain some of the Indian statements, there is an historical reality to which Indians can point as victims—unlike the indigenous Colored minority. The Indian press frequently editorializes on this deep-seated fear of historical repetitions: "There was a time when one thought that whatever else was objectionable in Communist methods, racism was not part of it."[28] However, happenings in Zanzibar, where "naked racialism was directed against Asians and Arabs,"[29] as well as White imperialist tendencies of Russia toward her own non-White Mongolian and Asian-inhabited states, would seem to cast doubt on Communist credibility. "Already some racist Africans have been making anti-Indian noises, and the fear is that the Communists will make tirades against 'capitalist exploiters,' and in the same way that President Amin of Uganda falsely claimed that it was the Indians who were the capitalist exploiters, and Hitler blamed it on the Jews, Indians will be the scapegoats here."[30]

As has been pointed out, one of the noticeable differences between the Indians and Coloreds in South Africa is the larger middle class of the Indians. Yet affluence alone would seem an insufficient explanation for their varying attitudes. The participation of the Chinese minority in the Communist movement in Malaya, for instance,[31] despite their general affluence, would seem to suggest that other explanations must be sought. A second difference between the two groups is the cultural and visible distinctiveness of Indians, bolstered by a host of traditional institutions and organizations. Throughout the history of Indian settlement in South Africa, the antagonism of the rulers toward them was expressed in varying degrees of severity—from informal discrimination to legislative exclusion. This discrimination, always more severe than that the indigenous Coloreds experienced, reinforced bonds of commonality among Indians. Religion, music, customs, traditions, and distinctive food tastes formed part of the construction of a womblike structure to act as a bulwark against a hostile environment. As Hilda Kuper points out: "It is because identification with their own sub-groups is so meaningful that the political role of minorities becomes less effective."[32]

This group identity which emerged in the process of retaliating against an antagonistic environment became reified. In so doing it generated confidence among the group members and insulated them from the White perceptions of them as a lower caste. In some instances this cultural narcissism was so successful that Indians believed themselves to be morally superior to the dominant group. The government's policy of Separate Development integrated these tendencies and gave them official status by pointing to their existence as the *raison d'etre* for separate development.

Political change has different connotations for the Indians than it does for the Coloreds. While both groups would benefit from egalitarian status and other political freedoms, political change of the kind that would be offered by joining decolonizing African forces presents the trauma of loss of identity for Indians. Since the preservation of their identity is seen by Indians as having enabled them to survive White oppression, its perpetuation has become synonymous with security and survival itself. For the Chinese minority in Malaya the main attraction offered by the Communists, apart from freedom from domination or oppression, would appear to have been its specifically "Chinese" character and the promise of a continued Chinese identity as opposed to incorporation into an alien Malay nation;[33] for South African Indians, on the other hand, joining the outside liberation forces means a merging of the group's identity into one political unit with no certainty of being free from persecution by the new regime.* Ambivalent attitudes of Africans toward Indians, especially in the Durban area, are documented in the Hanf study,[34] showing some basis for these anxieties.

In the present situation, Indians can feel certain of their survival through cultivating their group identity, but the future as they perceive it provides no such assurance.

*Leo Kuper formulated a similar conclusion in the following way: "A 'stranger' category, separated from the rest of society by discontinuities in structure and culture, and affording a likely target for persecution, can hardly fail to be aware of the multi-racial structure of society. One section may seek to align itself with the dominant race as a criterion for social relationships, but they can hardly escape awareness of a separate identity" (*Race, Class, and Power* [Chicago: Aldine, 1975], pp. 58-59). If this is true, the South African liberal dream of a common society in which group identifications are replaced by individualism seems rather unlikely.

CHANGE IN SOUTH AFRICA: OPPORTUNITIES AND CONSTRAINTS

Lawrence Schlemmer

INTRODUCTION

By now it is commonplace to describe the period from 1973 as a watershed in the recent history of South and southern Africa. In 1973 there was serious Black labor unrest in Natal and, to a lesser extent, on the Rand; in the same year the Arab oil boycott of South Africa was initiated as a reflection of external condemnation of South Africa's racial policies. Since then a series of events has occurred dramatically altering the political situation both in South Africa and the region as a whole. In newly independent Mozambique and Angola, Black Marxist-leaning regimes have come to power, eliminating two important buffer states between White-ruled southern Africa and the rest of Africa. And more recently, Zimbabwe-Rhodesia and Namibia have entered difficult periods of transition to majority rule.*

Within South Africa there was widespread Black† pupil and youth unrest in June 1976 that once suppressed took the form of a school boycott which dragged on until virtually the end of 1977. In addition, the Black Consciousness movement, founded in 1968 to foster pride and unity among Africans, Coloreds, and Indians, gained momentum after 1973, encouraging more and more militant stances by Black leaders. Many of these took up the cause of the rebellious youth in 1976 and 1977, which was probably one of the factors moving the state in October 1977 to detain many Transvaal Black leaders and to ban the important Black-read newspaper *The World* and all prominent Black Consciousness organizations. There have been a number of political trials of Blacks, as well as detentions without trial and deaths in detention (including that of the founder

*At this writing, Zimbabwe-Rhodesia has instituted an internal settlement in the form of a multiracial government.

†Unless otherwise stated, the word *Black* refers to all non-Whites—i.e., Africans, Coloreds, and Indians.

of the Black Consciousness movement, Steve Biko), which strongly suggest heightened political activity in recent years by the Black opposition to White rule. Very recently there have been a number of instances of urban terrorism and sabotage; some of the people involved have been refugees from police action in the 1976-77 township disturbances who have returned after receiving training and weapons in Eastern Europe.

In the wake of the international publicity given to the township riots and other political events, there has been increased moral and economic pressure on South Africa from the West. Previously, pressure on South Africa consisted largely of opposition to participation in international competitions by South African sportsmen. This sports boycott commenced at a time when sport was racially segregated in South Africa and has continued despite changes in policy which have led to substantial racial integration in South African sport. Since then a UN Security Council boycott on arms to South Africa has been imposed and, more important, various impediments to the much-needed flow of international investment capital and loan finance. These restrictions have undoubtedly retarded South Africa's economic growth significantly over the past few years—so much so that well-known South African economists like Dr. Jan Hupkes have claimed that were it not for these external economic pressures, by early 1978 the country would have been experiencing an export-led economic boom.[1]

These events are seen by many observers as the beginning of the end for White control and race segregation in South Africa. Certainly the quiescent years of Black political inactivity from the early 1960s to the beginning of the 1970s have passed. It would be naive, however, to see the system of White oligarchy as entering a final phase of instability, or even as faltering. Unlike the Whites in Zimbabwe-Rhodesia, Namibia, Angola, and Mozambique, the Whites in South Africa are sufficient in number to retain control of the police force and the army; their numbers also give them high morale and a sense of being well enough established to retain the initiative. South Africa's industry is sufficiently developed and diversified, with adequate access to local raw materials, to enable it to be self-sufficient if needs be. This having been said, there can be no doubt that the recent changes in the subcontinent and the pressures from abroad and from Blacks inside South Africa have had significant effects on government policies. The purpose of this analysis is to examine the nature of the response of South African Whites to the developments of the past five to six years.

At the end of 1974 the Prime Minister (optimistically and misleadingly perhaps) asked the world to give South Africa six months' chance: "They will be amazed at where the country stands in about six to twelve months' time." Since then the present Minister of Foreign Affairs and other important spokesmen have time and again committed South Africa to the abolition of what they describe as "unnecessary race discrimination." A number of policy changes have occurred. Their magnitude and significance may be questioned, but some at least should be briefly recorded here. The sports policy has shifted considerably. Sport, like other social activities, had been strictly segregated. The first major reaction to international pressure was to allow integration in international events. Then the words "international event" were adopted as a euphemism for inter-group competition within South Africa. Recently the policy was relaxed further, and fully integrated sport at club level is now possible. Some state departments have removed signs segregating the races in government buildings, and major local authorities have opened park facilities to all races. Hotels, restaurants, and social clubs have applied for international status to serve all races (although such concessions tend to be granted only to the more expensive facilities). African businessmen in urban Black township areas have had some of the restrictions on their trading activities removed, and very recently Africans qualifying for permanent urban residence were allowed occupancy rights to their homes in the form of 99-year leases, including rights to buy, sell, and bequeath property, but without granting full freehold title to the land on which houses stand.

From 1970-1975 average real wages of Blacks grew at a rate of 6.6 percent a year compared to 1.0 percent for White wages, slightly narrowing the racial gap in wages for the first time in South Africa's history.[2] Between 1975-1977 the trend continued despite an economic downturn, with wages of Blacks rising in real terms while those of Whites fell.[3] Recently Dr. P.J. Koornhof, then Minister of Education and Training, announced increases in salary scales of African teachers raising them close to parity with White scales for equivalent qualifications.

Constitutionally, the state proposes to amend the South African parliamentary system to allow for parallel White, Colored, and Indian parliaments and cabinets linked by an overarching Cabinet Council headed by a State President with executive powers (who is almost certain to be White because of a built-in majority of Whites on the Cabinet Council). Indians and Coloreds will enjoy full ministerial status equivalent to their White colleagues. The Cabinet Council will deal with "common" affairs of state such as finance, defense, economic affairs, etc., while the "ethnic" cabinets and parliaments will deal with separate group affairs. These proposals, which are not likely to be introduced until 1980, are ill understood at the moment, and there are many unanswered questions—for example, how will group affairs be distinguished from "common" affairs, and will an Indian or Colored be appointed a full minister-in-portfolio dealing with the "common" affairs of all races? Africans are excluded from the new proposals. Inasmuch as they imply continued White predominance in the political affairs of the country, these proposals are hardly a basic change in the direction of government policy, but they would represent at least a limited form of power-sharing among Whites, Indians, and Coloreds. Key political groups among the Coloreds have rejected the proposals, however, and at the present time the government has appointed a parliamentary commission to reconsider the constitutional plan.

A very recent development of considerable interest has been the government response to the reports of two statutory commissions—one known as the Wiehahn Commission and the other as the Riekert Commission (the names of their respective chairmen). The response to the Wiehahn Commission has been a government decision to allow the registration of African trade unions, to phase out "job reservation" and trade union "closed shop" agreements on a gradual basis (both being devices which served to protect non-African occupational privileges in industry), and to allow Africans the right to receive artisan skill training in so-called "White" areas. These concessions may ease impediments to Black job and wage advancement in industrial areas. Not unexpectedly, however, the proposals include important limitations: the political activities and economic initiatives of trade unions are to be more carefully controlled than ever before; migrant workers and commuters from Black homelands will not be allowed the benefits of union rights; and the entry of Black unions on to industrial councils can be vetoed by the White unions. The new system, therefore, will not include legalized race discrimination as such, but ensures a pervasive system of covert control.

A distinction with important future policy implications is being made between "urban insider" Africans (specifically, those with so-called Section 10 rights to continuous domicile and work in "White" areas)* and homeland contract and migrant workers.

*Section 10(i) of the Natives (Urban Areas) Consolidation Act, as amended,

This distinction will be reinforced by the implementation of the proposals in the Riekert Commission report. If these proposals are adopted, those Africans with Section 10 rights will have these rights ensconced, will be allowed greater mobility, and might even be allowed to own businesses in certain White trading areas; in addition, the urban African townships will be developed and improved. The "influx control" system (pass laws) will also be eased for urban Africans; control will be based on housing and job availability (theoretically) for all races.*

These limited concessions will go hand in hand with more sophisticated sociopolitical controls, and there is considerable doubt that the "insider" Africans' children, who are forced to take homeland citizenship, will enjoy the same rights as their parents. All this notwithstanding, these changes are an important departure from the ideology of Separate Development. Whereas previously it was an article of faith in government policy that all Africans were to formally associate to one or another homeland, and were ultimately temporary sojourners in White areas, now a new interstitial status is being created for the so-called urban African. Someday he might even enjoy the broad sociopolitical status of Colored and Indian people in the common area. In a very real sense this splitting of urban insiders from homeland-based Africans is a policy of divide and rule, but it raises the possibility of gradual, partial inclusion of urban Africans in the politics of the common area.

It should be emphasized, however, that at this stage the overall policy stance of the government of South Africa is still very firmly against any recognition of citizenship for Africans in the core area of South Africa and the rights to political privileges which citizenship would imply. In Parliament the Minister of Bantu Administration and Development (since changed to "Plural Relations" and then to "Cooperation and Development" in an attempt to create a more favorable image for the department among Blacks) stated as recently as February 1978 that "there will be no black South Africans." Under the existing Bantu Laws Amendment Bill, all urban Africans still can be deprived of the security of their Section 10 rights to permanent urban status outside the homelands.[4] The Minister of Cooperation and Development (African Affairs) has

provides that no African may remain for more than 72 hours in an urban area unless he or she (a) has resided there continuously since birth, or (b) has worked there continuously for one employer for 10 years or lived there lawfully working for different employers for 15 years.

*The government has subsequently dropped the distinction as far as trade union rights are concerned, but it remains in other respects.

recently taken the welcome step of setting up machinery to consult with, *inter alia*, the most outspoken Black critics of the government, but policy is clearly in a state of flux and contradiction.

Broadly speaking, while changes in race relations at the social level in *some* spheres of life are beginning to take the form of a *very* gradual evolution toward nonracialism, changes at the political level are taking a different structural course. The policy changes emphasize more complete sociopolitical separation of "homeland" Africans, while for Indians and Coloreds (and possibly Africans with statutory urban rights in due course), a framework of parallel political structures is developing, with the necessary interlocking of the different segments occurring only at the top of the political hierarchies, and with the White leadership retaining a balance of power.

It is important to note that all policy adaptations are introduced with extreme caution, with great emphasis on increasingly sophisticated control of social change, and with reluctance to be seen as going against what are believed to be the prevailing Nationalist voter preferences and attitudes. Early in 1978, for example, an Afrikaner newspaper reported that Black children in small numbers were being allowed to attend White private schools. Soon after, the responsible minister, in a by-election speech in which he displayed his sensitivity to public opinion, vehemently denied any change in the policy to segregate school children, minimizing the significance of the "exceptions" made under "special circumstances." In another example, top-level Defence Force instructions to White Commando (citizen volunteer) units to train Blacks have met with widespread resistance, influencing the Defence Force to take a "soft line" on the introduction of the program. In introducing the proposals flowing out of the Wiehahn Commission on labor matters, the government took care to obtain prior agreement from those sections of the conservative White labor movement which normally support the government; it managed to separate off and then confront only those White union leaders who are associated with the ultra-right wing Herstigte Nasionale Party. There are numerous other examples, but the agonizing process of policy change when it is constrained by fear of prevailing attitudes is well summed up by Dr. Willem de Klerk, editor of *The Transvaler*, in the following description of the rhythm of the stages of policy change: "*Never; no, not now; perhaps; yes but; yes, but keep it quiet; good, go ahead but beware of repercussions.*"[5]

Those government ministers prepared to make pragmatic

adaptations in policy have to contend with various very watchful audiences. The Afrikaner group is relatively highly mobilized in political terms. The large, cross-sectional membership of the National party has to be taken very seriously by the government executive, and its congresses regularly provide critical feedback up to cabinet level. In the National party parliamentary caucus the right wing is better organized than the left wing, according to the influential Nationalist academic Professor Sampie Terreblanche.[6] Then there is the very coherently organized Afrikaner Broederbond (League of Brothers), composed of 11,000 members of the Afrikaner middle- to top-level elite. The Broederbond, a complex organization fundamentally dedicated to the advancement of Afrikaner culture and Christian-National ideals, is frequently consulted and makes top-level representations to members of the Cabinet (who appear to be mostly Broederbonders themselves) on a great variety of political issues. Evidence suggests that Broederbond executive committee representations have significantly influenced key legislation of recent times, such as the new constitutional proposals.[7]

Thus no matter what external pressures for policy change or contingencies might arise, the government is relatively constrained in its decisions by various powerful formations of public opinion. Hence, for the purposes of analyzing the constraints on and opportunities for policy change in the short- to medium-term future, it is helpful to examine the results of studies of political attitudes among the White voting electorate and, toward the end of this article, among a small sample of urban Africans as well.

THE USE OF ATTITUDE STUDIES

There is a need for caution in the interpretation of attitude studies. It is widely recognized that under given circumstances (say forceful leadership, or pragmatic needs to alter behavior patterns) certain types of attitudes and opinions can change very quickly. Percy Cohen refers to such attitudes as "malleable," being little more than a reflection of social conventions and behaviors determined by the social or political structure at any given time. He also refers to "immalleable" attitudes, however, which may reflect what he calls "primordial" sentiments—deep-seated fears, identity threats, or (it might be added) deeply imbued basic values, which are much more resistant to change.[8] In White South African racial and political attitudes, one will inevitably encounter an admixture of more and less malleable attitudes. In this analysis, then, it is not assumed that *all* attitudes are predictors of behavior. Certain attitudes may be sufficiently rigid and intensely held to have a determining influence on behavior, but in general political attitudes will be treated only as indexes of change in the political "climate."

The notion of political "climate" requires some discussion. Key political decision-makers are unlikely to know in advance which attitudes will become modified under the stimulus of leadership and policy change, and which attitudes will provoke resistance and backlash. Social attitudes therefore produce a climate within which the politician operates cautiously. The politician himself may hold fairly typical community attitudes, in which case the climate of public opinion will seem all the more salient as a guide to his behavior.

With these considerations in mind we can turn to an assessment of the trends revealed in the results of attitude studies. The main set of results is derived from an investigation carried out by Market and Opinion Surveys (MOS), but designed and analyzed by the author. The sample, stratified by region and community size, was a nationwide, randomly selected panel of 1,352 Afrikaans-speaking Whites and 946 predominantly English-speaking Whites. The data collection method used was a postal questionnaire; the typical low-response rate of such questionnaires has been overcome to the extent that at least 90 percent rates of return are inevitably achieved by MOS.* The study was carried out in June and July 1977.

The results of this survey have been supplemented by those of an earlier investigation designed by the author and conducted by the organization Market Research Africa (MRA), involving personal interviews conducted among a nationwide stratified random sample of 641 Afrikaans-speaking Whites in March/April 1974, and by other polls conducted by MOS and MRA using essentially the same methods, approach, and sampling. (The 1974 MRA study did not include "deep rural" farm-dwelling respondents, but it did include very small towns and hamlets; perusal of the results by community size in the MOS results does not reveal distinctive attitude patterns among farm dwellers as opposed to small town dwellers.)

It is not claimed that perfect technical comparability of the

*The panel members enter into a contract to respond to questionnaires in return for which they receive free subscriptions to magazines of their choice. A measure of the success of this method is that since 1969 MOS has been able to predict the outcome of election results within a margin of 2 to 4 percent.

two major and the other investigations has been achieved. In this analysis, however, the interest does not lie in minute shifts of opinion or in the kind of precision which would make near-perfect comparability essential. Generalizations regarding change, for example, are based only on substantial differences between the findings of the various studies—differences well in excess of the effects of the particular approach used and also well in excess of differences statistically significant at the 95 percent level of confidence.

HOW HAVE RECENT EVENTS AFFECTED WHITE PERCEPTIONS?

Of fairly central importance to the analysis is the way in which recent events are perceived by Whites, the extent to which they are taken seriously, and how the interpretations of the political system may have been altered. In the MOS 1977 investigation a general question about recent events was posed in an open-ended form: *Think about our national affairs and politics over the last three years. Which events have influenced your political thinking the most?* The township disturbances of mid-1976 onward emerged as most prominent, more so among English-speakers than Afrikaners (32 percent mention versus 25 percent). The Angola situation was next in frequency, followed by the Rhodesian situation. Rather more English-speakers than Afrikaans-speakers saw the Angolan situation as threatening. Generally, the Afrikaners appear somewhat less threatened by events in the townships and in Angola than the English-speakers. External pressure as an important factor was mentioned only by some 5 to 7 percent among both English-speaking and Afrikaans Whites. Among Afrikaners, perception of the Rhodesian situation as a threat appears to be related to pessimism about the future of Whites in South Africa, whereas this relationship does not hold for other factors mentioned.

A direct question was posed: *At present, how do you feel about your future as a White in South Africa?* Some 8 percent of all Whites were very pessimistic and 24 percent fairly pessimistic; hence roughly one-third of Whites express pessimism. Afrikaners were less pessimistic than the English-speakers (29 percent to 37 percent). In 1969 an MRA poll among a sample of 1,000 Whites revealed only 5 percent to be "anxious" about the future of South Africa. Hence a substantial shift seems to have occurred, and it is highly likely that this trend has been maintained at least up to the present.

In the light of the townships disturbances and other events, the sample was asked: *How satisfied or dissatisfied do you think the majority of Black people is with conditions at the moment?* Roughly 16 percent of Afrikaners and 39 percent of English-speakers selected the alternative *very dissatisfied.* In the 1974 MRA study, among 641 Afrikaners the proportion giving the *very dissatisfied* response was 11 percent. Hence, although the perception of the seriousness of the situation seems to be increasing among Afrikaners, their views on African discontent not too long ago still deviated markedly from those of the English-speakers. There is a clear relationship between optimism about the future and perceptions of African discontent. Among Afrikaners, 56 percent of those who considered Africans *satisfied* were optimistic compared with 36 percent of those who saw them as *dissatisfied.*

How threatening are the various types of political developments to White South Africans? The question asked was: *With regard to the general security of Whites in South Africa, how do you view the following events?* The proportions viewing the events as a *serious threat to security* are shown in Table 1.

Table 1

Event(s)	Afrikaans	English-Speaking
Developments in Rhodesia	39%	49%
Turnhalle conference in Namibia (aimed at reaching an internal settlement and early independence)	5	7
Independence of Transkei	6	7
Statements of Chief Buthelezi	16	9
Riots in Soweto	36	46
Attitude of the U.S. and the West	33	35
Mozambique and Angola	43	54
The country's economy	18	26
Border war in Namibia	38	43

In general the English-speaking Whites tend to perceive greater threats in most of the developments (except the statements of Chief Buthelezi and the attitude of the U.S. and the West). Among the more obvious threats to Whites, the pressures emanating from the West tend to be perceived as least serious, although these may have come to be seen as more threatening in recent months. Internally the most manifest threat was clearly the unrest in the townships in 1976.

One way of analyzing the evaluations of the various types of "threats" is to consider the relationship between the perception of the threat and the degree of pessimism about the future. Generally the threats perceived as serious are associated with a greater degree of pessimism about the future of Whites. This is only to be expected: the threats may be causing the pessimism or the pessimists may be more sensitive to threats. Among Afrikaners there is an interesting deviation from the general relationship between perception of threat and pessimism about the future in regard to the two "minor" threats: the Turnhalle debate in Namibia and the independence of the Transkei. Here the relationship between perceived threat and general pessimism is much stronger than with the other threats. Either these events have been able to generate extreme pessimism among the small minority which perceives them as threatening, or else the extreme pessimists have their vision so colored by their feelings that even these events are perceived as seriously threatening. The latter is the more likely explanation. Whites who are deeply pessimistic about their future are likely to feel threatened by any sort of change in the racial order, even if it is a consequence of South African government policies. This is a group for whom nothing other than the status quo is comforting.

How are the traumatic events of 1976—the youth unrest in the townships—perceived? Respondents were asked to indicate what they thought the main causes of the 1976 unrest had been. A wide range of reasons was offered, which can be categorized into what might be called *authentic* causes—those emerging out of socio-economic and political conditions in the townships, such as poor quality of education, lack of facilities, inadequate housing, and unemployment—and *artificial* causes: agitators, Communists, external influences. Among English-speakers, the authentic reasons outweighed the artificial by a ratio of 2.6 to 1, whereas among Afrikaners the artificial reasons outweighed the authentic by 1.2 to 1. Generally, then, the message derived from the disturbances seems to differ significantly for Afrikaans and English-speaking Whites.

Finally, as regards the general situation, the respondents were asked: *How long do you think the present race situation will last without creating serious problems for the Whites?* The percentage breakdown of replies from Afrikaans and English-speaking Whites is given in comparison with the results of the 1974 MRA study (Afrikaners only) in Table 2.

Table 2

	English-Speaking 1977	Afrikaners 1977	Afrikaners 1974
Less than 1 year	8%	7%	2%
Up to 5 years	49	32	14
Longer than 5 years	8	8	20
Indefinitely	9	16	39
Don't know	26	37	25

Obviously English-speakers are far less sanguine about the future than Afrikaners. On the other hand, among Afrikaners a dramatic shift in perceptions occurred between 1974 and late 1977. Those seeing the present situation as lasting longer than five years or indefinitely dropped from 59 percent in 1974 to 24 percent in 1977. These results relate to optimism or pessimism about the future of Whites in the expected way. They also suggest that basic political thinking is in the process of shifting among Afrikaners, with more and more emphasis being placed on future security.

A few general statements about current perceptions of the situation may be hazarded. It is probably still true that Afrikaners reflect substantially lower levels of concern about conditions than English-speaking Whites. Among Afrikaners, though, the degree of pessimism about the future of Whites in South Africa seems to be increasing quite markedly. Pessimism about the future of Whites is related to the extent to which recent events are seen as being serious threats, among which events in Zimbabwe-Rhodesia, Mozambique, and Angola, and the Namibian border situation figure prominently for both Afrikaners and English-speakers. For the English-speaking community, the riots in Soweto are perceived as threats roughly equal in seriousness to the external threats in southern Africa. Afrikaners do not accord the same significance to internal unrest, largely because they do not see the reasons for Black discontent as predominantly internal. A situation of social upheaval is not likely to be regarded as very serious if it can be ascribed to the influence of a small number of agitators who can be tracked down and removed from the scene. A clear majority of English-speakers believe that time for the maintenance of the present political situation is limited to less than five years, whereas most Afrikaners do not see time as running out in this way. While the Afrikaners may still be much more hopeful than the English, their perceptions are shifting markedly under the impact of recent events.

Recent political developments, therefore, have not left any group of White South Africans undisturbed. If the pressure of events persists, then even the more sanguine group—the Afrikaners—may become more anxious over the next few years. However, at this stage many Afrikaners are still apparently remarkably complacent. Not all are complacent, however, and those who are worried about the situation seem to be of two types. One type, like the English-speaking groups, reflects a general concern about the internal stability of South Africa; the other type is a small group which worries about any change in the status quo—even events like the attempt to achieve an internal settlement in Namibia, which would be regarded by most Afrikaners as a positive development.

The greater complacency among Afrikaners than among English-speakers is due in part to the fact that Afrikaners find it easier to adopt scapegoat explanations for some of the threats to their future; as noted earlier, the disturbances in the townships tend to be seen by them as due largely or solely to external forces—agitators, Communists, and the like. It may also be in part a consequence of a firm belief in the policy of separate development as a blanket solution to racial problems. Strong beliefs and ideologies are insulators against anxiety and uncertainty. There may also be a tendency among Afrikaners to underrate the capacities of Africans to constitute an effective threat to stability. Thus racialist views may in themselves provide comfort for some Afrikaners. (It is not suggested that there is no racism among English-speakers, but the form it takes is generally different.)

CHANGES IN BASIC RACE ATTITUDES

The data afford an opportunity to consider whether or not basic race attitudes among Whites have changed in recent times. In the 1977 study, four statements about race were included which had been submitted to a nationwide sample of both English- and Afrikaans-speaking Whites in March 1974, and one statement submitted to Afrikaners only in April 1974. (Until recently the word used officially to designate Africans was "Bantu." For this reason and because the word "African" cannot be translated into Afrikaans, the word Bantu is used in the statements.) The comparison of the results of the two studies is shown in Table 3.

Table 3

Statement	Percentage Agreement	
	1974	1977
1. *It will be many years before the Bantus reach the same level of civilisation as the White man.*	86%	88%
2. *Inherently the Whites and the Bantus are equals.*	16	18
3. *Bantus should not be allowed to mix with Whites at all.*	33	26
4. *Even if the Bantus were to reach the same level of development as the White man, I should not want to mix with them on an equal footing.*	48	40
5. *It is natural for Whites to avoid social contact with Blacks.*	54[a]	48

[a]Afrikaners only.

It is evident that the belief in Black inferiority is alive and well and does not appear to have changed over the four-year interval. Perhaps the period was too short to allow for changes in *basic* racial beliefs to take place. However, the results show that while basic beliefs about race differences are quite stable (items 1 and 2), attitudes toward interracial contact are more open to change (items 3, 4, and 5).

CHANGES IN POLICY STANCES

The results of the various studies allow quite a few time-comparisons to be made about attitudes toward political policies. In the 1974 survey directed at Afrikaners, they were asked to assign points on a scale of 1 to 10 to indicate the importance of various social, moral, and political issues. This procedure was repeated in the 1977 survey. Table 4 illustrates both the persistence of certain public values as well as certain changes which have taken place.

Segregation and protection of White interests against competition appeared to fall in importance between 1974 and 1977, whereas

Table 4

RANK-ORDERING OF THE RATED IMPORTANCE OF SOCIAL AND POLITICAL ISSUES BY AFRIKANERS: 1974 AND 1977

Social/Political Issue	Rank-Ordering in Terms of Rated Importance[a]		
	1974		1977
To lead an honest and moral life	1	(highest importance)	1
To maintain a strictly religious view of life	2		2
To strive for a fair deal for all race groups	3		5
To achieve unity and loyalty to South Africa among Whites <u>*and*</u> *non-Whites*	4		3
To lead a happy and contented life	5		4
To maintain strict segregation of the races	6		9
To serve the Afrikaner community	7		7
Protection of Whites against non-White competition	8		11
Maintenance of morality in films, magazines, etc.	9		6
To promote the cultural affairs of the Afrikaner	10		10
To strive for personal success and achievement	11		8

[a]Based on proportion assigning 8 to 10 in importance on scale of 1 to 10.

the achievement of unity across race lines and the desire for personal happiness (perhaps in an increasingly insecure world) acquired heightened importance, at the expense of the value assigned to a fair deal for all race groups.

A similar exercise was the rating by Afrikaners of a list of "problems" for 1974 and 1977 (see Table 5).These results suggest a decrease in the perceived importance of protecting rank-and-file interests and an increase in the importance of reducing the effects of apartheid. It should be noted, however, that in terms of political "solutions," the issue of homeland independence increased in importance while consultation between Black and White leaders remained essentially unchanged.

As would be expected in view of government policy, great changes have taken place in attitudes toward mixed sport. Thus in

Table 5

RANK-ORDERING OF THE RATED IMPORTANCE BY AFRIKANERS OF THE SERIOUSNESS OF SELECTED "PROBLEMS": 1974 AND 1977

Problem	Rank-Ordering in Terms of Rated Seriousness[a]		
	1974		1977
Rising cost of living	1	(most serious)	1
Too much criticism of policy by newspapers	2		2
Too little attention to problems of ordinary Afrikaners	3		6
Too many apartheid regulations such as separate entrances, etc.	4		3
Too few discussions between White and Black leaders	5		5
Too slow a development of homelands to independence	6		4

[a]Based on the proportion assigning 8 to 10 in seriousness on scale of 1 to 10.

an MOS February 1970 survey, only 4 percent of Afrikaners were in favor of *competition between Whites and Blacks in all types of sport*, but in an MRA May 1975 study, 28 percent of Afrikaners agreed with *racially mixed sport being played at club level*. Then in an MOS October 1976 survey, 50 percent of Afrikaners agreed with *mixed sport at club level*; in July 1977, 61 percent of Afrikaners found *non-Whites and Whites together in sports teams* acceptable (author's study); and by November 1978 the proportion for whom mixed sports clubs were acceptable was 76 percent.

Similar changes appear to have taken place in attitudes toward occupations. Thus in a November 1974 MOS poll, only 32 percent of Afrikaners agreed with the statement that *non-Whites should be trained for the same jobs as Whites in industry and receive the same pay*, while in October 1976 MOS found that 42 percent of Afrikaners agreed to the *abolition of job reservation* (the regulations allowing certain jobs to be performed only by Whites or by Whites, Coloreds, and Indians), and in October 1977, 62 percent found the *admission of non-Whites to the same jobs as Whites* acceptable.

Changes have also taken place in attitudes toward other areas of social life. The July 1977 study showed 28 percent of Afrikaners accepting the *admission of Blacks to all cinemas, theaters, etc.*, while by November 1978 (MOS), the proportion accepting the *opening of theaters, restaurants, and other public facilities to all races where facilities cannot be duplicated* was 43 percent. (Since most people realize that in practice few facilities can be duplicated, the shift in percentages is meaningful, although not quite as significant as the figures suggest.) Agreement among Afrikaners to *shared worship in the same church* was found to be 20 percent by MOS in November 1974, rising to 32 percent in October 1977. In July 1973 (MOS), 11 percent of Afrikaners disagreed with the statement that *the Immorality Act should be retained* (the law which prohibits sexual relations between Whites and Blacks), but by July 1977 the proportion finding *abolition of the Immorality Act* acceptable was 23 percent, and in March and November 1978 (MOS), 27 and 28 percent respectively.

Attitudes in other areas have changed less rapidly or not at all. Some comparisons among Afrikaners between April 1974 and July 1977 are shown in Table 6 (both studies by the author).

Table 6

	Complete and Partial Agreement	
	1974	1977
There should be higher wages for Blacks.	77%	82%
Black trade unions should be recognized.	47	47
The race policy should be adjusted to allow for greater economic growth.	75	68
Whites should pay more taxes so that Blacks can be uplifted.	15	12

On a broader political level, the following question (with alternative responses proposed) was posed in 1974 and 1977: *Suppose that dissatisfaction among Blacks and demands by Black leaders become serious, what in your opinion should Whites do?* The percentages selecting each response are given in Table 7. Here the trend —if any—appears to be in a negative direction.

Respondents in the MOS 1974 and 1977 surveys were also asked whether they agreed with a policy of qualified franchise on a common voters' roll for all race groups. A time-comparison for Afrikaners is not possible (data were not subdivided by language groups in 1974), but a comparison for predominantly Afrikaans-

Table 7

	1974	1977
Try to satisfy the needs of Blacks within White areas.	12%	7%
More discussion with Black leaders.	16	13
Whites should show their authority and enforce order.	17	19
Blacks should be allowed to provide for their own needs in their own areas.	55	56

speaking National party supporters can be made. The proportion of Nationalists supporting the idea of a qualified franchise on a common roll rose from 5 percent to 12 percent between 1974 and 1977. This change is not consistent with the finding that no change (or change in a negative direction) occurred among Whites in regard to the issue of solving the race problem. The increased support for the qualified franchise could be due to more English-speakers in the National party, however.

The overall impressions emerging from this analysis of attitudinal changes among Afrikaners are that interest in White economic and occupational "protectionism" and support for race segregation in social affairs have declined, and that changes have also taken place in regard to the more "intimate" areas of social life (e.g., the Immorality Act and mixed worship)—the latter in particular beginning from a relatively low baseline. Changes have been greatest where policy shifts have occurred without negative outcomes (like the changes accompanying the emergence of the mixed sport policy).

In contrast to these types of attitude changes, there has been only a relatively slight shift (or *no* shift) on issues where the implication is that the proposed policy change will lead to political integration or may affect White material interests. This might seem to contradict the statement above about a declining interest in White economic protection, but that conclusion is based on attitudes about White *working class* issues rather than issues of general economic concern. It seems that specifically working class issues are emphasized less and less, but that general White material interests are of continuing concern. On issues of political policy, Afrikaners do not seem to have changed their views: they appear to favor basically "separationist" policy solutions to political problems to the same extent as in 1974, certainly as far as all Blacks are concerned. So far then, while Afrikaners seem to have become more pragmatic about race in everyday social affairs, this increased pragmatism does not seem to have penetrated attitudes surrounding political policy.

"HARD" AND "SOFT" ISSUES

In assessing how current attitudes toward different issues of race and politics compare with one another, only the results from the author's July 1977 study will be analyzed. The main aim will be to determine the pattern of attitudes that underlies and influences the present sociopolitical system. Specifically the interest is in identifying issues which are "hard" because of pervasively negative views and issues which appear "soft" because of a more liberal climate of response to them.

In order to see where the greatest present resistance to shifts in social policy may be, a range of aspects of race integration was presented to respondents in the form of a list of proposed social arrangements. The list is reproduced in Table 8, with the percentages of Afrikaners and English-speaking respondents accepting the proposed arrangement appearing after each listing.

Table 8

	Percentage Accepting	
	Afrikaans	English-Speaking
Admission of Blacks to the same jobs as Whites.	62%	85%
Equal salaries for Whites and Blacks.	62	83
Blacks and Whites together in sporting teams.	61	92
Admission of Blacks to White sporting facilities.	40	81
Blacks and Whites worshipping together in the same churches.	32	88
Admission of Blacks to all cinemas, theaters, etc.	28	66
Abolition of the Immorality Act.	23	53
Permission to Blacks to attend certain White schools.	19	69
Use by Blacks of White recreation areas.	19	53
Permission to certain Blacks to move into White residential areas.	18	53

Although English-speakers are more "liberal" throughout the range, something approaching consensus is found relating to job opportunities, salaries, and interracial sport. When informal inter-race contact is at issue, however, the degree of support by Afrikaners drops off very markedly, far below that among English-speaking Whites. A majority of English-speakers is prepared to accept forms of social integration that less than one-fifth of Afrikaners will countenance. But apart from proposals touching on the issue of the Immorality Act, the greatest overall resistance to integration by Whites—Afrikaners and English-speaking—lies in those areas of social interaction in which White lifestyles are likely to be affected—notably in recreation and residential areas.

Earlier, reference was made to a range of "problems" presented to respondents with the instruction to rate the seriousness of the problems on a scale of 1 to 10. The proportions of Afrikaans and English-speakers giving each problem 8, 9, or 10 points out of 10 are given in Table 9.

Quite dramatic differences emerge between Afrikaans and English-speakers. There is broad consensus about the cost of living

Table 9

	Percentage Giving 8, 9, or 10 Points	
	Afrikaans	English-Speaking
Rising cost of living.	76%	82%
Developments in Rhodesia, Mozambique, Angola.	68	73
Criticism of South Africa abroad.	58	51
Too much criticism of our policy by newspapers in South Africa.	42	25
Conditions, housing and facilities in Black residential areas.	41	69
Too many petty apartheid regulations.	35	64
Too slow a development of homelands to independence.	20	14
Too few discussions between Black and White leaders.	21	54
Too little attention to the problems of the ordinary Afrikaner.	17	4

and about external threats, but thereafter the two population groups diverge sharply. Whereas the English-speaking group assigns high importance to internal problems affecting race relations, these are downgraded by Afrikaners. Internal criticisms of policy are viewed as a fairly serious problem by Afrikaners, but not by English-speakers.

The same approach was adopted to assess the relative importance of different sociopolitical issues and values as was used to assess "problems": Afrikaners and English-speakers were asked to rate the importance of a list of different values on a scale of 1 to 10. The percentages giving 8, 9, or 10 points out of 10 for each value are given in Table 10.

Table 10

	Percentage Giving 8, 9, or 10 Points	
	Afrikaans	English-Speaking
To live an honest and moral life.	86%	90%
A strictly religious view of life.	82	35
Unity and loyalty among Whites and Blacks.	76	87
The military power position of Whites in South Africa.	73	55
To lead a happy and contented life.	67	89
A fair deal for all race groups.	66	82
Maintenance of the power position of Whites.	64	37
Maintenance of morality in films, magazines, etc.	63	33
To strive for personal success and achievement.	49	61
To serve the Afrikaner community.	47	8
Social and political development of Blacks.	46	58
To promote the cultural affairs of the Afrikaners.	44	8
Strict segregation of the races.	39	11
Protection of Whites against Black competition.	35	14

A somewhat surprising feature of these results is the relatively low average value assigned by Afrikaners to values relating to Afrikaner culture. This challenges the widely held view that Afrikaners are primarily concerned with the preservation of an ethnic in-group culture and lifestyle. Their concerns seem to be those of *Whites* rather than specifically of Afrikaners.

The item rated highest by both English and Afrikaners relates to conventional morality and is essentially a "filler" item. Its preeminence among both groups was expected. One other item reflects a very broad consensus between the two groups—*unity and loyalty among Whites and Blacks.* This shared sentiment is very significant in the light of threats to the system, and it has undoubtedly increased in importance in recent times.

On other items there is less agreement between the two groups. Afrikaners place more emphasis on the defense of the system, while the English tend to emphasize the improvement of internal race relations. Neither group any longer places much emphasis on segregation of the races in regard to access to public facilities—the English even less than the Afrikaners. The responses of the English-speakers tend to reflect greater emphasis on individualism and the private values of "happiness and contentment," whereas the Afrikaners emphasize religion and morality.

Respondents were also asked to indicate whether the values listed had become more important, less important, or had maintained the same importance for them over the previous three years. When the items are rank-ordered in terms of the percentages of people indicating that they had become *more* important over the previous three years, the same four items ranked highest among both Afrikaans and English-speaking groups, but in a different order:

Afrikaans	English-Speaking
Military power position of Whites.	*Unity and loyalty among Whites and Blacks.*
Unity and loyalty among Whites and Blacks.	*A fair deal for all races.*
A fair deal for all races.	*Social and political development of Blacks.*
Social and political development of Blacks.	*Military power position of Whites.*

These rank-orderings tend to confirm the differences between English-speaking and Afrikaans groups outlined above, but they also indicate that concerns about internal race relations and interracial cooperation are becoming more salient in the minds of Afrikaners.

Respondents were asked: *With regard to the political policy of any political party, which of the following in your opinion should be first and second most important?* The items presented and the *combined* percentages of first and second choices for Afrikaner and English-speaking respondents are given in Table 11.

Table 11

	Percent First and Second Choices Combined	
	Afrikaners	English-Speaking
The future security of Whites.	41%	32%
Justice for all race groups.	33	70
The preservation of moral standards.	28	26
Maintenance of White political power.	18	8
Economic prosperity for people like me.	11	12
The political future of Blacks.	4	19
The interests of my language/cultural group.	3	1
Protection of public facilities used by Whites.	3	1
Protection of the work and professions of Whites.	3	1

There is a quite dramatic difference between the two groups in the concern expressed about *justice for all races*; the English-speaking respondents appear to be concerned with this above all. Afrikaans and English-speaking people share a concern about the *future security of Whites* (Afrikaners emphasize it more) and the *preservation of moral standards.* As would be expected from the overall pattern of findings, the English are more concerned about the *political future of Blacks* than are Afrikaners. Again there is the somewhat surprising result that issues relating to in-group identity and the maintenance of specifically Afrikaner culture are relatively unimportant for Afrikaners.

Respondents were then asked to consider what they felt the most appropriate political arrangements for the different Black groups in South Africa would be. Offered a range of seven alternatives, they were asked to select the one they preferred. The results appear in Table 12.

The first alternative offered is the independent homeland concept; the second proposes separate political structures of inferior status; the third and fourth are forms of limited political integration but with clear emphasis on the maintenance of separate institutions and procedures for different races. The sixth alternative—qualified franchise—is the only "integrationist" proposal, albeit of such a nature as to preserve dominant power for the Whites for a long time hence. The results show clearly that the Afrikaners

Table 12

POLITICAL ARRANGEMENTS PREFERRED FOR DIFFERENT BLACK GROUPS ACCORDING TO LANGUAGE GROUP OF RESPONDENTS

(*In percent*)

Political Arrangement	Coloreds		Indians		Africans	
	Afrikaners	English-Speaking	Afrikaners	English-Speaking	Afrikaners	English-Speaking
Representation by own people in a separate parliament with sovereign powers in own territory.	19%	7%	16%	7%	45%	16%
Representation by own people in a separate parliament with powers determined by the central White government.	28	9	27	8	15	7
Limited representation in the central White parliament elected on separate voters' rolls.	20	12	19	12	6	6
Representation in a joint parliament for all population groups, the number of representatives and the powers of the joint parliament determined by the White parliament.	10	12	10	12	6	9
No representation whatsoever.	3	1	8	2	8	2
Representation of all races in the central parliament on common voters' roll but with qualified franchise.	9	52	9	52	9	52
No choice.	11	7	11	7	11	8

favor separatism much more than the English-speaking group. Whereas the English-speakers tend to endorse either the integrationist qualified franchise proposal or the more integrative of the other "solutions," the Afrikaners clearly favor the idea of separate and autonomous political institutions. With respect to the Africans, the independent homeland concept dominates among Afrikaners, as would be expected in view of the extent to which this concept has been applied under National party rule, but it is interesting that the proportion favoring it is not overwhelming (45 percent) and that the remainder of Afrikaners are scattered across the range of options (although mainly in the "separatist" categories).

The rank and file do not formulate policies, however: they are formulated by political leaders and "sold" to the electorate. A more realistic approach to assessing political options for the future was to offer alternative statements about the political rights of Blacks, phrased in such a way as to suggest a *present* government initiative, giving each respondent the opportunity to "support," "accept," or "oppose" the particular alternative. The statements and the responses of Afrikaners and English-speaking respondents are given in Table 13.

The results of this survey reflect the considerable scope for the introduction of reforms in political institutions afforded by the electorate at large. For Afrikaners the most acceptable alternative is a joint "super-parliament" with all groups, including Africans, represented in it. This goes well beyond the government's present constitutional proposals for the Colored and Indian groups, but it is probably a policy adaptation consistent with the trend implied by these proposals. Almost a majority of Afrikaners would support or accept such a policy, and in view of the large "uncertain" category, more support would likely accrue over time. The English are even more favorably disposed to this policy, as one would expect. It is interesting that the super-parliament idea (which implies separate ethnic legislative bodies "underneath" it) is more acceptable to Afrikaners than integration of only Coloreds and Indians, even though as proposed it completely deviates from government policy concerning Africans. (At present the Cabinet is still emphatic that Africans shall never be accommodated within the political structures of the common area.) It attests once again to the grass-roots appeal of political separatism for Afrikaners.

It is perhaps surprising that the alternative of increasing the viability of the homelands is the least acceptable among Afrikaners. It would seem that some measure of upper-level integration is pre-

Table 13

(1) *If the present government should decide to grant full citizenship, social equality and full franchise in our parliament to Coloreds and Indians, would you:*

	Afrikaans		English-Speaking	
Support the policy	11%	42%	37%	78%
Accept the policy	31		41	
Oppose the policy or withdraw your support	35		6	
Uncertain	23		16	

(2) *If the present government were to decide to considerably enlarge and make the Bantu homelands more viable by incorporating certain "White" areas (including industrial areas), would you:*

	Afrikaans		English-Speaking	
Support the policy	11%	38%	13%	42%
Accept the policy	27		29	
Oppose the policy	39		30	
Uncertain	23		28	

(3) *If the present government decided to create a new legislative body where White, Colored, and Indian leaders, homeland and urban Bantu leaders would have a say over national affairs without one group being dominated by another, would you:*

	Afrikaans		English-Speaking	
Support the policy	19%	47%	37%	69%
Accept the policy	28		32	
Oppose the policy	29		9	
Uncertain	24		22	

ferred to making sacrifices in land and resources to homelands likely to become independent. This suggests that there is not much popular support for the policy of Separate Development.

DIFFERENCES BETWEEN SUBGROUPS WITHIN THE WHITE ELECTORATE

Throughout the study significant differences between Afrikaans and English-speaking Whites have become apparent. The differences between these two language groups are greater than the differences between any subgroups *within* the Afrikaans and English-speaking groups. However, there are interesting patterns of differences between subgroups. The survey results indicating these differences cannot be presented in detail here, but some of the overall trends can be briefly discussed.

In response to questions relating to race integration or improvement in the opportunities and life chances of Blacks, the following subgroups within the Afrikaans-speaking group tend to emerge as the most "progressive": members of business organizations, college graduates, those with higher incomes, senior civil servants, and those with poor church attendance records. Groups emerging as most conservative tend to be those who are greatly interested in maintaining Afrikaner culture—the members of cultural organizations—and active members of political organizations (largely the National party).

In response to questions relating to political dispensations for Blacks (a broad category which includes a variety of policy alternatives), the groups found to be most "progressive" are college graduates, higher-income groups, members of most types of organizations, and people with poor church attendance records. On some issues youth tend to be more *conservative* than average.

The groups that emerge as most committed to the policy of African homeland development are graduates, higher-income groups, and members of political organizations. Members of business organizations are least committed to the homelands policy and tend rather to be more favorably disposed to alternatives like a qualified franchise, or dialogue between Black and White leaders. People who are concerned about maintaining Afrikaner culture tend to be authoritarian in political outlook, favoring a coercive response to Black political demands.

On questions relating to the political integration of Coloreds and Indians, the most "progressive" are members of business organizations, higher-income Afrikaners, graduates, and inactive church members. Least progressive are members of cultural organizations and those concerned about maintaining Afrikaner culture. Many groups who give more than average support to the political integration of Coloreds also tend to favor other "progressive" options. For example, the idea of concessions to make homelands more viable is favored by members of business organizations and graduates; members of political organizations and senior civil servants also tend to favor this option. The idea of a super-parliament involving all race groups is supported primarily by graduates, higher-income groups, members of business organizations, members of sports bodies, civil servants, and (rather surprisingly) office-bearers in church organizations, who differ in this respect from rank-and-file members. Those who are relatively less favorable to this solution are people concerned with preserving Afrikaner culture.

Thus it can be seen that many of the groups which emerge as "progressive" are open to a variety of forward-looking suggestions for South Africa's political future: they support more than one alternative to present policies. Of particular interest is that one of the "progressive" groups—members of business organizations—are fairly tough-minded about the future. They, together with those interested in Afrikaner culture, are relatively more insistent than others on the maintenance of the power position of Whites. Groups less concerned with "White power" are inactive church members and senior civil servants. The latter are often people who have to shoulder responsibility for the day-to-day administration of a system of imposed White control and who, despite the dogged rigidity of many of the junior officials in the civil service, possibly sense a futility in attempting to maintain the system forever.

The group concerned with the maintenance of Afrikaner culture has a consistently "conservative" profile of attitudes. Its members are more youthful and more religious than average, and while broadly speaking their attitudes are fairly close to those of the right-wing Herstigte Nasionale Party, the majority support the National party.

PARTY LOYALTY

The National party has long held an overwhelming majority of the seats in Parliament, and in the most recent election (November 1977) it increased the number of seats it held from 116 to 135 out of a total of 164. Opinion polls conducted by Market and Opinion Surveys (MOS) show that support for the National party has varied between 55 and 60 percent of the total electorate since 1970. In late 1976 its support exceeded 60 percent for the first time, and at the time of the election in late 1977 it was supported by between 62-65 percent of the electorate. (The election results themselves do not accurately reflect the degree of party support because some seats were uncontested.) In September 1978, according to an MOS poll, the support for the National party reached a high of 67 percent of the electorate. In the wake of the Information

Department scandal (South Africa's "Watergate"),* support for the National party recently dropped to 55 percent. This decline is probably only temporary, and most of the lost support will be retrieved in due course.†

Afrikaners have been consistently loyal to the National party over the past decade, their support for it seldom dropping below 80 percent of all Afrikaans-speaking voters. At the time of the 1977 election this support appeared to be about 85 percent. English-speaking support for the party, on the other hand, has fluctuated from slightly over 20 percent in early 1970 to slightly over 10 percent in 1972, increasing marginally to 13-15 percent in 1973. By 1975 English-speaking support for the party once again exceeded 20 percent, and from late 1976 to the end of 1978 this support neared 30 percent—a level it maintained during the most recent election. After the "Information" scandal, however, support among English-speakers dropped to some 18 percent, which largely accounted for the fall off in the popularity of the National party and showed that English-speakers are a "floating" component of party support.

English-speakers are only a minority, however, and one of the prospects for real change frequently discussed is the possibility of a move away from the National party by so-called *Verligte* ("enlightened") Afrikaners. Several questions related to this issue were included in a July 1977 MOS survey. People were asked how satisfied or dissatisfied they were with the policies of the parties they supported. (The results are given in Table 14.)

The results show quite dramatically that the supporters of the governing National party were significantly more satisfied with their party than were the supporters of opposition parties. The English-speaking Nationalists were not as satisfied as the majority of the the National party supporters—the Afrikaners—but even so their profile of responses was significantly more favorable to their party than that among English-speaking opposition party supporters to the opposition parties. More recent polls suggest that English-speaking supporters have become less satisfied with the National party, but there is nothing to suggest

*In two successive inquiries it has become apparent that government funds were improperly used to finance, *inter alia*, a National party-supporting English newspaper—*The Citizen*. In consequence the State President and former Prime Minister B.J. Vorster resigned, and Dr. Eschel Rhoodie, the former secretary of the Department of Information, is to be charged with fraud.

†The author gratefully acknowledges the cooperation of Market and Opinion Surveys for making their full range of polls available to him.

Table 14

VOTER SATISFACTION/DISSATISFACTION WITH PARTIES SUPPORTED ACCORDING TO LANGUAGE GROUPS AND PARTIES

(In percent)

	Afrikaans-Speaking			English-Speaking		
Attitude	National Party	Progressive Reform Party[a]	United Party[b]	National Party	Progressive Reform Party	United Party
Completely satisfied	57%	18%	28%	32%	25%	18%
Fairly satisfied	32	48	36	51	37	21
In between	6	—	19	9	25	28
Fairly dissatisfied	4	34	17	4	7	20
Very dissatisfied	—	—	—	1	3	10
No information	1	—	—	2	3	1

[a]Shortly afterwards changed to the Progressive *Federal* party.

[b]Changed to the New Republican party.

Note: Results are presented only for the three largest parties; results for other parties were unreliable due to small cell entries.

any substantial change in attitude among Afrikaners.*

Among the Afrikaans-speaking supporters of the National party, the reasons given for less than complete satisfaction with the party were: poor policy for dealing with rising cost of living/inflation (cited by 55 percent of respondents), too liberal or conciliatory race policy (cited by 33 percent), too conservative race policy (23 percent), too little attention to future White security (21 percent), impractical plan for political future of Blacks (13 percent), too little concern with national defense (4 percent), too little attention

*As this article was being prepared for publication, an MOS poll appeared which showed that support for the National party among Afrikaners dropped more than 15 percent since the first news of the Information Department scandal became available. The disaffected voters have not switched their support to the opposition, however.

to Afrikaans language and culture (3 percent), other reasons (23 percent). The results suggest that dissatisfaction with the party's "race policy" is more or less evenly balanced between "conservative" and "liberal" positions. Thus while there is some basis for fear of an exodus of party supporters to the right, there is also a basis for fear of a swing away to the more liberal opposition. Is either (or both) likely to happen?

All respondents were asked if they would be likely to support another party if they were or became dissatisfied with their own party. The results among Afrikaans National party supporters were: *No, definitely not*, 51 percent; *unlikely*, 26 percent; *likely*, 15 percent; *definitely*, 4 percent. Among Afrikaners who were ambivalent about or dissatisfied with the National party, the results regarding possible support for another party were: *No, definitely not*, 20 percent; *unlikely*, 32 percent; *likely*, 39 percent; *definitely*, 7 percent.

Using these and other results as a basis for prediction, it would seem that only about 5 percent of the total of Afrikaans National party supporters are likely to support another party, and roughly half of those (2.5 percent) are likely to support the more liberal opposition. Thus the prospects for a meaningful swing away from the National party by Afrikaners do not seem at all favorable in the short term. Those Afrikaners who were ambivalent about or dissatisfied with the National party, but who would not or were unlikely to support another party, offered the following reasons (in order of percentage mentioned): other parties have weak major national policies, are too small and weak, are alien to the Afrikaans language and culture, or do not know the Afrikaans group and its problems. It seems very unlikely that the opposition parties could draw supporters away from the National party at the present time.

BASIC FEARS OF CHANGE

Assuming that attitudes held in a climate of fear might prove especially resistant to change, it seemed appropriate to consider perceptions with regard to the outcome of change in South Africa to see if these reflect fears and insecurities which might be very inhibiting.

This question was posed: *Which two of the following would in your opinion be the most likely changes that would come about if non-Whites were to govern South Africa?* The alternative choices and the results for Afrikaners and English-speaking Whites are given in Table 15.

Table 15

Type of Change	Afrikaans	English-Speaking
The order and security of our society would be threatened.	80%	50%
The jobs and work security of Whites would be threatened.	37	29
The incomes and standard of living of Whites would be lowered.	34	42
The way of life and culture of the Whites would have to change.	18	46
The language and culture of the Afrikaner would be undermined.	14	9
Whites would intermarry with Blacks.	9	6
No serious or permanent dangers would exist for Whites.	3	9

A very basic, dire fear of total disruption of the order and security in society is clearly the dominant expectation of all respondents, but even more so among Afrikaners than among English-speakers. The latter are relatively more concerned than the Afrikaners about lifestyle and standards of living, while the Afrikaners appear to be more concerned about survival. Here is perhaps an indication of one reason why the Afrikaners' attitudes are so much more rigid than those of the English-speaking group. There may be a self-reinforcing circle of attitudes. Because fears of change are so dire, they produce attitudes highly resistant to change; these attitudes are rationalized by developing highly negative stereotypes of Black characteristics, which in turn reinforce the basic fears about what would happen if Blacks took over the country.

THE DANGER OF REACTION

In discussions of the effects of pressure for change on the White electorate, reference is often made to the possibility of a negative reaction leading to a "back-to-the-wall" stance. If the proposed changes are seen to be such that they cannot be accommodated without great sacrifice, or if very basic fears (such as those described above) are aroused, such a reaction is a very real possibility. The results of this survey give some tentative indications of the likelihood of such an outcome. In response to the statement *South Africa must ignore world opinion and follow its own course,* 47 percent of Afrikaners agreed, and 37 percent were partly in agreement. As has already been indicated, however, the proportion endorsing this hard-line view has dropped since 1974, and therefore a process of reaction does not seem to be building up. One indication of the defensiveness of Afrikaner attitudes is that 91 percent of the Afrikaners consider that the country's defense force has to be strengthened. (Fifty-two percent believe this is necessary even if it means higher taxes and a lower standard of living for Whites.) These rather disparate results are far from conclusive, however, concerning the likelihood of a negative reaction. What has to be borne in mind is the irrational quality of the fears surrounding the prospect of majority rule, which means that a negative reaction is always a possibility. Perhaps the most significant finding in this regard is that in the 1974 (MRA) survey, only 59 percent of Afrikaners felt that *the order and security of society would be threatened* under majority rule, whereas by July 1977 this feeling was expressed by 80 percent of Afrikaners. This suggests quite strongly that latent fears of the consequences of the ultimate demands of many Blacks and many agencies abroad are coming to the fore. Until these fears are reduced by legitimate political figures and the mass media debating the majority rule option coolly and rationally, the danger of a highly emotional reaction remains high.*

DISCUSSION OF WHITE ATTITUDES

The results of this analysis show quite clearly that some fairly substantial changes in attitudes toward race conflict among all Whites taken together, as well as among the government-supporting Afrikaners, have taken place over the recent period of mounting problems and pressures. This broad conclusion must be qualified immediately by noting that negative stereotypes about racial characteristics of Blacks have not changed, which makes the changes in Whites' attitudes toward race contact all the more noteworthy. Also, change has been fairly limited among Afrikaners on issues relating to the political integration of Africans, or where typical White material interests and lifestyles are threatened ("typical" as opposed to specifically working-class interests).

There has been movement away from the older, typically South African, highly normative rejection of inter-race contact; certainly the pre-conditions for policy moves away from blatant

*Recent by-elections in the Transvaal were marked by a massive stayaway by National party supporters. Whether this was due primarily to the "Information scandal," to outdated voters rolls, or to voter dissatisfaction with the new "liberalization" in National party stances cannot be assessed; the next few months will indicate how serious the right-wing resistance in the party might be.

public discrimination have improved substantially. There has also been a sharp diminution of interest in White working class "protectionism," which has for decades acted as a severe brake on the occupational and material advancement of Blacks. Attitudes of a strategic nature, such as (for example) views aimed at securing the loyalty and cooperation of Blacks, have come strongly to the fore in recent years. Afrikaners have by no means become "liberals," but rational conservatism seems to be emerging steadily to replace the earlier, often irrational stances which often involved the stigmatizing of inter-race contact—even in the public sphere. Two factors in particular, among others yet to be mentioned, may be preventing the emergence of a truly tolerant outlook among Afrikaners: the fear of political domination and the persistence of basic beliefs in Black inferiority.

The changes that have been noted interrelate with perceptions of threats to the "White" system and with the extent of awareness of looming internal and external problems. It is impossible to say whether the pressures on Whites have caused the changes directly, since it is possible that a modernization of attitudes has taken place coincidentally with political events in recent times. It is more than likely, however, that the pressures building up within and without South Africa have had a substantial influence on race attitudes: ordinarily, processes of modernization would take longer than the time-periods analyzed in this paper.

The perceptions of the emergent political situation seem to be changing all the time, with more and more serious concern being expressed about threats to the future security of Whites. There are marked differences in Afrikaans and English-speaking perceptions, however. Afrikaners as a group feel comparatively less "threatened" by events than the English-speaking Whites, and the focus of perceived threats tends to differ. Whereas the English place primary emphasis on South Africa's internal problems, the Afrikaners see the greatest dangers as external to the system. The English-speakers also interpret internal threats differently, in that they accord considerable legitimacy to Black problems, needs, and demands, while the Afrikaners still set great store by "agitator" theories to explain internal events. It should be emphasized, however, that despite these differences, Afrikaners are increasingly perceiving the reality of Black discontent and the limits on their power to secure compliance from Blacks through coercion alone. The stage has not yet been reached where a majority of Afrikaners is seriously concerned about the problems of economic survival and internal order, but there appears to be a fairly rapid trend of change in that direction.

While it is clear that there are rather dramatic differences in attitudes between Afrikaans and English-speakers, there are areas of concern where near-consensus has been reached. One example is the perceived need to move away from discrimination in jobs, wages, and sport. There is also consensus about the need for securing the unity and loyalty of Blacks and Whites, and about the seriousness of the threats emanating from Angola and Mozambique.

The attitudes of Afrikaans and English-speakers deviate markedly on issues of informal or "private" inter-race contact. Generally, the English-speakers are substantially more liberal in outlook in these areas. Some critics of attitude surveys attribute this to an Anglo-Saxon sense of propriety and perhaps a little hypocrisy in the way the English respond to social surveys. There may be some truth to this contention (if so, however, English-speakers may exhibit the same propriety and "pleasant" hypocrisy in everyday life), but nevertheless any impartial observer of the South African scene will notice a greater frequency of informal interracial mixing between English-speakers and Blacks and will also note that English-speakers are more likely than Afrikaners to support voluntary programs of Black advancement and development.

The Afrikaners, however, are the most important group in any consideration of prospects for change. As far as the attitudes of Afrikaners affect issues, certain "soft" areas for future change are discernible, including the spheres of occupational advancement, improvement in socioeconomic conditions for Blacks, and race integration over a range of formal or impersonal spheres of social interaction (like the sharing of certain *non-local* public facilities such as larger hotels, universities, public services, parks, and bus services). Greater resistance to change in the attitudes of Afrikaners is evident in the more private and intimate spheres of (possible) race contact, and in areas of interaction where race-mixing would affect the lifestyles of Whites (e.g., residential areas). It should be emphasized that segregation ensures for even middle- and lower-income Whites access to relatively uncrowded and pleasant amenities and residential areas; the pressure of competition from large numbers of Blacks is kept at bay by segregation. It is in these aspects of life that racial attitudes appear to be most anti-progressive and rigid.

Another area of strong resistance among Afrikaners is related to the question of political integration among rank-and-file South Africans. There is a deep sense that such integration would be a threat to Afrikaner autonomy. Although Afrikaners as a group no longer accord high priority to the preservation of a distinctive Afrikaner culture, they are still solidly organized politically, economically, and socially as a *corporate* group. They are long accustomed to seeing themselves as a sociopolitical "enterprise," no matter how "South African" they may privately feel. Political security for them seems to lie in the maintenance of this corporate political autonomy, and some of the reasons they give for their unwillingness to vote for alternative parties reflect this persistence of a "particularistic" political culture. (Among the reasons given for not voting for other parties was the fear that these were "alien" or did not understand the problems of the group.)

Hence Afrikaners, much more than English-speaking Whites, tend to insist on separatism in political organization. (Not all Afrikaners exclude Coloreds from political integration, however; many Afrikaners—roughly 50 percent—see the Coloreds as Brown Afrikaners and potentially part of the political in-group.) To the extent that there is an increasing awareness of the need to secure the cooperation and recognize the interdependence of the different races, Afrikaners tend to modify their separatist ideals by agreeing to the need for overarching linkages between separate ethnic political institutions. However, in contrast to attitudes among the English-speakers, the notion of even the notoriously conservative device of the qualified franchise on a common roll is anathema to Afrikaners.

Rank-and-file Afrikaners seem to have moved away from a self-conscious concern with in-group culture (if indeed ordinary Afrikaners ever had much interest in it), and their dominant perception of themselves is that of being White South Africans. Yet their attitudes on racial and race-political issues differ markedly from those of other White South Africans, and these differences, according to the results of this analysis, cannot be accounted for by differences in background characteristics such as education, urbanization, and social status. There is not sufficient space here to attempt what would have to be a lengthy explanation of the reasons for this difference; suffice it to say that while self-conscious concern with Afrikaner culture may have receded into the background, a heritage of values remains within the group which deeply influences its racial views.

Thus in the 1977 study, for example, whereas 37 percent of English-speakers disagreed with the statement *The interests of a group are more important than the rights of individuals*, only 25 percent of Afrikaners rejected this view. Results presented earlier have shown that the English-speaking Whites, far more than the Afrikaners, tend to emphasize private values and individualism; the Afrikaners, on the other hand, are still fairly traditional in outlook, and emphasize *public* morality and religiosity. Furthermore, in the Afrikaans community (which became industrialized much later than the English-speaking community), different socioeconomic classes have not yet crystallized as clearly as in the Anglo-Saxon group. The Afrikaner still has more of a sense of community with fellow Afrikaners across class lines; hence he does not realize fully that class and status differences make for social barriers in what might otherwise be integrated situations.

Milton Rokeach has pointed to the importance of the perception of a similarity or identity of beliefs for the acceptance of other races.[9] People fear or avoid the "stranger" who may have beliefs different from their own. Anglo-Saxons, with their well-developed barriers of class and status, can live in social juxtaposition with strangers more easily than Afrikaners. Also, the Anglo-Saxons' sociopolitical beliefs now are fairly "universal" and tend to be reference points for other groups. The Afrikaners, on the other hand—no matter how they may currently downplay their own culture publicly—have strong community-based socio-religious beliefs which, as remnants of an older Calvinist-Puritan tradition, are not as "universal" as those of the English-speaking Whites. The Black as "stranger" is all the more threatening to Afrikaners when they do not have the security of knowing (as the English-speakers do) that he will accept their beliefs and standards. (It should be recalled here that the group of Afrikaners who are consistently most progressive are those who are inactive church members—a group which presumably has broken out of the nexus of Afrikaner beliefs and sentiments.)

If a cross-section of Afrikaner attitudes is taken as an indication of constraints on and opportunities for political change, then it is possible to make several tentative predictions. For example, moves to eliminate discrimination in public places are likely to proceed apace. Formal job reservation will probably be eliminated soon, and even informal job reservation is likely to erode fairly rapidly at the many levels where skill shortages exist—in part because there is an ever-more widely held appreciation of the need for economic growth. A publicly supported drive to win over the "hearts and minds" of the Black population may also be likely. What cannot be expected, however, are moves to desegregate residential areas, local schools, or those "close contact" public facilities which are very popular among rank-and-file Whites (such as cinemas, for example). Even though attitudes concerning integration of these facilities have changed, there is still too great a risk of a sharp reaction from fairly influential groups.

At the political level, the government would have considerable freedom of choice in policy formulation. If it provided firm leadership, it could with only slight difficulty integrate Colored people socially and politically. A clear majority of National party voters, particularly in the Cape, would accept this initiative. (A retired Minister of Transport, now National party M.P.—Mr. Ben Schoeman—is on record as recommending this step.)[10] It could also incorporate leaders of Colored, Indian, and African groups into some form of joint decision-making. Such a move would be congruent with the present constitutional debate and would be far more popular with the White electorate than enlarging the homelands. The survey results indicate that the National party is unlikely to split or even to lose more than a few percent of its overall support to the right if it embarks on meaningful political reform. Party loyalty within the National party is very high, and the government can count on widespread acquiescence if not enthusiasm for its policies.

Such speculation is one-sided, however. The government has to consider not only the general electorate, but also a range of pressure groups. On one side there is the small but effective category of Afrikaners who are *kultuurbehoudend* (cultural chauvinists at worst and cultural idealists at best), who are consistently more conservative than rank-and-file Afrikaners. These people are sometimes referred to as "super Afrikaners," and they are remarkably well-organized. They sit on myriad important committees, some are organized into letter-writing groups (*Briewekringe*), and they quite probably have a disproportionate influence in the Afrikaner Broederbond. Their disapproval is a powerful deterrent to rapid change. Small and atypical though their demographic base might be, they are likely to constrain the government for quite some time to come. Another generally more conservative group is the card-carrying members of the National party. Party morale depends to a considerable extent on accommodating the interests of this powerful pressure group. Furthermore, attitudes in a substantial section of the party caucus and cabinet are similar to those within the party as a whole.

On the other side of the scale, able to exert pressure in a progressive direction, are the business leaders and a substantial proportion of senior civil servants. The latter, as civil servants, are not supposed to participate openly in political affairs, but it can be assumed that they can exercise considerable covert influence. Business leaders, however, are the obvious category of persons to countervail against the conservative "cultural" and political establishments. Although Afrikaner businessmen place very definite limits on their "progressiveness," they are nonetheless quite favorably disposed to most of the changes that would produce a more open society.

It is impossible to accurately assess the relative influence of right- and left-wing lobbies on the government at this stage. A careful reading of the media suggests that both have their successes and failures. The important point to emphasize is that given the orientations of the Afrikaner electorate which the analysis reveals, and given the fact that such potentially influential groups as business-leaders and better-educated Afrikaners generally are relatively progressive, the government enjoys considerable freedom to introduce policy innovations. These will be more readily accepted if they do not *too soon* affect the popular lifestyle interests of rank-and-file Whites. There may well be great scope for the type of innovation which will counter the well-nigh total political alienation of urban Blacks, which is a more serious concern at the present time than issues like Blacks in White residential areas or swimming pools. There does not seem to be much faith even among Afrikaners in the policy of homeland independence as a means of solving critical internal problems. The time is clearly auspicious for bolder moves than hitherto in the direction of a constitutional arrangement which will embrace all South Africans and will allow for steady evolutionary changes toward a stable, just, and open society with constitutional protection of group interests.

THE RELEVANCE OF ATTITUDES AMONG BLACKS

The discussion in the opening section of this article suggests that in recent months the South African government has become somewhat more responsive to attitudes and grievances among Blacks. The recent establishment by the Minister for African Affairs of consultative committees all over the country is perhaps most significant, particularly since some very outspoken Black leaders have been invited to serve on these bodies. (Whether or not they accept is a separate issue.) There is also an increasing realization that any internal conflict or unrest among Blacks will weaken the image of economic stability abroad, which would be very costly for an external investment-hungry economy.

How do Black attitudes and expectations in South Africa relate to the possibilities for change which the previous discussion has revealed? In March and April 1978 a small attitudinal survey among Africans was undertaken by this author (in cooperation with the market research firm International Marketing Services Africa [Pty] Ltd.). It was decided to conduct the research among men in Soweto. Soweto, the scene of the first eruption of urban unrest in 1976, is the largest concentration of urban Africans in the Republic, and is commonly considered to represent the political vanguard of Black South Africa. The intention was to poll the thinking of the most politicized groups of urban Africans because it is assumed that they represent the most critical challenge to the government's policy of separate development and to White domination generally. In pursuit of this Black political vanguard, the sample was limited to somewhat better-educated people—those with Standard 8 (mid-high school) qualifications and above—and to people permanently settled in the urban area. The sample was a carefully controlled interrelated "quota" sample of 150 males, sixteen years and older. (The quota controls were age, socioeconomic status, education, area of Soweto, and home language.) The interviewing was conducted by highly experienced Black interviewers in homes or private locations at places of work, and interviews were quality-controlled and subject to a random 10 percent back-check in the normal way. No noteworthy resistance to the study was encountered: the interviewers were generally known in the area as regular commercial researchers whose discretion could be trusted.

The African respondents were asked to look at a range of five diagrammatic representations of faces showing various degrees of discontent, linked to explicit descriptive statements. A slightly "projective" form of questioning was used: *Which face (and statement) shows the way African people like yourself feel about life in South Africa now?* The responses were as follows: *angry and impatient*, 40 percent; *unhappy*, 32 percent; *in the middle*, 20 percent; *happy* and *very happy*, 8 percent. The better educated tended to be the most discontented: 56 percent of those with tertiary education were *angry and impatient*.

Following this, respondents were asked (the question and percentage responses follow): *If you think of your life in about five years' time, do you think things will be: much better*, 15 percent; *not much better but better*, 25 percent; *the same*, 20 percent; *worse*, 41 percent. The item which followed was: *Which two of the following do you think about most when you say your life will be* [option selected]? The alternatives, with percentage choices, were: *political rights for Africans*, 57 percent; *influx control or "pass laws,"* 33 percent; *housing and township conditions*, 29 percent; *opportunities for education*, 29 percent; *wages and salaries*, 22 percent; *opportunities for promotion at work*, 19 percent. Those who tended to perceive future conditions as worse were relatively more likely to think of political rights.

On the issue of leadership, respondents were asked: *Think of the people like yourself in Soweto—people who live and work around you. Who would they see to be their real leaders?* The alternatives, with percentage selection, were: *Soweto Committee of Ten* (a group of prominent professionals and others, very progressive and critical of the status quo—some having been detained—claiming to be the authentic voice of Soweto), 54 percent; *African National Congress people in jail or outside South Africa*, 21 percent; *people who used to belong to the Black People's Congress* (a fairly outspoken Black Consciousness organization, now banned), 7 percent; *Black Parents Association* (a group of outspoken community leaders sympathetic to the youth disturbances, similar in composition to the "Committee of Ten"), 7 percent; *Chief Gatsha Buthelezi* (the KwaZulu Chief Minister and President of Inkatha), 5 percent; *other homeland leaders*, 2 percent; *Pan African Congress leaders*, 1 percent; *elected community councillors* (the government-established local consultative committee), 1 percent; *others*, 3 percent.

The sample was asked about preventing disturbances: *There were serious disturbances in the townships in 1976. What should the government do to prevent such disturbances happening again?* This time the question was open-ended. The most common responses, with percentages, were as follows: *establishment of political equality*, 63 percent; *improvement of education*, 60 percent; *serious consultation with real leaders*, 47 percent; *improvement of economic conditions*, 40 percent; *improvement of housing and community circumstances*, 37 percent; *abolition of "pass laws,"* 21 percent; *abolition of social segregation* (apartheid), 15 percent. (Other responses were less frequent.)

These results seem to show that better-educated Africans in Soweto are highly politicized. They recognize political interests as preeminent, and tend to select as leaders the more progressive or radical figures (present and past) over those in any way connected with government institutions. They favor the OAU-UN General Assembly alternative for Zimbabwe-Rhodesia—i.e., majority rule without the entrenchment of White interests.* Very few of them are happy or contented with their circumstances in South Africa at the moment. They are the sort of people who would surely tend to favor majority rule—in effect, Black majority rule. A perfect recipe for polarization?

With respect to power-sharing in government, the sample was asked: *Think of people like yourself who live and work around you. What kind of government would such people (like yourself) be prepared to accept and be happy with in the future?* The alternatives offered were formulated so as to force a choice for or against clear Black majority rule. The alternative of a "non-racial" color-blind government was not given, although opportunity was provided for it to be mentioned. The primary reason for this omission was that "non-racial" rule, which would almost certainly in effect be Black majority rule (and thus has been the platform of the more progressive groups and Black Consciousness leaders), would be too easy to endorse in a display of political idealism. (The survey results should be interpreted with this omission in mind.)

The alternatives, with percentage selections, were as follows: *Would accept and be happy to live with—government of equal numbers of Blacks and Whites in cabinet*, 57 percent; *government in which Blacks, as the majority, rule the Whites*, 35 percent; *Blacks ruling half the country and Whites the other half*, 4 percent; *independent homelands with more land and towns added to them*, 2 percent. Additional answers (respondents were asked for "any alternative answer," etc.) were: *"non-racial"/integrated rule*, 5 percent; *rule by the highly educated*, 2 percent; other diverse responses, 8 percent. As noted above, if non-racial rule had been presented as an alternative, many more would have selected it than those who volunteered it. Without it, however, these highly politicized and deeply discontented urban Africans preferred a shared rule or "consociational" alternative to Black majority rule. The partition alternative was firmly rejected, as was the expanded homelands option.

The preference for shared rule involving balanced Black and White power is, of course, due in some measure to the fact that it would be such a substantial advance on the present dispensation. Further insight can be derived from the responses to another ques-

*On the issue of Zimbabwe-Rhodesia, 62 percent favored a settlement including the guerillas, 21 percent favored the current internal settlement between the White parties and internal leaders, and 13 percent considered that the guerillas alone should rule.

tion: *What problems do you think might arise in the future if Black people should rule South Africa?* Once again, in an attempt to avert the danger of too many facile and idealistic "no problem" answers, the question was somewhat loaded in the direction of problems. The percentage responses to this open-ended question were as follows: *inter-ethnic problems*, 37 percent; *no problems* (or similar answer), 29 percent; *economic problems/inefficiency*, 29 percent; *danger of losing/alienating Whites*, 19 percent. Those respondents who mentioned ethnic problems, the danger of an exodus of Whites, or the possibility of economic problems tended less than others to support the Black majority rule option. Hence, as would be expected, the preference for "shared" (consociational) rule over Black majority rule appears to be conditioned by perceptions of probable outcomes. The selection of the shared rule alternative, therefore, is not necessarily an "Uncle Tom" option—that is, not a choice of an inferior alternative made in a sense of helplessness simply because it appears so much better than the present dispensation. There is some evidence, therefore, that in a group of highly politicized and discontented Black South Africans, a preference for consociational rule is based to some extent on an awareness of major sociopolitical problems characteristic of a highly diversified society.

DISCUSSION

Within the constraints of broad White voter expectations, traditional policy development, and established precedent, the government could select one of two basic political strategies for the medium- to long-term. One has been briefly alluded to already—i.e., a form of "grand coalition" of ethnic leaders—an overarching cabinet council or "super-cabinet" in which members from separate "ethnic" assemblies covering all groups are represented. We have seen that substantial proportions of both Whites and Blacks would accept such an option. The other strategy would be to make the homeland policy more viable and comprehensive by adjustments of territory. This option has relatively strong support over a range of White interest groups. The White political elites tend to favor this alternative exclusively, but among urban Blacks there appears to be virtually no support for it. Furthermore, no amount of homeland development or of territorial concessions which are feasible will solve the problem of the urban Africans in a way which will be convincing to South African critics abroad. Therefore, the two alternative strategies should not be seen as mutually exclusive, and—as noted—White *and* Black voters are receptive to the concept of a super-cabinet, including representation of Africans not embraced by the homeland independence policy.*

There is at present, then, some scope and need for some form of internal negotiated settlement as an interim step in a process of change toward an open society. Such an interim solution might involve a mixed cabinet, as already noted, or (if a cabinet is considered in the light of South African tradition to be most appropriately representative of only one party) a mixed Executive Council representing common area Africans, Coloreds, Indians, Whites, and with representation for those homelands not wishing to become independent. (Obviously there could be no prescription that permanent common area Africans have to be citizens of any homelands wishing to become independent.) Such a step is broadly congruent with an extrapolation of current trends discussed at the beginning of this article and with substantial proportions of popular White expectations and even larger proportions of Black political expectations.

The extrapolation of current trends, however, can only be made on the basis of certain assumptions. The first assumption is that the present White political leaders will grasp the full implications for South Africa of the Zimbabwe-Rhodesian and Namibian situations. This is not to suggest that the two situations are similar, but the key implication in both is that if change occurs too slowly, it allows externally based refugee groups and their supporters to gain a degree of credibility, material support, and legitimacy as norm-establishing agencies which it is virtually impossible for any internal government to counteract effectively. The price of a pace of change which is too slow is a loss of political initiative. Sections of the Afrikaans Nationalist press have recognized this implication and so have a range of notable Afrikaner opinion-leaders, including certain top generals in the Defence Force. Thus there appears to be a real possibility for such an interim solution.

The emergence of this type of solution would require forceful and gifted leadership. On the White side the influence of very conservative lobbies would have to be counteracted by such leadership. On the Black side the emergence of a strong and legitimate, constituency-based leadership would be required to give full weight to popular attitudes and realistic possibilities and to counteract

*Independence may be acceptable to many homeland-based Africans whose lives and work are conducted solely within the homeland.

the by now well-established popular wisdom among the more articulate Black elites that one person-one vote in a unitary system is the only respectable alternative for South Africa.

It is assumed that a fairly substantial equalization of life-chances, services, and material rewards for different races at given levels of skill and education is possible without Whites perceiving this equalization as a direct threat to their own interests. For a while this would have to involve a duplication rather than an integration of particularly "sensitive" services and amenities. (Of course no "separate" amenity can be fully equal—the reference here is to a pace of reform rather than an ideal.) In this regard Whites, by virtue of their hitherto privileged access to education and training, would retain much the same broad level of relative advantage even in a non-racial democracy, provided there was no discrimination against them and that a free-enterprise economy prevailed. (Change is not necessarily a zero-sum game in South Africa.)

Is there time for these developments to emerge? Will events not overtake ameliorative trends in White politics? One possibility is a "White backlash." We have seen that fears of Black majority rule have deepened and that there are strong popular reactions to pressure from abroad and to insurgency on the borders. By and large, however, the policy reactions of Whites have tended to be pragmatic and strategic. Pressure, provided it is aimed at realistic adjustments, seems likely to have a constructive influence. What of Black reactions and the danger of internal unrest in the near future? David Welsh points out that there are no immediate prospects of political upheaval in South Africa.[11] Rank-and-file Blacks, who by virtue of their dominance in the labor force could pose the greatest challenge to the established order, as yet have shown little serious inclination to emulate the 1976 youth confrontation of authority in the townships. For the moment, the mass of ordinary Black people perhaps would rather take comfort in whatever signs of reform exist than risk massive retaliation from White authority. Yet events in the wider southern African region are a powerful stimulus to Black political expectations, and the government is still too much concerned with control and too fearful of right-wing White reaction to implement a policy of clear and unambiguous reform. Whites still have the time to secure the future peace and stability of their country, but that time is surely very limited.

SOUTH AFRICA IN THE CONTEMPORARY WORLD

Colin Legum

The Republic of South Africa occupies a unique place as the loneliest and probably the most reviled country in the world. Although militarily one of the strongest of the smaller powers, it lives in a state of paranoidal anxiety about the danger of external attacks; and while it is the richest and most industrially advanced country in Africa, its trading partners are sensitively concerned to distance themselves politically from it. The Republic is the only UN member-state which is under constant threat of economic sanctions designed to bring about its total isolation.

South Africa's strange situation has no close parallel in modern history, although there are some similarities with Mussolini's Italy at the time of the invasion of Ethiopia, as well as with Nazi Germany and Franco's Spain in the 1930s. Other contemporary states attract widespread hostility—notably Israel, Cuba, Albania, Kampuchea, and more recently Egypt—but with the exception of idiosyncratic Albania, each of these other states can rely on the backing of at least one of the major powers as well as other allies. South Africa, virtually friendless, cannot count on the support of any of the major powers. Were it not for its great economic resources, it would probably long since have achieved the unenviable distinction of having been sent to Coventry by the entire world community—thus fulfilling a fear expressed at the time of Sharpeville in 1960 by a pro-government Afrikaner newspaper that South Africa would become a "skunk among the nations" unless it changed its apartheid policies.[1]

Afrikanerdom had committed itself to the concept of apartheid —an ideology of racial separation—at a watershed period in Africa's history when the rest of the continent was approaching the end of its colonial history and new states, deeply opposed to alien rule and to any form of White supremacy on the continent, were emerging. This post-imperial development had two important consequences inimical to the survival of South Africa's status quo. The first was the evolution of a Pan-African continental system which had no place for a White minority-ruled state; as a result, White South Africa was bound to find itself increasingly estranged from its continental neighbors, and drawn inevitably into political confrontation and, eventually, into open conflict with them. The second consequence was that the process of decolonization created new national interests for South Africa's traditional friends in the West—i.e., the need to establish friendly relations with the newly independent Black states as well as with the wider, emergent Third World—which the Western nations would find it increasingly difficult to reconcile with friendship for a state committed to racial policies completely at variance with those in the rest of Africa.

White South Africa's commitment to apartheid also added an international dimension to the country's internal problems because the new kind of world society which emerged after World War II was irresistibly drawn toward involvement in the affairs of any country which practiced racial discrimination—especially one in which a White minority pursued a policy of race supremacy in a Third World country. (Even the United States became increasingly sensitive to the international dimension of its domestic policies toward Blacks in the 1950s and 1960s.) International involvement in the "domestic affairs" of South Africa was intensified by the dialectic of the apartheid process. Thus attempts to implement "separate development" provoked militant Black resistance; this resulted in greater internal police repression which, in turn, sharpened internal resistance and so fed the sources of international opposition to South Africa. Every new internal crisis resulted in greater external pressures.

As is necessarily true of the foreign relations of all ideological states, and especially of those with an authoritarian basis, South Africa's foreign policies have been increasingly affected by its domestic policies. At the end of three decades of apartheid, the Pretoria regime has had to move toward a policy of isolationism, and has had to think seriously about the feasibility of South Africa establishing itself as the center of local regional power in the southern African subcontinent.

THE BASIS OF SOUTH AFRICA'S FOREIGN POLICY

Successive governments have explicitly defined South Africa's foreign policy in terms of a commitment to defend the country's "right and necessity" to maintain the status quo, the essence of which is the maintenance of White political control over at least two-thirds of the country. From the first Prime Minister at the time of union, General Louis Botha, down to J.B. Vorster and now P.W.

Botha, this has remained a constant factor in South Africa's foreign policy. A particularly striking example of how this "national interest" translates into international practice was offered by Dr. Verwoerd in January 1966 in defining South Africa's attitude toward the Rhodesian regime of Ian Smith:

> If I have to judge the situation in Rhodesia, the attitude of the people and the resistance they will put up, by what we would do in South Africa under precisely similar circumstances—if our way of life were threatened; *if there were an attempt to remove the supremacy of the white man here, even in the course of time*; if we were subjected to sanctions or embargoes or boycotts; and if we had to put up a struggle for survival, in which we would have to conquer or die—then I am quite convinced that the Rhodesians in their own circumstances will show no less determination.[2]

For South Africa's ruling minority the crucial problem has always been how to defend White supremacy, both at home and abroad. The world community has always been more sensitive—and for a time, more militant—after dramatic events inside the Republic reflecting Black resistance, especially when they result in violence, such as the protests at Sharpeville in 1960, the general strike in Namibia in 1972-73, the urban Black unrest triggered by the Soweto student demonstrations in 1976, and the explosion of Black anger over the martyrdom of Steve Biko in 1976. It is on such occasions that the close connection between internal explosions and external pressures is seen most clearly. During times when South Africa appears to have its Black population under effective control ("stability"), pressures from the Western community slacken and the temperature of Black Africa is relatively low. This close connection between violent explosions in the Republic and Western pressures does not augur well for the future, since it suggests that the West will commit itself fully only when the challengers to apartheid succeed in producing serious armed violence, as they have done recently in Zimbabwe/Rhodesia. South Africa's overriding concern is its Western connections because if the West were ever to sever its connections completely with South Africa, the consequences would be catastrophic.

SOUTH AFRICA'S STRATEGY FOR SURVIVAL

There are four main elements in South Africa's strategy for survival. The first is to maintain a firm base of political control at home so as to ensure internal political stability while pursuing its "grand design of Separate Development." Since this program depends for its success on a strong economy, the second aim is to maintain rapid economic growth. Such growth is very largely dependent on a continuing supply of foreign capital investment and expanding overseas markets for South African exports. The third element in the strategy is to build up a powerful defense system to counter local and external threats to its security, and to obtain membership in as wide a military alliance system as possible to protect itself against threats from any major foreign powers (generally characterized as "Communist"). The fourth is to improve its relations with African states in order (1) to reduce the danger of attacks on its frontiers from Black Africa (and to resist Chinese and Russian penetration),* (2) to gain greater access to the African market, its natural trading area, and (3) to make its international posture more acceptable (especially in the West) by demonstrating that not all Black people are its enemies. In 1977 Vorster went so far as to acknowledge that the only hope of regaining Western friendship was "to sell ourselves to Africa" but, he was quick to add, not to "sell out" to Africa.

The essential condition for the success of this foreign policy strategy is that the Republic avoid becoming completely discredited in the West and deprived of any important friends in Africa. How the four elements in this strategy fit together can perhaps best be illustrated by considering their external aspects.

THE ECONOMIC IMPERATIVE IN SOUTH AFRICA'S FOREIGN POLICY

South Africa's foreign relations are crucial to expanding its economy, which is basic to the survival of its political system. To a greater degree than other countries, it must overcome political obstacles to trade, as well as face normal trade competition, and it suffers the disadvantage of not belonging to any of the major international trading alliances.

South Africa's well-developed economy depends for its continuing expansion on a number of factors—*inter alia*, the price of gold, industrial peace (especially among its Black workers), fresh external capital to complement its own large internal sources, acqui-

*E.g., Mr. Vorster justified opening diplomatic relations with Malawi in 1967 on the ground that it was necessary to prevent the Communists from cutting Africa in two (SA House of Assembly, *Debates*, 23 April 1969, cols. 4577-78).

sition of new technology, guaranteed supplies of oil (all of which must be imported), and, above all, expanding overseas markets. By slowing its expansion South Africa could make itself less reliant on imports (except for oil), but this could carry the risk of political troubles at home; by adopting a "siege economy" it could become self-reliant for many years, provided it had an assured supply of oil. However, for normal peacetime conditions South Africa's economy depends, like most developed economies, on large-scale exports. While it has no difficulty finding markets for its gold and other mineral exports, it is much less well-placed when it comes to manufactured goods and agricultural exports and in gaining access to foreign capital markets. South Africa's manufactured and agricultural exports must compete in the world market mainly with the major industrial countries and with the African associates of the European Economic Community (EEC). Because South Africa has, in some respects, a high-cost economy and its exports carry high transport costs, they are not easily competitive.

The Republic's economy has suffered two crucial setbacks as a direct consequence of its apartheid policies: (1) virtual exclusion from the larger part of the African market and (2) denial of special access rights to the EEC. If it had been allowed to remain a member of the Commonwealth, it could have qualified for special consideration when Britain negotiated its terms for membership in the EEC, especially with respect to its manufactured agricultural products—sugar, fruit, and wine—as well as semi-processed steel. As it is, South Africa lost not only its privileged access to traditional markets in Britain, but also the opportunity to freely expand its exports to the vitally important Common Market.

Even more serious is the denial to the Republic of what under normal circumstances should be its greatest trading area—the African continent. In the long term, only the African market can offer South Africa the chance of competing successfully with the major trading nations, but so long as its regime is viewed with hostility by the great majority of African states, the opportunities for participation in their markets will be severely restricted. This compels South Africa to compete in the much more difficult markets of North America and Latin America, where its transport costs make its exports (other than minerals) less competitive.

Trade with Africa is seen not only as important to South Africa's economy but also as a means of promoting diplomatic and other ties. The policymakers in Pretoria continue to believe, like Vorster, that "economic realities will force Africa to change its attitude towards South Africa."[3] Since Pretoria has for some years stopped publishing trade figures with individual African countries, no clear picture can be formed of its trade pattern. Official sources put South Africa's direct trade with the continent in 1979 at 800 million Rand a year (R0.84 = $1). However, this figure includes trade with the Customs Union members (Lesotho, Botswana, and Swaziland) as well as Transkei. By far the biggest element in this total is trade with Rhodesia. Although the trend has been upward in recent years, it still shows a significant decline since 1969. Throughout the 1960s about 19 percent of South Africa's export trade was with the rest of the continent. The share was still 18.6 percent in 1971, but in the following six years it dropped by half to 9.3 percent in the first nine months of 1977. By far the greatest component of South African exports to its neighboring countries is food—particularly to Zambia and Zaire. Trade with Malawi has increased steadily to the point where South African exports now account for 37 percent of all Malawi's imports as against Britain's 19 percent. Lesotho's share of the Customs Union revenues went up from R11 million to over R56 million from 1975-78, while over the same period Swaziland's share doubled to about R75 million, and Botswana's share more than doubled to over R52 million. However, contrary to the belief that greater trade will inevitably result in greater political friendship, the hostility of (especially) Lesotho and Botswana toward South Africa has continued to increase despite the more favorable trade between the countries.

The Republic has been able to increase its "backdoor trade" with a number of African states for mainly adventitious reasons. First, the "hostage" neighboring states have little alternative option since their economies and communication systems are integrated with South Africa's (e.g., Lesotho, Botswana, Swaziland, and Mozambique). Second, the impact of sanctions on Rhodesia and the peculiar circumstances which surrounded Angola's independence compelled countries like Zambia and Zaire to use the transport links and other facilities offered by South Africa. Third, the French connection for military supplies (until late 1977) resulted in rapidly expanding trade with both metropolitan France and a number of Francophone African states—notably Ivory Coast, Gabon, and Senegal. Working through some African countries, it became possible to conceal the original source of South African manufactured goods to facilitate their entry into other African states. These channels have also been used to develop a "backdoor" entry for certain South African goods into the EEC. Finally, Malawi's maverick

President, Dr. H.K. Banda, has chosen to ignore the Organization of African Unity (OAU) boycott against economic and diplomatic links with Pretoria. But none of these relationships offers a satisfactory basis on which to develop a dependable export market.

The Republic's pattern of economic growth, under the constraints imposed by its apartheid policies and by external factors, has deepened its internal contradictions. Thus, although it achieved an average real growth rate of 4.5 percent from 1967-1972, this expansion was accompanied by a high rate of inflation and by a current account deficit in its balance-of-payments of about £200 million annually. Since 1977 the growth rate has dropped by more than half to around 2 percent. The Republic's balance of trade has worsened, and it has experienced growing difficulty finding the new capital it needs on the international capital market. This contraction of new capital began in mid-1977 after the Black urban violence triggered by the demonstrations in Soweto. The significance of Soweto is that it destroyed the myth of South Africa as a stable country which was safe for long-term foreign investment. Perhaps even more important than the political reactions to Soweto were the boardroom reactions of major Western firms. The European loan market has marked the Republic down as a risk country. As a result, only short-term and medium-term loans can be raised by South African borrowers—on terms much stiffer than before 1977. Even then, South Africa has been able to raise only half the new capital it needs.

The beginning of the loss of business confidence has facilitated a shift in Western foreign policy because foreign investment is now *becoming* (though it has not yet *become*) less of a constraint on foreign policymakers at a time when the West has begun to seriously reexamine its overall interests in Africa. This change in the economic climate has contributed to a slowing of South Africa's growth, which has resulted in a sharp rise in unemployment among Black workers (now estimated at c. 600,000). This will inevitably feed Black urban unrest, and so increase the loss of confidence on the part of investors.

THE MILITARY IMPERATIVE IN SOUTH AFRICA'S FOREIGN POLICY

The Republic's military expenditure has soared since 1960—the year of Sharpeville, which brought the first cold chill of Western hostility to South Africa. That year also saw the achievement of independence by an array of African states. In 1960-61, South

Africa's expenditure on defense was still less than $50 million; this rose almost fivefold to over $210 million in 1964-65, and to over $2 billion in 1977-78—a rise of 4000 percent in less than twenty years. The total number of its armed forces rose to almost 300,000 in 1977. In response to threats of an arms embargo, South Africa quickly established its own arms industry. One thousand firms are contracted to the Armaments Board (ARMSCOR), and South Africa now produces about 80 percent of all its weapons. It established its own shipping industry capable of producing smaller ships, and it has spent almost $20 million to establish a submarine base at Simonstown. It also established its own aircraft industry, based on the Atlas Aircraft Corporation, and under mainly French and Italian licenses, it now builds Mirages and Aermacchis, as well as its own trainer aircraft. It manufactures rocket missiles capable of carrying a nuclear warhead, and it has made great strides in the field of nuclear power. It has refused to sign the nuclear non-proliferation treaty.

South Africa's success in building up its military strength, despite the 1966 United Nations' and other arms embargoes, was mainly the result of its ability to exploit its economic strength to acquire new friends in the West. Although most Western countries observed the first arms embargo—some more than others—there were a number of gaps, which allowed serious evasions and gave South Africa twelve years in which to build up its armory of sophisticated weapons and lay the foundations for its own arms industry. The French connection was the decisive factor. France used the opportunity both to expand its valuable arms exports and to profit from greater trade with South Africa at the expense of Britain, which observed the UN arms embargo with a minimum of reservations. France cooperated with South Africa (both at government and private levels) in developing the Republic's Cactus ground-to-air missile system; it supplied submarines, helicopters, and Panhard armored cars, and it sold Mirages to be built under license in the Republic. It was also closely involved in assisting the growth of South Africa's nuclear power program. France rapidly became one of the most favored countries in South Africa until October 1977, when it finally agreed to support the mandatory arms embargo imposed by the Security Council.

South Africa has also profited militarily from Israeli cooperation, although this has been minor compared to the French contribution and has existed over a shorter period. The South Africa-Israel military connection developed only after Golda Meir relinquished office following the October 1973 war. It grew stronger after (and partly in consequence of) the UN General Assembly resolution equating Zionism with racism, which seemed to produce among Israelis an injured (and a self-wounding) spirit of "why not have the game, if the Africans give us the name?" Another reason for this cooperation was the feeling in Israel that, however much it abhorred the racism of apartheid, the two countries had some common interest in standing together—thereby giving some credibility to the attempts by its enemies to justify the Zionism = racism charge. Israel, like France, has promised to honor the mandatory arms embargo. Although there are bound to be evasions of the arms embargo, it is becoming harder for South Africa to find loopholes for getting around the sanctions. In a world where weapons systems become outmoded almost as rapidly as automobile models, the problems of acquiring the latest sophisticated weapons exceed the capacities of even a country as industrially advanced as South Africa.

South Africa's external and internal military objectives have remained as stated in 1961 by its then Minister of Defense, J.J. Fouché, when he gave three reasons for strengthening the Republic militarily: (1) to preserve internal security, (2) to make its contribution on the side of the West against Communism, and (3) to meet the threat of external invasion.[4] The Republic has failed to make any progress toward fulfilling the second of these objectives: acceptance into one of the Western defense alliance systems. It has variously tried to form an African/Middle East defense system, a South Atlantic defense system, an Indian Ocean defense system (with Australia and New Zealand), and most recently, a naval defense system with Argentina and Brazil. Nothing so far has come of any of these initiatives, and the Republic still remains outside any military alliance. Even Britain's earlier commitment to the Simonstown naval base as a defense post on the Atlantic route has been abandoned.

While no serious military threat has yet developed internally, anxieties about the possible emergence of effective guerrilla action continue to grow. This concern extends over four areas. First is the border of Namibia with Angola because of the great effectiveness of the South West Africa People's Organization (SWAPO) guerrilla campaign—especially after the victory in Angola of the Movimiento Popular de Libertacao de Angola (MPLA) regime, heavily backed by the Soviet bloc and Cuba. Second is the threat of guerrillas—mainly from the African National Congress, with the support of the South African Communist Party—operating across the Mozambique border and along the Swaziland frontier. (The ANC, which enjoys strong Soviet backing, now has camps in Mozambique and Tanzania. According to the South African Chief of Police Security, Brigadier Zietsman, there are four thousand ANC guerrillas training for insurgent activities.) Third is the risk of violence spilling over from Zimbabwe/Rhodesia following the successes of the Patriotic Front's armed struggle. Fourth is the growing risk of urban guerrilla activities—an essential part of the external liberation movement's strategy. In addition, the guerrilla movements of southern Africa have introduced a new element of international involvement in the area because of the support they get from the OAU, the non-aligned nations, and the Communist countries, as well as from some Scandinavian countries and the Netherlands.

The danger of escalating armed struggles in southern Africa has forced itself to the top of the Republic's priorities. The likely impact on South Africa of growing armed violence has been described by the Republic's army chief, Lieutenant-General Magnus Malan. Borrowing (as he admits) from Maoist ideas, Malan takes the view that South Africa is already involved in a type of enemy activity—

> if you want to call it a war, then do so—which is of low and high intensity. Resulting from this there is one tremendous danger staring us in the face. This is that we are becoming conditioned by circumstances. We are involved in a war. . . . The first terrorist crossed our border in 1967. But today we have become used to it. It's everyday news. It is not real any more; we cannot observe it objectively. . . . [I]t is important . . . that we analyse our involvement and determine to what degree this struggle really affects us. The conclusion I must reach, particularly if the internationalistic spirit to be found at present is taken into account, is that African states can fight and lose, recover and fight again. But can we? I am afraid that we can lose only once. And therefore I say that we must be watchful that we do not become conditioned and over-confident.[5]

THE AFRICAN IMPERATIVE IN SOUTH AFRICA'S FOREIGN POLICY

South Africa can never escape from the consequences of its geographic position. A regime like the present one can secure itself effectively only by achieving two essential objectives in its African diplomacy: (1) peaceful frontiers and (2) opportunities to trade in its natural hinterland. The former is essential to its external security, and the latter to its economy. Both objectives depend on the chances of establishing peaceful coexistence between White-ruled and Black-ruled regimes. This is Pretoria's key objective. Winning acceptance by a substantial number of African states is also important as a means of satisfying Western pressures since deepening hostilities in the subcontinent must affect Western policymakers' calculations in determining their best long-term interests. The dilemma is plain: how can a regime committed to White supremacy hope to win acceptance in African eyes? South Africa continues to believe it is possible on the assumption that economic imperatives outweigh ideologies.

The collapse of Portuguese colonialism in 1974 marked a critical turning-point in South Africa's position on the continent.[6] It brought the loss of its *cordon sanitaire*, which had kept its major borders physically isolated from Black Africa because of the presence of minority White regimes in Mozambique, Angola, and Rhodesia. With the departure of the Portuguese, the pressures on Rhodesia became irresistible, while the South African presence in Namibia gave it a direct border with Angola, where the civil war had introduced a substantial Russian and Cuban military presence.

The Vorster regime's recognition of the historic changes produced by the collapse of Portuguese colonialism led it to reshape its African policy to enable it to pursue, more energetically than before, a policy of detentism with Black Africa. However, the South African army's disastrous intervention in Angola in 1976 virtually paralyzed its efforts to sustain a dialogue with the rest of the continent.[7]

For South Africa the defeat of the "dialogue" initiative (which it had been carefully preparing since 1969 to promote its "outward-looking policies") was especially serious because it blocked the way to achieving a substantial diplomatic and economic breakthrough against the African trade boycott. It exploded the highly optimistic forecast that the Republic was on the way to breaking out of its continental straitjacket, which its friends in the major Western powers felt was essential if they were to adopt a more forthright policy in support of the Republic's struggle to fight off international isolation. The result of the controversy over "dialogue" was to stir up even more African opposition to South Africa in countries previously lukewarm about their commitment to the struggle against apartheid.[8] Thus, far from improving its position inside Africa through its "outward-looking policies," the Republic's relations have in fact continued to decline.

The new administration of Prime Minister Botha has decided to refurbish the African policy originated by Dr. Verwoerd at the beginning of the era of apartheid. The only essential difference is that whereas Verwoerd proposed "a commonwealth of African states" which would link Lesotho, Botswana, Swaziland, the "independent homelands," and South Africa, Botha has elaborated a plan for a larger "constellation of southern African states" which would revolve around South Africa. The rationale underlying this concept is that the Republic's economic and technological strength can provide the stimulus for an economic and political grouping which would include an independent Zimbabwe and Namibia, Lesotho, Botswana, Swaziland, the "independent homelands," and possibly Malawi, Zambia, and Zaire. According to Pretoria's thinking, this plan can succeed only if the regimes of the new Namibia and Zimbabwe are broadly sympathetic to South Africa's aims, which would rule out a SWAPO-dominated Namibia or a Patriotic Front-dominated Zimbabwe. Hence Pretoria's current policies are determined by an overriding interest in ensuring that neither of these two liberation movements should form the government of its country at the time of its independence. There is little reason to suppose that Botha's notion of a new "constellation of southern African states" is any likelier to succeed than Verwoerd's earlier proposal for a "commonwealth"—at least not before apartheid has ceased to be the state policy in South Africa.

THE WESTERN IMPERATIVE IN SOUTH AFRICA'S FOREIGN POLICY

Because the present political system in South Africa was originally produced and subsequently buttressed by Western Europe (and by Britain in particular), it is natural that White South Africa should have come to regard itself as an integral part of the Western community. To remain an accepted member of this community—which nobody seriously questioned up to the time of General Smuts's defeat in 1948—is crucially important to the Republic.

South Africa's oldest haunting fear has been that it might one day find itself "abandoned" by the West—to which its White leadership feels it belongs—and so end up totally isolated within the world community. Although its only hope of averting this disaster lay in adopting policies that could more easily be defended by Western governments, it chose instead to move in precisely the opposite direction—as exemplified by its further repression of Black opposition in October 1977. The Vorster regime thereby created for itself a double crisis: the one external, the other internal. A resolution of the external crisis depended on overcoming, or at least diminishing, the internal crisis, whereas the deepening of the internal crisis could only widen the gulf between the Republic and the West.

The propaganda hostility of the Communist world and of much of the Third World has never seriously troubled the Pretoria regime; what mattered was its ability to keep communications open with a sizable part of Black Africa and with the major Western powers. However, after the South African army's intervention in Angola in 1976, the only significant Black states still willing to talk to Pretoria were the Ivory Coast, Zaire, and Malawi; Senegal refused to have any further talks. This meant that it was no longer possible for the Pretoria regime to take any independent diplomatic initiative in Africa. Yet, as noted above, Vorster himself acknowledged in 1977 that South Africa's only way of winning back the West lay in winning over Africa. Although he no longer expected friendship from the Western nations, he still continued to hope for Western "understanding" of the Republic's difficulties and, above all, for continuing economic, military, and diplomatic links, which, he argued, were necessary to defend mutual interests. He could not understand why the West failed to see that its best interests lay in a strong South Africa. On the other hand, the Western leadership could not understand why Vorster failed to appreciate that a Western alliance with the apartheid Republic would marvelously suit Russian interests.

In the hope of reaching some *modus vivendi* with the new Carter administration, Vorster went to Vienna in May 1977 for talks with Vice-President Walter Mondale. But far from getting on a better footing with Washington, Vorster found himself faced with what could properly be regarded as an ultimatum. Carter's message was that White South Africa could expect no support from the United States unless there was progress on "majority rule for Rhodesia and Namibia, and a progressive transformation of South African society to the same end."[9] Mondale made it clear that the United States did not expect changes to come overnight, but that steps should be taken toward the ultimate goal of a democratic society. The decisive change in Washington's position was marked by Mondale's carefully worded warning:

> We hope that South Africa will carefully review the implications of our policy and the changed circumstances which it creates.

> We hope that South Africans will not rely on any illusions that the United States will in the end intervene to save South Africa from the policies it is pursuing, for we will not do so.

In other words, if South Africa found itself in a military conflict with Africans—even if they had Communist support—the United States would not intervene militarily to defend apartheid.

After his Vienna meeting with Mondale, Vorster threatened that if the West took any action which was tantamount to "putting out our eyes," it should remember the biblical story of Samson and be aware that "South Africa will pull down the pillars with us." In an interview with the American Broadcasting Corporation, Vorster said that the United States had started to turn against South Africa when Carter took office: "Whereas it appears to us at the moment that the Soviets want to kill us off by force, the United States wants to strangle us with finesse."

Vorster's successor, P.W. Botha, has for some years been an advocate of neutrality between the Western community and the Soviet bloc. He emphasized this aspect of his policy in a statement to his Parliament on April 19, 1979 in which he said that the Republic should remain "as far removed as possible from the East-West dispute," and should be guided only by regional interests. His foreign minister, "Pik" Botha, spoke along similar lines in a speech in Geneva a month earlier. In his view, South Africa's "sole commitment ought to be towards security and advancement of our Southern African region" by establishing "a sub-continental solidarity which could form the basis for cooperation in important spheres of life."

The idea of neutrality has frequently come up in the past at times when South Africa's relations with the West were under particular strain; it reflects the Africaners' essentially ambivalent feelings toward the West—especially toward Britain and the United States. A prominent South African establishment political commentator, Deon Geldenhuys, suggested that the idea of the Republic moving toward a neutral position should be treated with some reserve, but added:

> If, however, the government this time intends seriously to go beyond stylistic adjustments and is planning to embark on structural changes in South Africa's foreign relations, the proposed options need careful examination lest they too be added to the growing list of typical South African responses under pressure. There is indeed a case to be made for lessening South Af-

rica's Western fixation by, for example, further diversifying diplomatic and economic ties. Closer association with Africa is not only advisable but imperative. South Africa's freedom of action on the international scene is, however, severely circumscribed by the constraints imposed by its domestic policy. In the final analysis, structural changes in foreign policy cannot be considered in isolation from structural domestic policy change.[10]

CONCLUSIONS

The main thesis of this paper is that change in the Republic of South Africa will come primarily through effective Black militancy posed against White militancy, which will sharpen both the internal and external contradictions of the apartheid society. This confrontation will increasingly weaken the status quo. In the context of this thesis, international pressures have played an important role—although not as important as the role of apartheid itself—in radicalizing Black attitudes and in making Whites more sensitive to the nature of the challenge they face.

South Africa's present position, internally and externally, is far less secure than it was in 1948 when the rallying cry of apartheid brought the diehard defenders of the status quo to power. Threats of international isolation have come close to realization, but so far external pressures have produced only limited results of a kind that can be measured. The most important of these are that the Republic has been locked out of most of Africa, that it has come to be felt as an increasing liability to its friends in the West, and that there is much greater international understanding of and support for the aims of Black and White opponents of apartheid inside the Republic as well as for the externally based liberation movements.

These developments have not weakened South Africa's determination or capacity to defend its system of White supremacy. In fact its ability to defend itself economically and militarily has increased. However, behind this strength of will lie gnawing doubts about the "reliability" of the West—especially at a time when the other major world powers and the Third World have openly joined the African camp against the Republic—and, even more important, doubts about the efficacy of apartheid itself.

Nevertheless, despite all these doubts, despite the censure of world opinion, and despite the open hostility of Black Africa, the Republic has not been deflected from its course. Apartheid is being pursued in disregard of any considerations but those thought to be in the best interest of the White economy and White political power. South Africa has adjusted itself to changing circumstances abroad, but without changing any of the fundamentals of its internal policies. Thus, while a number of remarkable changes have been made, none touches on the core problem of political rights: only Whites are to be allowed the right to vote for the central Parliament where all political power resides.

APARTHEID AND WHITE SUPREMACY: THE MEANING OF GOVERNMENT-LED REFORM IN THE SOUTH AFRICAN CONTEXT

Robert M. Price

Currently, when attention is focused on the Republic of South Africa, political change is almost inevitably the subject of discussion. Foreign governments claim to desire it and sometimes to require it; spokesmen for the African, Colored, and Indian populations that constitute four-fifths of the Republic's population demand it; the Nationalist government of the country alternatively promises and proclaims it; sympathetic observers detect it, while their more critical colleagues deny it. At the end of the decade of the 1970s this focus on political change is more pronounced than ever as the South African government has with great fanfare proclaimed its commitment to a major effort at liberalizing reform. During 1979 certain aspects of the South African system of official discrimination and segregation, hitherto thought to be nearly sacred in the thinking of official circles, were slated for abolition. Concurrently senior government officials were publicly condemning the system of apartheid and committing themselves to its elimination. "Apartheid as you have come to know it is dying and dead," announced cabinet minister Dr. Piet Koornhof on a speaking tour of the United States.[1] "Apartheid was a recipe for permanent conflict," the Prime Minister, P.W. Botha, told the Natal Congress of the ruling National party, and "the only alternative to revolution" was change.[2] Considering that for over thirty years the essential "rightness" of apartheid had been a sacred truth within Afrikanerdom, and that during that time political leaders had stressed above all that apartheid was the only way to avoid racial friction, these statements and the government acts they refer to must be viewed as nothing less than startling. But before ascribing meaning to recent government-inspired alterations in even core aspects of the apartheid system and to the anti-apartheid statements of Koornhof and Botha, one should note the comments of another senior government official. Foreign Minister R.F. "Pik" Botha, universally identified as one of the most reform-minded Afrikaans politicians and a close political associate of Koornhof and P.W. Botha in the National party ruling circle, told a West

German television audience in 1977 that his government will "never in 100 years agree to share power with blacks, coloured, and Asians": "It is our birthright to govern this country of ours. . . . No one can take that birthright away."[3]

What is one to make of this apparent contradiction in the statements of the most senior and influential members of the South African government? Is it an indication of duplicity on the part of Koornhof and Prime Minister Botha? Or does it reveal that the foreign minister is out of step with government thinking? The basic thesis of this chapter is that the answer to both of these questions is *no*, that the statements of all three of these officials accurately reflect government thinking and policy, and that the apparent contradiction is instead a rather easily resolved paradox. Comprehending that paradox and its resolution is, I believe, the key to understanding the motivation for the current reform effort, its likely future course, and its long-term significance for meaningful change in the South African system. The starting point for resolving the paradox is an understanding of the relationship between the apartheid system, on the one hand, and White supremacy, on the other.

APARTHEID AND WHITE SUPREMACY

White supremacy in South Africa, as commonly understood, involves the phenomenon of a small European (White) minority—12 percent of the population—maintaining complete political domination over a Black* majority so as to guarantee for itself a position of economic and social privilege. In recent years it has become commonplace to treat the system of apartheid as if it were synonymous with White supremacy. Thus the phrase "the apartheid regime" is commonly used as a referent for the political and social system of South Africa, and those seeking fundamental change in that country usually demand "an end to apartheid." However, it is essential to understand that apartheid is but one, and by no means the only, strategy for maintaining the condition of White supremacy. As such it is only a particular form of White supremacy, and the form can change while the basic condition remains the same. The failure to draw a distinction between apartheid and White supremacy is a serious analytic mistake and contributes a good deal of

*Here we use the term "Black" in the way it has come to be used by the majority group in South Africa—to encompass the Indian and Colored communities as well as the African population.

confusion and misunderstanding to discussions about whether changes occurring in South Africa are really meaningful or only cosmetic. The distinction is also crucial to providing a proper perspective on the current government-initiated reform effort.[4]

Apartheid originated as an ideology of race relations that took hold within the Afrikaner intellectual and political elite in the mid-1940s. With the 1948 electoral victory of the Nationalists, the party of the Afrikaner community, the ideology evolved and was implemented in an elaborate system of laws. A single principle underlay both the ideology and the institutional system it spawned—*the complete separation* of Black and White races in South Africa. After 1948, and especially after the assumption of the prime ministership by Verwoerd in 1958, government domestic policy was directed at enforcing race separation in every conceivable sphere—in interpersonal relations, in social and economic organization, in residential patterns, in the political organization of the state. The political sphere was the most important for the effort of separation. Through the creation of separate states for the Black population out of the old native reserves, which covered some 13 percent of the country's land area, the Afrikaner elite hoped to eliminate Africans from the South African heartland altogether, except as foreigners in search of temporary employment.

In understanding the manner in which apartheid doctrine has been implemented, it is important to recognize that for post-World War II Afrikaner political leaders the endeavor of "separation" upon which they had embarked had both consummatory and instrumental significance. Something possesses *consummatory significance* when it represents an ultimate goal or value, or when its achievement is so closely linked with the realization of some other ultimate goal/value that the two are in reality inseparable. Something has *instrumental significance* when it is an agent or tool for the accomplishment of something else; it is significant only as a means to an end, and it has little virtue in and of itself. The consummatory significance of apartheid in the history of Afrikanerdom lies in its connection to two closely related things. The first is what Dunbar Moodie, in his seminal work *The Rise of Afrikanerdom*, calls the Afrikaner civil religion;[5] the second is what by the mid-twentieth century had become a collective obsession among the Afrikaner ethnic community—the maintenance of their group identity. At the heart of their civil religion is the notion of the Afrikaners as God's chosen people with an ordained calling or mission.[6] "God created the Afrikaner People with a unique language, a unique philosophy of life, and their own history and tradition in order that they might fulfill a particular calling and destiny here in the southern corner of Africa."[7] Afrikaner doctrinal writings do not go very far in spelling out the nature of Afrikanerdom's national calling, except insofar as understanding it to be simply vigilance in the maintenance of its cultural uniqueness.[8] Thus J.C. van Rooy, chairman of the Afrikaner Broederbond during the 1940s, defined his people's divine mission this way: "We must stand guard on all that is peculiar to us and build upon it . . . to continue with the struggle to maintain our language and culture."[9]

Apartheid—the doctrine and practice of complete group separation—can be seen as the operationalization of this Afrikaner national calling to the maintenance of unity and group identity. If as Moodie has said, the purpose of the Afrikaner on earth "was to remain true to his express particularity,"[10] then "apartness" was a necessary corollary. The genetic mixing and cultural diffusion that were seen as the natural concomitants of intergroup contact would erode unity and identity among the *volk*, thus undermining its God-given mission.* Separation, then, becomes within this logic an ordained enterprise. It also follows that within the domain he defines as his own, the political sovereignty of the Afrikaner is divinely required. As van Rooy stated in 1944: "The Christian republican state is the only constitutional form for the proper completion of our calling."[11] Earlier he had expounded on the nature of such a Christian republic: "A completely independent, truly Afrikaans government for South Africa—a government which by its embodiment of our own personal head of state, bone of our bone, flesh of our flesh, will inspire us and bind us together to irresistible unity and power."[12]

Although there is much in Afrikaner thought that seeks to justify Afrikaner political supremacy and/or White supremacy in terms of alleged racial or ethnic superiority, the main thrust of apartheid ideology is on the cultural difference between groups and the importance of maintaining that difference and the identity that goes with it. It is this emphasis which permitted, in the full flowering of separate development ideology under Verwoerd, the justification

*In the words of G. Cronje, one of the intellectual founders of apartheid: "The more radically racial segregation is carried through, the better it will be; and the more consistently we apply the policy of apartheid, the more efficient our purity of blood and our unadulterated European racial survival will be guaranteed" (quoted in Johannes Degennar, *Afrikaner Nationalism* [Centre for Intergroup Studies, University of Cape Town, 1978], p. 21).

of the entire apartheid effort in terms of the values of equality and self-determination:

> Every People in the world, of whatever race or color, just like every individual, has an inherent right to live and to develop. Every People is entitled to the right of self-preservation. . . . [I]t is our deep conviction that the personal and national ideals of every individual and of every ethnic group can best be developed within its own national community. . . . This is the philosophic basis of the policy of apartheid.[13]

Since the South African government accompanied the implementation of separate development with very heavy use of ideological rhetoric, many observers of the South African scene have focused on the ideological aspects of apartheid—what we have called its consummatory significance. There is, however, another face to apartheid which is equally if not more important for the unfolding of South African politics—what we have called its instrumental significance. Apartheid offered to the Afrikaner political elite a method for overcoming its most basic political challenge—a challenge built into the very structure of the South African sociopolitical system: how to maintain in perpetuity the domination of a White minority over a vastly more numerous Black majority. The simple demographic realities had always raised very serious doubts about the viability of White supremacy on the southern tip of Africa, but for the White political leadership this problem was particularly vexing in the aftermath of World War II. The global political currents set loose by the war contained potentially serious consequences for White South Africa's domestic and international security. The domestic security threat lay in the forces of mass nationalism which spread, in the early postwar years, throughout the non-Western world, undermining the foundations of European colonial domination. In sub-Saharan Africa, the late 1940s saw the birth of anticolonial movements in Ghana and Nigeria that shattered the assumed stability of these two bastions of British rule. By 1958, when Verwoerd announced his separate development policy—i.e., the creation of Black homelands which would eventually become independent states—the process begun in Ghana had "infected" virtually every colony in sub-Saharan Africa, and the entire enterprise of European colonialism on the continent entered its eleventh hour. Seen from Pretoria the picture of European political retreat in the face of mass politicization and mobilization was something that could not be ignored with equanimity. Left unchecked the forces of modern mass nationalism might well be the ingredient that the African National Congress (ANC) needed to emerge as an irresistible force in South African politics, spelling doom for White rule. Indeed, in the early postwar years the Afrikaner leadership could find considerable basis for such a fear. As Philip Bonner points out in an earlier chapter in this volume (pp. 174-93), wartime conditions had created a context whereby African trade unions, in league with the South African Communist Party, had developed sufficient membership and levels of organization to sustain a serious challenge to the White-dominated economic system. And as Roland Stanbridge details in another chapter (pp. 66-98), in the immediate aftermath of the war the ANC began to move toward a new militancy and toward closer cooperation with other forces opposed to the White government, especially the Communist party. In sum, then, as the National party took power in 1948, political trends in the non-Western world generally, and in sub-Saharan Africa particularly, were such as to make the political demography of South Africa even more forboding than usual from the vantage point of the Afrikaner leadership.

The aftermath of World War II was no more propitious for South Africa's international posture than for its long-term domestic political stability. In the immediate wake of the fight against Nazism, a sociopolitical system based upon racial supremacy and political domination, such as existed in South Africa, did not constitute a very attractive friend or ally for the Western powers. And it was to these Western industrial states that South Africa looked. They were its main trading partners, purchasing South African minerals and selling it manufactured goods; they were the prime source for the new technology and capital needed for South African industrial expansion; and perhaps most important, they were the hoped-for source of diplomatic and military support in the event the country was attacked or subverted from without—most especially by the "forces of world communism." In addition, in a general cultural sense, White South Africans—and the Afrikaners in particular—self-consciously identified themselves as a part of, indeed as a forward outpost of, Western civilization. Now, after the fight against Nazism, South Africa's system of racial domination threatened to turn the country into an international pariah. Moreover, the strains between South Africa and the community of Western nations were likely to increase as the government took repressive measures to deal with the heightened effort for equality and political power being launched by the Black majority.

Put simply, from the vantage point of the Afrikaner leadership seeking to maintain White supremacy in South Africa, the postwar situation posed this basic dilemma: how to suppress the emerging challenge of Black political and economic power and at the same time gain legitimacy internationally. Apartheid in its instrumental aspects was an attempted solution to this dilemma.[14] It was a strategy for maintaining White supremacy under particular historical circumstances. However much the Afrikaner leadership held to the ideological or consummatory justification for apartheid, there can be little doubt that the political elite was fully conscious of the instrumental significance of the apartheid system which they developed and implemented. No less authoritative source than Prime Minister Verwoerd declared in defense of his separate development program:

> [We] cannot govern without taking into account the tendencies in the world and in Africa. We must have regard to them. . . .[15]
>
> [The political partition of South Africa] is not something we would have liked to see. It is a form of fragmentation that we would not have liked if we were able to avoid it. In the light of the pressure being exerted on South Africa, there is however no doubt that eventually this will have to be done, thereby buying for the White man his freedom and the right to retain his domination in what is his country.[16]

Numerous detailed analyses of the apartheid laws and their consequences are available, and it is not my intention to provide yet another one here.[17] Rather, let me highlight the instrumental benefits sought by the ruling political elite. While the apartheid system holds many practical economic and social benefits for the White population, my concern is how the system was designed to maintain White political domination through tackling the twin problems of domestic security and international legitimation. With respect to internal security, the intended "benefits" were threefold: (1) insulation of the minority White population from potential uprisings by the Black majority and the creation of physical conditions that would allow for the effective repression of such uprisings should they occur; (2) "improvement" in the White-Black demographic ratio in what was officially designated as White South Africa; and (3) elimination of opportunities for effective and autonomous political organization on the part of the Black majority. A central role in securing these internal security benefits was played by the "group areas" aspect of apartheid policy. Given the need for African labor in domestic and industrial service, the presence of millions of Black people in the cities of South Africa was an unavoidable reality for South African Whites. The Group Areas Act was a means of reducing the political liabilities inherent in the necessities imposed by the economic system. The National party sought to consolidate and systematize the existing segregated neighborhoods so as to create a pattern of racially homogeneous and physically separated residential areas. In each city it set about to create peri-urban townships for the African, Indian, and Colored population groups that were several miles distant from the centers of White residence and business enterprise.* By carefully linking the satellite Black townships to their respective metropoles with only one or two transportation arteries, which could easily be cut, the government was in a position to swiftly and effectively insulate the White cities from the townships and their numerous, potentially hostile inhabitants. This was the first "security benefit" of group areas. In the event of a mass uprising the rebellion could be literally fenced off and contained, and any direct threat to the greatly outnumbered White population could be avoided. A second security benefit of group areas was the ease with which any rebellion could be suppressed. The newly created peri-urban townships were physically planned with internal security considerations clearly in mind.[18] Thus the group areas policy seemed to offer the means to both contain and defeat any uprising in the urban areas before it directly impacted upon the White minority.

A second area of benefits offered by apartheid was a method for altering the racial demography so as to reduce the size of the Black population in what was officially designated White South Africa. Here the system of "influx control" based upon the enforcement of complex pass laws was the key to an attempt to remove from the South African core area all but those Africans required by economic necessity. Under the apartheid system the already extensive mechanisms for controlling and monitoring the movement of the African population were systematized and further extended.

*In the cities of Cape Town and Durban, the concern was primarily with the Colored and Indian population groups respectively, rather than with Africans, and the immediate impact of this policy was more disruptive for the Coloreds in Cape Town and the Indians in Durban than it was for the Africans living in urban areas. The neighborhoods of the Colored and Indian groups were in the centers of the cities; thus the implementation of the Group Areas Act entailed large-scale forced population movement and near total destruction of existing patterns of economic enterprise and community life.

Most important was Section 10 of the Natives (Urban Areas) Consolidation Act of 1945, which provided that no African could remain in an urban area for more than seventy-two hours except under certain specified conditions—essentially that he or she had a record of long-term and continuous employment in the area, or that the government had granted special permission for him (or her) to be there.[19] The effort expended by the government to enforce this and ancillary laws restricting the African presence in White South Africa attests to the importance assigned by the political elite to this aspect of the apartheid strategy. Over the decade 1966-1975 prosecutions under laws restricting the movement of Africans numbered an extraordinary 5.8 million.[20]

Reducing the African presence in White areas was only one aspect of the benefits to be derived from the influx control apparatus. Others fall within the third category of the internal security "benefits package"—the elimination of opportunities for effective political organization on the part of the Black majority. One consequence of the influx control system is the creation of a condition of permanent insecurity for the African population in the urban areas. Those lacking Section 10 rights have to live with the constant threat of apprehension and immediate rustication to one of the homelands. Those fortunate enough to possess rights under Section 10 are only marginally better off since they can lose these rights for a variety of legal infractions or because the government deems them "undesirable" persons. Thus they too can easily be "endorsed out" of the urban areas. Since forceable removal from the cities usually means not only disruption of family life, but also permanent loss of access to the main sources of livelihood, it is an eventuality that cannot be taken lightly. The implication of this for political organization is that such a state of insecurity creates powerful incentives for the individual to avoid calling himself to the attention of officialdom, and in the South African situation there is probably no better way to attract such attention than by political activity. Thus, since survival under the system of group areas, influx control, and pass laws requires the maintaining of a "low profile," individuals are discouraged from joining in political action organizations.

The 1968 Prohibition of Political Interference Act is another way in which apartheid severely limits the Black majority's opportunities for the creation of effective organizations of political opposition. The culmination of a long series of efforts, this act was intended to put an end to interracial cooperation at the political party level.[21] The key provisions of the act are summarized by Muriel Horrell as follows:

> It was rendered illegal for anyone:
>
> (a) to belong to a racially-mixed political party;
> (b) to assist a political party that had members drawn from a population group other than his own . . .;
> (c) to address any meeting to further the interests of a political party . . . if the greater majority of those present belonged to a population group other than his own.[22]

This law had at least two important internal security consequences. Anti-apartheid elements in the White community, especially its English-speaking segment, had been an important potential source of financial aid, assistance in the development of organizational cadre, and general political support for fledgling African organizations. The 1968 law cut the Black community off from this source of organization-building resources by making such assistance illegal.* Additionally, the law placed a major obstacle in the path of political cooperation among the three disenfranchised communities --the African, Colored, and Indian groups. Because apartheid's race classification laws designated these three groupings as separate racial categories, the Prohibition of Political Interference Act had the effect of making political cooperation or alliance among them at the organizational level illegal. Preventing united opposition to its rule is a major concern of the Afrikaner elite, and this legislation is one among a number of mechanisms in the apartheid arsenal designed to serve this purpose.

Political parties were not the only target of the government effort to deny the Black community a significant organizational capacity. Because the South African economy was very heavily dependent upon African labor for its operation, a significant trade union organization among African workers would not only be a threat to the low-wage structure of the economy, but also could easily be transformed into a political weapon. Thus a very important element in the apartheid system is a set of laws which places severe obstacles in the path of strong and autonomous African trade union

*The history of the growth of nationalist movements in colonial territories is replete with examples of the important role played by opposition organizations in the metropole in assisting the development of trade union and political organization among the colonized. The apartheid system virtually eliminated this process in South Africa.

organization. The Native Labour Act of 1953 prohibited the registration of African trade unions and denied African employees the right to strike. The law did not outlaw African trade unions as such, but by denying them official status it placed them at considerable disadvantage in negotiating with employers and denied them very important organizing resources, such as dues check-off and access to the workplace by union organizers.[23] In addition, as was the case in regard to political party organization, apartheid legislation outlawed racially mixed unions and prevented cooperation between unions representing workers of different racial designations.

After 1959 the core of apartheid strategy became the Verwoerdian plan for the partition of South Africa. Separate development, as the partition plan was called, had two instrumental political functions. First, it would contribute to the security of White rule by dividing the African population and directing its political attention away from racial rule in the South African heartland. To achieve this end there were four interrelated elements: (1) the creation of eight ethnic homelands out of the existing native reserves, (2) the requirement that all Africans become citizens of one of the designated homelands and the concomitant stripping from them of all citizenship rights in what was designated as White South Africa, (3) the gradual granting of internal self-government status and then independent statehood to the ethnic homelands, and (4) the ruthless elimination of any political "space" for Africans in White South Africa. By, on the one hand, denying the African population any opportunity for political expression within South Africa and, on the other hand, opening up channels for genuine although limited political power and economic mobility within the homelands, the South African government hoped to channel the political energy of the Africans away from White rule and into the homeland structures. The key to this plan was not in the absolute level of power and economic resources made available through the homeland governments, which would be severely limited by the economic destitution of the territory they controlled, but rather in the political and economic opportunities available to Africans *relative* to the base-zero existing for them within White South Africa.

The second instrumental function of separate development policy related to White South Africa's problem of international legitimation—i.e., the untenability, in the post-World War II era, of the disenfranchisement of the majority of a country's population on racial grounds. Separate development policy involved doing away with this problem by simply eliminating South Africa's African majority by means of legal definition. Africans would become citizens of the independent states evolving out of the homelands, within which they would be free to exercise their political rights; those found in South Africa could then be considered temporary sojourners in search of employment. Thus separate development—the metamorphosis of native reserves into sovereign states—would have the effect of legally transforming the members of the African majority into citizens of other independent countries. As such they would have no more legitimate claim to participate in the governance of South Africa than Yugoslav migrants have to participate in the governance of West Germany or Mexican laborers in the governance of the United States. By this means the South African system could be brought into line with the "standards" of Western civilization. Moreover, the entire exercise could be explained, justified, and defended—i.e., sold to the world—in terms of the two values that were at the core of postwar liberalism: equality and self-determination. Thus the Minister of Bantu Affairs in the Verwoerd cabinet defended separate development in this manner:

> Every people in the world finds its highest expression and fulfillment in managing its own affairs and in the creation of a material and spiritual heritage for its prosperity. We want to give the Bantu that right also. The demand for self-determination on the part of the non-white nations is one of the outstanding features of the past decade. . . . If the white man is entitled to separate national existence, what right have we to deny that these People have a right to it also? Nationalism is one of the forces which has led to the most beautiful deeds of idealism. . . . Should the Bantu not have it? It will always be my task not only to respect these things of the Bantu, but to assist them to develop it as something beautiful.[24]

To summarize: While "separateness" was something that acquired an inherent goodness within Afrikaner national political culture—indeed it was required by the people's Christian national mission—apartheid at the same time had a very basic utilitarian significance. It was developed and implemented as a strategy for the maintenance of White supremacy in the face of the domestic and international challenges confronting the Afrikaner political elite in the post-World War II era. As an instrumental undertaking apartheid was an effort to combine the repression of any challenge by South Africa's Black majority to the White minority's monopoly of political power with the gaining of international legitimacy for South Africa's political arrangement.

THE UTILITY OF APARTHEID IN A CHANGED ENVIRONMENT

Because utilitarian considerations are so important in the genesis and development of apartheid policy, it should not be surprising that the Afrikaner political elite implemented it with a good deal of pragmatism, relaxing the principle of separation when economic exigencies or the conduct of international diplomacy appeared to require flexibility. Thus when faced with shortages of White skilled workers, the government ignored the violations of job reservation laws which reserved such skilled employment for Whites; when the goal of establishing diplomatic relations with independent states of sub-Saharan Africa was being pursued, certain hotels and restaurants were designated "international class" and were exempted from the segregation laws that applied to all other public facilities; when segregated sports made it difficult and then impossible for South Africa to compete internationally, enforced race separation in athletic activity was gradually relaxed. Two things characterized these and other instances of pragmatic apartheid policy prior to 1978. First, they took place at the same time that commitment to the principle of apartheid was being resoundingly reiterated by officialdom. Second, they were focused on what critics came to call "petty apartheid": they altered, to a minor extent, the pattern of interpersonal segregation, but they did not affect the core of the system—i.e., those aspects that worked to guarantee for Whites a monopoly of organized political power. By contrast, the reforms being implemented (and contemplated) at the end of the 1970s do affect what are generally considered core elements of the apartheid system, and they do not take place while officials are declaring their commitment to apartheid. Instead, the head of government describes apartheid as a recipe for permanent conflict, and the various elite institutions of Afrikanerdom—the press, the regional congresses of the National party, and by inference the Broederbond—support him. What explains this change of orientation among the Afrikaner political elite, and what are the implications of the current reform effort? In the remainder of this chapter these questions will be addressed.

By the mid-1970s it had become clear that apartheid had fallen short of achieving its two major instrumental goals—internal security and international legitimation. As a strategy for legitimation, separate development had been a complete failure. The international community had simply refused to accept the program as a genuine exercise in self-determination, and thus not a single country recognized the Transkei when it became an "independent state" in 1976—or Bophuthatswana or Venda when they followed in 1978 and 1979 respectively. On the internal security dimension, apartheid's failure was not as complete or obvious. During the 1960s the apartheid system, in combination with an elaborate apparatus of coercion, had been quite effective in eliminating significant African political and trade union organization within South Africa, but events in the 1970s dramatically demonstrated that Black political and economic alienation could still find expression with telling effect. Two events were crucial in this regard: the Natal strikes of 1973 and the Soweto uprising of 1976. The pattern of labor quiescence that followed the crushing of Black trade union organization in the mid-1960s was startlingly upset by a series of illegal strikes that convulsed the Natal during 1973—strikes which involved some sixty thousand workers and led to the hiking of Black wages by up to 20 percent throughout South Africa. Even more significant, the success of the Natal workers led to heightened worker militancy throughout South Africa.[25]

As in the trade union sphere, by the mid-1960s the South African government had crushed the existing African political organizations, and had seemingly created conditions which would make the formation of new ones impossible. Nevertheless, by 1970 an African student organization—the South African Students Organization (SASO)—had taken on the role of political leadership among Black intellectuals, had reached a wide audience with its politico-cultural ideology of Black Consciousness, and had launched a political movement—the Black People's Convention—dedicated "to unite . . . the Black People . . . with a view to liberating and emancipating them."[26] The emergence and popularity of the Black Consciousness movement indicated the failure of apartheid as a method for ending the expression of majority opposition to White supremacy, and the Soweto uprising dramatically punctuated this failure. What began as a protest against government education policy by school children in the Johannesburg African township of Soweto quickly developed into a movement of mass defiance in which various symbols of government authority—police stations, administrative office buildings, beer halls, and the like—were attacked and destroyed. The rebellion spread to practically all South African urban areas and beyond, and received support across generations from a broad spectrum of the Black population.

The internal security threat that the Natal strikes and Soweto uprising by themselves posed for the South African regime was not particularly grave. The higher wages forced by the strike action could be absorbed without difficulty by the economic system; indeed the expanded market which would result from an increase in the Black population's disposable income was likely to enhance the outlook for the manufacturing sector. For the most part the uprising begun in Soweto was contained within the confines of apartheid's geographically separated residential areas, and thus the lives, property, and general sense of well-being of the White minority were insulated from any direct danger. Moreover, the rebellion was effectively suppressed with only a fraction of the state's coercive apparatus committed. Indeed one could calculate some direct security benefits from the uprising. By its brutal suppression, involving the deaths of many hundreds and perhaps over a thousand youths, the South African government may well have eliminated, through death or exile, a sizable portion of the Black population's next generation of political leadership.

Although the Natal strikes and the Soweto rebellion did not pose a significant direct danger to the internal security of the regime, they interacted with South Africa's international situation so as to create serious short-term, and potentially ominous long-term, problems for the government. This was especially true in the case of Soweto, where the rebellion and its brutal suppression galvanized the attention of the international public. The increasing labor militancy which the Natal strikes initiated also had international implications. Bonner's analysis shows that these implications had two aspects. First, by making the plight of South Africa's Black workers more salient, labor militancy threatened to produce "undesirable" reactions from well-organized and strategically placed foreign and international labor unions. These began to call for recognition of Black trade unions in South Africa, and they were capable of providing material support and leadership training for the fledgling unregistered Black unions which appeared after 1973. Moreover, they were often in a position to threaten costly actions against a South African economy heavily dependent on international trade. In this regard the most pointed lesson for the South African government was provided by the American Mineworkers Union and the dock workers of Mobile, Alabama, who launched a boycott of South African coal in 1974 on the grounds that it was produced by indentured labor. The sensitivity of the South African government to this kind of action was revealed when it rapidly removed the penal provisions of the Masters and Servants legislation, which had been on the law books for 120 years.[27] Second, foreign-owned multinational corporations, which increasingly came to play a central role in the South African economy during the 1960s, were more favorably disposed to the recognition of African trade unions than was the South African government; the experience of these companies with trade unions both in their home countries and in their overseas operations encouraged such a disposition. But even more important, in the wake of Soweto the recognition of African trade unions seemed a useful way for the multinationals to satisfy home governments and dissident shareholders who were raising embarrassing questions about their South African operations and, in some instances, calling for divestment.

Soweto and its aftermath of repression emphasized anew and in especially dramatic form the pariah status that South Africa's domestic arrangements conferred upon it within the international community. It revived the whole issue of the international unacceptability of racial rule that Verwoerd had sought to lay to rest through his separate development program, and it subjected South Africa to the type of international pressures that policy was designed to avert. Moreover, South Africa was more vulnerable on the international dimension in the 1970s than it had been two decades earlier when the apartheid program was devised. Strategically its position had rapidly deteriorated. The collapse of Portugal's African empire in 1975-76 and the imminent end to White rule in Rhodesia meant the disappearance of the *cordon sanitaire* that had previously separated the Republic from the Black-ruled countries to the north. In its place were two, and potentially three, Marxist-oriented African states whose long-term goals would most certainly include the elimination of the White redoubt to the south. Economically also, South Africa was more exposed than it had been in an earlier era. The 1960s had seen the maturation of the South African industrial economy—a process which was based upon large-scale involvement of foreign-owned multinational corporations. This meant that to the existing trade dependence of the South African economy, which was a function of its large mineral export sector, was added the need to maintain ready access to international markets for capital and technology and to foreign outlets for its manufactures.

The international repercussions that followed Soweto struck at these very strategic and economic vulnerabilities. Since the late

1960s the South African government had worked carefully, and with considerable success, to create a cooperative diplomatic and strategic relationship, albeit a non-public one, between itself and the Western powers—in particular the United States.[28] Soweto dramatically reversed this process, producing the greatest diplomatic estrangement of South Africa from the West in that country's modern history. Concretely this meant that South Africa found it increasingly difficult to purchase sophisticated military equipment and so-called "grey area" technology—e.g., civilian equipment such as computers or light aircraft with a potential military use. More important was the psychological impact of its isolation. Recent events in Angola and Ethiopia had raised the specter of future direct intervention by Communist powers in support of attacks on South Africa by neighboring African states or by domestic revolutionaries. The U.S. reaction to Soweto, projected in statements by the President, Vice-President, secretary of state, and UN ambassador, strongly indicated to the South Africans that they could no longer count on the world's great anti-Soviet power even in the event of a direct assault by the Communists. Admittedly this did not constitute an immediate danger, since the African states to the north and the revolutionaries within lacked the capability to launch sizable attacks against it. But a long-term future in which it stood alone against increasingly capable African countries who were closely supported by the military might of the Soviet Union could hardly be contemplated with equanimity by the Afrikaner government of South Africa.

The international economic repercussions of Soweto were felt almost immediately. Like the impact in the strategic sphere, these were not of such magnitude as to threaten the collapse of the existing politico-economic system, but they contained significant short- and long-term constraints on the growth of the South African industrial economy. These repercussions can be classified in three categories:

1. *Constraints on Access to Foreign Capital and Technology*. During the previous decade and a half, foreign-owned multinational corporations had been very active investors in the South African economy, and their capital and technology played a central role in the modernization and maturation of the South African industrial system. Following Soweto, the flow of foreign direct investment slowed to a trickle. The MNCs, either because they had doubts about the long-term stability of the Republic, or because they were under pressure from their shareholders or their home governments, or for a combination of these reasons, no longer considered South

Africa a particularly attractive place for investment purposes. Some of the largest foreign corporations active in the economy publicly announced that they would not expand their South African investments, and explicitly linked this decision to the country's domestic political and social arrangements. Thus the General Motors Corporation issued a statement that reads as follows:

> The Corporation has no present need for, and has no intention of, further expanding its productive capacity in South Africa.
>
> The single most important factor in the creation of a more promising investment climate in South Africa is a positive resolution of the country's pressing social problems, which have their origin in the apartheid system.[29]

A potential alternative to the MNCs as a source of foreign capital is the international banking system. This source had been utilized during the early 1970s to finance the development of South Africa's state-owned industrial sector and a major upgrading of its defense capability.[30] After Soweto, however, South Africa's access to international credit, like its access to direct foreign investment, was severely constrained. Some of the largest international banking institutions became distinctly less interested than they had previously been in arranging loans to South Africa. "Most British and some American banks," stated the chairman of Barclay's South African subsidiary, "were of the opinion that their exposure to South Africa at the present time was as far as they were prepared to go, bearing in mind the recent disturbances in our black townships."[31] Although not cut off completely from sources of foreign loans, the South African government has found that it must pay premium interest rates for the credit it does manage to obtain.

Not only has the flow of new capital funds been woefully inadequate after Soweto, but foreign firms began to repatriate an unusually large proportion of their local earnings rather than reinvest them in South Africa. This, together with the constraints on foreign borrowing and the lack of new direct foreign investment, produced a dramatic turnabout in the country's net capital flow. Within six months of Soweto the South African economy faced a situation in which the amount of capital leaving the country greatly exceeded that which was coming in. Thus the capital account swung from a net inflow of R528 million in the last half of 1976 to a R810m net outflow in 1977, and an even more dramatic R1,370m net outflow in 1978.[32]

2. Constraints on Foreign Trade. Because the expansion of

exports is an important element in the development and growth of the South African economy, political constraints on foreign trade pose a significant threat to the country's long-term economic well-being. The potential problem is less severe in the area of minerals than it is for the manufacturing sector, since in the former area South Africa is the sole feasible source of a number of essential minerals for the industrial economies of the West and Japan. But in the manufacturing sector, which in the last decade has been the most dynamic part of the economy, the threat to South Africa is far more serious. The skewed structure of domestic income distribution excludes the majority of the country's population from the market for consumer manufactured goods, and thus foreign markets must be found to provide effective demand for a growing manufacturing sector. Consequently if domestic political affairs threaten to interfere with the ability to export manufactures to foreign markets, it is a matter that cannot be taken lightly by the South African government. The events of Soweto had just such an effect. They gave new impetus to the effort by sub-Saharan African countries to have the United Nations launch a campaign of sanctions against South Africa. Although the chances of an effective total embargo on South African goods are very remote, the mere fact that it is the subject of international consideration has forced the South African government to spend considerable diplomatic time and effort in blocking such an undertaking. Moreover, there were more immediate repercussions in the area of trade. First, short-term commercial credits for trading with South Africa have become more difficult to obtain, and domestic political pressures on the private Western banks and government agencies which provide this credit have threatened a wholesale curtailment of such trade-supporting activities. (The salience of South Africa's negative political image might well produce a degree of consumer hostility toward its products, thus reducing the attractiveness of South African manufactured goods to businesses who could easily switch to alternative sources.) Second, international hostility has led the main oil-producing countries to embargo South Africa, forcing reliance on the "spot market," where the cost is in excess of OPEC prices, and raising questions about the security of supplies over the medium term.

3. "Directed Investment." In the wake of Soweto, various governments, private agencies, and international organizations have sought to encourage foreign companies active in South Africa to conduct their operations in ways that are at odds with apartheid. These efforts have been directed primarily at elements of "personal apartheid"—the desegregation of eating facilities, restrooms, and the like—and economic apartheid: equal opportunities in job allocation and equal pay for equal work. The most far-reaching effort thus far has been produced by the European Economic Community, which in September 1977 announced a "code of conduct" for member country corporations that have operations in South Africa. Most significant among the code's provisions was one calling upon firms to engage in collective bargaining with African trade unions.* The emergence of a trend toward "directed investment"—especially should it continue and evolve an enforcement component—would pose a serious dilemma for the South Africans. A situation would develop in which they might have to choose between the foreign capital and technology they sorely need and the wholesale violation of apartheid laws.

In summary: Political developments in the latter half of the 1970s provided the Afrikaner governing elite with dramatic evidence of apartheid's weakness as a long-term strategy for the maintenance of White supremacy. Its lack of success in eliminating Black domestic opposition made its utter failure to secure international legitimation for the South African regime very costly. Ironically the apartheid system which had been in part devised to make White supremacy in South Africa internationally palatable had become the very symbol of South Africa's opprobrium within the international community. It is within this context that the South African government has undertaken to reform the apartheid system. A pattern can be discerned in the reforms underway which, I believe, reveals the overall purpose of these efforts. The aim is to eliminate those aspects of apartheid which have drawn the most international attention and criticism, while at the same time tightening state control in those areas where apartheid has proved less than fully effective. In the 1950s apartheid was adopted in order to achieve internal security and international legitimacy for the regime of White supremacy, but as South Africa approaches the 1980s, apartheid—or at least substantial aspects of it—is viewed by the White governing elite as a *threat* to security and legitimation. They are therefore in search of an alternative strategy to secure White supremacy domestically and internationally.

The ability of the South African government to move forward with such a new strategy is not based solely on apartheid's demon-

*Several large foreign firms began moving in this direction on their own as a means of deflecting pressure by dissident stockholders for divestment from South Africa.

strated lack of instrumental effectiveness. The context which has given birth to the current reform effort and which permits its implementation is also informed by a decline in the consummatory significance of apartheid. The two faces of apartheid—instrumental and consummatory—were always in tension: a commitment to the doctrine of separateness as a necessary condition for the maintenance of Afrikaner identity inherently limited the flexibility that policymakers could exhibit in their efforts to preserve White supremacy. This tension gave rise to two political tendencies within Afrikanerdom: (1) *verligtheid*—an orientation toward apartheid's utilitarian aspects, and thus a willingness to abandon those aspects of racial separation which on practical grounds were perceived as counterproductive to the security of White rule; (2) *verkramptheid*—an orientation to apartheid as doctrine rather than strategy, and thus a dogmatic insistence on the necessity of racial separation in all spheres. As long as *verligt* political leaders continued to share with their *verkrampt* colleagues an obsession with Afrikaner identity, and as long as the unity of Afrikanerdom continued to be a primary political objective, they were trapped within the basic structure of the apartheid strategy. Such was the case during the 1960s and much of the 1970s. However, by the mid-1970s the environment which in an earlier era had made ethnic identity the Afrikaner's primary concern no longer existed. Some twenty-five years of unchallenged and increasing National party domination of every aspect of the state apparatus, and a concomitant, albeit less complete, penetration of the industrial economy by the Afrikaner community, had served to eliminate the sense of political, economic, and cultural insecurity that gave rise to the obsessions with unity and identity. Reflecting this change, the political coalition represented by the Botha cabinet has been able to detach the goal of White survival from the more parochial concern for Afrikaner identity, and to give the former clear priority.[33] Attitudinal data presented by Lawrence Schlemmer in an earlier chapter in this volume (pp. 236-80) reveal a similar shift away from identity concerns by the Afrikaner public generally. Among Schlemmer's representative sample of Afrikaners, cultural matters currently have a surprisingly low salience. His data also show that a sizable proportion of the Afrikaner public would grant the government considerable latitude to modify the apartheid system; however, this flexible attitude toward change does not extend to modifications that might adversely affect White material interests or physical security. Thus while there appears to be a considerable base of support for the government's efforts to "reform" apartheid, there is also considerable scope for the mobilization of popular opposition to change among those who fear an erosion of their economic and social position. Faced with this situation among its constituents, the National party government has been rather cautious in its movement away from conventional apartheid or separate development. It has accepted far more reform in principle than it has actually implemented in practice. But this does not render current moves insignificant. In contrast, past Afrikaner governments had always been steadfast in their claim to be adhering to the principle of apartheid even when pragmatically violating it.[34] Thus the acceptance "in principle" of reforms that move away from apartheid should probably be read as the creation of "roadsigns" for a new strategic thrust by a government that as yet lacks the political confidence to move full throttle in the newly charted direction. The reform effort sketched below is, then, an ongoing process whose direction seems clear, but whose extent is at this writing undetermined.

THE REFORM OF APARTHEID

The reforms that have come in the wake of Soweto affect various aspects of apartheid. For analytic purposes we can view these as representing change in six areas of the apartheid regime.

1. Personal Apartheid. During 1979 South African government spokesmen have frequently proclaimed a commitment to the removal of "unnecessary race discrimination." Although little has been done concretely in this regard, what they apparently plan is the gradual elimination of legally mandated racial segregation in the realm of personal and social interaction. The gradual relaxation of enforced segregation in public facilities can be expected, as can the lifting of legal prohibitions against "race mixing" in various social organizations. Even the "Immorality Act," which makes interracial sexual intercourse a criminal offense, may be dropped.* This area of reform aims at what is generally referred to as "petty apartheid"—i.e., those laws which perform for the White population a largely symbolic function, emphasizing race distinction as an end-in-itself, rather than directly serving the functions of economic and political domination.[35] Note that the government has not committed itself to ending racial discrimination, but rather to ending *unnecessary* racial discrim-

*Soon after this was written, Prime Minister Botha indicated his government's intention to scrap the Immorality Act.

ination. By implication then, the government is pledging itself to maintain "necessary" discrimination. Thus "acceptance of the principle of separate schools and amenities" was announced by the Prime Minister along with the "scrapping of unnecessary discriminatory measures" as two of twelve principles underlying his alternative to apartheid.[36] In other words, when segregation or discrimination is more than symbolic—when it enhances the political, economic, and social position of Whites, or when it affects their sense of group well-being—it is deemed necessary and will be retained.

The pledge to scrap unnecessary race discrimination, and any action that follows from it, performs functions for the South African government with respect to three separate audiences at the same time. For the Black population group it eliminates points of friction which serve no purpose other than generating animosity toward the regime of racial rule; for the Whites it provides assurance that the changes introduced will not significantly affect their "way of life"; and most important, for the world community it serves to reduce the stigma of official racism which marks the South African system. Since much of the international criticism of South Africa is focused on its official segregationist practices and on racialist laws like the Immorality and Prohibition of Mixed Marriages Acts, their elimination would not be an insignificant step in creating a more "enlightened" image for the country.

2. African Trade Union Organization. In September 1979 the South African government announced with great fanfare the granting of formal trade union rights to African workers. This was the culmination of a process begun with the appointment in 1977 of a government commission of inquiry into existing labor legislation (the Wiehahn Commission). Since the denial of trade union rights to Africans has generally been considered one of the core aspects of apartheid,[37] the Wiehahn Commission report, which recommended lifting the prohibition against registration of Black unions, and the government action which implemented the report's recommendation have been hailed by many liberal critics, both domestic and foreign, as major positive steps toward a more equitable arrangement within South Africa.* However, if one looks carefully

*The first government draft legislation was sharply criticized as being far less liberal than the Wiehahn Commission recommendations because it excluded from union rights migrant and "commuter" workers, who constitute a majority of the African work force. In order to recoup some of the public relations advantage generated by the Wiehahn Commission report, the government reversed itself, and in the end made all South African workers legally eligible for membership in registered trade unions.

at the Wiehahn report and places the labor reform effort in its historical context, a very different perspective on the government's intentions emerges.

As noted earlier, the failure of the apartheid system to effectively terminate large-scale agitation by African workers posed a problem for the South African government. Not only were African laborers able to mount a challenge to the low-wage system —a challenge that might be extended into the realm of political change—but their strike action drew international attention to the denial of trade union rights in the Republic. The introduction to the Wiehahn report reveals that the commission clearly understood its genesis as based in the existence of this problem and its task as providing a solution to it. The report comments that in recent years unregistered trade unions have grown and "can only continue to grow in strength and importance," and that these unions are enjoying financial and moral support "on a broad front."[38] The report continues:

> The fact that their existence is not prohibited, while at the same time they are not registerable . . . serves as an incentive to foreign labour and political organisations to aid them overtly and covertly. Added to this is the fact that other non-labour organisations regard these unions as vehicles for change, using them also in matters other than those of a purely labour character (Para 1.10).

Thus the related problems of domestic control and international legitimation were identified by the Wiehahn Commission as the reason for seeking modifications in the existing apartheid system. It rejected efforts to suppress the existing unregistered unions as infeasible and counterproductive, and instead called for bringing Black unions under the "*protective and stabilising elements of the system [and] its essential discipline and control*" (Para. 3.35.5; emphasis added).

The Wiehahn Commission had recognized the "two-edged" character of legalizing the registration of Black trade unions. While on the one hand registration would enhance union organizational capabilities, on the other hand it would provide the government with significant means of control. As the commission report observes:

> Registered trade unions are under certain statutory restrictions and obligations designed to protect and nurture a system that has proved its success in practice. . . .

> The Industrial Conciliation Act, 1956, provides for matters such as the annual auditing of the trade unions' financial affairs; the maintenance of membership registers; the submission of annual reports, statements of income and expenditure and balance sheets to a meeting of members and to the Department of Labour; the strict control of constitutions and memberships; and a prohibition on affiliation with any political party or to a candidate for election to Parliament, a provincial council or any local authority (Paras. 3.35.4 and 3.35.5).

Moreover, on the Wiehahn Commission's recommendation the government created a new control mechanism—the National Manpower Commission (NMC). This body will consult with the Industrial Registrar on the registration and de-registration of unions, taking into account "a wide spectrum of considerations [including] . . . *the implications for the country as a whole in social, economic and political aspects*" (Para. 3.71; emphasis added). Through this and other functions to be performed by the NMC, a mechanism has been created to facilitate the Department of Labour's rapid intervention in union activities regarded as undesirable by the government. Thus at the same time that union rights are being extended, a watchdog on labor has been created.

In sum, then, the overall purpose for the extension of union rights in the current South African context would appear to be the establishment of control over existing unregistered unions in a manner that will bring South Africa's system of worker rights more into line with international standards.[39]

3. *Influx Control and Pass Laws.* As previously noted, one of apartheid's primary goals has been the reduction of the Black population within the South African core area. The mechanism designed to achieve this end was influx control, a system based upon two key elements: (1) a requirement that all Africans carry a reference or "pass book" giving detailed particulars regarding their residence and employment and (2) a law prohibiting unauthorized Africans from remaining in White South Africa for longer than seventy-two hours. In practice, influx control has proved not only ineffective, but also exceedingly costly both in financial and political terms. The Black population in South Africa's cities continues to expand, and the number of arrests and prosecutions for pass law violations (5.8 million between 1965 and 1975) provides strong indication that influx control has not discouraged Africans from leaving the impoverished homelands in which they are required by law to live and illegally entering White South Africa. Meanwhile, the financial costs

of administering the system have been tremendous. Michael Savage found the administration of influx control to have an annual price tag in excess of $130 million.[40] Beyond the monetary costs, the pass laws have been a constant irritant for the Black population, generating intense opposition to the existing system. Because for all Africans it is a constant reminder of their inferior status, and because it brings the arm of the state directly to bear on so many of them, the pass has become a symbol of their oppression. And because it has historically been the focus of numerous mass protests, and is such a concrete, easily understood symbol of indignity, the pass has become identified internationally as a prime example of the odious nature of the South African system.

Given the lack of effectiveness and high cost, both domestically and internationally, of influx control and the pass laws, the analysis presented here would predict that they would be prime targets of the Botha government's "reform" effort. And indeed there are very clear signs that change in this area is on the government's agenda. First, there was a statement made by the current reform effort's bellwether, minister Piet Koornhof, that he "strongly disapproved" of the pass book system and was determined to eradicate it, and that he was in the process of reviewing the whole system of influx control.[41] Second, there was the report of the Riekert Commission, another government appointed board of inquiry, which recommended abolishing the 72-hour rule and scrapping the pass books. As might be expected, the commission was not proposing to give up on attempts to control the number of Africans within the South African heartland; rather, as one government publication noted, the question for the commission "was not whether there should be influx control, but what would be the right mechanism for influx control."[42] The mechanism hit upon by the Riekert Commission was to shift the focus of government enforcement efforts from the African population to the White employers of African labor. The commission recommended that penalties on employers who hired "illegal" Africans—those lacking Section 10 rights or special permission to be in a White area—be drastically raised so as to deter such practice. If such penalties were imposed, homeland Africans could have little hope of obtaining employment through unauthorized migration, and without such an incentive presumably they would remain in their designated homelands. Whether or not this would be the outcome of the Riekert Commission alternative to the pass book system is less important for this analysis than is the type of strategic thinking that such a recommendation represents. "The accent," one Afrikaans newspaper commented enthusiastically, "has in important respects been shifted from central control to control by the people who have to live with their decisions."[43] In other words, the underlying principle of the Riekert Commission recommendation is the devolution of the control functions to agencies outside the central government structure (i.e., employers), thereby reducing both the budgetary and political costs to the government of its influx control program.*

4. *"Urban" Africans.* A central tenet of apartheid is that Africans in what is officially designated as White South Africa are only "temporary sojourners" (from the homelands) in search of work, and therefore have no permanent place in South Africa. A large proportion of apartheid legislation is designed to deny to these "temporary sojourners" economic rights, residential security, and political participation. Like other elements of apartheid this aspect has proved in practice to be both ineffective and costly, and has consequently become the target of reform under the Botha government. By the mid-1970s a significant portion of the National party leadership had come to recognize that the South African manufacturing economy required a very sizable, permanent African labor force, and thus the burgeoning Black population of cities like Johannesburg could no longer be regarded as a temporary aberration. Moreover, the official posture toward the African residential areas on the outskirts of South Africa's cities—i.e., acting as if they were refugee camps whose inhabitants must eventually be returned to where they really belonged—was proving costly on both the domestic and international fronts. Domestically, the lack of amenities available to the urban African population, the efforts to expel large numbers of urban residents into the poverty-ridden homelands, and the general climate of insecurity created and manipulated by the government produced intense alienation. And the nature of urban life meant that this alienation could relatively easily be trans-

*At the moment the government has adopted the Riekert Commission recommendation that penalties against the employers of "illegal" Africans be raised, but has accepted only the *principle* that the 72-hour stipulation be repealed, while maintaining it in practice. The immediate consequence of adopting the Riekert Commission recommendation was summed up by the Johannesburg weekly, the *Sunday Express*, in these terms: "The huge penalties about to be introduced for employing illegal labour can only have the effect of pushing thousands, perhaps tens of thousands, out of the work they need to survive. They are going to have to go away to places they may never have seen where . . . there is no work they can do" (see *South African Digest* [Pretoria], June 22, 1979).

lated into political opposition. Moreover, because of the proximity of the urban areas to the international communication system, the existence of this alienation and opposition could be instantaneously and graphically transmitted to the outside world. (This was a prime lesson of Soweto.) Beyond this, a policy which forced vast numbers of South Africa's African population to leave their homes and take up residence in a "country" with which they had no psychological or social connection, and in which the means of earning a livelihood were severely limited, provided an easy target for South Africa's international critics.

In this context the South African government has moved away from the orthodox apartheid position toward the acceptance of a permanent African population outside of the homelands. Although not explicit about his intentions, Prime Minister Botha has subtly indicated this new direction. For example, he recently told the Natal Congress of the National party that South Africa had no alternative but to accept the principle of "a multinational society and the existence of minority groups."[44] But more important than words have been a series of steps taken during 1979 directed at the so-called "urban Black" population. These steps include:

(1) A decision not to demolish Crossroads, a squatter shantytown of twenty thousand outside of Cape Town which exists in violation of the Group Areas Act, and the abandonment of plans to move Black families out of Alexandria, a suburb of Johannesburg.
(2) Announcement of a 99-year leasehold scheme for Black townships. (Previously security of home occupancy for Africans could only be obtained in one of the homelands.)
(3) Promises to commit substantial new resources to the improvement of amenities, such as housing and electrification, in the Black urban townships.
(4) Announcement that the wives and children of those with legal rights to be in a city will be allowed to live with their spouse or parent in the urban area. (Previously they were required to remain in the homelands.)
(5) Announcement that some restrictions on business and commercial activity by Black entrepreneurs will be lifted, easing the limits on the size of Black-owned shops and the restrictions on areas in which Blacks can operate businesses. The possibility that Black entrepreneurs will be permitted to operate in "White" areas has been hinted.

(6) Appointment of multiracial regional commissions to advise the government on the problems of Black people in urban areas. (This represents perhaps the first time since the initiation of separate development that the government has acknowledged a role for Africans in the formation of policy regarding White South Africa.)

(7) A visit by Prime Minister Botha to Soweto. (This event, carried out with the fanfare of a state visit, marked the first occasion when a South African head of government officially set foot in a Black township. The extraordinary attention paid to it by the government and media in South Africa suggests that it was invested with great symbolic significance.)

Although they are largely still-to-be-implemented promises, in the South African context these steps—all taken within a short period of time—reflect a government decision to move away from orthodox apartheid strategy. At the same time, it is essential to note that simultaneously with the announcement of these changes in policy toward urban Africans, the government was publicly recommitting itself to strict limitations on the number of Africans allowed in urban areas and to firm enforcement of influx control measures. It is this combination of improvements in the situation of the urban-based Africans with the effort to maintain the basic homelands policy that reveals the overall implications of the recent reforms within a strategy of White supremacy. For these reforms, if fully carried through, will serve to make Africans with Section 10 rights in the cities a privileged stratum—separated from the rest of the African population by access to economic opportunities, homeownership, freedom of movement, availability of education, and general standard of living. Hypothetically at least, these advantages can be viewed as giving the legally recognized urban African a stake in the stability of South Africa's capitalist system. The emergent Black urban-based middle class could then be expected to stand against revolutionary activities since these would be a threat to their newly constructed homes and expanded professional and entrepreneurial activities. They could also be expected to be a strong prop for influx control, since the overcrowding and social instability that come with illegal rural migration would be a threat to their middle-class family-oriented life style, their secure jobs, and the property interests they manage to acquire. Correlatively the reforms, limited as they are to those with Section 10 rights, will serve to create a clash of political, economic, and social interests between the city-based Africans and their rural compatriots. An urban-rural cleavage will be added to the ethnic divisions institutionalized within the homeland structure. Thus from the vantage point of domestic control, the reforms directed at urban Africans can be seen as simultaneously performing two functions—division and cooptation. From an international vantage point, a general improvement in the standard of living among this group—the most visible portion of South Africa's Black majority—would serve to improve South Africa's image abroad.

5. *"A New Political Dispensation."* Of all the areas of reform discussed here, the government's intentions in regard to South Africa's political structure are the most murky. While a commitment to "a new political dispensation" which will include "full political participation for all within a plural setup" has been proclaimed, the specifics of this new "plural" structure have not been set forth, and may not yet be worked out. However, on the basis of various statements by the Prime Minister and inferences drawn from recent government actions, it is possible to speculate on the broad outlines of the strategy that is now evolving.

The first indication that alterations in political structure were on the agenda came with the announcement in 1977 by then Prime Minister Vorster of proposals for a new constitution. As discussed in an earlier chapter by Hermann Giliomee (pp. 14-44), these proposals envisage the creation of three separate parliaments—one each for the Indian, Colored, and White population groups—which would have legislative responsibility for affairs within their own communities. In addition it was proposed that an office of State President be created which would be served by a cabinet in which all three groups would be represented, but in which the White group would be guaranteed a dominant position. This reform was met with less than enthusiasm by the leaders of the Indian and Colored communities, as well as by international opinion (at whom it was also directed). The fact that the proposed constitution would not fundamentally alter the White group's ability to control affairs in "their own area"—i.e., in the South African economic and geographic heartland—was an important element in its negative reception. Equally if not more important, however, was the fact that the constitutional reform continued to exclude all Africans from political participation, and therefore represented a continuation of apartheid policies. In particular, the domestic and foreign media focused on the failure of the proposals to politically recognize the existence of the large, permanent African population in and around South

Africa's cities. This probably explains the evolution of government policy, under Prime Minister Botha's leadership, to a position where urban Africans—i.e., those with Section 10 rights—will in some manner be incorporated as a political unit within a new governmental structure. Thus during the summer of 1979 National party leaders began speaking of granting distinct political status to urban Black areas, with self-governing authority over matters such as social welfare, housing, education, and the maintenance of law and order (the term "city-state" has been used in influential circles).[45] The Prime Minister has stated that he foresees for the urban Blacks "a place in the constellation of Southern African states" that will become "a bulwark against Marxist penetration."[46]

In creating a new political dispensation for urban-based Africans, the government will probably move in one of two directions: either it will group a number of the larger urban African townships into yet another self-governing homeland (along the way officially creating a new ethnic identity—"urban Black"), or it will incorporate Africans with Section 10 rights into the parallel structure of the new constitutional proposal, along with Indians and Coloreds.* At the same time, the government is likely to continue to pressure homeland leaders to cooperate in a transition to independence, following the example set by the Transkei, Bophuthatswana, and Venda. However, the present government will probably differ from its predecessor in two respects. First, it is likely to be far more receptive to further consolidations of the fragmented homeland territories, which will necessitate ceding additional lands to the Black states and the consequent abandonment of the previously "sacred" 1936 Land Act. Second, it is likely to be more willing to live permanently with self-governing homeland status for Bantustans such as QwaZulu which refuse independence. What is evolving, then, is a governmental structure that will probably contain four types of political units: (1) White South Africa, containing Indian, Colored, and perhaps "urban Black" minority communities, with each group internally governed under parallel structures (what is referred to as a "plural" setup); (2) rural internally self-governing homelands, made up of those Bantustans whose political leadership has refused independence; (3) an internally self-governing urban African city-state (unless this group is given minority status in White South Africa); and (4) enlarged and consolidated "independent"

*The latter would be a greater break with separate development policy than the former, since it would acknowledge that at least some Africans have political rights outside of the homeland structure.

homelands tied to White South Africa in some type of confederal arrangement.

The governmental structure that is emerging reflects a strategic choice by the current Afrikaner leadership. It is opting for an "indirect rule" approach rather than separation as the method of maintaining White supremacy. (This new strategy is analyzed by Andre du Toit in an earlier chapter of this volume—pp. 1-13.) It entails the devolution of various financially and politically costly tasks—tax collection, social welfare, the enforcement of influx control, and the maintenance of law and order—to political units which are tied to and ultimately controlled by the White South African state through economic dependence, financial subsidies, and overwhelming inferiority in the instruments of coercion. There are similarities here to orthodox separate development strategy, except that indirect rule does not require the political removal of the majority of the population (i.e., all Africans) from the Republic of South Africa. It accepts that a certain portion of the African population will remain within South Africa, and provides it with political representation and responsibility, albeit of a limited type. It is a strategy designed to achieve the cooptation of Black leadership domestically, and the placating (or at the very least, confusing) of opinion internationally.

6. Media Controls. Simultaneously with the reforms outlined above, the Botha government has moved to establish significant controls over South Africa's news media. The purpose of controls is to reduce South Africa's international vulnerability, and they thus should be seen as part of the Botha government's new strategic thrust. To many outside observers a major irony of the apartheid regime was the existence within South Africa of a free and critical press. The explanations most often given for its continued existence in the face of the many "police state" aspects of the South African system were that the National party was so securely in power that a critical press did not threaten it, and that to be able to point to the existence of a free press was useful for international propaganda purposes. After 1976, however, South Africa's press became a significant element in the government's international legitimation problem. Through its reporting of the police suppression of the Soweto uprising and its investigation into the police torture and murder of Black Consciousness movement leader Steve Biko, the South African press fed information to the international community which led directly to diplomatic and economic difficulties for the country. In addition, a newspaper investigation into the Department of Information begun in 1976 uncovered a secret slush fund used in covert domestic and international operations. The revelations of these covert activities and of the illegal actions taken by government officials in connection with them not only undermined the government domestically, but also embarrassed and constrained it internationally.

During 1979 the Botha government succeeded in enacting two pieces of legislation directed at preventing repetitions of these events. One law creates a kind of special prosecutor in matters of official misconduct who has the power to stop newspapers from publishing reports about official misbehavior simply by declaring that he is investigating the matter. Moreover, he can permanently suppress such reports when he deems that their publication could threaten state security. The second law, called the Police Amendment Act, requires that newspapers clear any story containing allegations of police misconduct with the police themselves.* The international impact of Soweto and of the death of Steve Biko may well have been of very different magnitude had such a "handy" piece of legislation been on the books in 1976.

CONCLUSION

Apartheid emerged in the years after World War II as the national ideology and political program of South Africa's Afrikaner community. It was in essence a response to the political and cultural insecurity of that community. Contained within the general Afrikaner political concern for the survival of White rule in the face of opposition from a domestic Black majority and an unsympathetic international community was a parochial concern—indeed obsession—with the maintenance of their ethnic identity. Apartheid as practice served the first of these concerns—the survival of White supremacy—and apartheid as doctrine served the second—the maintenance of Afrikaner identity. Despite apartheid's rigorous implementation, some thirty years after its initiation White supremacy continued to face threats from the domestic majority and the international community. Its survival thus continued to be of grave concern to the Afrikaner leadership. Ethnic identity, however, was a less salient matter. Apparently the three decades in which

*A similar law affecting reporting about South Africa's prison system has been in effect for a number of years, and has effectively silenced reports on conditions within the prisons.

Afrikanerdom had maintained its total domination of the state apparatus had provided the sense of group security that had been lacking in the 1940s. Consequently by the mid-1970s the Afrikaner governing elite felt free to pursue "survival" unencumbered by the doctrinal constraints imposed by the earlier obsession with ethnic identity. Once freed from the dogmatic commitment to the principle of separation, which apartheid as ethnic ideology necessitated, the Afrikaner elite could recognize that major aspects of apartheid were counterproductive to its survival concerns. It then proceeded to jettison some, and modify other, aspects of the previously sacred apartheid program in the hope of improving domestic control of the Black majority and overcoming international hostility. Thus Prime Minister Botha has repeatedly defended his reform efforts to the National party membership as the only alternative to revolution by the Black majority, while senior officials have described with great fanfare the "liberalizing" face of the new South Africa as they traveled abroad seeking new foreign investment.*

The question remains "Will the new strategy adopted by the Botha government work?" The answer, of course, can only be speculated upon. My guess is that it will not. The various efforts to eliminate official race discrimination, to grant trade union rights to African workers, to provide some political status for Blacks who live permanently in the cities, and to devolve "unpleasant" governmental functions to a set of plural self-governing political units may well have a salutary effect on South Africa's international posture. But this is likely to be true only so long as Black opposition does not make itself highly visible. This latter condition, however, is hardly likely to hold. The level of political mobilization among the Black population of South Africa's urban areas is such as to likely preclude the success of the current strategy over the medium term. Cooptation requires relatively low levels of expectation among

*Following the publication of the Wiehahn and Riekert Commission reports, Minister of Plural Relations Piet Koornof and Minister of Finance Owen Horwood traveled to the United States and Europe respectively to announce the end of apartheid to audiences of prospective investors. The official South African Broadcasting Company, analyzing the foreign investment picture, noted that race discrimination under existing international circumstances put South Africa at a disadvantage, but that "the Wiehahn and Riekert commissions have done much to remove this single impediment to foreign participation in the country's economy." This is the backdrop, it noted, "to the extremely *favourable* loan which South Africa has just made in Britain" (*South African Digest*, July 6, 1979, pp. 23-24 [emphasis in original]; for report of Horwood in Europe, see *ibid.*, p. 3).

the target group; otherwise its price involves cutting into the real interests of the dominant community. Considerable evidence exists that the demands for equality—social, economic, and political—have become so extensive, at least among South Africa's Black city-dwellers, as to make the current reform effort a complex example of the simple adage "too late with too little."

Hermann Giliomee: The National Party and the Afrikaner Broederbond

1. René de Villiers, "Afrikaner Nationalism," in *Oxford History of South Africa*, eds. Monica Wilson and Leonard M. Thompson (Oxford: Clarendon Press, 1971), p. 370.

2. Three outstanding recent contributions to the study of Afrikaner nationalism are the complementary essays by André du Toit and F. van Zyl Slabbert in *Change in Contemporary South Africa*, eds. Leonard Thompson and Jeffrey Butler (Berkeley: University of California Press, 1975), pp. 3-50, and a class analysis by Dan O'Meara, "White Trade Unionism, Political Power and Afrikaner Nationalism," *South African Labour Bulletin* 1, 10 (1975): 31-51. I elaborate on Afrikaner politics and culture in a book co-authored with Heribert Adam: *Ethnic Power Mobilized* (forthcoming). I wish to thank André du Toit for incisive criticism of a first draft of this paper.

3. This paragraph is based on two excellent studies by Dan O'Meara: "Analysing Afrikaner Nationalism" and "The Afrikaner Broederbond 1927-1948: Class Vanguard of Afrikaner Nationalism," *Journal of Southern African Studies* 3, 2 (1977): 156-86. It will be seen that my analysis differs from O'Meara in that I attach separate weight to the factors of ethnicity and class.

4. For an analysis of statements such as these, see D.J. Kriek, "General J.B.M. Hertzog se Opvattings oor die Afrikaans—en Engelssprekendes na Uniewording" (doctoral dissertation, University of Pretoria, 1971).

5. See Malan's series of articles entitled "Op die Wagtoring," published in *Die Burger*—esp. the articles published on 16 and 23 December 1933.

6. The term is used by Crawford Young, *The Politics of Cultural Pluralism* (Madison: University of Wisconsin Press, 1976), p. 45.

7. O'Meara, "Analysing Afrikaner Nationalism."

8. T. Dunbar Moodie, *The Rise of Afrikanerdom* (Berkeley: University of California Press, 1975), p. 21.

9. See the argument of Newell M. Stultz, *The Nationalists in Opposition, 1934-1948* (Cape Town: Human and Rousseau, 1974).

10. See Malan's unpublished ms., "Op die Wagtoring" [c. 1946] (D.F. Malan collection, Carnegie Library, University of Stellenbosch).

11. Stultz, pp. 136-43.

12. F. van Zyl Slabbert, "Afrikaner Nationalism, White Politics, and Political Change in South Africa," in Thompson and Butler, eds., pp. 3-19. This short piece is, to my mind, the best analysis of the sociology of Afrikaner nationalism.

13. For a further analysis see A. James Gregor, *Contemporary Radical Ideologies* (New York, 1968), pp. 221-76. Gregor gives a succinct account, based on primary sources, of the ideology of apartheid. My analysis differs from his in that I do not consider separate development as the dominant ideology.

14. André du Toit, "Ideological Change, Afrikaner Nationalism and Pragmatic Racial Domination in South Africa," in Thompson and Butler, eds., p. 39.

15. Willem A. Kleynhans, *Political Parties in South Africa* (Pretoria: University of South Africa, 1973), p. 104; Kenneth A. Heard, *General Elections in South Africa* (London: Oxford University Press, 1974), p. 73.

16. Kleynhans; Jan J. van Rooyen, *Die Nasionale Party: Sy Opkoms en Oorwinning—Kaapland se aandeel* (Cape Town: Nasionale Handelsdrukkery, 1956), pp. 177-85. For an analysis of the decision-making process in the National party by a political scientist, see R.A. Schrire, "The Formulation of Public Policy" (unpublished paper, 1978). Schrire first used the term "chairman of the board" to describe Vorster's prime ministerial style.

17. See B.M. Schoeman, *Van Malan tot Verwoerd* (Cape Town: Human and Rousseau, 1973), pp. 65, 173-75. Based on the diary of Albert Hertzog, this book and its sequel, *Vorster se 1000 dae* (Cape Town: Human and Rousseau, 1974), are valuable sources of information on struggles behind the scenes in the party. Despite his obvious conservative and racial bias, Schoeman seems intent on telling the story as he received it from his sources. The main problem is to establish whether his sources told the truth. In this case the evidence is corroborated by the personal notes of Mr. Japie Basson, a caucus member who on this occasion clashed with Verwoerd and was eventually expelled. I wish to thank Mr. Basson for permission to consult his notes.

18. Personal interview with a close confidant of Verwoerd and Vorster.

19. *Ibid.*

20. Schoeman, *Van Malan tot Verwoerd*, pp. 214-15, 253-54.

21. Schoeman, *Vorster se 1000 dae*, p. 14.

22. Jan J. van Rooyen, *P.W. Botha: 40 Jaar* (Cape Town: Cape Province National Party, 1976), p. 32.

23. *House of Assembly Debates*, 12 April 1978, col. 4552.

24. B.M. Schoeman, *Parlementêre Verkiesing in Suid-Afrika, 1910-1976* (Pretoria: Aktuele Publikasies, 1977), pp. 312-13, 438-39; *S.A. Foundation News*, December 1977.

25. W.H.B. Dean, *Whither the Constitution?* (Cape Town: University of Cape Town, 1975), and subsequent comments by Dean cited in John de St. Jorre, *A House Divided: South Africa's Uncertain Future* (New York: Carnegie, 1977), p. 19.

26. *House of Assembly Debates*, 12 April 1978, col. 4552.

27. Marinus Wiechers, "Current Constitutional Proposals" (unpublished paper, February 1978).

28. William J. Foltz, "The Foreign Factor in New Constitutional Provisions for South Africa" (unpublished paper, July 1978).

29. G.E. Devenish, "The New Constitutional Proposals: The Politics of Reconciliation or Dictatorial Rule" (unpublished paper, February 1978).

30. Lawrence Schlemmer, "White Voters and Change in South Africa: Constraints and Opportunities," *Optima* 27, 4 (1978); Theodor Hanf, Heribert Weiland, and Gerda Vierdag, *Südafrika: Friedlicher Wandel?* (München: Kaiser, 1978).

31. *Rapport*, 6 February 1977.

32. Hanf et al., pp. 421-22.

33. Interview of Gerrit Viljoen with Helen Zille, *Rand Daily Mail*, 1 August 1978.

34. See O'Meara, "The Afrikaner Broederbond, 1927-1948."

35. Schoeman, *Van Malan tot Verwoerd*, p. 120.

36. The preceding two paragraphs are based on disclosures published in the *Sunday Times* of 24 September, 5, 8, and 15 October 1972; 28 January and 4 February 1973; and 20 January 1978. See also the comprehensive study by Ivor Wilkins and Hans Strydom, *The Super-Afrikaners: Inside the Afrikaner Broederbond* (Johannesburg: Jonathan Ball, 1978).

37. Schalk Pienaar, "Broederbond: Vrae en Bedenkinge," *Rapport*, 24 September 1972.

38. Dirk Richard, "Na my mening," *Dagbreek en Sondagnuus*, 13 September 1970.

39. *Sunday Times*, 24 September 1972.

40. *Ibid.*, 20 January 1978.

Heribert Adam: The Failure of Political Liberalism in South Africa

1. I am grateful to a truly liberal scholar, Leonard Thompson, who has sensitized me to the difficulties of pursuing a humanistic ideal under South African conditions.

2. For a good overview of this period, see Phyllis Lewson, "The Cape Liberal Tradition--Myth or Reality," in London Institute of Commonwealth Studies, *Collected Seminar Papers* 1, 10 (1970):72-88.

3. An analysis with a focus on the unique class relationships in the Cape Colony in conjunction with the need to restore stability and the British authority through enfranchisement is provided by Stanley Trapido, "Liberalism in the Cape in the 19th and 20th Centuries," in London Institute of Commonwealth Studies, *Collected Seminar Papers* 4, 17 (1974):53-66.

4. C.W. de Kiewiet, "Loneliness in the Beloved Country," *Foreign Affairs* (April 1964):413-27.

5. Alan Paton, *Reality*, September 1977. In a subsequent controversy a fellow liberal, John Aitchison, challenged Paton publicly to "admit that you no longer stand for what the Liberal party stood for." Paton replied: "I no longer stand for majority rule in a unitary state in our present circumstances, but for majority rule in a federal state" (*Reality*, September 1978, pp.6-7).

6. David Welsh, *The Roots of Segregation: Native Policy in Colonial Natal, 1845-1919* (Cape Town: Oxford University Press, 1971), p. 322.

7. Theodor Hanf et al., *Südafrika: Friedlicher Wandel?* (München: Kaiser, 1978), p. 95. This survey is cited as the "Freiburg study."

8. Pierre L. van den Berghe, "The Impossibility of a Liberal Solution in South Africa," in *The Liberal Dilemma in South Africa*, ed. P.L. van den Berghe (London: Croom Helm, 1979), p. 59. See also his "Race and Ethnicity: A Sociobiological Look " (unpublished manuscript, 1978); italics added.

9. Hamish Dickie-Clark, "On the Liberal Definition of the South African Situation," in *The Liberal Dilemma in South Africa*, ed. P.L. van den Berghe, p. 51.

10. See on this point esp. two instructive essays: Martin Legassick, "The Rise of Modern South African Liberalism: Its Assumptions and Its Social Base" (unpublished paper), and Paul Rich, "Liberalism and Ethnicity in South African Politics, 1921-1948," *African Studies* 35, 3-4 (1976): 229-51.

11. Leo Kuper, *The Pity of It All: Polarization of Racial and Ethnic Relations* (London: Duckworth, 1977), p. 9; emphasis added.

12. N.P. van Wyk Louw, *Liberale Nasionalisme* (Cape Town: Nasionale Boekhandel, 1958).

13. Alan Paton, *Hope for South Africa* (London: Pall Mall, 1958), p. 5.

14. Paton, *Reality*, September 1977.

15. Jordan K. Ngubane, "The Road to and from Soweto," *Journal of Southern African Affairs* 2, 2 (April 1977): 167-82.

16. Joel Mervis, *Star Weekly*, October 22, 1977.

17. Donald Woods, *New York Times*, January 8, 1978.

18. A revealing analysis by an activist of the failure of the ANC and PAC campaign of armed resistance, with emphasis on the elitist nature of sabotage and the lack of preparedness for superior police techniques, is Ben Turok, "South Africa: The Search for a Strategy," *Socialist Register 1973* (London: Merlin, 1974).

19. Paton, *Knocking on the Door*, p. 212.

20. Janet Robertson, *Liberalism in South Africa 1948-63* (London: Oxford University Press, 1971), pp. 161-83.

21. Ezekiel Mphahlele, "South Africa: Two Communities and the Struggle for a Birthright," *Journal of African Studies* 4, 4 (Spring 1977): 49.

22. Paton, *Hope for South Africa*, p. 62.

23. Van den Berghe, ed., *The Liberal Dilemma*, p. 63.

24. Leo Kuper, *Race, Class and Power* (Chicago: Aldine, 1975), p. 274.

25. R.F. Alfred Hoernle, *South African Native Policy and the Liberal Spirit* (Cape Town: University of Cape Town, 1939), pp. 135-36.

26. The most explicit recent elaboration of this position is found in Alex Callinicos and John Rogers, *Southern Africa after Soweto* (London: Pluto Press, 1977), pp. 212ff.

27. Ann Seidman, *Contemporary Crisis* 1, 3 (July 1977): 336.

28. *The Nation*, November 12, 1977, pp. 489-92.

29. Paton, *Knocking on the Door*, p. 258.

30. Kuper, *Pity of It All*, p. 9.

31. A recent biography of Helen Suzman (Joanna Strangwayes-Booth, *The Cricket in the Thorn Tree: Helen Suzman and the Progressive Party of South Africa* [Bloomington: Indiana University Press, 1978]) describes her as "one of the bravest political figures in South Africa." As long as the Security Police can control the lunatic fringe, it probably requires much less bravery for a national figure, such as Suzman, to express well-tempered disdain to benches of Nationalists than for an ordinary African worker to join a walkout or an African student at a tribal university to question his Afrikaner instructor; but in the absence of other legitimate channels, Suzman has often served as the lone ombudsman for African grievances.

32. Arend Lijphart, *Democracy in Plural Societies: A Comparative Exploration* (New Haven and London: Yale University Press, 1977).

33. Arend Lijphart, "Majority Rule versus Democracy in Deeply Divided Societies," *Politikon* 4, 2 (December 1977): 123.

34. Nic Rhoodie, "Instead of Crude Apartheid," *Daily Telegraph*, September 1977.

35. *Ibid.*

36. *Ibid.*

37. Lijphart, *Democracy*, p. 53. On this crucial point, see also Eric Nordlinger, *Conflict Regulation in Divided Societies* (Cambridge, Mass.: Harvard University Press, 1972), ch. V.

38. Lijphart, *Democracy*, p. 169.

Roland Stanbridge: Contemporary African Political Organizations and Movements

1. *Sechaba*, 60th anniversary issue.

2. *Ibid.*

3. *Ibid.*, September-November 1968.

4. P.W. Walshe, *Black Nationalism in South Africa* (Johannesburg: SPRO-CAS Publications, Ravan Press, 1973).

5. "ANC Youth League Constitution" (SA Institute of Race Relations, c. 1944: mimeo).

6. R. Gibson, *African Liberation Movements* (London: Oxford University Press, 1972), and T. Karis and G. Carter, *From Protest to Challenge* (Stanford: Hoover Institution Press, 1973).

7. Walshe, p. 29.

8. World Council of Churches, *A Profile of the African National Congress*, January 1971.

9. 1949 Programme of Action; quoted in Helen Joseph, *If This Be Treason* (Andre Deutsch, 1963).

10. Y.M. Dadoo, "The Role of the Indian People in the South African Revolution," *Sechaba*, March/April 1969 (Special Issue), p. 15.

11. South African Institute of Race Relations (SAIRR), *Annual Report*, 1951-52, p. 11.

12. *Sechaba*, June 1969.

13. *Ibid.*

14. *Ibid.*

15. SAIRR, *Annual Survey*, 1958-59.

16. *Azania News*, July-September 1977.

17. *Ibid.*, July 1969.

18. SAIRR, *Annual Survey*, 1960-61, and B. Turok, *Strategic Problems of South Africa's Liberation Struggle* (Richmond, Can.: LSM Information Centre, 1974).

19. Alfred Nzo, "Ten Years of Armed Struggle, 1961-1971," January 1972.

20. D. Woods, *Biko* (London: Paddington Press, 1978).

21. *Azania News*, April 1973 ("Thirteen Years of Resistance").

22. B. Turok, *Strategic Problems.*

23. *Ibid.*, p. 45.

24. SAIRR, *Annual Report*, 1961.

25. Nzo.

26. B. Turok, *Strategic Problems*, note 76.

27. Quoted in *Africa Contemporary Record*, 1975-76.

28. SAIRR, *Annual Report*, 1963.

29. *Azania News*, July 1968.
30. SAIRR, *Annual Report*, 1968.
31. SAIRR, *Annual Report*, 1971.
32. *Azania News*, September 1972.
33. *Sechaba*, March 1967.
34. *Azania News*, January 1973.
35. *Africa Confidential*, 1978; various issues.
36. *Reality* (Johannesburg), March 1972.
37. *SASO Newsletter*, July/August 1975, p. 21.
38. Woods, *Biko*, p. 30.
39. *SASO Newsletter*, 1969.
40. *Africa Contemporary Record*, 1972-73, p. B370.
41. *Ibid.* See also SAIRR, *Annual Report*, 1972.
42. Participation in the debate in *Reality* was between March 1972 and September 1973.
43. Undated 1978 leaflet issued by Count Pietersen, chief representative of the PAC in the Nordic countries.
44. Quoted in *Azania News*, June 1973.
45. *Reality*, May 1975.
46. *Sechaba*, 2nd quarter, 1978.
47. *Z* (journal of the radical students' society at the University of Cape Town), Vol. 2, No. 5.
48. Information about student leaders gleaned from a series of articles in *The World* (Johannesburg) before the SA government closed it down in October 1977.
49. *Africa Contemporary Record*, 1976-77.
50. *The World*, July 17, 1977.
51. *Africa Contemporary Record*, 1977-78.
52. *Sechaba*, 1st quarter, 1977.
53. SAIRR *Annual Report*, 1977; introductory essay on major events.
54. Press handout: "Statement of the ANC of South Africa on the Rustenburg Battle," August 11, 1978.
55. *Africa Confidential*, April 1978.
56. Quoted in *ibid.*, June 9, 1978.

57. *Ibid.*, August 1978.

58. *Africa Contemporary Record*, 1977-78.

59. "Strategy and Tactics of the ANC," adopted at the consultative conference in Morogoro, Tanzania, in 1969; reprint by ANC Information and Publicity, London.

60. *Ibid.*

61. *Ibid.*

62. *Ibid.*

63. *Ibid.*

64. *Ibid.*

65. PAC Mission to the Nordic Countries, 1978 Report.

66. Joe Slovo, "South Africa—No Middle Road," in B. Davidson, J. Slovo, and A.R. Wilkinson, *Southern Africa: The New Politics of Revolution* (Penguin, 1976).

Lawrence Schlemmer: The Stirring Giant

1. This brief account is drawn mainly from Peter Walshe, *The Rise of African Nationalism in South Africa* (Berkeley: University of California Press, 1971); Mary Benson, *South Africa: The Struggle for a Birthright* (Penguin Books, 1966); Gwendolen M. Carter, "African Concepts of Nationalism in South Africa," in *South Africa: Sociological Perspectives*, ed. Heribert Adam (London: Oxford University Press, 1971), pp. 103-20; Fatima Meer, "African Nationalism: Some Inhibiting Factors," in *ibid.*, pp. 121-57; Edward Feit, *African Opposition in South Africa: The Failure of Passive Resistance* (Stanford: Hoover Institution, 1967).

2. See Feit, ch. 3.

3. Cf. Feit, and Leo Kuper, *An African Bourgeoisie: Race, Class and Politics in South Africa* (New Haven: Yale University Press, 1965).

4. Theodor Hanf and Gerda Vierdag, *People's College: 'The World's' Educational Supplement* (Frankfurt: Deutsches Institut für Internationale Pädagogische Forschung, 1977), sect. 3-1-1.

5. Thomas Ross, "Erst mussen wir wie Lowen werden," Bilder and Zeitung, *Frankfurter Allgemeine Zeitung*, 16-4-1977.

6. *Black Review* [ed. Bennie Khoapa], 1972 (Durban, 1973), pp. 41-42.

7. *Ibid.*

8. Ross.

9. Philip Mayer, *Urban Africans and the Bantustans* (Johannesburg: South African Institute of Race Relations, 1972), pp. 7-8; Lawrence Schlemmer,

Black Attitudes: Reaction and Adaptation (Durban: Centre for Applied Social Sciences, University of Natal, 1975).

10. Theodor Hanf et al., *Südafrika: Friedlicher Wandel?* (Munich/Mainz: Kaiser/Grunwald, 1978), p. 371.

11. Hanf and Vierdag.

12. *Ibid.*

13. For a brief account, see M.A. du Toit, *South African Trade Unions: History, Legislation, Policy* (McGraw-Hill, 1976).

14. See Institute for Industrial Education, *The Durban Strikes, 1973* (Ravan Press, 1974).

15. Buthelezi, speech at Soweto, March 14, 1976.

16. Buthelezi, speech on Namibia Day, Windhoek, September 25, 1976.

17. *Ibid.*

18. L. Schlemmer and T. Muil, "Social and Political Change in the African Areas: A Case Study of KwaZulu," in *Change in Contemporary South Africa*, eds. L. Thompson and J. Butler (Berkeley and Los Angeles: University of California Press, 1975), p. 136.

19. S.M. Bengu, address at the annual council meeting of the South African Institute of Race Relations, Durban, January 1976.

20. Buthelezi, speech at Portland University, Oregon, March 1, 1977.

21. M.G. Buthelezi, *White and Black Nationalism: Ethnicity and the Future of the Homelands* (Johannesburg: South African Institute of Race Relations, 1974).

22. Schlemmer and Muil, pp. 131, 132.

23. Buthelezi, speech at the Jabulani Amphitheatre, Soweto, March 14, 1976.

24. Buthelezi, speech at the University of Cape Town, September 8, 1976.

25. Buthelezi, speech on Namibia Day, Windhoek, September 25, 1976. (Emphasis added.)

26. Buthelezi, speech at Portland University, March 1, 1977.

27. *Ibid.*

28. Buthelezi, speech at Jabulani Amphitheatre, Soweto, January 29, 1978. (Emphasis added.)

29. Buthelezi, speech at the University of Willamette, Oregon, February 23, 1977. Recently Buthelezi sharply condemned a call for sanctions against South Africa by exiled editor Donald Woods (*Natal Mercury*, January 30, 1978).

30. Buthelezi, speech at Conference on Race Discrimination, December 3-4, 1976.

31. Buthelezi, speech at Portland University.

32. The information in the ensuing paragraphs has been furnished by officials in the organization itself known to the author, extracted from data compiled by Toni Tickton of the South African Institute of Race Relations (Information Sheet No. 1, 18/11/77), or obtained from Tim Muil, African Affairs correspondent of the *Natal Mercury*, who is closely acquainted with the organization.

33. See Schlemmer and Muil.

34. Hanf et al., ch. 11.

35. See debate in KwaZulu Legislative Assembly, *Daily News*, May 10, 1978.

36. See statement by Mr. Dhlomo, Councillor for Education, *Natal Mercury*, May 12, 1978.

37. See, for example, report on the Black Alliance rally at Chatsworth (an Indian area), *Daily News*, July 24, 1978.

38. See opinions expressed in Hanf et al., pp. 315-16; see also Schlemmer and Muil.

39. Colin Legum, "Political Leadership in the Bantustans," *Third World* 2 (1973): 17. Legum sees the "stooge" labels as both insulting and misleading.

40. Buthelezi, speech at Jabulani Amphitheatre, Soweto, March 14, 1976.

41. Tom Duff, "A Huge Zulu Force on the Move," *The Star*, August 6, 1977. There is also evidence that support for Buthelezi exists among ANC members in exile, particularly among some in the Dar es Salaam group of the ANC (African Nationalists)—Private correspondence to Buthelezi.

42. See David Hammond-Tooke, "Tribal Cohesion and the Incorporative Process in the Transkei, South Africa," in *From Tribe to Nation in Africa*, eds. R. Cohen and J. Middleton (Philadelphia, 1970).

43. B.G.M. Sundkler, *The Christian Ministry in Africa* (Uppsala, 1960), p. 102.

44. Schlemmer, *Black Attitudes*.

45. Buthelezi, speech at Shaka Day rally, September 24, 1977.

46. See, *inter alia*, Buthelezi, speech at Black Alliance rally, Chatsworth, July 24, 1978.

47. Hanf et al., pp. 373-74.

48. Interview with Dr. Connie Mulder, *Rand Daily Mail*, March 15, 1978.

Martin West: The "Apex of Subordination"

1. The phrase "apex of subordination" is taken from L. Kuper, *An African Bourgeoisie* (New Haven: Yale University Press, 1965), p. 8.

2. See D. Welsh, "Social Research in a Divided Society," *Social Dynamics* 1 (1975).

3. See in particular M. Wilson and L. Thompson, eds., *Oxford History of South Africa*, vol. 1 (Oxford: Clarendon Press, 1969), and R.R. Inskeep, *The Peopling of Southern Africa* (New York: Barnes and Noble, 1979).

4. See Wilson and Thompson, vol. 1; W.D. Hammond-Tooke, ed., *The Bantu-speaking Peoples of South Africa* (London: Routledge & Kegan Paul, 1974).

5. Cited in M. Savage, "Urban Africans" (unpublished ms., University of Cape Town, 1977).

6. F. Wilson, "The Political Implications for Blacks of Economic Changes Now Taking Place in South Africa," in *Change in Contemporary South Africa*, eds. L. Thompson and J. Butler (Berkeley: University of California Press, 1975), p. 175.

7. P. Mayer, "Class, Status and Ethnicity as Perceived by Johannesburg Africans," in Thompson and Butler, p. 140; *Survey of Race Relations* (Johannesburg: S.A. Institute of Race Relations, 1977), p. 51.

8. D. Welsh, "The Growth of Towns" in *Oxford History of South Africa*, eds. M. Wilson and L. Thompson (Oxford: Clarendon Press, 1971), vol. 2; M. Horrell, *Legislation and Race Relations* (Johannesburg: S.A. Institute of Race Relations, 1971). See also annual *Survey of Race Relations* (Johannesburg: S.A. Institute of Race Relations).

9. Wilson, "Political Implications for Blacks," p. 181.

10. Quoted in Welsh, "The Growth of Towns," pp. 177-78, 185.

11. *Ibid.*, p. 185.

12. *Ibid.*, p. 187.

13. Horrell, *Legislation*, p. 3.

14. Welsh, "The Growth of Towns," p. 190.

15. *Ibid.*, p. 191.

16. Horrell, *Legislation*, pp. 35-46.

17. P. Lewis, *The Creation of Soweto* (Johannesburg: City Council, 1966).

18. Horrell, *Legislation*, p. 35.

19. *Ibid.*, p. 36.

20. *Ibid.*, p. 40.

21. *Ibid.*, pp. 1-2.

22. *Ibid.*, p. 22.

23. *Ibid.*, p. 23.

24. *Ibid.*, p. 28; *Survey of Race Relations* (Johannesburg: S.A. Institute of Race Relations, 1978), p. 89.

25. *Survey* (1977), pp. 380-83.

26. *Laws Affecting Race Relations in South Africa, 1948-1976* (Johannesburg: S.A. Institute of Race Relations, 1978), p. 68.

27. *Survey* (1978), p. 341.

28. *Survey* (1976), pp. 181-82.

29. *Survey* (1975), pp. 81-82; *Survey* (1978), p. 335.

30. Savage, "Urban Africans," pp. 19-20.

31. *Ibid.*, p. 21; *Hansard* (South Africa), v. 9, 1979, col. 636.

32. Wilson, "Political Implications for Blacks," p. 174n.

33. Welsh, "The Growth of Towns," p. 187.

34. Horrell, *Legislation*, pp. 29-30.

35. *Survey* (1976), p. 208.

36. *Ibid.*, pp. 207-8. Subsequent figures on arrests under the pass laws (*Survey* [1977], pp. 385-86; *Survey* [1978], p. 323) show a marked decline, but the 1976-77 period was atypical in view of the uprising in urban areas and prosecutions under other legislation. The 1978-79 figures will show whether the decrease has continued.

37. Wilson, "Political Implications for Blacks," p. 175.

38. F. Wilson, "Why Modderdam?," *South African Outlook*, August 1977, p. 123.

39. *Survey* (1976), p. 208.

40. *Ibid.*, p. 152.

41. Horrell, *Legislation*, p. 12.

42. *Survey* (1976), pp. 229-30.

43. Quoted in *ibid.*, p. 233.

44. *Ibid.*, p. 45.

45. *Ibid.*, p. 84.

46. *Ibid.*, pp. 233-34.

47. *Ibid.*, p. 231.

48. "South Africa's New Constitutional Plan," (South African Embassy, Washington, 1977); *Survey* (1976), p. 183.

49. An article in the *Sunday Times* (London), 19 February 1978, notes that nearly half of South Africa's police force are technically foreigners.

50. *Survey* (1976), p. 181.

51. See Wilson and Thompson, vol. 1; Hammond-Tooke.

52. Mayer, "Class, Status and Ethnicity," p. 142.

53. *Ibid.*, pp. 151-60.

54. See B.A. Pauw, *The Second Generation* (Cape Town: Oxford University Press, 1963); P. Mayer, *Townsmen or Tribesmen*, 2d ed. (Cape Town: Oxford University Press, 1971); M. Wilson and A. Mafeje, *Langa* (Cape Town: Oxford University Press, 1963); M. Brandel-Syrier, *Reeftown Elite* (London: Routledge & Kegan Paul, 1971); Hellmann, *Soweto*; M. West, *Bishops and Prophets in a Black City* (London: Rex Collings, 1975).

55. Mayer, *Townsmen.*

56. *Ibid.*, pp. 299ff. See also B. Magubane, "The Xhosa in Town Revisited: Urban Anthropology; A Failure of Method and Theory," *American Anthropologist* 75 (1973).

57. Kuper, *Bourgeoisie*; Wilson and Mafeje, *Langa*; Mayer, "Class, Status and Ethnicity"; Welsh, "The Growth of Towns," p. 218.

58. Mayer, "Class, Status and Ethnicity," p. 152.

59. See *ibid.*; Mayer, *Townsmen*; Wilson and Mafeje, p. 35; Wilson, "Political Implications for Blacks," p. 174.

60. *Survey* (1975), p. 85.

61. Wilson, "Political Implications for Blacks," p. 174.

62. Kuper, p. 7. I make a similar argument for people classified as Colored: see M.E. West, *Divided Community* (Cape Town: A.A. Balkema, 1971).

63. Kuper, p. 6.

64. Mayer, "Class, Status and Ethnicity," p. 141. See also P. Mayer, *Urban Africans and the Bantustans* (Johannesburg: S.A. Institute of Race Relations), and B. Magubane: "A Critical Look at Indices Used in the Study of Social Change in Colonial Africa," *Current Anthropology* 12 (1971), and "Xhosa in Town."

65. Mayer, "Class, Status and Ethnicity," pp. 141-42.

66. *Ibid.*, pp. 145ff.

67. *Ibid.*, p. 151.

68. Mayer, *Urban Africans*, p. 17.

69. Mayer, "Class, Status and Ethnicity," p. 153.

70. This section is based upon material drawn from the work of Philip Mayer; Hellmann, *Soweto*; and West, *Bishops and Prophets.* (I worked as an anthropologist in Soweto during the period 1969-71.)

71. Mayer, "Class, Status and Ethnicity," p. 150.

72. Welsh, "The Growth of Towns," p. 241.

73. See Lewis, *Creation of Soweto.*

74. *Survey* (1975), p. 84.

75. *Survey* (1976), pp. 189-200. The official waiting list rose to 12,000 families in 1977 (*Survey* [1978], p. 337), while the Black Sash estimated that 25,000 families were wanting housing (*ibid.*).

76. Mayer, "Class, Status and Ethnicity," pp. 138-40.

77. West, *Bishops and Prophets*, p. 11.

78. A.A. Dubb, "The Impact of the City," in *Bantu-speaking Peoples*, ed. Hammond-Tooke, p. 465.

79. E. Hellmann, "Social Change Among Urban Africans" in *South Africa: Sociological Perspectives*, ed. H. Adam (London: Oxford University Press, 1971), p. 161.

80. West, *Bishops and Prophets*, p. 13.

81. *Survey* (1976), pp. 275-80.

82. *Financial Mail* (Johannesburg), December 1977.

83. West, *Bishops and Prophets*, p. 13.

84. *Survey* (1975), p. 53.

85. Welsh, "The Growth of Towns," p. 225.

86. *Ibid.*, p. 224.

87. *Survey* (1976), p. 321.

88. *Ibid.*, p. 327; West, *Bishops and Prophets*, p. 15.

89. *Financial Mail*, December 1977, pp. 10-11.

90. M.L. Edelstein, *What Do Young Africans Think?* (Johannesburg: S.A. Insttute of Race Relations, 1971).

91. Savage, "Urban Africans," p. 1.

92. See, for example, reports by June Goodwin in *Christian Science Monitor*, 11 November 1977, 2 February 1978, and March 2, 22, and 27, 1978.

93. R.W. Johnson, *How Long Can South Africa Survive?* (New York: Oxford University Press, 1977), p. 23.

94. See *ibid.*, p. 295, on the role that the ANC might play—despite itself—in the future.

95. *Ibid.*, pp. 295-96.

96. L. Thompson, "White Over Black in South Africa: What of the Future?," in Thompson and Butler, p. 412.

97. *Survey* (1975), p. 211; *Survey* (1976), p. 316.

98. Johnson, *How Long*, p. 296. See also Wilson, "Political Implications for Blacks," pp. 186ff.

99. Johnson, *How Long*, pp. 196-201, 298.

100. *Christian Science Monitor*, 2 March 1978.

101. Johnson, *How Long*, p. 300.

102. Wilson, "Political Implications for Blacks," pp. 192-93.

103. Johnson, *How Long*, p. 305.

104. *Ibid.*, p. 297.

105. White Paper on the *Report on the Commission of Inquiry into Legislation Affecting the Utilisation of Manpower* (Pretoria: Government Printer, 1979).

106. *Ibid.*, Sect. A (I) 10 and A (II) 11.

107. *Ibid.*, Sect. A (I) 7 and A (II) 1.

Francis Wilson: Current Labor Issues in South Africa

1. Department of Labour and Mines, *Report of the Commission of Inquiry into Labour Legislation (Wiehahn), Part 1* (Pretoria, RP 47/1979); Republic of South Africa, *Report of the Commission of Inquiry into Legislation Affecting the Utilisation of Manpower (Excluding the Legislation Administered by the Departments of Labour and Mines) (Riekert)* (Pretoria, RP 32/1979).

2. Dudley Horner and Alide Kooy, *Conflict in South African Mines, 1972-1976* (Saldru Working Paper No. 5; Cape Town, 1976).

3. Three pioneering studies in this area are G. Sack, "Black Railwaymen in a Durban Compound" (M.A. diss. in preparation, Rhodes University); Agency for Industrial Mission, *Another Blanket* (Johannesburg, 1976); Anglo-American Corporation, Industrial Relations Department, *The Perceptions and Behaviour Patterns of Black Mine Workers in a Group Gold Mine* (Johannesburg, 1976). See also Robert J. Gordon, *Mines, Masters and Migrants: Life in a Namibian Compound* (Johanessburg: Ravan Press, 1977).

4. Horner and Kooy.

5. Cf. *ibid.*

6. Francis Wilson, "Unresolved Issues in the South African Economy: Labour," *South African Journal of Economics* 43, 4 (1975): 533.

7. For an incisive analysis, see Dan O'Meara, "The 1946 African Mineworkers' Strike and the Political Economy of South Africa," *Journal of Commonwealth and Comparative Politics* 13, 1 (1975).

8. Francis Wilson, *Labour in the South African Gold Mines 1911-1969* (Cambridge: Cambridge University Press, 1972), pp. 77-79, 66.

9. See D.G. Clarke, *Contract Labour from Rhodesia to the South African Gold Mines: A Study in the International Division of a Labour Reserve* (Saldru Working Paper No. 6; Cape Town, 1976), for discussion of this transition.
10. For detailed history and analysis of the color-bar in the mining industry, see Frederick A. Johnstone, *Class, Race and Gold* (London: Routledge & Kegan Paul, 1976), and Wilson, *Labour in the South African Gold Mines*, pp. 110ff.
11. Republic of South Africa, *White Paper on Part 1 of the Report of Commission of Inquiry into Labour Legislation.*
12. Francis Wilson, Alide Kooy, and Delia Hendrie, eds., *Farm Labour in South Africa* (Cape Town: David Philip, 1977), p. 196.
13. Republic of South Africa, *Report of the Commission of Inquiry into Legislation Affecting the Utilisation of Manpower.*
14. Wilson, Kooy, and Hendrie, eds.
15. *Ibid.*, ch. 11.
16. Johann Maree and Judith Cornell, *Sample Survey of Squatters in Crossroads, December 1977* (Saldru Working Paper No. 17; Cape Town, 1978).
17. Budget speech delivered by Minister of Finance (Senator Horwood), 28 March 1979.
18. Leonard Thompson and Jeffrey Butler, eds., *Change in Contemporary South Africa* (Berkeley: University of California Press, 1975), p. 185.
19. For a summary of current research, see Norman Bromberger, "Unemployment in South Africa: A Survey of Research," *Social Dynamics* 4, 1 (1978), and Johann Maree, "The Dimensions and Causes of Unemployment and Underemployment in South Africa," *South African Labour Bulletin* 4, 4 (1978).
20. Charles Simkins and Duncan Clarke, *Structural Unemployment in Southern Africa* (Pietermaritzburg: University of Natal Press, 1978); P.J. van der Merwe, "Black Employment Problems in South Africa," *Finance and Trade Review* 12, 4 (1976).
21. The best guide to an understanding of the difficulties of obtaining a precise measure of unemployment is John Knight, *Labour Supply in the South African Economy* (Saldru Working Paper No. 7; Cape Town, 1977), which analyzes the numerical consequences of different assumptions.
22. Manpower Utilisation, *Current Population Survey as Information Source* (Pretoria: South African Human Sciences Research Council, 1979).
23. Lieb J. Loots, *A Profile of Black Unemployment in South Africa: Two Area Surveys* (Saldru Working Paper No. 19; Cape Town, 1978).
24. For more detailed discussion and further references, see Francis Wilson, "International Migration in Southern Africa," *International Migration Review* 10, 4 (1976).

Philip Bonner: Black Trade Unions in South Africa Since World War II

1. *Africa News*, 1 May 1978.
2. See, for example, *Financial Mail*, 18 November 1977.
3. J. Lever, "Capital and Labour in South Africa: The Passage of the Industrial Conciliation Act of 1924," *South African Labour Bulletin (SALB)* 3, 10 (December 1977); R. Davies, "The Class Character of South Africa's Industrial Legislation," *SALB* 2, 6 (January 1976).
4. G.V. Doxey, *The Industrial Colour Bar in South Africa* (Cape Town, 1961), pp. 111, 115-16, 126-27; W.H. Hutt, *The Economics of the Colour Bar* (London, 1964), pp. 76-78.
5. Lever, p. 28; Davies, pp. 15-16.
6. *Ibid.*; D. O'Meara, "Analysing Afrikaner Nationalism: The 'Christian National' Assault on White Trade Unionism in South Africa, 1934-48," *African Affairs* 77, 306 (January 1978): 48.
7. Horrell, *Trade Unionism*, pp. 60-64; F.A. Johnstone, *Class, Race and Gold* (London, 1976), pp. 20-25, 34-39. Johnstone is primarily concerned with mine labor, but much of what he says applies equally to all spheres of Black employment.
8. P.L. Bonner, "The Decline and Fall of the I.C.U.—A Case of Self Destruction?," *SALB* 1, 6 (September-October 1974).
9. *Ibid.* I argue that the number of Black workers in urban areas provided an adequate base for Black industrial trade unionism which the ICU neglected. However, this constituency was infinitely smaller than that ultimately reached by the ICU, as is shown by the experience of the Non-European Trade Union Federation, which organized along orthodox trade union lines from 1928 on. (See M. Stein, "African Trade Unionism on the Witwatersrand, 1928-40" [Honors dissertation, University of the Witwatersrand, 1977], ch. 4.)
10. See, for example, P.L. Bonner, "The 1920 Black Mine Workers Strike: A Preliminary Account" (paper presented to the History Workshop, University of the Witwatersrand, 3-7 February 1978); A.M.D. Humphrey, "South African Agriculture in a Period of Transition, 1913-1924" (Honors dissertation, University of the Witwatersrand, 1978).
11. Bonner, "I.C.U."; for the notion of populism used in this paper, see J.S. Saul, "On African Populism," in *Essays in the Political Economy of Africa*, eds. G. Arrighi and J.S. Saul (London, 1973).
12. Bonner, "I.C.U."; R.M. Swanson, "Alison Wessels Champion" (paper presented to the U.S. African Studies Association, 1971).
13. D.O'Meara, "The 1946 African Mine-Workers Strike in the Political Economy of South Africa," in *Working Papers in Southern African Studies*, ed. P.L. Bonner (Johannesburg, 1977), pp. 185-86. (This is a slightly modified version of the article that appears in the *Journal of Commonwealth and Comparative Politics* 12, 2 [July 1975].)
14. *Ibid.*, p. 187.

15. O'Meara, "Analysing Afrikaner Nationalism," p. 48.

16. L. Douwes-Dekker, D. Hemson et al., "Case Studies in African Labour Action in South Africa and Namibia (South West Africa)," in *The Development of an African Working Class*, eds. R. Sandbrook and R. Cohen (London, 1975), p. 209.

17. See, for example, *The Industrial Review*, November 1950-November 1956—esp. November 1950 (I am grateful to Jon Lewis for this reference); M.C. Morris, "Capitalism and Apartheid: A Critique of Some Current Conceptions of Cheap Labour Power," in *Perspectives on South Africa*, ed. T. Adler (Johannesburg, 1976), pp. 63, 74, 81.

18. O'Meara, "Mine-Workers Strike," p. 187.

19. *Ibid.*, pp. 212-14.

20. *Ibid.*, p. 192.

21. *Ibid.*, pp. 193-94.

22. T. Karis and G.M. Carter, eds., *From Protest to Challenge* (4 vols.; Stanford, 1972-77), vol. 2, pp. 80-81, 115-16; P. Walshe, *The Rise of African Nationalism in South Africa* (London, 1970), pp. 303-4; A. Stadler, "Birds in the Cornfield: Squatter Movements in Johannesburg, 1944-47" (paper presented to the History Workshop, University of the Witwatersrand, 3-7 February 1978).

23. D. Lewis, "African Trade Unions and the South African State, 1947-53" (unpublished paper, Cape Town, 1976), pp. 15-19; R. Davies, D. Kaplan, M. Morris, D. O'Meara, "Class Struggle and the Periodisation of the State in South Africa," *Review of African Political Economy* 7 (September-December 1976): 21-30; A. Brooks, "The Communist Party of South Africa between 1940 and 1950," in *Collected Seminar Papers* (University of London, Institute of Commonwealth Studies), vol. 2, p. 2.

24. Cited in Lewis, "African Trade Unions," p. 20.

25. *Ibid.*, p. 23; R. Davies and D. Lewis, "Industrial Relations Legislation: One of Capital's Defences," *Review of African Political Economy* 7 (September-December 1976): 63.

26. Brooks, "Communist Party," pp. 5-6; Karis and Carter, eds., pp. 80-81, 115-16.

27. O'Meara, "Mine-Workers Strike," p. 203.

28. Report of the Industrial Legislation Commission of Enquiry (UG 62/1951), para. 1540.

29. Horrell, *Trade Unionism*, p. 62.

30. Report of Commission of Enquiry, para. 1616, 1693, 1703, 1719, 1743 (cited in Davies and Lewis, pp. 63-64).

31. Horrell, *Trade Unionism*, pp. 18-19; E. Feit, *Workers Without Weapons* (Hamden, Conn., 1975), pp. 59-61; M. Horrell, *Action, Reaction and Counter-Action* (Johannesburg, 1963).

32. Horrell, *Trade Unionism*, pp. 63, 93-95.

33. Horrell: *Action, Reaction*, pp. 6-20, 30-94; *Legislation and Race Relations* (Johannesburg, 1963); and *South Africa's Workers* (Johannesburg, 1969), p. 77; Hoover Institution, "South Africa: A Collection of Miscellaneous Documents": Presidential Address to the Fourth Annual Conference of SACTU, March 1959 (citing Government Notice 2715 of 1952).

34. Lewis, "African Trade Unions," pp. 38-39.

35. Horrell, *Trade Unionism*, pp. 21-23.

36. Hoover Institution, Vatcher Collection, Box 5, File SACTU: Statement of Policy submitted to the First Annual SACTU Conference, 1-3 March 1956.

37. SACTU, *Basebetai Mekoting. Mine Workers Condition in South Africa* (1976, pamphlet), p. 21.

38. Feit, *Workers*, pp. 33, 50-126.

39. Hoover Institution, "South Africa . . . Documents," Reel 8, Lectures prepared by SACTU (n.d.).

40. R. Hyman, *Marxism and the Sociology of Trade Unionism* (London, 1971), pp. 23-27, 37-43.

41. The argument about the two strands in SACTU's thinking does not come from Feit. I am referring here only to his view of the organizational failings of SACTU.

42. Feit, *Workers*, pp. 50-126.

43. O'Meara, "Afrikaner Nationalism," p. 71; M. Legassick and D. Innes, "Capital Restructuring and Apartheid: A Critique of Constructive Engagement," *African Affairs* 76, 305 (October 1977): 440; Hoover Institution, "South Africa . . . Documents": Presidential Address to the Third Annual Conference of SACTU, March 1958.

44. *Ibid.*, according to which the promise given during the Alexandra bus boycott to institute Wage Board investigations into twenty or so undertakings was followed by wage determinations which specified new minimum wages *below* those already being paid; see also Report of the General Secretary to the Third Annual National Conference of SACTU, March 1958, pp. 5-9; Presidential Address to the Fourth Annual National Conference of SACTU, March 1959, p. 7; Report of the Secretariat presented to the Fifth Annual National Conference of SACTU, October 1960, p. 3; SACTU memo "The Urgent Need for a General Increase of Wages, Particularly for the Lower Paid Categories of Workers, and a National Minimum Wage of £1 a Day," n.d. In addition, Africans were also excluded from the Unemployment Insurance Fund in this period.

45. A glance through SACTU's annual reports makes this abundantly clear: see *Annual Reports* 1957-62; Horrell, *Trade Unionism*, p. 79.

46. L. Ensor, "TUCSA's Relationship with African Trade Unions: An Attempt at Control 1954-1962," *SALB* 3, 4 (January-February 1977): 32.

47. M. Horrell, ed., *A Survey of Race Relations in South Africa 1963* (Johannesburg, 1964), p. 215; *Survey . . . 1964* (Johannesburg, 1965), p. 266; Feit, *Workers*, p. 177.

48. M. Lipton, "British Investment in South Africa: Is Constructive Engagement Possible?," *SALB* 3, 3 (October 1976): 16-17; see also Legassick and Innes, pp. 440-41, 470.

49. Institute for Industrial Education, *The Durban Strikes 1973* (Durban-Johannesburg, 1974), pp. 52, 84; Douwes-Dekker et al., pp. 209, 223.

50. I.I.E., *Durban Strikes*, pp. 11, 39-40, 43.

51. *Ibid.*, p. 46; Lipton, pp. 16-17.

52. Horrell, *Survey . . . Race Relations 1974* (Johannesburg, 1975), pp. 325-26; *Survey . . . 1975* (Johannesburg, 1976), pp. 210-11.

53. *Ibid.*, pp. 206-7; J. Lewson, "The Role of Registered Unions in the Black Trade Union Movement," *SALB* 3, 4 (January-February 1977): 50-52.

54. T. Mbanjwa, ed., *Black Review 1974/5* (Johannesburg, 1975), p. 136; Lewson, p. 52; Horrell, *Survey . . . Race Relations 1975*, pp. 55-59; *Review of African Political Economy*, No. 7, p. 115.

55. T.U.C., *Trade Unionism in South Africa: Report of a Delegation from the Trade Union Congress* (London, 1974), p. 22; *Review of African Political Economy* 7 (September-December 1976): 118.

56. *Ibid.*

57. Horrell, *Survey . . . Race Relations 1976* (Johannesburg, 1977), p. 315.

58. *Review of African Political Economy* 7 (September-December 1976): 118; D. Horner, "The Western Province Workers' Advice Bureau," *SALB* 3, 2 (September 1976): 74-79.

59. Horrell, *Survey . . . Race Relations 1974*, p. 332; Horrell, *South Africa's Workers*, p. 78.

60. *Daily Despatch*, 30 August 1977.

61. B. Godsell, "A Comparative Study of Works and Liaison Committee Legislation," *SALB* 2, 6 (January 1976): 34-39; D. Horner, "Metal and Allied Workers Union. Workers Under the Baton. An Examination of the Labour Dispute at Heinemann Electric Company," *SALB* 3, 7 (June-July 1977): 49-59; M. Kirkwood, "The Defy Dispute: Questions of Solidarity," *SALB* 2, 1 (May-June 1975): 55-63; Case Studies by Cape Town and Durban Editors, *SALB* 2, 9 and 10 (May-June 1976).

62. Glass and Allied Workers Union, "Report on the Strike at Armourplate Safety Glass," in *ibid.*, pp. 60-72.

63. D. Horner, "African Labour Representation and the Draft Bill to Amend the Bantu Labour Relations Regulation Act (No. 48 of 1953)," *SALB* 2, 9 and 10 (May-June 1976): 31-35; *Financial Mail*, 6 May 1977.

64. Douwes-Dekker, "Case Studies," p. 232.

65. Horrell, *Survey . . . Race Relations 1974*, pp. 336-37.

66. See, for example, ICFTU, *Free Labour World*, January-December 1977, pp. 319-29.

67. M. Legassick, "Capital Accumulation and Violence," *Economy and Society* 3, 3 (August 1974): 270-72; R. Sandbrook, *Proletarians and African Capitalism: The Kenyan Case, 1960-72* (Cambridge, 1975).

68. ICFTU, 7th Meeting of the Coordinating Committee on South Africa, mins.
69. *Rand Daily Mail*, 5 July 1977.
70. *Financial Mail*, 18 November 1977.
71. *Ibid.*
72. *Ibid.*
73. Act 107 (1978).
74. Horrell, *Survey . . . Race Relations 1976*, p. 319.

Newell M. Stultz: Some Implications of African "Homelands" in South Africa

1. Only three of the ten "homelands" have been studied in depth: KwaZulu, Bophuthatswana, and Transkei. See Jeffrey Butler, Robert I. Rotberg, and John Adams, *The Black Homelands of South Africa: The Political and Economic Development of Bophuthatswana and KwaZulu* (Berkeley: University of California Press, 1977), and Patrick Laurence, *The Transkei: South Africa's Politics of Partition* (Johannesburg: Ravan Press, 1976).
2. Howard Rogers, *Native Administration in the Union of South Africa* (Pretoria: Government Printer, 1949), p. 97.
3. *Ibid.*, p. 100.
4. *Ibid.*, p. 97.
5. See Gwendolen M. Carter, Thomas Karis, and Newell M. Stultz, *South Africa's Transkei: The Politics of Domestic Colonialism* (Evanston: Northwestern University Press, 1967), ch. 7.
6. *New York Times*, October 27, 1976.
7. Dennis Austin, "White Power: Cohesion Without Consensus?" (unpublished ms.).
8. This information about Lesotho is taken largely from *Lesotho: A Development Challenge* (Washington: The World Bank, 1975).
9. Roger Southall, "The Beneficiaries of Transkeian 'Independence,'" *Journal of Modern African Studies* 15, 1 (1977): 8.
10. See Butler, Rotberg, and Adams, p. 125.
11. Richard F. Weisfelder, "Lesotho," in *Southern Africa in Perspective*, eds. C.P. Potholm and R. Dale (New York: The Free Press, 1972), pp. 33-34.
12. See "Assistance to Lesotho: Report of the United Nations Mission to Lesotho," *Objective: Justice* 9, 2 (Summer 1977): 22-37.
13. See Newell M. Stultz, "Transkei Independence in Separatist Perspective," *Journal of African Studies* 4, 4 (Winter 1977): 414-32.
14. Austin Turk, "The Futures of South Africa," *Social Forces* 15, 3 (March 1967): 410.
15. Heribert Adam, "Three Perspectives on the Future of South Africa" (unpublished ms.), p. 10.

16. *Sechaba* 11, 2 (1977): 48.

17. The most thorough examination to date of the application of the federal idea to South Africa was provided by the late Leo Marquard in *A Federation of Southern Africa* (London: Oxford University Press, 1971).

18. In a recent article Nelson Kasfir notes that in 1970 all the states in Nigeria except Lagos received 70 percent or more of their total revenues from the federal government; see "Soldiers as Policymakers in Nigeria," *American Universities Field Staff Reports* 17, 3 (October 1977): 10.

19. Southall, pp. 22-23.

20. Pierre van den Berghe, *South Africa: A Study in Conflict* (Berkeley: University of California Press, 1965), p. 119.

21. Chief Gatsha Mangosuthu Buthelezi, untitled contribution to *Transkei Independence* (Durban: Black Community Programs, 1976), pp. 27-28.

22. Leonard Thompson and Jeffrey Butler, eds., *Change in Contemporary South Africa* (Berkeley: University of California Press, 1975), p. xi.

23. Johann Maree and P.J. de Vos, *Underemployment, Poverty and Migrant Labour in the Transkei and Ciskei* (Johannesburg: S.A. Institute of Race Relations, 1975), pp. 2, 17, 21, 22; Johann Maree, "Bantustan Economics," *Third World* 2, 6 (June 1973): 27.

24. Bureau of Economic Research re Bantu Development, *Transkei, Economic Review, 1975* (Pretoria: Benbo, 1975), p. 11.

25. Heribert Adam, "When the Chips Are Down: Confrontation and Accommodation in South Africa," *Contemporary Crises*, No. 1 (1977), p. 423.

26. In 1973 the leadership of KwaZulu involved itself at least briefly with labor matters affecting Zulu workers in Natal; see Lawrence Schlemmer and Tim J. Muil, "Social and Political Change in the African Areas: A Case Study of KwaZulu," in *Change in Contemporary South Africa*, eds. L. Thompson and J. Butler, pp. 128-30.

Kogila A. Moodley: Structural Inequality and Minority Anxiety

1. South African Institute of Race Relations (SAIRR), *A Survey of Race Relations in South Africa* (1978) (Johannesburg), p. 50.

2. Austin Turk, "The Future of South Africa," *Social Forces* 45, 3 (March 1967).

3. Frene Ginwala, *Indian South Africans, Minority Rights Group* (London, 1977).

4. A.L. Muller, *Minority Interests: The Political Economy of the Coloured and Indian Communities in South Africa* (Johannesburg: South African Institute of Race Relations, 1968).

5. *Die Transvaler*, February 18, 1978.

6. *The Star*, February 14, 1978.

7. L. Schlemmer, "Employment Opportunity and Race in South Africa," *Studies in Race and Nations* 4, 3 (Denver: University of Denver, 1973), p. 39; Institute for Industrial Education, *Durban Strikes 1973* (Durban: Ravan Press, 1974), p. 58.

8. *Ibid.*, p. 59.

9. *Ibid.*, p. 62.

10. *Graphic*, September 20, 1974.

11. *Ibid.*

12. *Survey of Race Relations* (1973), pp. 378-90.

13. *Ibid.*, p. 390.

14. K.A. Moodley, "South African Indians: The Wavering Minority," in *Change in Contemporary South Africa*, eds. L. Thompson and J. Butler (Berkeley: University of California Press, 1975), pp. 250-79.

15. Schlemmer.

16. *Survey* (1978), pp. 243, 241.

17. *Financial Mail*, January 10, 1975.

18. *Ibid.*, February 13, 1976.

19. *Survey* (1976), p. 272.

20. H.W. van der Merwe and C.J. Groenewald, eds., *Occupational and Social Change among Coloured People in South Africa* (Capetown: June, 1976).

21. M. Webb and K. Kirkwood, *The Durban Riots and After* (Johannesburg: SAIRR, 1949), p. 20.

22. Eric Walker, *A History of South Africa* (London: Longman, 1964), p. 783.

23. Webb and Kirkwood, p. 30.

24. *Ibid.*, p. 4.

25. *Ibid.*, p. 5.

26. *The Leader*, October 11, 1974.

27. *The Post*, June 13, 1976.

28. *Graphic*, January 1, 1976.

29. *Ibid.*

30. *Ibid.*

31. L. Pye, *Guerrilla Communism in Malaya* (Princeton: Princeton University Press, 1954).

32. H. Kuper, "Strangers in Plural Societies: Asians in South Africa and Uganda," in *Pluralism in Africa*, eds. L. Kuper and M.G. Smith (Berkeley: University of California Press, 1969), pp. 247-82.

33. E. Staley, *The Future of Underdeveloped Countries* (New York: Doubleday, 1954), pp. 207-9.

34. T. Hanf, H. Weiland, and G. Vierdag, *Südafrika: Friedlicher Wandel?* (München: Kaiser, Grunewald, 1978).

Lawrence Schlemmer: Change in South Africa: Opportunities and Constraints

1. *Rapport*, Business Supplement, March 26, 1978.
2. Jill Nattrass, "Narrowing Wage Differentials: Some Dynamic Implications for Income Distribution in South Africa," *South African Journal of Economics* 45, 4 (December 1977).
3. Standard Bank Review, March 1978.
4. Ellen Hellman, "Urban Rights Hit by New Act," *Race Relations News* 40, 3 (March 1978).
5. "Sê die ding tog soos dit is" [For goodness sake tell it like it is], *Rapport*, February 26, 1978.
6. *Sunday Express*, July 3, 1977.
7. *Sunday Times*, January 22, 1978 to February 5, 1978. See also J.H.P. Serfontein, *Brotherhood of Power* (London: Rex Collings, 1979), and Ivor Wilkens and Hans Strydom, *The Super Afrikaners* (Johannesburg: Jonathan Ball, 1978). Both these works are excellent treatises on the Broederbond.
8. Percy Cohen, "Social Attitudes and Sociological Enquiry," *British Journal of Sociology* 14 (1966).
9. Milton Rokeach, "Race and Shared Belief as Factors in Social Choice," in *Racial Attitudes in America*, eds. J.C. Brigham and T.A. Weissbach (New York: Harper and Row, 1972).
10. *Rapport*, September 23, 1979.
11. David Welsh, "Politics of Conflict Negotiation in South Africa," *Optima* 3 (1977).

Colin Legum: South Africa in the Contemporary World

1. *Die Burger* (Cape Town), 1960.
2. South Africa House of Assembly, *Debates*, 25 January 1966, cols. 46-70. (Emphasis added.)
3. Quoted by S.A. Broadcasting Corporation, Johannesburg, 9 March 1979.
4. SA House of Assembly, *Debates*, 6 June 1961, cols. 7378-79.
5. *Cape Times* (Cape Town), 12 September 1973.
6. See Colin Legum and Tony Hodges, *After Angola: A Study of International Intervention* (New York: Africana Publications, 1976).
7. See *Africa Contemporary Record 1975-76*, pp. A39ff.

8. See Colin Legum, *Vorster's Gamble for Africa* (London: Rex Collings, 1976).

9. See Colin Legum, *The Western Crisis over Southern Africa* (New York: Africana, 1979).

10. Deon Geldenhuys, *The Neutral Option and Sub-continental Solidarity* (Johannesburg: SA Institute of International Affairs, March 1979).

Robert M. Price: Apartheid and White Supremacy: The Meaning of Government-Led Reform in the South African Context

1. "Koornhof Says Apartheid Dying," *Africa News*, July 6, 1979.

2. *South African Digest* (Pretoria), August 24, 1979, p. 1; see also *ibid.*, August 31, 1979, p. 4.

3. *The Argus* (Cape Town), July 12, 1977, p. 13.

4. For an important treatment of the distinction between White supremacy and apartheid, see Frederick A. Johnstone, "White Prosperity and White Supremacy in South Africa Today," *African Affairs* 67, 275 (April 1970): 124-40.

5. Dunbar Moodie, *The Rise of Afrikanerdom: Power, Apartheid, and the Afrikaner Civil Religion* (Berkeley: University of California Press, 1975).

6. *Ibid.*, p. ix.

7. *Die Burger*, October 11, 1944; quoted in Moodie, p. 110.

8. *Ibid.*, p. 164.

9. *Ibid.*, pp. 110 and 111.

10. *Ibid.*, p. 111.

11. Quoted in *ibid.*, p. 111.

12. Address to the 1933 Congress of the Broederbond; quoted in *ibid.*, p. 112.

13. M.D.C. de Wet Nel, Minister of Bantu Administration and Development, 1959; reported in *Hansard*, May 18, 1959, cols. 6001-2.

14. For a detailed analysis of the instrumental aspects of apartheid, see Heribert Adam, *Modernizing Racial Domination: The Dynamics of South African Politics* (Berkeley: University of California Press, 1971).

15. Quoted in Moodie, p. 264.

16. Quoted in André du Toit, "Ideological Change, Afrikaner Nationalism, and Pragmatic Racial Domination in South Africa," in *Change in Contemporary South Africa*, eds. L. Thompson and J. Butler (Berkeley: University of California Press, 1975), p. 41.

17. For a good summary account, see T.R.H. Davenport, *South Africa: A Modern History* (Toronto, 1977), sect. 3; see also Adam, *Modernizing Racial Domination*, ch. 4.

18. See Pierre L. van den Berghe, "Racial Segregation in South Africa: Degrees

and Kinds," in *South Africa: Sociological Perspectives*, ed. Heribert Adam (Oxford, 1971), pp. 39-40.

19. See the discussion by Martin West in an earlier chapter of this volume (pp. 127-51).

20. Michael Savage, "Costs of Enforcing Apartheid and Problems of Change," *African Affairs* 76 (1977): 295; see also Davenport, p. 346.

21. See David Welsh, "The Politics of White Supremacy," in Thompson and Butler, eds., pp. 62-63.

22. Muriel Horrell, *Legislation and Race Relations* (Johannesburg: S.A. Institute of Race Relations, 1971), pp. 17-18.

23. *Ibid.*, pp. 57-58.

24. De Wet Nel; quoted in Moodie, pp. 266 and 268.

25. See pp. 186-87 above.

26. See p. 86 above.

27. See p. 190 above.

28. For a discussion of the trend toward closer relations between South Africa and the United States during the Nixon years, see Mohamed A. El-Kawas and Barry Cohen, *The Kissinger Study on South Africa: National Security Study Memorandum 39* [Secret] (Westport: Lawrence Hill, 1976).

29. Quoted in Timothy Smith, "U.S. Firms and Apartheid: Belated Steps Analyzed," *Africa Today* 24, 2 (1977): 29-33.

30. See U.S. Congress, Senate, Committee on Foreign Relations, Subcommittee on African Affairs, *U.S. Corporate Interests in South Africa*, 1978.

31. See Martin Bailey, "Foreign Loans are Drying Up for White South Africa," *New African*, June 1977, p. 575.

32. South Africa, *Barclay's Country Report*, 3 May 1979; see also *Africa Research Bulletin*, August 15-September 14, 1977, p. 4402.

33. For an analysis of the shift from the politics of identity to the politics of survival, see Heribert Adam, "Survival Politics: Afrikanerdom in Search of a New Ideology," *Journal of Modern African Studies* 16, 4 (December 1978): 657-69.

34. See Welsh, pp. 51-78, and Du Toit.

35. See Albie Sachs, "The Instruments of Domination in South Africa," in Thompson and Butler, eds., p. 248.

36. See *South African Digest*, August 24, 1979, pp. 1 and 3.

37. See Johnstone.

38. All quotations from the Wiehahn Commission report are taken from *The Wiehahn Commission: A Critique and Some Reactions* (Cape Town: Southern Africa Labour and Development Research Unit, Working Paper No. 25).

39. For a detailed examination of the control implications of the Wiehahn Commission recommendations, see *ibid*.

40. Savage, p. 299.

41. *South African Digest*, June 29, 1979, p. 27.

42. *Ibid*., p. 3.

43. *Die Beeld*, May 9, 1979; reprinted in *South African Digest*, May 11, 1979, p. 23.

44. *South African Digest*, August 24, 1979, p. 1.

45. *Die Burger*, August 13, 1979; reprinted in *South African Digest*, August 17, 1979, p. 21. See also "Soweto: The Government's Big Step Forward," *To The Point*, September 7, 1979, p. 15.

46. *Die Burger*, August 13, 1979.

SELECTED BIBLIOGRAPHY

GENERAL

Adam, Heribert. *Modernizing Racial Domination: The Dynamics of South African Politics.* Berkeley: University of California Press, 1971.

__________ et al., eds. *South Africa: Sociological Perspectives.* London: Oxford University Press, 1971.

Ballinger, Margaret. *From Union to Apartheid.* Cape Town: Juta, 1969.

Carter, Gwendolyn M. *The Politics of Inequality: South Africa Since 1948.* New York: Farrar, Strauss and Giroux, 1977.

__________, and O'Meara, Patrick, eds. *Southern Africa in Crisis.* Bloomington: University of Indiana Press, 1977.

Davidson, Basil, Slovo, Joe, and Wilkinson, Anthony R. *Southern Africa: The New Politics of Revolution.* London: Penguin, 1976.

De Kiewiet, C.W. *A History of South Africa.* London: Clarendon Press, 1941.

Gerhart, Gail. *Black Power in South Africa.* Berkeley: University of California Press, 1978.

Grundy, Kenneth W. *Confrontation and Accommodation in Southern Africa: The Limits of Independence.* Berkeley: University of California Press, 1974.

Horwitz, Ralph. *The Political Economy of South Africa.* London: Weidenfeld and Nicolson, 1967.

Johnson, R.W. *How Long Will South Africa Survive?* London: Oxford University Press, 1977.

Johnstone, Frederick A. *Class, Race and Gold: A Study of Class Relations and Racial Discrimination in South Africa.* London: Routledge and Kegan Paul, 1976.

Kuper, Leo. *An African Bourgeoisie: Race, Class and Politics in South Africa.* New Haven: Yale University Press, 1965.

Leftwich, Adrian, ed. *South Africa: Economic Growth and Political Change.* London: Allison and Busby, 1974.

Marquard, Leo. *The Peoples and Policies of South Africa.* London: Oxford University Press, 1969.

Mathews, Anthony S. *Law, Order and Liberty in South Africa.* Berkeley: University of California Press, 1972.

The editors wish to express their gratitude to Ardath Grant for her assistance in the preparation of this bibliography.

Mbeki, Govan A.M. *South Africa: The Peasant's Revolt*. Baltimore and Harmondsworth: Penguin, 1964.

Moodie, T. Dunbar. *The Rise of Afrikanerdom: Power, Apartheid, and the Afrikaner Civil Religion*. Berkeley: University of California Press, 1974.

Munger, Edwin S. *Afrikaner and African Nationalism: South African Parallels and Parameters*. London: Oxford University Press, 1967.

Palmer, Robin, and Parsons, Neil, eds. *The Roots of Rural Poverty in Central and Southern Africa*. Berkeley: University of California Press, 1978.

Plaatje, S.T. *Native Life in South Africa*. London: P.S. King and Son, 1916.

Roux, Edward. *Time Longer Than Rope: A History of the Black Man's Struggle for Freedom in South Africa*. Madison: University of Wisconsin Press, 1964.

Sachs, Albie. *Justice in South Africa*. Berkeley: University of California Press, 1973.

Simons, H.J., and Simons, R.E. *Class and Colour in South Africa 1850-1950*. London: Penguin, 1969.

Stultz, Newell M. *Afrikaner Politics in South Africa 1934-1948*. Berkeley: University of California Press, 1974.

Thompson, Leonard, and Butler, Jeffrey, eds. *Change in Contemporary South Africa*. Berkeley: University of California Press, 1975.

Van den Berghe, Pierre L. *South Africa: A Study in Conflict*. Middletown, Conn.: Wesleyan University Press, 1965.

Walshe, Peter. *The Rise of African Nationalism in South Africa*. Berkeley: University of California Press, 1971.

Wilson, Francis. *Labour in the South African Gold Mines 1911-1969*. Cambridge: Cambridge University Press, 1972.

Wilson, Monica, and Thompson, Leonard, eds. *Oxford History of South Africa*. 2 vols. New York and Cape Town: Oxford University Press, 1969 and 1971.

WHITE POLITICS

Adam, Heribert. *Modernizing Racial Domination: The Dynamics of South African Politics*. Berkeley: University of California Press, 1971.

__________. "Survival Politics: Afrikanerdom in Search of a New Ideology." *Journal of Modern African Studies* 16, 4 (1978).

__________. "The South African Power-Elite: A Survey of Ideological Commitment." *Canadian Journal of Political Science* 4, 1 (March 1971): 79-96.

Austin, Dennis. "White Power in South Africa: Cohesion Without Consensus?" *Government and Opposition* 13 (Winter 1978): 21-38.

Brett, E.A. *African Attitudes: A Study of the Social, Racial and Political Attitudes of Some Middle-Class Africans*. Johannesburg: South African Institute of Race Relations, 1963.

Brotz, Howard. *The Politics of South Africa: Democracy and Racial Diversity*. London: Oxford University Press, 1971.

SELECTED BIBLIOGRAPHY

Davenport, T.R.H. *The Afrikaner Bond: The History of a South African Political Party, 1880-1911.* Cape Town: Oxford University Press, 1966.

Drew, Archibald. "The Afrikaners as an Emergent Minority." *British Journal of Sociology* 20 (December 1969): 416-25.

Du Toit, André. "Ideological Change, Afrikaner Nationalism and Pragmatic Racial Domination in South Africa." In *Change in Contemporary South Africa*, eds. L. Thompson and J. Butler. Berkeley: University of California Press, 1975.

Hill, Christopher R. "South Africa: The Future of the Liberal Spirit." In *South Africa: Economic Growth and Political Change*, ed. A. Leftwich. London: Allison and Busby, 1974.

Kallaway, P., and Malan, F.S. "The Cape Liberal Tradition and South African Politics." *Journal of African History* 15, 1 (1974): 113-29.

Klerk, W.A. *The Puritan Africans: A Story of Afrikanerdom.* London: Collings, 1975.

Loubser, Jan J. "Calvinism, Equality and Inclusion: The Case of Afrikaner Nationalism." In *The Protestant Ethic and Modernization: A Comparative View*, ed. S.N. Eisenstadt. New York: Basic Books, 1968.

Marquard, Leo. *Liberalism in South Africa.* Johannesburg: South African Institute of Race Relations, 1965.

Michelman, Cherry. *The Black Sash of South Africa: A Case Study in Liberalism.* London: Oxford University Press, 1975.

Moodie, T. Dunbar. *The Rise of Afrikanerdom.* Berkeley: University of California Press, 1974.

__________. "The Rise of Afrikanerdom as an Imminent Critique of Marxist Theory of Social Class." In *Working Papers in Southern African Studies*, ed. P.L. Bonner. Johannesburg: ASI African Studies Seminar, University of Witwatersrand African Studies Institute, 1977.

Munger, Edwin S. *Afrikaner and African Nationalism: South African Parallels and Parameters.* London: Oxford University Press, 1967.

Nolutshungu, Sam C. "Issues of the Afrikaner Enlightenment." *African Affairs* 70, 278 (January 1971): 23-36.

O'Meara, D. "Analyzing Afrikaner Nationalism: Christian-National Assault on White Trade Unionism in South Africa, 1934-1948." *African Affairs* 77, 306 (1978).

__________. "The Afrikaner Broederbond 1927-1948: Class Vanguard of Afrikaner Nationalism." *Journal of Southern African Studies* 3, 2 (April 1977): 156-86.

__________. "Puritans in Africa: Story of Afrikanerdom." *Journal of Southern African Studies* 4, 2 (1978).

Rich, P.B. "Liberalism and Ethnicity in South African Politics 1921-1948." *African Studies* 35, 3-4 (1976): 229-51.

Robertson, Janet. *Liberalism in South Africa: 1948-1963.* London: Oxford University Press, 1971.

SELECTED BIBLIOGRAPHY

Schlemmer, Lawrence. *Privilege, Prejudice and Parties: A Study of Political Motivation Among White Voters in Durban.* Johannesburg: South African Institute of Race Relations, 1973.

Stokes, R.G. "The Afrikaner Industrial Entrepreneur and Afrikaner Nationalism." *Economic Development and Cultural Change* 22, 4 (July 1974): 557-79.

Stultz, Newell M. *Afrikaner Politics in South Africa 1934-1948.* Berkeley: University of California Press, 1975.

__________. *The Nationalists in Opposition 1934-1948.* Cape Town: Human and Rousseau, 1974.

Turner, Richard. *The Eye of the Needle: Toward Participatory Democracy in South Africa.* Maryknoll, N.Y.: Orbis Books, 1978.

Vatcher, William H. *White Laager: The Rise of Afrikaner Nationalism.* London: Pall Mall, 1965.

Worrall, D.J. "Afrikaner Nationalism: A Contemporary Analysis." In *Southern Africa in Perspective: Essays in Regional Politics*, eds. C. Potholm and R. Dale. New York: Free Press, 1972.

NATIONALIST POLICIES AND THEIR IMPLEMENTATION

Baldwin, A. "Mass Removals and Separate Development." *Journal of Southern African Studies* 1, 2 (April 1975): 215-27.

Butler, Jeffrey, Rotberg, R., and Adams, J. *The Black Homelands of South Africa.* Berkeley: University of California Press, 1977.

Carter, Gwendolyn M. *Separate Development: The Challenge of the Transkei.* Johannesburg: South African Institute of Race Relations, 1966.

__________, and Stultz, N.M. *South Africa's Transkei: The Politics of Domestic Colonialism.* Evanston: Northwestern University Press, 1967.

Datta, A.K. "Urbanization and Apartheid in the Republic of South Africa." *Africa Quarterly* 3 (July-September 1963): 82-91.

Horrell, Muriel. *The African Homelands of South Africa.* Johannesburg: South African Institute of Race Relations, 1973.

Lombard, J.A. "The Economic Philosophy of Homeland Development." In *South African Dialogue: Contrasts on South African Thinking on Basic Race Issues*, ed. N.J. Rhoodie. Johannesburg: McGraw-Hill, 1972.

Rich, P.B. "Ministering to the White Man's Needs: Development of Urban Segregation in South Africa 1913-1923." *African Studies* 37, 2 (1978).

Rogers, Barbara. *Divide and Rule: South African Bantustans.* London: International Defence and Aid, 1976.

Schlemmer, Lawrence. *Political Policy and Social Change in South Africa: An Assessment of the Future of Separate Development and of Possible Alternatives to the Policy.* Johannesburg: South African Institute of Race Relations, 1970.

SELECTED BIBLIOGRAPHY

BLACK PROTEST AND POLITICAL ORGANIZATION

Adam, Heribert. "The Rise of Black Consciousness in South Africa." *Race* 15, 2 (October 1973): 149-63.

Benson, Mary. *The African Patriots: The Story of the African National Congress of South Africa.* London: Faber and Faber, 1963.

__________. *South Africa: The Struggle for a Birthright.* London: Minerva Press, 1966.

Brett, E.A. *African Attitudes: A Study of the Social, Racial and Political Attitudes of Some Middle-Class Africans.* Johannesburg: South African Institute of Race Relations, 1963.

Burgess, Julian. *Interdependence in Southern Africa.* London: Economics Intelligence Unit, 1976.

Buthelezi, M. Gatsha. *White and Black Nationalism, Ethnicity and the Future of the Homelands.* Johannesburg: South African Institute of Race Relations, 1974.

Carter, Gwendolyn M. "Black Initiatives for Change in Southern Africa." *Issue* 4, 1 (Spring 1974): 6-13.

__________. "Challenges to Minority Rule in Southern Africa." *International Journal* 25, 3 (Summer 1970): 486-96.

Crewe, A. "SASO and Black Consciousness in South Africa." *Reality* 3, 4 (September 1971): 8-13.

De Villiers, René. *The Role and Challenge of the Student in South Africa.* Johannesburg: South African Institute of Race Relations, 1967.

Feit, Edward. *African Opposition in South Africa: The Failure of Passive Resistance.* Stanford: Hoover Institution, 1967.

__________. *South Africa: The Dynamics of the African National Congress.* London: Oxford University Press, 1962.

__________. "Generational Conflict and African Nationalism in South Africa: The African National Congress, 1949-1959." *International Journal of African Historical Studies* 5, 2 (1972): 181-202.

__________. "Urban Revolt in South Africa." *Journal of Modern African Studies* 8, 1 (1970): 55-72.

Gerhart, Gail. *Black Power in South Africa.* Berkeley: University of California Press, 1978.

Horrell, Muriel. *Action, Reaction and Counteraction: A Review of Non-White Opposition to Apartheid Policy, Countermeasures by the Government and New Waves of Unrest.* Johannesburg: South African Institute of Race Relations, 1963.

Jaspan, M.A. "South Africa 1960-1961: The Transition From Passive Resistance to Rebellion." *Science and Society* 25, 2, pp. 97-106.

Jeeves, A. "African Protest in Southern Africa 1945-1960." *International Journal* 28, 3 (Summer 1973): 465-510.

SELECTED BIBLIOGRAPHY

Karis, Thomas G. "The South African Treason Trial." *Political Science Quarterly* 56 (1961): 217-41.

Kuper, Leo. *Passive Resistance in South Africa*. New Haven: Yale University Press, 1957.

Magubane, Ben. "African Opposition in South Africa." *Africa Review* 2, 3 (1972): 433-47.

Mbata, J. Congress. "Race Resistance in South Africa." In *The African Experience*, eds. John N. Paden and Edward Soja. Vol. 1. Evanston: Northwestern University Press, 1970.

Moodley, Kogila A. "South African Indians: The Wavering Minority." In *Change in Contemporary South Africa*," eds. L. Thompson and J. Butler. Berkeley: University of California Press, 1975.

Morlan, Gail. "The Student Revolt Against Racism in South Africa." *Africa Today* 17 (May-June 1970): 12-20.

Ntebe, S. "Soweto and After: A Diary of Urban Unrest in 1976." *South African Outlook* 107, 1269 (February 1977): 19-33.

Pettigrew, Thomas. "Social Distance Attitudes of South African Students." *Social Forces* 38 (1960): 246-53.

Rathbone, R. "Students and Politics in South Africa." *Journal of Commonwealth and Comparative Politics* 15, 2 (1977).

Roux, Edward. *Time Longer Than Rope: A History of the Black Man's Struggle for Freedom in South Africa*. Madison: University of Wisconsin Press, 1968.

Simons, H.J., and Simons, R.E. *Class and Colour in South Africa 1850-1950*. Harmondsworth: Penguin, 1969.

Spence, J.E. "The Origins of Extra-Parliamentary Opposition in South Africa." *Government and Opposition* 1 (October 1965): 55-84.

Walshe, Peter. *Black Nationalism in South Africa: A Short History*. Johannesburg: SPROCAS-Raven Press, 1973.

__________. *The Rise of African Nationalism in South Africa*. Berkeley: University of California Press, 1971.

__________. "Black American Thought and African Political Attitudes in Southern Africa." *Review of Politics* (January 1970): 51-77.

__________. "The Origins of African Political Consciousness in South Africa." *Journal of Modern African Studies* 7 (1969): 583-610.

Webster, E.E. "The Durban Riots: A Case Study in Race and Class." In *Working Papers in Southern African Studies*, ed. P.L. Bonner. Johannesburg: ASI African Studies Seminar, University of Witwatersrand African Studies Institute, 1977.

Wood, E. "Community Action, Urban Protest and Change in Zimbabwe and South Africa." *African Affairs* 77, 307 (1978).

SELECTED BIBLIOGRAPHY

SOCIOECONOMIC CONDITIONS AMONG THE BLACK POPULATION

Black, P.A. "Regional Economic Strategy and the Black Homelands." In *Public Policy and the South African Economy*, ed. M.L. Truu. Cape Town: Oxford University Press, 1977.

Bloom, Len. "Some Problems of Urbanization in South Africa." *Phylon* (Winter 1964): 347-68.

Dickie-Clark, H.F. *The Marginal Situation: A Sociological Study of a Coloured Group*. London: Routledge and Kegan Paul, 1966.

Duncan, Sheena. "The Plight of the Urban African." In *Topical Talks* 23. Johannesburg: South African Institute of Race Relations, 1970.

Folscher, G.C.K. "The Economic and Fiscal Relationships of the Transkei vis-ā-vis the Rest of the Republic as Determinants of Its Economic Development." *South African Journal of Economics* 35 (September 1967): 203-18.

Hellmann, Ellen. *Soweto: Johannesburg's African City*. Johannesburg: South African Institute of Race Relations, 1968.

__________. "Social Change Among Urban Africans." In *South Africa: Sociological Perspectives*, ed. Heribert Adam. London: Oxford University Press, 1971.

Kuper, Hilda. *Indian People in Natal*. Natal: Natal University Press, 1960.

Marais, J.S. *The Cape Coloured People 1652-1937*. Johannesburg: Witwatersrand University Press, 1968.

Mayer, Phillip. *Urban Africans and the Bantustans*. Johannesburg: South African Institute of Race Relations, 1972.

__________. "Migrancy and the Study of Africans in Towns," Pt. 1. *American Anthropologist* 64, 3 (June 1962): 576-92.

Muller, A.L. *Minority Interests: The Political Economy of the Coloured and Indian Communities in South Africa*. Johannesburg: South African Institute of Race Relations, 1968.

Patterson, Sheila. *Colour and Culture in South Africa*. London: Routledge and Kegan Paul, 1953.

Pauw, B.A. *The Second Generation: A Study of the Family Among Urbanized Bantu in East London*. Cape Town: Oxford University Press, 1963.

Reader, D.H. *The Black Man's Portion: History, Demography and Living Conditions in the Native Locations of East London Cape Province*. Cape Town: Oxford University Press, 1961.

Rheinallt, J.D. "Social and Economic Conditions of the Urban Native." In *Western Civilization and the Natives of South Africa*, ed. I. Schapera. New York: Humanities Press, 1967.

South African Institute of Race Relations. *The Future of the Homelands: Papers Given at the 44th Annual Council Meeting of the SAIRR*. Johannesburg, 1974.

Southall, Roger. "The Beneficiaries of Transkeian Independence." *Journal of Modern African Studies* 15, 1 (1977).

Van den Berghe, Pierre L. *Caneville: The Social Structure of a South African Town*. Middletown, Conn.: Wesleyan University Press, 1964.

Van der Horst, Sheila. "The Economic Problems of the Homelands." In *South African Dialogue*, ed. N.J. Rhoodie. Johannesburg: McGraw-Hill, 1972.

Whisson, Michael G. *The Fairest Cape? An Account of the Coloured People in the District of Simonstown*. Johannesburg: South African Institute of Race Relations, 1972.

THE ORGANIZATION OF AFRICAN LABOR

Alexander, Ray, and Simons, H. *Job Reservation and the Trade Unions*. Cape Town: Enterprise, 1959.

Alverson, Hoyt. "Africans in South African Industry: The Human Dimension." Paper delivered to African Studies Seminar, University of Witwatersrand, December 1971.

Birley, Sir Robert. *The African Worker in South Africa*. Leeds: University Press, 1971.

Douwes Dekker, L., et al. "Case Studies in African Labour Action in South Africa and Namibia." In *The Development of an African Working Class*, eds. R. Sandbrook and R. Cohen. Toronto: University of Toronto Press, 1975.

Doxey, G.V. *The Industrial Colour Bar in South Africa*. Cape Town: Oxford University Press, 1961.

Du Toit, M.A. *South African Trade Unions: History, Legislation, Policy*. Johannesburg: McGraw-Hill, 1976.

Feit, Edward. *Workers Without Weapons: The South African Congress of Trade Unions and the Organization of the African Workers*. Archon Books, 1975.

Horner, D.B., ed. *Labour Organization and the African*. Johannesburg: South African Institute of Race Relations, 1975.

Horrell, Muriel. *South African Trade Unionism: A Study of a Divided Working Class*. Johannesburg: South African Institute of Race Relations, 1961.

__________. *South African Workers: Their Organization and Patterns of Employment*. Johannesburg: South African Institute of Race Relations, 1969.

Hutt, W.H. *The Economics of the Colour Bar*. London: Andre Deutsch for the Institute of Economic Affairs, 1964.

Jeeves, A.H. "The Administration and Control of Migratory Labour on the South African Gold-mines: Capitalism and the State in the Era of Kruger and Milner." In *Working Papers in Southern African Studies*, ed. P.L. Bonner. Johannesburg: University of Witwatersrand African Studies Institute, 1977, pp. 123-78.

Johns, Sheridan W. "The Birth of Non-White Trade Unionism in South Africa." *Race* 9 (October 1967): 173-92.

Johnstone, F.A. *Class, Race and Gold*. London: Routledge and Kegan Paul, 1976.

SELECTED BIBLIOGRAPHY

Kraft, R.L. "Labour: South Africa's Challenge of the Seventies." *Optima* 21, 1 (March 1977): 2-11.

Legassick, Martin. "South African Forced Labour, Industrialization and Racial Discrimination." In *The Political Economy of Africa*, ed. R. Harris. Boston: Schenkman, 1974.

Leistner, G.M.E. "Foreign Bantu Workers in South Africa: Their Present Position in the Economy." *South African Journal of Economics* 35 (March 1967): 30-56.

Leys, Roger. "South African Gold Mining in 1974: The Gold of Migrant Labour." *African Affairs* 74, 295 (April 1975).

Natal University Department of Economics. *The African Factory Worker.* London: Oxford University Press, 1950.

O'Meara, D. "The 1946 African Mineworkers Strike in the Political Economy of South Africa." *Journal of Commonwealth and Comparative Politics* 12, 2 (July 1975).

Randall, Peter. *Migratory Labour in South Africa.* Johannesburg: South African Institute of Race Relations, 1967.

Roux, Edward. *Time Longer Than Rope.* Madison: University of Wisconsin Press, 1964.

Simons, H.J., and Simons, R.E. *Class and Colour in South Africa 1850-1950.* London: Penguin, 1969.

Thomas, W.H. *Labour Perspectives on South Africa: Proceedings of a Workshop on Organized Labour in South African Society.* Cape Town: David Phillip, 1974.

Trapido, Stanley. "South Africa in a Comparative Study of Industrialization." *Journal of Development Studies* 7, 3 (1971): 309-20.

Van der Horst, S.T. "Labour Policy in South Africa 1948-1976: A Sketch." In *Public Policy and the South African Economy*, ed. M.L. Truu. Cape Town: Oxford University Press, 1976.

Wickins, P.L. "The One Big Union Movement Among Black Workers in South Africa." *International Journal of African Historical Studies* 7, 3 (1974): 391-416.

Wilson, Francis. *Labour in the South African Gold Mines 1911-1969.* Cambridge: Cambridge University Press, 1972.

__________. *Migrant Labour: Report to the South African Council of Churches.* Johannesburg: South African Council of Churches and SPROCAS, 1972.

__________. "Labour Problems in South Africa." *Rhodesian Journal of Economics* 6, 4 (December 1972): 46-68.

Wolpe, Harold. "Capitalism and Cheap Labour Power in South Africa: From Segregation to Apartheid." *Economy and Society* 1, 4 (November 1972): 425-56.

SELECTED BIBLIOGRAPHY

FOREIGN POLICY

Adelman, K.L. "Strategy of Defiance—South Africa." *Comparative Strategy* 1, 1-2 (1978).

Amin, Samir. "The Future of South Africa." *Journal of Southern African Affairs* 2, 3 (July 1977).

Anglin, Douglas G., Shaw, Timothy M., and Widstrand, Carl G., eds. *Conflict and Change in Southern Africa: Papers From a Scandinavian-Canadian Conference*. Washington, D.C.: University Press of America, 1978.

Baker, Pauline H. "South Africa's Strategic Vulnerabilities: The Citadel Assumption Reconsidered." *African Studies Review* 20, 2 (September 1977).

Barber, J. *South Africa's Foreign Policy 1945-1970*. London: Oxford University Press, 1973.

Egeland, L. "South Africa's Role in Africa." *Rivista di studi politici internazionali* (April-June 1968): 276-89.

Hirschmann, P. "Southern Africa: Detente?" *Journal of Modern African Studies* 14, 1 (March 1976): 107-26.

Legum, Colin. *Southern Africa: The Secret Diplomacy of Detente*. New York: Africana, 1976.

Munger, Edwin S. *Notes on the Formation of South African Foreign Policy*. Pasadena: Castle Press, 1965.

Nolutshungu, Sam C. *South Africa in Africa: A Study in Ideology and Foreign Policy*. Manchester: Manchester University Press, 1975.

Seiler, John. "South African Perspectives and Responses to External Pressures." *Journal of Modern African Studies* (1975): 447-68.

Spence, J.E. *South Africa's Foreign Policy in Today's World*. Johannesburg: South African Institute of International Relations, 1975.

__________. "South African Foreign Policy: The Outward Movement." In *Southern Africa in Perspective: Essays in Regional Politics*, eds. C.P. Potholm and R. Dale. New York: Free Press, 1972.

__________. "South Africa's 'New Look' Foreign Policy." *World Today* (April 1968): 137-45.

Stockholm International Peace Research Institute. *Southern Africa: The Escalation of a Conflict*. Stockholm: SIPRI, 1976.

Vandenbosch, Amry. *South Africa and the World: Foreign Policy and Apartheid*. Lexington: University Press of Kentucky, 1970.

Woldring, K. "South Africa's Africa Policy Reconsidered." *African Review* 5, 1 (1975): 77-93.

INDEX

"African Claims," 69
African National Congress (ANC): 3, 66-77, 83, 99; Defiance Campaign of, 72, 99, 220; evolution of policies of, 96-98; guerrilla activities of, 92, 93, 289-90; in exile, 79-81; involvement in labor movement, 68, 109, 182; opposition to apartheid, 57-58, 72; Program of Action of, 70-71; resurgence of, 92-94; and SACP, 57, 58, 67, 69, 71, 81, 97; turn toward violence of, 77-79
African National Congress Youth League (ANCYL), 68-69, 70, 99
African People's Democratic Union of South Africa (APDUSA), 69, 82
African People's Organization, 71
African population: ethnic groups, 138-43; franchise rights, 2, 131-32, 197-98; freehold rights of, 134, 196, 238, 324; Freedom Charter, 74; survey opinions of, 275-78; under proposed constitutional reforms, 326-28; urban, 42, 127-51, 151n, 323-26
African Student Movement (ASM), 89
African Students' Association, 101
African Students' Union of South Africa, 101
Afrikaans, 90, 104, 146. *See also* Bantu education
Afrikaans-speaking whites. *See* Afrikaners
Afrikaner Broederbond, 16-17, 37-42, 242
Afrikaner party, 25, 38
Afrikaner supremacy, 5, 7. *See also* White supremacy
Afrikaners, 14-19, 30-31, 299-301; political attitudes of, 244-74
Afrikanerdom, 16, 17, 63, 218
American Mineworkers Union, 190, 311
Angola, 1, 142, 233, 236, 244, 247, 289, 291
Apartheid, 1-2; consummatory significance of, 299-301, 317; economic consequences of, 285-87; and election of 1948, 18-19; instrumental significance of, 299, 301-10; and South African liberalism, 49-50; organized opposition to, 47, 57-59; "petty apartheid," 26, 211, 216, 309, 318-19; political consequences of, 281-82; reforms in, 26-30, 238, 297, 316, 318-29; restrictive legislation of, 70, 181; survey responses to, 250; and White supremacy, 5-6, 298-99. *See also* National party; Separate development; White supremacy
Arms embargoes, 288, 289
Asian population. *See* Indian population
Azania, 54, 206-7
Azania People's Organization, 92

Bantu Administration Department, 150
Bantu Affairs Adminstration Boards, 133-34
Bantu authorities, 72, 76n
Bantu Authorities Act (1951), 131, 196
Bantu education, 87, 89, 91, 103, 104, 106-7, 146-47, 224
Bantu Homelands Citizenship Act (1970), 135, 198-99

INDEX

Bantu Homelands Constitution Act (1971), 198
Bantu Labour (Settlement of Disputes) Act (1953), 174n, 181; amended (1959), 181
Bantu Laws Amendment Act (1964), 131
Bantu Laws Amendment Act (1978), 169n
Bantu Relations Regulations Amendment Act (1975), 192
Bantustan policy, 165, 171. *See also* Homelands policy; Separate development
Bantustans. *See* Homelands
Basutoland (Lesotho), 204
Battle of Blood River, 17
Biko, Steve, 84, 85, 91, 92, 101, 237, 328, 329
"Black," definition of, 218-19n
Black Alliance. *See* South African Black Alliance
Black [and] Allied Workers Union (BAWU), 101, 110, 187, 222
Black Consciousness, 4, 84-92, 97n, 101-3; as aspect of Black solidarity, 10, cleavages in 140, 148; and SACP, 67; opposition to apartheid, 57-58, 310
Black labor, 15, 108-11, 165, 236; in agriculture, 161-64; in manufacturing, 155; in mining, 152-53, 155; trade unions, 108, 108n, 178-79, 319-21; unemployment, 149, 170; wages, 153-55, 157, 162-63, 178, 186, 238
Black Parents Association, 90, 91-92, 117n, 276
Black People's Congress, 227-28
Black People's Convention, 85-86, 88, 91-92, 101, 310
Black Renaissance Convention (BRC), 89
Black Sash, 48
Black United Front, 66n, 96
Black Unity Front, 91, 121
Blacks (Urban Areas) Consolidation Act (1945). *See* Natives (Urban Areas) Consolidation Act (1945)
Bophuthatswana, 136, 194, 201, 202, 211
Bophuthatswana Democratic party, 204
Botha Commission, 180
Botha, M.C., 136-37
Botha, P.W., 23-25, 30, 36, 292, 297-98, 324-25, 327-28
Botswana, 202, 203
Broederbond. *See* Afrikaner Broederbond
Bus boycotts, 178, 185
Buthelezi, Chief Gatsha, 7, 64n, 212-13, 232-33, 245; Inkatha movement of, 4, 57, 66n, 95-96, 111-26, 148

Champion, A.W.G., 176
Chinsamy, Y.S., 221
Cindi, Zitulele, 88
Ciskei, 198, 201
Colored Labor Party, 4, 95, 121, 213
Colored population: cultural differentiation of 226-29; franchise, 72; impact of group areas policy on, 304, 304n; labor preference policy of, 134, 165, 166, 167; origins and status of, 217-19; political activity of, 219-23, 233; relations with African population, 57, 63, 74, 85, 86; socioeconomic differentiation of, 223-26; under homelands policy, 199; under proposed constitutional reforms, 11-12, 27, 29, 218
Colored Persons Representative Council, 8
Commission on Native Education, 146
Communist Party of South Africa (CPSA), 68, 87. *See also* South African Communist Party (SACP)
Community Councils, 106, 132, 137
Community Councils Act (1977), 132
Congress Alliance, 73-74, 77, 182
Congress of Democrats, 73
Congress of Non-European Trade Unions (CNETU), 178, 180
Congress of the People, 73-74, 75, 213
Consociationalism, 62-65, 277, 278
Constitutional reforms, proposed, 11-12, 27-30, 35-36, 238-39, 326-28

Cooperation and Development, Department of, 150
Council of Cabinets, 11-12, 218, 238-39
Council of Industrial Workers of the Witwatersrand, 187
Crossroads, 150, 166, 167, 168, 324

Dadoo, Dr. Yusuf, 70, 72, 74
Defense, spending and strategy, 6, 93-94, 287-90
Defiance Campaign. *See under* African National Congress
De Kiewiet, C.W., 48
De Klerk, Dr. Willem, 241
Demonstrations, 104-8, 152-54. *See also* Durban riots; Soweto
Devenish, G.E., 30
De Villiers, René, 14
"Dialogue" policy, 291
Dickie-Clark, Hamish, 50-51
"Dipping" of Africans, 176, 176n
Donges, T.E., 24
Durban Institute for Industrial Education, 222
Durban riots, 229-31

Economic development, 176-78, 284-87, 302
Edelstein, Dr. M.L., 147
Election of 1948, 18-19, 25, 61
English-speaking Whites, political attitudes of, 244-74
European Economic Community (EEC), 122, 285, 316

Fagan Commission. *See* Natives Laws Commission
Federal Council (National party), 20
Federation of Free African Trade Unions of South Africa (FOFATUSA), 185
Feit, Edward, 183
Fingloland, 196
Foreign investment, 287, 313-14
Foreign policy, 282-84, 290-95
Foreign trade, 314-15
Fouche, J.J., 289
France, 288
Freedom Charter, 74-75, 98, 220
Freiburg study, 57, 64n
FRELIMO, 88, 89, 94, 172
Front-line states, 59
Fund Raising Act (1978), 192
Fusion, 14-16

Gazankulu, 121, 201
Geldenhuys, Deon, 294-95
General Laws Amendment Act (Sabotage Act), 77
Ghetto Act, 70
Gordon, Max, 178, 181
Great Trek, 17
Group Areas Act, 223, 224-25, 304
Guerrilla activities, 5, 92, 93, 289-90

Havenga, N.C., 38
Herstigte Nasionale Party, 241
Hertzog, Albert, 22
Hertzog, J.B.M.,14, 16, 17-18
Hoernle, Alfred, 55
Hofmeyr, Onze Jan, 61
Homelands: African identification with, 64, 64n, 91; citizenship in, 107, 137, 201-2; as "decolonization" process, 5, 199-209; economics of, 205-6, 213-15; by ethnic group and size, 197 (table); international opinion of, 194, 199, 216; and South African labor policy, 149, 162; survey opinions on, 250, 278-79
Homelands policy, 4, 5, 6-7, 20, 125, 136-38; background of, 194-99
Household Subsistence Level, 145

Immorality Act, 34, 229, 252, 318
Indian-African Congress, 231
Indian Congress, 227, 277n
Indian Council, 219
Indian population: cultural differentiation of, 226-29, 233-35; impact of group areas policy on, 304, 304n; militancy of, 69-70; origins and status of, 217-19; political activity of, 219-23, 233; relations with African population, 57, 74, 85, 86, 222-23, 229-33; socioeconomic differentiation of, 223-

26; strike participation of, 109; under proposed constitutional reforms, 11-12, 27, 29, 218, 241
Indian Reform party, 95, 121, 213
Indirect rule, 6-10, 35, 328
Industrial and Commercial Workers' Union (ICU), 68, 108-9, 175-76, 180
Industrial Conciliation Act (1924), 174, 175
Industrial Conciliation Act (1956), 174n, 182
Industrial Council (Natives) Bill (1947), 180
Industrial Legislation Commission of Enquiry, 180
Industrial relations legislation, 174-75, 179-81. *See also* Riekert Commission; Wiehahn Commission
Industrial Socialist League, 68
Influx control, 129-38, 135, 150, 304-5, 321-23. *See also* Pass laws
Information, Department of, 24, 263-64, 265n, 268n, 328-29
Inkatha movement, 4, 57, 58, 66n, 111-26, 221. *See also* Buthelezi, Chief Gatsha
International Confederation of Free Trade Unions (ICFTU), 185, 190

Job reservation, 34, 35, 159, 160, 174n, 251
Johnson, R.W., 148-49

Kadalie, Clements, 108
Kaunda, Kenneth, 59
Koornhof, Piet, 24, 150, 168, 238, 297-98, 322
Kotane, Moses, 74
Kuper, Hilda, 234
Kuper, Leo, 140-41
KwaZulu, 112, 115-16, 118, 123, 125, 201, 327

Labor: in agriculture, 161-64; in manufacturing, 164-69; in mining, 152-61, 171-73; policy changes, 241; unemployment, 169-73; wages, 109, 154, 157, 225. *See also* Black labor; Migrant labor; Riekert Commission; Wiehahn Commission
Labor unions. *See* Trade unions
Labour Party, 4, 180
Land Act (1913). *See* Native Land Act (1913)
Langa, 76-77
Leballo, Potlako, 80, 81, 83, 85
Lebowa, 121, 198, 201
Legum, Colin, 119
Lesotho, 200-6
Liaison committees, 108, 110, 188, 189. *See also* Trade unions
Liberalism: background, 45-48; failure of, 49-56; functions of, 60-62
Liberal party (1953-68), 46-47
Liberation Committee (OAU), 81
Liberation movements. *See* African National Congress; Black Consciousness; Pan Africanist Congress
Lijphart, Arend, 62, 65
Luthuli, Chief Albert, 57, 71, 73, 74, 100, 226

Makiwane, Ambrose, 81
Malan, D.F., 15-16, 18
Malan, Magnus, 290
Malawi, 163, 286
Mandela, Nelson, 78
Mangope, Chief Lucas, 204
Manufacturing. *See* Economic development
Mashinini, Tsietsi, 90
Masters and Servants legislation, 175, 190
Matanzima, Paramount Chief Kaiser, 198, 204, 205, 213
Mayer, Philip, 103, 139-40, 141, 142-43, 144
Mbeo, Menziwe, 222
Migrant labor, 2, 135, 140, 175, 215; contract labor, 166; in agriculture, 163-64; in manufacturing, 164, 168-69; in mining, 153-54, 172
Mixed Marriages Act, 34
Mkhatshwa, Rev. Smangaliso, 89
Modderdam, 135, 166, 168
Mondale, Walter, 49, 293-94
Montsitsi, Daniel Sechaba, 91
Moodie, Dunbar, 17, 299-300

Morogoro, 80, 81, 97
Movimiento Popular de Libertacao de Angola (MPLA), 94, 289
Mozambique, 1, 142, 158-59, 172, 173, 233, 236, 247, 289-90
Mphahlele, Ezekiel, 53
Mulder, Dr. C.P., 24, 150
Multinationals, 190-91, 312-14

Namibia, 85, 94, 142, 173, 236, 246, 279, 289, 291, 292
Nasionale Pers, 23, 24-25
Natal Indian Congress (NIC), 119
National Manpower Commission (NMC), 321
National party: and Afrikaner Broederbond, 37-42; cleavages within, 30-37; labor policies of, 160, 180-81; historical survey of, 14-19; one-party rule, 25-26; organizational framework of, 3-5, 19-25, 32-33, 242; proposed constitutional reforms of, 11-12, 27-30; 218; "Purified" party, 15, 16, 18; racial ideologies of, 1-3, 18, 26-30; strategical options of, 5-10, 12-13, 278-80; support for in surveys, 263-66, 268n, 273
National Union of South African Students (NUSAS), 47, 54, 84, 85, 101
Native Affairs, Department of, 195
Native Affairs Commission, 129, 179, 196
Native Labour Act (1953), 307
Native Labour Bill, 181
Native Land Act (1913), 67-68, 129, 196
Native Laws Amendment Act (1952), 130
Native National Congress, 67
Native Trust and Land Act (1936), 196
Natives Laws Commission, 130
Natives' Representative Council, 131
Natives Resettlement Act (1954), 134
Natives (Urban Areas) Act (1923), 129-30
Natives (Urban Areas) Consolidation Act (1945), 131, 132, 169n, 305; Section 10 of, 64n, 136, 151, 167, 169n, 239, 305, 322, 325-26
Ndebele, 138
Ngubane, Jordan K., 52
Ntsanwisi, Hudson, 91, 121
Nyerere, Julius, 59
Nzo, Alfred, 77, 80, 94

Oppenheimer, Harry, 47
Organization of African Unity (OAU), 81-82, 83, 93, 94, 204
Ossewa Brandwag, 38, 179

Pan Africanist Congress (PAC), 3, 66, 67, 99; and Black Consciousness, 57, 87; decline of, 94-95; in exile, 79-82; guerrilla activities of, 92, 93; policies of, 75-76, 98; and SACP, 67, 83, 97; turn toward violence of, 77, 78-79
Partition, 206-9
Pass laws, 2, 76-77, 99, 175, 178, 179, 180, 321-23. *See also* Influx control
Paton, Alan, 45, 47n, 60, 86-87
Patriotic Front, 94
"Petty apartheid," 26, 211, 216, 309, 318-19
Plural Relations, Department of, 32, 150, 168
Police Amendment Act, 329
Poqo, 78-79, 81, 99
Poverty Datum Line, 109
Power-sharing, 5, 7, 12-13, 66, 125, 209-13, 218, 239
President's Advisory Council, 11
Prevention of Illegal Squatting Amendment Act (1976), 135
Progressive Federal Party (PFP), 4, 7, 12-13, 28n
Progressive National Students' Organization, 101
Progressive party, 60
Prohibition of Political Interference Act (1968), 132, 305-6
Promotion of Bantu Self-Government Act (1959), 131-32, 196-97

QwaQwa, 121, 201, 202
QwaZulu. *See* KwaZulu

Race Relations, South African Institute of, 48, 104
Rand rebellion, 160
Red/School division, 139, 139n
Reference books. *See* Pass laws
Reform party, 221
Representation of Natives Act (1936), 198
Resettlement areas/camps, 161-62
Rhodesia, 1, 142, 159, 233, 236 244, 245, 283, 291. *See also* Zimbabwe
Riekert Commission, 36-37, 150-51, 151n, 162, 168-69, 239-40, 322-23, 330n
Rivonia trial, 78

Sabotage Act, 77
Schlebush, Alwyn, 24
Seathlolo, Khotso, 90-91
Seme, Dr. Pixley ka Izaka, 67
Separate development, 2, 67, 165, 240; and Afrikaner Broederbond, 38-39; and Bantu education, 104; homeland opposition to, 213; and Indian population, 234; and Inkatha movement, 119; as instrumental strategy, 307-8, 309-10; under proposed constitutional reforms, 11; in *verlig-verkramp* dichotomy, 33-34
Sharpeville, 46, 69, 76-77, 92, 99
Slovo, Joe, 98
Smuts, J.C., 14, 18, 61, 69, 70
Sobukwe, Robert, 75, 76, 78, 94-95, 118
South Africa Act (1909), 61, 203
South African Black Alliance (SABA), 66n, 95-96, 121
South African Colored People's Organization (SACPO), 71, 73
South African Communist Party (SACP), 57, 58, 67, 69, 71, 81, 97, 180. *See also* Communist Party of South Africa (CPSA)
South African Congress of Democrats, 73
South African Congress of Trade Unions (SACTU), 74, 74n, 109, 181, 182-86, 187
South African Indian Council (SAIC), 70, 71, 72, 73
South African Native Affairs Commission. *See* Native Affairs Commission
South African party, 14
South African Students' Movement (SASM), 89-90, 108
South African Students' Organization (SASO), 54, 57, 84-93, 101, 310
South African United Front, 79-80
South West Africa People's Organization (SWAPO), 68n, 94, 120n, 289
Soweto, 1, 4-5, 7-8, 64, 143-47, 167; cleavages in, 139-40; economic significance of, 287, 312-16; protests of 1976, 8, 43, 58, 90-92, 133, 310-11; restrictive legislation on, 130, 133; school boycott in, 90, 104, 108; survey attitudes on, 275-78
Soweto Committee of Ten, 9, 42, 92, 117n, 276
Soweto Students' Representative Council (SSRC), 90-91, 105
Sports, multiracial, 20, 220, 237, 238, 250-51
Squatters/squatting, 135, 150, 166-69, 178
Status of the Transkei Act (1976), 136
Strijdom, J.G., 38
Strikes: in Durban, 154, 156; Indian participation in, 221-22; in industry, 99, 109, 148-49; legislation against, 175, 189; in mining, 153-56, 159-60, 174; Rand rebellion, 160; and trade union movement, 188, 310, 311; and worker militancy, 178, 186-87, 311
Sundkler, B.G.M., 121
Suppression of Communism Act, 70, 71n, 72, 90, 180-81
Suzman, Helen, 60
Swazi, 121, 138, 201, 202
Swaziland, 203

Tambo, Oliver, 80
Theron report, 226

Thula, Gibson, 95
Trade Union Advisory and Coordinating Council (TUACC), 187, 188
Trade Union Advisory Committee, 110
Trade Union Council of South Africa (TUCSA), 181, 185-86
Trade unions, 71, 108-11, 174-93, 306-7, 311-12. *See also* Riekert Commission; Wiehahn Commission
Transkei, 4, 136, 194-98, 200-11, 214
Transkei Constitution Act, 198, 211
Transkei National Independence party, 204
Tswana, 64, 138, 202
Turnhalle conference, 245, 246
Turok, B., 79, 80

Umkhonto we Sizwe, 77, 78, 79, 94, 99
Unibel, 166, 168
Unilateral Declaration of Independence (Rhodesia), 157
United Liberation Front for Azania (ULFA), 83
United Nations, 194, 199, 206, 216, 219, 237
United party, 4, 14, 15, 18 25, 61, 180
United States, relations with South Africa, 49, 293-94, 313
Unity Movement of South Africa (UMSA), 69, 82-83, 229
University Christian Movement (UCM), 84, 86, 101
Urban Areas Act. *See* Natives (Urban Areas) Consolidation Act
Urban Bantu Councils (UBCs), 91, 92, 106, 106n, 132
Urban Bantu Councils Act (1961), 132
Urban Training Project, 109, 110, 187-88

Van den Berghe, Pierre, 50, 211
Venda, 138, 198, 201
Verlig vs. *verkramp*, 24, 33-34, 39n, 143, 264, 317. *See also* National party, cleavages within
Verwoerd, Hendrik, 14, 20-25, 31, 301, 303
Viljoen, Gerrit, 33-34
Vorster, John, 20-28, 41-42, 137-38, 199, 201-2, 284, 293-94

Wage Act (1925), 174
Wages. *See* Labor, wages
Wallerstein, Immanuel, 59
Walvis Bay, 201
Western Province Workers Advice Bureau, 187, 188
White Mineworkers Strike (1922), 174
White population, survey attitudes of, 244-74
White supremacy, 5, 33, 283, 298
Wiechers, Marinus, 29
Wiehahn Commission, 36-37, 108n, 159-60, 174-75, 191-92, 239, 319-21, 330n
Wilson, Francis, 129
Woods, Donald, 52, 85
Works committees, 108, 110, 188-89
World Bank, 205-6

Xuma, Dr. A.B., 69, 71, 123

Youth League. *See* African National Congress Youth League (ANCYL)

Zimbabwe, 94, 173, 244, 247, 276 279, 290. *See also* Rhodesia

INSTITUTE OF INTERNATIONAL STUDIES
UNIVERSITY OF CALIFORNIA, BERKELEY

CARL G. ROSBERG,
Director

Monographs published by the Institute include:

RESEARCH SERIES

1. *The Chinese Anarchist Movement*, by Robert A. Scalapino and George T. Yu. ($1.00)
7. *Birth Rates in Latin America: New Estimates of Historical Trends*, by O. Andrew Collver. ($2.50)
15. *Central American Economic Integration: The Politics of Unequal Benefits*, by Stuart I. Fagan. ($2.00)
16. *The International Imperatives of Technology: Technological Development and the International Political System*, by Eugene B. Skolnikoff. ($2.95)
17. *Autonomy or Dependence as Regional Integration Outcomes: Central America*, by Philippe C. Schmitter. ($1.75)
19. *Entry of New Competitors in Yugoslav Market Socialism*, by S.R. Sacks. ($2.50)
20. *Political Integration in French-Speaking Africa*, by Abdul A. Jalloh. ($3.50)
21. *The Desert and the Sown: Nomads in the Wider Society*, ed. by Cynthia Nelson. ($5.50)
22. *U.S.-Japanese Competition in International Markets: A Study of the Trade-Investment Cycle in Modern Capitalism*, by John E. Roemer. ($3.95)
23. *Political Disaffection Among British University Students: Concepts, Measurement, and Causes*, by Jack Citrin and David J. Elkins. ($2.00)
24. *Urban Inequality and Housing Policy in Tanzania: The Problem of Squatting*, by Richard E. Stren. ($2.95)
25. *The Obsolescence of Regional Integration Theory*, by Ernst B. Haas. ($4.95)
26. *The Voluntary Service Agency in Israel*, by Ralph M. Kramer. ($2.00)
27. *The SOCSIM Demographic-Sociological Microsimulation Program: Operating Manual*, by Eugene A. Hammel et al. ($4.50)
28. *Authoritarian Politics in Communist Europe: Uniformity & Diversity in One-Party States*, ed. by Andrew C. Janos. ($3.95)
29. *The Anglo-Icelandic Cod War of 1972-1973: A Case Study of a Fishery Dispute*, by Jeffrey A. Hart. ($2.00)
30. *Plural Societies and New States: A Conceptual Analysis*, by Robert Jackson ($2.00)
31. *The Politics of Crude Oil Pricing in the Middle East, 1970-1975: A Study in International Bargaining*, by Richard Chadbourn Weisberg. ($4.95)
32. *Agricultural Policy and Performance in Zambia: History, Prospects, and Proposals for Change*, by Doris Jansen Dodge. ($4.95)
33. *Five Classy Programs: Computer Procedures for the Classification of Households*, by E.A. Hammel and R.Z. Deuel. ($3.75)
34. *Housing the Urban Poor in Africa: Policy, Politics, and Bureaucracy in Mombasa*, by Richard E. Stren. ($5.95)
35. *The Russian New Right: Right-Wing Ideologies in the Contemporary USSR*, by Alexander Yanov. ($4.50)
36. *Social Change in Romania, 1860-1940: A Debate on Development in a European Nation*, ed. by Kenneth Jowitt. ($4.50)
37. *The Leninist Response to National Dependency*, by Kenneth Jowitt. ($3.25)
38. *Socialism in Sub-Saharan Africa: A New Assessment*, ed. by Carl G. Rosberg and Thomas M. Callaghy. ($10.50)
39. *Tanzania's Ujamaa Villages: The Implementation of a Rural Development Strategy*, by Dean E. McHenry, Jr. ($5.95)
40. *Who Gains from Deep Ocean Mining: Simulating the Impact of Regimes for Regulating Nodule Exploitation*, by I.G. Bulkley. ($3.50)

INSTITUTE OF INTERNATIONAL STUDIES MONOGRAPHS (continued)

41. *Industrialization, Industrialists, and the Nation-State in Peru: A Comparative/Sociological Analysis*, by Frits Wils. ($5.95)
42. *Ideology, Public Opinion, and Welfare Policy: Attitudes toward Taxes and Spending in Industrialized Societies*, by Richard M. Coughlin. ($6.50)
43. *The Apartheid Regime: Political Power and Racial Domination*, ed. by Robert M. Price and Carl G. Rosberg. ($10.95)
44. *The Yugoslav Economic System and Its Performance in the 1970s*, by Laura D'Andrea Tyson. ($4.95)
45. *Conflict in Chad*, by Virginia Thompson and Richard Adloff. ($7.50)
46. *Conflict and Coexistence in Belgium: The Dynamics of a Culturally Divided Society*, ed. by Arend Lijphart. ($7.50)

POLITICS OF MODERNIZATION SERIES

1. *Spanish Bureaucratic-Patrimonialism in America*, by Magali Sarfatti. ($2.00)
2. *Civil-Military Relations in Argentina, Chile, and Peru*, by Liisa North. ($2.00)
3. *Notes on the Process of Industrialization in Argentina, Chile, and Peru*, by Alcira Leiserson. ($1.75)
9. *Modernization and Bureaucratic-Authoritarianism: Studies in South American Politics*, by Guillermo O'Donnell. ($7.50)

POLICY PAPERS IN INTERNATIONAL AFFAIRS

1. *Images of Detente and the Soviet Political Order*, by Kenneth Jowitt. ($1.25)
2. *Detente After Brezhnev: The Domestic Roots of Soviet Foreign Policy*, by Alexander Yanov. ($3.00)
3. *The Mature Neighbor Policy: A New United States Economic Policy for Latin America*, by Albert Fishlow. ($2.00)
4. *Five Images of the Soviet Future: A Critical Review and Synthesis*, by George W. Breslauer. ($2.95)
5. *Global Evangelism Rides Again: How to Protect Human Rights Without Really Trying*, by Ernst B. Haas. ($2.00)
6. *Israel and Jordan: Implications of an Adversarial Partnership*, by Ian Lustick ($2.00)
7. *Political Syncretism in Italy: Historical Coalition Strategies and the Present Crisis*, by Giuseppe Di Palma. ($2.00)
8. *U.S. Foreign Policy in Sub-Saharan Africa: National Interest and Global Strategy*, by Robert M. Price. ($2.25)
9. *East-West Technology Transfer in Perspective*, by R.J. Carrick. ($2.75)
10. *NATO's Unremarked Demise*, by Earl C. Ravenal. ($2.00)
11. *Toward an Africanized U.S. Policy for Southern Africa: A Strategy for Increasing Political Leverage*, by Ronald T. Libby. ($3.95)
12. *The Taiwan Relations Act and the Defense of the Republic of China*, by Edwin K. Snyder et al. ($3.95)
13. *Cuba's Policy in Africa, 1959-1980*, by William M. LeoGrande. ($4.50)
14. *Norway, NATO, and the Forgotten Soviet Challenge*, by Kirsten Amundsen. ($2.95)
15. *Japanese Industrial Policy*, by Ira C. Magaziner and Thomas M. Hout. ($5.50)
16. *Containment, Soviet Behavior, and Grand Strategy*, by Robert E. Osgood. ($5.50)

Address correspondence to:

Institute of International Studies
215 Moses Hall
University of California
Berkeley, California 94720